Waldenses

For my parents

Waldenses

Rejections of Holy Church in Medieval Europe

Euan Cameron

First published 2000

2 4 6 8 10 9 7 5 3 1

Blackwell Publishers Ltd
108 Cowley Road
Oxford OX4 1JF
UK

Blackwell Publishers Inc.
350 Main Street
Malden, Massachusetts 02148
USA

British Library Cataloguing in Publication Data

A CIP catalogue record for this book is available from the British Library.

Library of Congress Cataloging-in-Publication Data

Cameron, Euan.
Waldenses: rejections of holy church in medieval Europe/Euan Cameron.
p. cm.
Includes bibliographical references and index.
ISBN 0-631-15339-X (alk. paper) – ISBN 0-631-22497-1
1. Waldenses – History – To 1500. 2. Church history – Middle Ages, 600–1500.
3. Waldenses – History – 16th century. 4. Church history – 16th century. I. Title.
BX4881.2.C37 2001
273'.6–dc21

00-034329

Typeset in 10.5 on 12 pt Galliard
by Best-set Typesetter Ltd., Hong Kong

This book is printed on acid-free paper.

Contents

List of Plates

List of Maps

Preface

The Waldensian heresy has experienced periods of great popularity, and also periods of relative neglect down the centuries since its history began to be written systematically in the sixteenth and seventeenth centuries. The last two decades have seen a flowering and broadening of interest in the heresy across much of Europe, but there has not been a comprehensive academic work dedicated solely to the medieval Waldenses written in English. My earlier monograph, *The Reformation of the Heretics: The Waldenses of the Alps 1480–1580* (1984), addressed only one hundred years in the history of one segment of the Waldensian phenomenon, the Waldenses of the southwestern Alps in the Dauphiné and Piedmont. The present book embraces a much larger expanse of both time and distance. Only the latter half of chapter 7, chapters 9 and 10, and the epilogue, overlap with the previous book; and even in those chapters there is significant new material. This book, written at the suggestion of Blackwell Publishers, is intended to make an extended survey of Waldensian history, based on primary sources, available to an anglophone readership. It offers a conspectus of the long, interwoven and intermittently documented story of the people known as 'Waldenses'.

Several parallel and independent research projects which came to fruition in the late 1970s and 1980s have considerably increased scholarly interest in these diverse, durable and intriguing dissenters. International conferences and symposia have taken the subject to a wider readership than that defined by the Società di Studi Valdesi (international as that body is). I have not, however, attempted to address all the more recherché or technical issues of interpretation which have been raised in the specialist literature since about 1980. Such a response belongs (if anywhere) rather in the specialist journals than in a monograph. Although some of the scholarly debate has centred around my own work, this present book offers neither a retraction nor a summation of those controversies. To clarify those issues would involve rectifying several misunderstandings (and occasional misrepresentations) of my earlier work, and would yield little benefit or interest to most historians. Although this book does have a distinct thesis, I nevertheless hope, by presenting some of the most important sources for the controversial periods and episodes here in English translation, to leave the reader free to judge for his or herself. For the same reason, the references are used principally to indicate where the primary sources for any given point may be found. To have cited every earlier discussion of each issue would have generated a huge and cumbersome apparatus, of little help to the general historian. The Waldensian bibliography, as many others have already remarked, is vast.

I acknowledge with thanks the support and patience of Blackwell Publishers during the time that this book has been in gestation, in particular successive History editors, most especially Tessa Harvey. I am obliged to the University of Newcastle upon Tyne, and my colleagues in the Department of History, for periods of study leave and teaching relief during which the book has been researched and written; and especially to Bob Moore for his interest and support. I wish particularly to thank the reader who has read the manuscript for Blackwell and commented on it with great thoroughness and care. Though he and I do not agree on all points, I have undoubtedly profited from a careful and balanced assessment, and have tried to respond to his comments where I felt able. Thanks are due to the libraries of the universities of Newcastle, Oxford, Cambridge, and Trinity College, Dublin, which have all facilitated access to important source materials; also to the libraries and archives in Paris and Grenoble which supplied vital microfilms of key documents. I also acknowledge with gratitude and respect the many contributions made to this subject by other scholars and editors on which this work chiefly depends. Finally, I thank my family for their patience while a large part of our home has been taken over by stacks of notes, documents, and books.

Euan Cameron
Gosforth

Introduction

An anonymous but well-informed ecclesiastical writer claimed, in a treatise probably first composed in the 1260s, that the Waldenses were the most dangerous of all the heretics faced by the Church of his time. This was, he said, for three reasons: they were the most long-lived of all; they were the most widespread; and finally, while other heretics taught repellent errors of faith, the Waldenses lived piously, believed everything in the Christian creeds, and differed from the rest only in the 'blasphemies' with which they attacked the Roman Church, its clergy, and its rituals.[1] Without sharing the anonymous writer's value judgements, one can readily agree with these insights, which hold good for most of the people who were called 'Waldenses'. They were durable and persistent; they were scattered over a wide area of Europe; they were largely orthodox in most of their beliefs; and they were opposed to the authority and pretensions of the Western Church.

The Waldensian heresy existed from the end of the twelfth to the early sixteenth centuries. During that period it was found, at one time or another, in places as far away as Pyrenean France, Northeastern Germany, and the extreme south of Italy. By the Reformation era, Waldenses were chiefly associated with a heartland district in the Alpine valleys of Piedmont just west of Turin. There, they were transformed into a settled Protestant Church in the reformed or 'Calvinist' tradition. By the 1560s, this particular group of Waldenses had succeeded in preserving their name and identity, while abandoning nearly all their traditional patterns of behaviour: and as such, despite many hardships, they have survived and remain to this day. Elsewhere in Europe they were either subsumed into another movement in the great religious upheavals of the sixteenth century, or had already disappeared before then.

1 The so-called 'Anonymous of Passau', in A. Patschovsky and K.-V. Selge (eds), *Quellen zur Geschichte der Waldenser*, Texte zur Kirchen- und Theologiegeschichte, 18 (Gütersloh, 1973), p. 73; also in J. Gretser, *Lucae Tudensis episcopi scriptores aliquot succedanei contra sectam Waldensium*, in M. de la Bigne (ed.), *Magna Bibliotheca Veterum Patrum*, 15 vols (Cologne, 1618–22), vol. 13, p. 299.

Waldenses and the Catholic Church

The medieval Waldenses were a 'heresy' opposed to, and to some extent also defined by, the Western Catholic Church of the high and later middle ages. They only arose where medieval Catholicism prevailed. They lived in a curious, ambivalent relationship with the Catholic clergy. In the very beginnings the first Waldenses sought clerical approval for their mission. Throughout their history they depended on the clergy to give them the traditional sacraments, such as baptism or the eucharist. At intervals, various groups of Waldensian brothers defected to join the ranks of the Catholics, and sometimes even became clerics themselves. Yet the Waldenses also routinely denounced the clergy as a sink of vice, and rejected its claim to control access to the means of grace. The clergy, for its turn, regarded the Waldenses as a menace, and pursued them with a vigour which never relented and occasionally erupted into mass persecution.

A heresy is defined by the orthodoxy which condemns it: this is a truism. However, the relationship between Waldensianism and medieval Catholicism was more complex and reciprocal than that truism implies. In the movement's earliest days, the followers of 'Valdesius' sought to preach entirely conventional Catholic doctrine as poor apostolic preachers, and thereby to make up what they saw as a deficiency in the ministry of the clergy. They aimed to supplement the Church's efforts rather than to contradict them, although their preaching against the dualist Cathar or Albigensian heresy contained an implicit (and sometimes overt) criticism that the ordained priesthood was failing in its tasks. These first 'Waldenses' became heretics when they refused to submit to Catholic bishops who forbade them to preach and teach. Disobedience, rather than wrong belief as such, first marked them out. For preaching without authority, they were duly condemned as roundly as the Cathars they strove against.

The subsequent heresy of the Waldenses thus reacted against the assertion by the Catholic Church that it alone could control and restrict access to certain ministries, especially preaching and penitential discipline. By the logic of its situation, Waldensianism also challenged the Church's authority to channel and direct saving grace: it had to devise alternative beliefs about the way to heaven. As the emphases within Catholic belief and worship shifted across three centuries, therefore, the salient features of Waldensian *disbelief* also appeared in a somewhat different perspective. Rejection of masses or indulgences for souls in purgatory, for example, grew more significant as those particular rites assumed an ever greater place in Catholic devotion towards the end of the middle ages. By refusing to take part in customary religious acts which were in theory voluntary, Waldenses could single themselves out and expose themselves to criticism, even if they lived as 'good Catholics' to the extent that they performed all the duties required of the faithful by canon law.

Finally, Waldensian belief was sometimes permeated by other, contradictory belief systems. This tendency was seen mostly among the lay followers, but also in some of the 'apostolic preachers' as well. In the early days, and in the fourteenth century, some of the practices and even the beliefs of Cathar 'perfect' brothers leaked into Waldensian custom. In the fifteenth century German and other Eastern European Waldenses made contacts with branches of the Hussite movements; by the early sixteenth century this literary exchange also reached the Waldenses in the southwestern Alps. Perhaps the most corrosive inroads, however, were those made into Waldensianism by Catholicism itself. Constantly exposed to Catholic rites and preaching, Waldensian followers seem to have found it very hard to stay at a logically consistent distance from the majority religious culture. Supposedly hostile to the cult of the saints or the service of the dead, they may be found nevertheless to have participated in these alongside the Catholics at least some of the time.

The Changing Shape of the Sources

The movements described by the Church as 'Waldensian' persisted over such a long period that the nature and preservation of records and documents is vastly different at the end of the story to its state at the start. Between c.1170 and c.1230 most sources consist of narratives or theological writings, chronicles or treatises against the heresy, written by ecclesiastics. In several of these the Waldenses played a minor role alongside the greater threat of Catharism. From time to time the Waldenses figured in official documents such as papal registers or conciliar decrees. From this primitive period also dates the one surviving extended theological piece actually written by a Waldensian, the *Liber antiheresis* or 'Book against the [Cathar] Heresy' of Durand of Osca, one of the most erudite of the first generation of Waldensian teachers.[2] Apart from an important and literate dossier of correspondence between German and Italian brothers in the 1360s,[3] the Waldensian brotherhood would rarely thereafter yield surviving written records of itself. Only at the very eve of the Reformation do we again find theological literature in its posses-

---

2 On the *Liber Antiheresis*, see below, chapter 2.1–2; also K.-V. Selge, *Die ersten Waldenser mit Edition des Liber antiheresis des Durandus von Osca*, 2 vols (Berlin, 1967).
3 See below, chapter 6.4.

sion. That literature, moreover, poses special problems of its own, as will be seen.[4]

From the 1230s onwards the figure of the inquisitor begins to dominate the sources.[5] Inquisitors, and those prelates who followed inquisitorial procedure, kept various kinds of records of their activities. The most immediate are the protocols of trials of individual heretics, containing sometimes minute transcripts of the interrogations. At best, these dossiers show us in often moving detail the struggle of wills between inquisitor and accused, and yield much circumstantial detail of the life and customs of Waldensian communities. Such full records are rare before the 1330s, but become quite abundant thereafter. At a slightly further remove from the actual interrogation stand collections of final sentences, like those of the Toulouse inquisitors from 1307–23.[6] For the earliest inquisitors, such as Pierre Seila, active in Quercy in the 1240s, these books of sentences, or even more fragmentary books of sample formulae, are the only surviving record.[7] More remote still were the extended treatises which inquisitors and other experts from time to time wrote attacking the heretics. These works often combined a derivative literary description of the origins and past history of the movement, and a similarly derivative theological résumé of its teachings, with evidence drawn from the personal experiences and face-to-face testimonies extracted by the authors in the course of their work. Since these collections sometimes formed the manuals used by a later generation of inquisitors to interrogate further suspects,[8] the ecclesiastical view of the Waldenses evolved as a sort of continual dialogue between literary tradition and direct testimony, each overlaying and merging into the other.

Inquisitorial records are not all alike. Even within one of the categories just described, the quality and subtlety of the evidence varies enormously. It is clear that inquisitors routinely used leading questions to elicit infor-

---

4   See below, chapter 8.2–3.

5   For the rise of the procedure of 'inquisition' in the middle ages, see the introduction to part two and notes 1–12.

6   See the Book of Sentences of the inquisitors of Toulouse, as printed in Philippus van Limborch, *Historia Inquisitionis. Cui Subjungitur Liber sententiarum inquisitionis Tholosanae ab anno Christi MCCCVII ad annum MCCCXXIII* (Amsterdam, 1692) in a separately paginated appendix.

7   For some extracts from Pierre Seila's handbook (Paris, Bibliothèque Nationale, Collection Doat, vol. 21), see H. C. Lea, *History of the Inquisition of the Middle Ages*, 3 vols (London, 1888), vol. 2, pp. 579–84. Comparable documents are found in Patschovsky and Selge, *Quellen*, pp. 55–69, and in A. Patschovsky, *Die Anfänge einer Ständigen Inquisition in Böhmen; Ein Prager Inquisitoren-Handbuch aus der ersten Hälfte des 14. Jahrhunderts*, Beiträge zur Geschichte und Quellenkunde des Mittelalters, Bd. 3 (Berlin, 1975), based on Wolfenbüttel MS. 311 Helmst.

8   For a primary example see Bernard Gui, *Manuel de l'inquisiteur*, ed. and trans. G. Mollat and G. Drioux, 2 vols (Paris, 1964).

mation.[9] Some crude, impatient investigators simply recorded routine confession to a formulaic list of theological 'crimes', and thereby suppressed any signs of individuality in the accused. Others, more subtle and more patient, documented a wide range of doubts and hesitations, only asking detailed theological questions of those who were sufficiently educated to understand their meaning.[10] Worst of all were the minority who tried to extract sensational admissions of fundamental disbelief, diabolism or sexual immorality from their victims: these recur in eras as far apart as the 1230s and the 1480s.[11] While some scholars have sought to establish ground-rules for the sifting and sorting of these records,[12] there is really no substitute for the careful and sympathetic weighing of one source against another. Deciding which evidence to believe when there is conflict, as there so often is with the Waldenses, will always be a matter of sensitive judgement.

Some Questions Arising

No recent scholarly survey book written in English has been wholly devoted to the medieval Waldenses over the entire time-span of their existence.[13] They have figured in more general works on medieval heresy; and many theses, books and articles have addressed particular aspects of the story.[14] Meanwhile, scholars writing in French, Italian and German

9   See, for instance, the 'questionnaire' discovered by the editor of the inquisitorial protocols of Peter Zwicker in Brandenburg: D. Kurze (ed.), *Quellen zur Ketzergeschichte Brandenburgs und Pommerns*, Veröffentlichungen der historischen Kommission zu Berlin, Bd. 45, Quellenwerke Bd. 6 (Berlin, 1975), pp. 17–18, 73–5, and evidence of its use, in ibid., pp. 30–1.
10   For instances where an inquisitor refrained from asking detailed questions about doctrine of those who could not understand them, see Kurze, *Quellen*, pp. 240, 245.
11   For accusations of diabolism and lechery see below, chapters 6.1 and 7.2–4.
12   For suggestions about the use of sources, see J.-F. Gilmont, 'Sources et critique des sources', in G. Audisio (ed.), *Les Vaudois des origines à leur fin (xiie–xvie siècles): Colloque international . . . Aix-en-Provence, 8–10 avril 1988* (Turin, 1990), pp. 105–13; G. Audisio, *Les 'Vaudois': naissance, vie et mort d'une dissidence (xiie–xve siècles)* (Turin, 1989), pp. 34–6; E. Cameron, *The Reformation of the Heretics: The Waldenses of the Alps 1480–1580* (Oxford, 1984), pp. 53–5, 67–70; compare also the methodologies proposed by historians of witchcraft, esp. R. Kieckhefer, *European Witch Trials: Their Foundation in Popular and Learned Culture, 1300–1500* (London, 1976).
13   G. Audisio, *The Waldensian Dissent: Persecution and Survival, c.1170–c.1570*, trans. Claire Davison (Cambridge, 1999) is a translation of Audisio's *Les 'Vaudois'*, as above, n. 12. Though by an scholar of wide experience in the subject, the book lacks full scholarly apparatus.
14   Of the general works on medieval heresy, see esp. M. Lambert, *Medieval Heresy: Popular Movements from the Gregorian Reform to the Reformation*, 2nd edn (Oxford, 1992); for other monographs and articles, see the references below, *passim*.

have made vital contributions to the subject in recent years, including a number of substantial survey works.[15] The expansion of the subject, and related developments in the study of other medieval religious movements, have raised a number of highly interesting questions, the importance of which reaches far beyond the narrow confines of the Waldensian movement, and which needs to be made accessible to non-specialist anglophone readers.

The first and most pressing question is one of identity: what did the term 'Waldensian' mean, and how specific was it? Were all those called 'Waldenses' recognizably similar, in the wide range of locations and at the diverse periods in which they appeared? One Italian scholar has in recent years decided to write of medieval Waldensian*isms*, on the grounds that the plurality and diversity of the various heretics forbids us to speak of a single movement.[16] Related to this is the issue of continuity: what line of descent, if any, linked the Waldenses of the end of the middle ages to those of the early thirteenth century? How far were they aware of their ancestry, and how accurate were their perceptions?[17]

The identity and sense of belonging of the Waldenses entails a further set of questions, regarding the consistency and comprehensiveness of their dissent. Between the sixteenth and the nineteenth centuries they were regularly cited by Protestant controversial writers as evidence that there had survived down the ages a counter-Church, or 'true Church' of orthodox but anti-Roman Christian believers detached from and opposed to the Roman 'Antichrist'.[18] This apologetic stance would not now be taken seriously by any modern scholarly historian. However, one of its implications, that the Waldensian movement was an articulate and coherent thread of non-Catholic spirituality, persists in some of the older literature and needs careful consideration. For example, how literate or learned were the Waldensian pastors? How far were they qualified or equipped to define a coherent religious position, or teach it to their followers? How far was their religious culture a developed, or indeed a developing thing? Such questions need to be addressed for the Waldenses

---

15   The most important survey work is still J. Gonnet and A. Molnar, *Les Vaudois au moyen âge* (Turin, 1974); other general surveys include A. Armand Hugon, A. Molnar, and V. Vinay, *Storia dei Valdesi*, 3 vols (Turin, 1974–80); G. Tourn, *L'É-tonnante aventure d'un peuple-église* (Tournon and Turin, 1980).

16   G. G. Merlo, *Valdesi e valdismi medievali: itinerari e proposte di ricerca* (Turin, 1984); G. G. Merlo, *Valdesi e valdismi medievali II: Identità valdesi nella storia e nella storiografia: studi e discussioni* (Turin, 1991).

17   See discussions of this point in chapter 6.4, chapter 7 and n. 9, chapter 8.1.

18   E. Cameron, 'Medieval Heretics as Protestant Martyrs', in D. Wood (ed.), *Martyrs and Martyrologies: Papers read at the 1992 summer meeting and the 1993 winter meeting of the Ecclesiastical History Society*, Studies in Church History, vol. 30 (Oxford, 1993), pp. 198–200; also Cameron, *Reformation of the Heretics*, pp. 243–52.

no less, and possibly more so, than for other movements such as Catharism, Lollardy, the 'Free Spirits', or any others.[19]

The acid test of the relationship between Waldenses and reformed Protestants (the 'first and second Reformations', as a work published in 1975 described them)[20] is the process by which Alpine Waldenses and Genevan Protestants combined forces in the mid-sixteenth century. The model proposed by nineteenth- and most twentieth-century historians was that of a conscious merger, initiated by the Waldensian pastors, discussed in a series of synods, and enacted in dialogue with early Protestant clerics in the 1530s. However, close reconsideration of the known sources, and discovery of a number of new pieces of evidence, led two quite independent researchers, in works published almost simultaneously in 1984, to assign a quite different date, around 1560, for the *effective* transformation of the Waldensian communities into reformed parishes.[21] The re-dating is less important than the new interpretation of the relationship which it entails. An early date implies a merger, as it were, of equal partners; a later date implies a takeover, a suppression of old ways by new ones and of old preachers by new ministers.

One important lesson has emerged from the preparatory study undertaken for this book. Despite the patchy survival of the source material, the Waldensian movements constitute a very large subject indeed. Most historians, including those who have written survey books on the subject, have been specialists in only a part or parts of the story. The part tends to colour one's view of the whole. It is an easy and dangerous pitfall to assume that the lessons of research in one branch of the subject ought to hold good in another. Looked at from different angles, different and even contradictory aspects of the subject present themselves: which helps to explain some of the disagreements charted in recent published work.[22] While no one contribution to the subject can resolve these differences, this book aspires at least to help the search for a synthesis. It will do so by careful dissection of as many of the primary sources as possible in the light of the recent literature. If the Waldensian movement of each time and place is studied by itself and for itself, without presuppositions, some helpful comparative suggestions, at least, may emerge.

19   On this see esp. Peter Biller and Anne Hudson (eds), *Heresy and Literacy, 1000–1530* (Cambridge, 1994).

20   V. Vinay, *Le Confessioni di fede dei Valdesi riformati, con i documenti del dialogo fra la 'prima' e la 'seconda' riforma*, Collana della Facoltà valdese di teologia, 12 (Turin, 1975).

21   Cameron, *Reformation of the Heretics*, pp. 155–66; G. Audisio, *Les Vaudois du Luberon: une minorité en Provence, 1460–1560* (Aix-en-Provence, 1984), pp. 409–39.

22   For an example of the debates, see Audisio, *Les Vaudois des origines à leur fin*. The proceedings of a further conference held in Aix-en-Provence in 1998 are edited by G. Audisio in *Revue de l'histoire des religions*, vol. 217, fasc. 1 (2000), forming the whole of that number of the periodical.

Part I
The First Phase

1

Before Heresy: Valdesius and the Poor Brethren at Lyon to 1184

The Waldenses of the later middle ages had no very precise idea of their own origins. Some believed their movement to be as old as the apostles; some thought that it dated from the fourth century, in the time of Pope Sylvester I (314–35).[1] Years later, some Protestant apologists tried to argue for a similarly ancient origin, at least as far back as the ninth century and possibly before.[2] Nevertheless, the overwhelming weight of modern opinion follows that of medieval Catholic chroniclers. These ascribed the origin of the 'Waldenses' to a citizen of Lyon called Valdesius, who lived in the late twelfth century, and after whom the movement was named.

1.1 Poverty and Bible Reading (c.1170–c.1177)

Two chronicles, the *Universal Chronicle* of the Laon Anonymous and the *Life of Pope Alexander III* of Richard of Poitiers, offer overlapping accounts of the course of events which led Valdesius, the rich citizen of

1 The so called 'Anonymous of Passau', in A. Patschovsky and K.-V. Selge (eds), *Quellen zur Geschichte der Waldenser*, Texte zur Kirchen- und Theologiegeschichte, 18 (Gütersloh, 1973), p. 73. The most elaborate incorporation of the Waldenses into the medieval Sylvester legend is found in the fourteenth-century *Liber Electorum*, as edited in J. J. Ignaz von Döllinger (ed.), *Beiträge zur Sektengeschichte des Mittelaters*, 2 vols (Munich, 1890), vol. 2 (*Dokumente vornehmlich zur Geschichte der Valdesier und Katharer*), pp. 352–5; also in P. P. A. Biller, 'Aspects of the Waldenses in the fourteenth century including an edition of their correspondence' (Oxford University D. Phil. thesis, 1977), pp. 264–70.
2 It used to be quite common to tie in the history of the Waldenses with Bishop Claudius of Turin (d. 827), who attacked a wide range of Church rituals and repudiated much of the authority of the Roman Church. Some of Claudius's works are in J.-P. Migne, *Patrologiae Cursus Completus*, Series Latina, vol. 104, cols 615–928.

Lyon, into his extraordinary religious career.[3] They agree on the essential point, that the founder of the movement was a rich layman, who suddenly decided to abandon all his wealth and seek a life of perfection through apostolic poverty.

Many otherwise unknown details are supplied by the Laon Anonymous. Valdesius, he tells us, had made his fortune through the 'iniquity of usury', which may mean no more than that he was a merchant obliged to use, in business, forms of dealing in money which the Church condemned as usurious.[4] One Sunday in the earlier part of 1173 (according to the chronicle's questionable dating) he saw a *jongleur* who had gathered a crowd to hear him speak, and called the *jongleur* back to his house. There Valdesius heard from him the story of St Alexis, a fifth-century Roman patrician who had left a wealthy bride for a life of mendicancy and almsgiving in Syria.[5] The following day, anxious for the sake of his soul, Valdesius went to ask the local theologians which was the most 'certain and perfect' way to reach God. He was duly told of Jesus's advice to the rich young man: 'If you wish to be perfect, go and sell everything that you possess'.[6]

Rather than 'going away sorrowing' as the young man in the gospel had done, Valdesius apparently took the text, and the example of St Alexis, absolutely literally. He offered his wife the choice of either his immovable property, reportedly including land, rivers, woods, fields, houses, rents, and so forth, or his movable property. She chose the

---

3   *Chronicon universale anonymi Laudunensis*, in *Monumenta Germaniae Historica, Scriptores*, vol. 26, pp. 447–9; trans. in R. I. Moore (ed.), *The Birth of Popular Heresy*, Documents of Medieval History 1 (London, 1975), pp. 111–13, and W. L. Wakefield and A. P. Evans (eds), *Heresies of the High Middle Ages: Selected Sources Translated and Annotated* (New York and London, 1969), pp. 200–3. For Richard of Poitiers' *Vita Alexandri Papae III* see G. Gonnet (ed.), *Enchiridion fontium valdensium (Recueil critique des sources concernant les Vaudois au moyen âge) du IIIe Concile de Latran au Synode de Chanforan (1179–1532)*, vol. 1 (Torre Pellice, 1958), pp. 164–6.

4   On the relevance of the charge of usury in Valdesius's context, see R. I. Moore, *The Origins of European Dissent* (London, 1977), pp. 228–9; on canon law on usury see J. T. Noonan, *The Scholastic Analysis of Usury* (Cambridge, Mass., 1957). M. Rubellin, 'Au temps où Valdès n'était pas hérétique: hypothèses sur le rôle de Valdès à Lyon (1170–1183)', in M. Zerner (ed.), *Inventer l'hérésie? Discours polémiques et pouvoirs avant l'inquisition*, Collection du Centre d'Études médiévales de Nice, vol. 2 (Nice, 1998), p. 202, points out that there is no firm evidence for the often repeated statement that Valdesius was a merchant; and reports (ibid., pp. 205–6) the suggestion that he may have been a financial administrator for the rich diocese.

5   On St Alexis, see the article 'Alexis of Rome' in D. H. Farmer, *The Oxford Dictionary of Saints*, 3rd edn (Oxford, 1992), p. 15 and refs. Farmer concludes that Alexis probably never existed. For the poem and its currency in the middle ages, see Wakefield and Evans, *Heresies*, p. 707, n. 6.

6   Matthew 19:21.

former. So, from the movables Valdesius made restitution to those from whom he had charged interest;[7] he settled a large amount on his daughters, whom he placed 'without their mother's knowledge' in a house of the order of Fontevrault reformed earlier in the century by Robert d'Arbrissel;[8] most he gave to the poor. Between 27 May and 1 August, while a very serious famine afflicted France and Germany, he gave regular doles three days a week of bread, soup and meat to whoever asked for it.[9] On 15 August, the Feast of the Assumption, he scattered money around to the poor in the streets, saying that no one could serve God and Mammon.[10] The chronicler relates, plausibly enough, that the bystanders assumed that he had gone mad. Nevertheless, he reportedly justified his actions as a 'vengeance on the enemies' which had enslaved him to money and created things, and also said that he had done this to teach his hearers to trust in God rather than riches. There is some pathos about the sequel. Valdesius found himself begging food from someone who had been his friend in his past life. The friend promptly offered to take him in and support him. Valdesius's wife, however, complained bitterly to the Archbishop of Lyon[11] that he had sought food from anyone other than herself; the archbishop agreed to order Valdesius to receive alms only from his wife.

There are serious grounds for regarding the Anonymous of Laon's account as a moral tale rather than a strictly factual account. Elements of the story have been recognized as *topoi*, typical themes found in medieval saints' lives. The sudden conversion under the influence of a saint's life told by a minstrel, recurs in the life of St Aybertus, for example.[12] Another *topos*, conversion under the effects of a sudden shock, crops up in the very different account of Valdesius's conversion by a rather later writer, the Anonymous of Passau. He told how the 'greater citizens' of Lyon were gathered together when one of their number died suddenly: so

---

7   Restitution was in principle required under canon law; there may also be an allusion here to the story of Zacchaeus in Luke 19:1–10.

8   On the order of Fontevrault, see F. L. Cross and E. A. Livingstone (eds), *The Oxford Dictionary of the Christian Church*, 3rd edn (Oxford, 1997), art. 'Fontevrault, Order of', p. 622 and refs. Rubellin, 'Au temps où Valdès n'était pas hérétique', p. 203, speculates that it may have been the priory of Jourcey in the Fontevrault Order to which Valdesius's daughters were consigned.

9   K.-V. Selge, *Die ersten Waldenser mit Edition des Liber antiheresis des Durandus von Osca*, 2 vols (Berlin, 1967) vol. 1, pp. 238–9; also K.-V. Selge, 'Caractéristiques du premier mouvement vaudois et crises au cours de son expansion', in *Cahiers de Fanjeaux* 2, 'Vaudois languedociens et pauvres catholiques' (1967), p. 110, dates this to 1176.

10   Matthew 6:24.

11   Guichard de Pontigny, 1165–80/1.

12   Selge, *Die ersten Waldenser*, vol. 1, pp. 232ff. and refs; Selge, 'Caractéristiques', pp. 118–19.

frightened was Valdesius by the spectacle of this sudden proof of human mortality, that he gave prodigally to the poor and attracted a crowd of poor followers.[13] The fact of Valdesius's sudden conversion to apostolic poverty seems agreed; the rest may well be embellishments – though even clichés sometimes contain some truth.

Valdesius's dilemma, as described by the Anonymous of Laon, highlights the predicament of lay people at this stage in the development of medieval Christianity. One could seek the 'perfect' way of celibacy, monastic renunciation, or ordination early in life; or one could seek the 'unperfect' way of marriage, involvement in the lay world, business and property.[14] Once the decision was taken, however, one was expected to stay on one's chosen path. Clergy were to remain clergy; married lay people were to remain married, unless widowhood released them for a celibate existence.[15] This ordering of Christian society did not leave room for the sudden, inconvenient, inappropriate experience of late conversion.[16] Archbishop Guichard, in ordering Valdesius to take support from his wife, denied any validity to his self-imposed religious divorce.

One very important factual detail of the early story is lacking in the Laon Chronicle. According to Richard of Poitiers and the inquisitor Étienne de Bourbon (d. 1261), Valdesius (whom they call Valdensis) at the very outset sought to have some passages of the Bible and the Fathers translated for him. Étienne de Bourbon named the translator as a 'grammarian' called Stephanus de Ansa, and said that he dictated to a scribe called Bernardus Ydros, later to become a prosperous and successful priest.[17] The recent discovery of the testament of Stephanus de Ansa has corroborated this account.[18] It should be emphasized that Richard and

13   Patschovsky and Selge, *Quellen*, p. 19.
14   For the attitude of the post-Hildebrandine clergy to the laity, see for example the description of lay people in Gratian's *Decretum*: 'there are Christians of another sort, called laymen . . . these are allowed to possess temporal goods . . . they are allowed to marry, to till the earth, to pronounce judgment on men's disputes and to plead in court, to lay their offerings on the altar, to pay their tithes; and so they can be saved, if they do good and avoid evil': in A. L. Richter and E. A. Friedberg (eds), *Corpus Juris Canonici* (repr. Graz, 1955), vol. 1, p. 678; see also I. S. Robinson, 'Gregory VII and the Soldiers of Christ', in *History* 58 (1973), pp. 169ff.
15   On the canon law of marriage see R. Naz (ed.), *Dictionnaire de droit canonique*, 7 vols (1935–65), vol. 6, cols 731–802; see also C. N. L. Brooke, *The Medieval Idea of Marriage* (Oxford, 1989).
16   Though Moore, *Birth of Popular Heresy*, p. 111, alludes to some instances where such religious conversion was contained within orthodoxy.
17   Patschovsky and Selge, *Quellen*, pp. 15–16.
18   A. Patschovsky, 'The Literacy of Waldensianism from Valdes to *c*.1400', in Peter Biller and Anne Hudson (eds), *Heresy and Literacy, 1000–1530* (Cambridge, 1994), p. 115.

Étienne speak of 'books of the Bible' and 'sentences of the holy [Fathers]': this suggests extracts rather than a complete text of scripture. The translation itself has not survived. Stephanus de Ansa and Bernardus Ydros were entirely orthodox, and clearly saw nothing untoward in preparing translations of Latin religious works for a pious, literate layman.[19] Valdesius was somewhat unusual, for the period, in that he could evidently read the vernacular, but not Latin: Latinity and literacy usually went together. Bourgeois merchants would have been some of the few people to use written materials without needing formal schooling in Latin.[20]

1.2   The Instinct to Preach (1177–1179)

The Laon Anonymous makes the point that Valdesius made his show of poverty and renunciation of wealth 'publicly',[21] and that he spoke out to show bystanders not to trust in their riches. In other words, he supposedly saw it as his mission, not just to be poor for his own soul's sake, but to encourage others to do likewise. However accurate the details, all the authorities agree that Valdesius quite soon began to preach his mission of apostolic poverty in public, and to attract a band of followers, men and women alike. The Laon Anonymous dates this development to 1177: 'those who followed his example, giving everything to the poor, became exponents of voluntary poverty'.[22] Gradually, the chronicle adds, they began to criticize their own and others' sins both privately and in public. The closely related accounts of Richard of Poitiers and Étienne de Bourbon agree; the latter described Valdesius's preaching as repeating in public what he had learned by heart from his Bible translations.[23]

In retrospect, some Catholic writers could denounce the 'presumptuous usurpation' implicit in Valdesius's and his followers' decision to preach in public. Certainly, at a time when the boundaries between laity and clergy were becoming ever more sharply defined,[24] the spectacle of spontaneous lay preaching might have frightened some. However, the movement may have seemed more threatening in retrospect than at the time. This was the eve of the age of the friars as well as that of new here-

---

19   Patschovsky, 'Literacy', p. 117.
20   See discussion in Patschovsky, 'Literacy', pp. 116–18 and refs.
21   The original reads *in manifesto: Chronicon universale anonymi Laudunensis* (as note 3), p. 448.
22   Ibid., p. 449; Moore, *Birth of Popular Heresy*, p. 112.
23   Selge, 'Caractéristiques', pp. 114–20, argued that preaching, not poverty as such, was always the core activity envisaged by Valdesius.
24   See above, n. 14.

sies.[25] The details of the story rather suggest that Valdesius was placed under a form of probation by the Church. Richard and Étienne claim that he was forbidden to preach by the Archbishop of Lyon *before* he was summoned to the Lateran Council, presumably the Third Lateran Council of 1179, which we know that some followers of Valdesius attended. However, these two related sources name the archbishop as Jean Bellesmains,[26] who was not appointed to the see until at least 1181, *after* the Council. Once again, hindsight may explain this report of an early prohibition on preaching.

Several sources agree that Valdesius, or some of his followers, did attend the Third Lateran Council. There is, however, less agreement as to what actually happened there. Richard and Étienne affirmed that they were 'summoned' to the Council and there adjudged schismatics.[27] This is contradicted by Canon 27 of the Council itself, which named only the Cathars, Publicani, and Patarenes.[28] The English curial commentator Walter Map described how some people named 'Valdesii' after their founder, from Lyon, presented a French translation of parts of scripture to the pope (Alexander III) at this Council, and asked to have their right to preach 'confirmed' to them. Map, who speaks of the group with sarcastic condescension, says that he was appointed to examine them on their learning. He asked them if they believed in each person of the Trinity, one by one; to each question they replied that they believed in him. Then he asked, in the same terms, if they believed in the Virgin Mary: they said, yes, they believed in her too, at which the assembled company collapsed in laughter at their ignorance. Map rounded off his report by claiming that however humbly they behaved now, they were a threat; and said how wrong it was to assume that 'ancient times', presumably meaning the apostolic age, were necessarily better than the present.[29] He leaves the impression that the followers of Valdesius were humiliated, but says nothing about their being banned or condemned. The Laon Anonymous goes further: it reports that the pope 'embraced'

25 See Wakefield and Evans, *Heresies*, p. 707, n. 3, for parallels with St Francis; Rubellin, 'Au temps où Valdès n'était pas hérétique', p. 211 and nn., cites evidence that not all clerics in the late twelfth century disapproved uniformly of lay preachers, and that there was considerable debate on this issue.

26 Note his alternative English title, 'John of Canterbury': see M. Lambert, *Medieval Heresy: Popular Movements from the Gregorian Reform to the Reformation*, 2nd edn (Oxford, 1992), p. 65.

27 For Richard and Étienne see Patschovsky and Selge, *Quellen*, p. 17 and refs.

28 For Canon 27 of the Third Lateran Council, see G. Alberigo (ed.), *Conciliorum Oecumenicorum Decreta: The Decrees of the Ecumenical Councils*, 2 vols, trans. N. P. Tanner (London and Washington, DC, 1990), pp. 224–5.

29 The story is found in Walter Map, *De nugis curialium*, ed. M. R. James (Oxford, 1914), pp. 60–2; edited in Gonnet, *Enchiridion*, vol. 1, pp. 122–4, and trans. in Wakefield and Evans, *Heresies*, pp. 203–4.

Valdesius, and approved his vow of voluntary poverty; but that he told him not to take on preaching *unless asked to do so by the priests*. These two accounts can be reconciled: the followers of Valdesius had shown humility by presenting themselves for papal approval, but were sorely wanting in theological depth: so it made sense to endorse their poverty, which the Church had long approved in others, but to restrain their enthusiasm for the sermon within limits to be set by the ordained clergy. In the passage immediately following, the Laon Anonymous describes a very similar papal response to the movement of the Humiliati in Lombardy, at much the same period.[30]

The fervour of the late convert had confronted officialdom. The pope, remote from the pastoral situation, could afford to be conditionally benevolent. The unease of the local clergy, on the other hand, can easily be understood. In the previous century or so France had seen a series of charismatic religious leaders spring up, often in defiance of the hierarchy, and sometimes propagating alarming heresies. After the experience of Henry of Lausanne and Peter of Bruis,[31] caution was the very least to be expected of the Lyonnais clergy.

1.3   Explicit Rejection of Dualist Heresy (1180–1181)

There was a further worry, remote from Lyon perhaps, but as serious a challenge as was ever faced by the churches of southern France. The Cathar heresy was spreading in the Languedoc in the mid to late twelfth century, barely impeded by a demoralized clergy. The fear of Catharism seems likely to explain, at least in part, the next phase in the story of Valdesius.

Geoffroy of Auxerre, abbot of Hautecombe, reported that Archbishop Guichard of Lyon summoned a council in the city, which was presided over by the prominent Cistercian Henri de Marcy, newly appointed cardinal-legate, in 1180 or 1181.[32] At that council, as Geoffroy reported in his *Super Apocalypsim*, the founder of a 'sect' whom he names Wandesius, abjured his heresy in the presence of the attendant church-men. The followers of this sect, he said, had been 'usurping the office of preaching' and travelling around the towns living off the food of others without labour 'on the pretext of poverty'. Geoffroy was apparently an eye-witness: however, his report of an 'abjuration' by Valdesius does not

---

30   *Chronicon universale anonymi Laudunensis* (as note 3), pp. 449–50; Wakefield and Evans, *Heresies*, pp. 158–9.
31   On these, see sources in Wakefield and Evans, *Heresies*, pp. 107–26; discussions in Lambert, *Medieval Heresy*, pp. 44–50; also Moore, *Origins*, pp. 82–114.
32   For the sources which cast doubt on the date of this council see Wakefield and Evans, *Heresies*, pp. 204, 709–10 and refs.

accord with the surviving text of a 'profession of faith and proposal of a way of life' which seems to have been subscribed by Valdesius on this occasion, and which has survived.

The Profession of Faith has been shown to occupy a pivotal position in the development of a formal summary of Western Catholic doctrine at this period. The text was not original to Valdesius and was almost certainly not drafted by him: it may originate with Henri de Marcy. Earlier versions of its wording have been traced in the *Statuta Ecclesiae Antiqua* dated to the fifth century, and the ordination formularies of the Gallican rite from the sixth to the eleventh centuries. After its use to confirm the orthodoxy of Valdesius, the text was adapted slightly for the declarations of two groups of former Waldenses who reconciled themselves to the Church in 1208 and 1210, and for the reconciliation of other heretics under Innocent III. Its influence has been detected in the First Constitution of the Fourth Lateran Council of 1215 and the formulae for reconciling heretics in the canon law.[33]

In the Profession of Faith, Valdesius confirmed that he believed in and accepted the Trinity, the three main creeds of the Church, and the divine origin of both Old and New Testaments. He accepted the divine inspiration of John the Baptist. He affirmed that only the Son of God became incarnate; and that Christ had a true physical nature. He confessed to believing in one Catholic Church, and in all its seven sacraments, even if these were administered by a sinful priest. He affirmed that the devil was made evil by an act of will, not nature; that eating meat was not blameworthy; that those to be resurrected will rise in their own flesh and no other; and that alms, masses and other works benefited the dead.[34]

The principal point of the profession, in the form in which Valdesius subscribed it, was evidently to refute any suggestion that he subscribed to the Cathar heresy. Most Cathars rejected the Old Testament, believed that John the Baptist was damned, and denied the orthodox view of the

33 For the council see Geoffroy of Auxerre in Gonnet, *Enchiridion*, vol. 1, pp. 45–9. An alternative version of Geoffroy's report in another work reads 'juravit' for 'abjuravit', so the report of an 'abjuration' by Valdesius may have been a simple misreading with hindsight: Rubellin, 'Au temps où Valdès n'était pas hérétique', p. 198, n. 16.

34 For the Profession of Faith see A. Dondaine, 'Aux origines du valdéisme. Une profession de foi de Valdès', in *Archivum Fratrum Praedicatorum* 16 (1946), pp. 191–235; C. Thouzellier, *Catharisme et valdéisme en Languedoc à la fin du xiie et au début du xiiie siècle* (Paris, 1966), pp. 27–34; also in Gonnet, *Enchiridion*, vol. 1, pp. 32–6. J. Duvernoy, 'Le Mouvement vaudois: origines', in *Mouvements dissidents et novateurs, Heresis*, nos 13–14 (1990), pp. 173–98, argued that the Profession might have originated not with Valdesius but with Durandis of Osca (as chapter 4.1, below). Rubellin, 'Au temps où Valdès n'était pas hérétique', pp. 198–9, presents valid arguments for the traditional interpretation.

Incarnation. Their 'perfect' masters refused to eat meat, and they believed in the transmigration of souls from one body to another at death.[35] In some of its later forms the confession would be directed more specifically to a refutation of the errors of the 'Waldenses'.[36] At this stage, however, there were simply no such errors to abjure or to refute. The confession tells us more about the worries of the prelates, and about the essential orthodoxy of Valdesius and his followers, than it does about any distinctive beliefs which they may have had.

The document closed with a 'proposal of [a way of] life'. In this Valdesius and his 'brethren' affirmed that they had 'renounced the world' and had resolved to give their goods to the poor and become poor themselves. They would keep no money for themselves, and would accept nothing but their immediate supplies of food and clothing from others. They proposed to keep the 'evangelical counsels' as rules: that is, to follow all the advice found in the gospels about the apostolic way of life literally.[37] The inclusion of this proposal in the confession is singularly important. It has been remarked that it gives a form of ecclesiastical authorization for the life-style of Valdesius and his 'brethren'. Preaching is neither permitted, nor explicitly forbidden; and practically speaking, it would have been naive of the prelates at the council to expect the brethren to follow their proposal, without giving some form of teaching verbally as well as by example.[38] On the face of it, this document appears to mark an accommodation of the followers of Valdesius within the Church, as well as an affirmation of their orthodox faith. It may even signify that they had temporarily overcome the scepticism of Henri de Marcy and Geoffroy of Auxerre regarding their vocation.

1.4   Dispersal and Condemnation at Verona (1182–1184)

Yet this relationship, if such it was, broke down almost immediately. Even the relatively sympathetic account of the Laon Anonymous relates how the poor brethren obeyed for a while the command to preach only with

---

35   For Cathar belief, besides Thouzellier, *Catharisme et valdéisme*, see also M. Lambert, *The Cathars* (Oxford, 1998), pp. 19–32 and *passim*.
36   Compare the versions of the 'propositum' adopted later, as below, chapter 4.1, 4.3.
37   See Dondaine, 'Aux origines', p. 232: 'quia fides secundum iacobum apostolum "sine operibus mortua est", seculo abrenunciavimus, et que abeabamus, velut a domino consultum est, pauperibus erogavimus et pauperes esse decrevimus, ita ut de crastino solliciti esse non curamus, nec aurum nec argentum vel aliquid tale preter victum et vestitum cotidianum a quoquam accepturi sumus. Concilia quoque evangelica velut precepta servare proposuimus'. The 'evangelical counsels' were generally taken to include the three traditional monastic vows.
38   Selge, *Die ersten Waldenser*, vol. 2, p. 5, n.

priestly permission; but later they disobeyed it, bringing 'scandal to many and ruin to themselves'. Richard of Poitiers, despite some chronological confusion, reported that when faced with an order to desist from preaching and expounding scripture, they quoted the apostles to the effect that 'one should obey God rather than men'.[39] They were then declared disobedient and contumacious, and excommunicated, and ultimately driven from the territory.[40]

So Archbishop Jean Bellesmains expelled the followers of Valdesius from Lyon. This decision does not appear to be attested by any formal document, nor is its date certain: it presumably took place between Archbishop Jean's arrival in the see, c.1182 and the Council of Verona of 1184.[41] When the inevitability born of hindsight is peeled away, this collapse in the relationship between Valdesius and the local Church marks a critical and a somewhat surprising turning-point. Both the local Church and the papacy had, it seems, been willing to accommodate the poor brethren between c.1173 and c.1181 without taking any hostile action; then the policy was reversed. Perhaps the offer to recognize their poverty, but not their preaching mission, had been only half sincere. It may be that the cardinal-legate, or Archbishop Guichard, had been more hopeful of keeping them within the Church than the next archbishop, Jean Bellesmains, felt able to be; and that under a new archbishop relations grew worse.

This speculation seems particularly plausible in the case of Guichard de Pontigny, who had gained the archbishopric after a disputed election and a struggle, c.1164–7. Guichard was a Cistercian and a vigorous, controversial reformer: he may well have seen in Valdesius's spectacular voluntary poverty a welcome contrast to the wealth and self-indulgence which he deplored in some of the cathedral canons. On Guichard's death, the canons of Lyon elected in Jean Bellesmains a secular priest, an experienced and hierarchically minded prelate who would have had much less time than Guichard de Pontigny for a small group of semi-disciplined lay preachers. Moreover, Archbishop Jean did not inherit the disputes in the chapter which made Guichard seek for allies outside. Such an attitude on the part of the earlier archbishop – if this speculation about his motives is correct – ties in perfectly with the interpretation whereby the origins of popular lay heresy in the middle ages may be seen in movements for reform within the Church, which were then exiled from the fold when

39   Acts 5:29.
40   The expulsion from Lyon is inferred from the chronicles listed above; neither is precise as to date.
41   It was similar to the event portrayed in a thirteenth-century relief on Porta Romana at Milan, as in J. Gonnet and A. Molnar, *Les Vaudois au moyen âge* (Turin, 1974), p. ii.

they grew out of hand or when opponents of reform seized the political initiative against them.[42] Papal policy towards such groups may also have changed when Pope Lucius III succeeded Alexander III. Whatever the reason, this decision to drive Valdesius and his followers from the fold ensured that their name would hereafter be associated with a heresy, while that of Francis was associated with a religious order.

On 4 November 1184 the Council of Verona under Pope Lucius III promulgated the decree *Ad Abolendam*.[43] This decree placed under anathema the Cathar and Patarene heresies, as before; but also, and for the first time, it anathematized 'those who falsely call themselves *Humiliati* or *Poor of Lyon*'. It went on to decree that all those who claimed authority to preach, or who presumed to preach publicly or privately against the orders or without the permission of pope or bishop, were under anathema. This specific reference to unlicensed preaching, apart from any doctrinal error as such, appears to address the case of the Waldenses quite specifically. It is also one of the earliest documents to use the term 'Poor of Lyon', which would thereafter become a standard ecclesiastical term for the scattered followers of Valdesius. The inclusion of the Humiliati of Lombardy in the same sentence as the Waldenses is interesting: both had been given conditional approval around 1179; both were condemned when that approval was withdrawn.

Only after 1184 can one meaningfully or properly speak of the 'heresy' of the Waldenses or Poor of Lyon; even then, there is some doubt as to when heterodox belief, rather than irregular preaching, became their primary characteristic. Before 1184, the issue of Valdesius was a pastoral problem within the Catholic faithful. Broadly speaking, it exemplified the conflict between a very potent inner call to missionary poverty, and the ritual, legal rights of an institutional clergy. Valdesius and his followers were expected to submit their zeal to the jurisdiction of a hierarchy, which did not share their fervent aspiration to apostolic poverty or their reborn sense of mission. The priestly hierarchy, in the period *c*.1177–*c*.1183, was asked to accommodate the enthusiasm of a group of lay people who had no proper place within the estate of the 'clergy' and whose insistence on poverty must have appeared a standing reproach to the clergy's own prosperous condition. Each group expected too much of the other. On the other hand, if the Archbishop of Lyon had been more patient, or Valdesius more obedient, there would probably still have been irregular,

---

42   See Rubellin, 'Au temps où Valdès n'était pas hérétique', pp. 193–217. On the wider theory, see Moore, *Origins*, pp. 38–136, 261–83; also R. I. Moore, *The Formation of a Persecuting Society: Power and Deviance in Western Europe, 950–1250* (Oxford, 1987), pp. 68–72.
43   For the Council of Verona see Richter and Friedberg, *Corpus Juris Canonici*, vol. 2, cols 780–2; Gonnet, *Enchiridion*, vol. 1, pp. 50–3.

unlicensed lay evangelists at work in twelfth-century Europe. They might not have been called Waldenses; but there would still have emerged some groups who preferred the self-proclaimed mission to the legally sanctioned hierarchy. The speed with which the movement of the Waldensian preachers spread in the following twenty years implies that the first Waldenses had somehow or other caught a mood in the age, which needed to find expression.

2

Disobedient Preachers, 1184–c.1210

In the conclusion to his account of 'Valdensis', Richard of Poitiers told how, after their excommunication, the 'heretics were scattered through Provence and Lombardy, where they mingled with other heretics, and imbibed and spread around their errors'.[1] During the quarter of a century or so after the Council of Verona the first generation of the Waldensian movement took shape. Itinerant, poor preachers travelled in small groups among the Catholic laity of southern France and northern Italy. They preached to anyone who would listen: there does not seem to have been any clearly defined 'membership' of their hearers and followers at this stage. For some, at least, their primary goal was to defend and uphold Catholic doctrine against the Cathar heresy so prevalent in these regions.

However, the brethren's illegal status in the eyes of the Church gradually forced them to devise arguments to justify their own work. They taught Catholic doctrine, but (paradoxically) did not believe in the Catholic Church's right to forbid them to do so. A complex question of authority arose, which was never really to be resolved as long as the Waldensian movements existed. This was the beginning of Waldensian 'heresy': the questioning of the apostolic authority of the visible hierarchy. With time, other doctrinal issues arose to trouble and divide the movement. It spread so rapidly, and tended so easily to merge or be confused with other movements, that no single, simple core of 'Waldensian' belief could be sustained.[2] The spread of the brethren into Lombardy proved specially fertile in such problems. In this chapter the focus will be on the followers of Valdesius in southern France: the Lombards will be considered in chapter 3.

---

1 For Richard's account see G. Gonnet (ed.), *Enchiridion fontium valdensium (Recueil critique des sources concernant les Vaudois au moyen âge) du IIIe Concile de Latran au Synode de Chanforan (1179–1532)*, vol. 1 (Torre Pellice, 1958), pp. 164–6.
2 See K.-V. Selge, *Die ersten Waldenser mit Edition des Liber antiheresis des Durandus von Osca*, 2 vols (Berlin, 1967), vol. 1, pp. 129–88.

2.1   Preachers Despite the Church

The vital issue, in this first generation, was the claim made by Valdesius
and his followers that all of them might preach, and ought to preach.
Some of the clearest and earliest evidence for this issue comes from the
province of Narbonne in Languedoc. Some time before 1191 Archbishop
Bernard Gaucelin (or d'Arsac) of Narbonne discovered that his efforts
to condemn the Waldensian preachers in his diocese were ignored: as
after the 1184 anathema, they simply ignored the sentence. A disputation was called at which both sides presented their views under the presidency of a cleric called Raymundus de Daventria.[3] The arguments of both
parties were summarized in the *Book against the Sect of the Waldenses*
written by Bernard, the Premonstratensian abbot of Fontcaude, shortly
after the disputation. Bernard produced the work as a debating tool for
Catholic priests who, he feared, were too inexperienced or unable to
resist the heretics by preaching.[4]

Bernard first attacked the Waldenses for their disobedience: he noted
the bald fact that they ignored the commands of pope and prelates, but
did not suggest that they used any particular arguments to justify their
stance.[5] It was heresy, he remarked later, to say that one ought not to
obey bishops, priests or the Church.[6] He argued at some length that the
dignity of prelates demanded respect, and that one should not criticize
or speak ill of them.[7] On their insistence that everyone including laymen
must preach, however, he cited an arsenal of their proof-texts and arguments. They applied the text of James 4:17 ('the man who knows the
good he ought to do and does not do it is a sinner') to their preaching,
likewise Revelation 22:17 as expounded by Gregory the Great. They
cited the man who cast out demons in Christ's name even though he
was not an apostle.[8] They quoted Paul's rejoicing at the truth of Christ
being announced in any way whatever.[9] Nor did they rely narrowly on
biblical authority: they cited instances of lay preachers such as Honora-
tus of Lerins, St Equitius, or more recently St Raymond Paulus; and even
the lay, unlettered apostles themselves.[10] The other argument to which
Bernard of Fontcaude devoted some time was their application of the

3   Most probably to be translated 'of Deventer'.
4   Bernard's work is found in J.-P. Migne, *Patrologiae Cursus Completus*, Series
Latina, vol. 204, cols 793–840.
5   Ibid., cols 795–8.
6   Ibid., col 817.
7   Ibid., cols 798–805.
8   Mark 9:38–40.
9   Philippians 1:15–18.
10 Migne, *Patrologiae*, vol. 204, cols 805–9.

apostles' defence that 'one should obey God rather than men',[11] already attributed to the Waldenses on an earlier occasion by Richard of Poitiers.[12] Since Christ had told the disciples 'to go out and preach to all the world', that message they applied to themselves. Bernard somewhat testily pointed out that the Waldenses were not the apostles, nor were the clergy to be equated with the Jews who had crucified Christ.[13]

Did the Waldenses simply disobey the prelates and clergy who banned their preaching, or did they have some more elaborate theoretical justification for their disobedience? A significant historical point is at issue here. Many (not all) later Waldenses would reportedly claim that a sinful priest lost his authority, even his ritual power, and *because of his sinfulness* should not be obeyed. This is the argument sometimes called the Donatist doctrine.[14] The issue of the validity of sinful priests' ministries was to be one of the most serious and divisive points for debate between different wings of the movement in the period leading up to the conference at Bergamo in 1218.[15] It is important to decide, then, how far mere pragmatic disobedience among the earliest Waldenses developed into theological heresy.

Bernard de Fontcaude gives no hint that the Waldenses justified their disobedience with a Donatist argument. However, the poet and controversial theologian Alain of Lille (?1128–1203) presented a different picture in his *Work in Four Parts against Heretics, Waldenses, Jews, and Saracens*, possibly written in the late 1180s or 1190s at Montpellier.[16] Alain's work, to judge by the large number of surviving manuscripts, seems to have been one of the most successful and influential treatises on its subject in the high middle ages.[17] The second part of the work dealt with the Waldenses, distinguished from the 'heretics', i.e. the Cathars, who were discussed in the first part. Alain corroborated Bernard in defining the origin of the movement with the presumption of 'Waldus', who had chosen on his own inspiration to preach 'without the authority of his bishop, without divine inspiration, without knowledge, without learning'. He claimed that without a special miracle they could not claim to have been called to preach over the heads, as it were,

---

11 Acts 5:29.
12 See above, chapter 1, note 39.
13 Migne, *Patrologiae*, vol. 204, cols 817–18.
14 For the earlier history of Donatism within the church of fourth-century North Africa, see F. L. Cross and E. A. Livingstone (eds), *The Oxford Dictionary of the Christian Church*, 3rd edn (Oxford, 1997), art. 'Donatism', pp. 499–500 and references.
15 For the conference of Bergamo, see below, chapter 3.5.
16 Selge, *Die ersten Waldenser*, vol. 1, pp. 166ff.; W. L. Wakefield and A. P. Evans (eds), *Heresies of the High Middle Ages: Selected Sources Translated and Annotated* (New York and London, 1969), p. 214.
17 See Wakefield and Evans, *Heresies*, p. 746 and references.

of the clergy.[18] At some length, and in line with Bernard of Fontcaude's arguments, Alain reproached the Waldenses for their disobedience to the hierarchy.[19] However, he went on to say that 'perhaps some heretics may say, that one should obey good prelates, who stand in place of the apostles by life and work; but not those who do not follow the life of the apostles or perform their work, because these are hirelings and not shepherds'.[20] Developing this argument against Donatist arguments occupied ten chapters of Alain's work. All priests had the power to bind and loose, regardless of their conduct. He attacked the view, which he attributed to the Waldenses, that a good moral character conferred more spiritual authority than ritual orders.[21] He insisted that true contrition required confession of sins to a priest: confession to a layman, or to God alone, was insufficient, though the heretics said it was preferable.[22] Prayers offered by the Church were valid, he said, whether the priest who offered them was good or bad.[23]

If Alain of Lille's account were entirely accurate, the Waldenses would within a decade or so of their condemnation have adopted a set of highly destructive arguments against the value of an ordained clergy. The positions attributed to them go far beyond what is necessary to justify their rejection of a ban on lay preaching, and strike at the spiritual value, not just the jurisdictional power, of the Catholic priesthood. However, there are various reasons to doubt Alain's report of Waldensian arguments. The internal evidence of the work betrays no personal contact with the heretics: indeed the structure of some sentences ('*perhaps* the heretics may say . . .') suggests that he may have been, in the manner of the schools, summoning up analogous arguments, originating with the Patarenes or the followers of Arnaldo of Brescia,[24] in order to refute them; or at best, he may have depicted only one wing of the early movement.[25] The question may be partly resolved by looking at the one major theological composition from the hands of an authentic Waldensian

---

18 Alain of Lille, *De fide catholica: contra haereticos sui temporis, praesertim Albigenses*, in Migne, *Patrologiae*, vol. 210, cols 377–80.
19 Ibid., cols 380–2.
20 Ibid., col. 383.
21 Ibid., col. 385.
22 Ibid., cols 385–7.
23 Ibid., cols 388–90.
24 On the Patarenes and Arnaldists, see the references in chapter 3, note 4.
25 Compare the discussion in Selge, *Die ersten Waldenser*, vol. 1, pp. 169–72; and also the corresponding remarks in K.-V. Selge, 'Caractéristiques du premier mouvement vaudois et crises au cours de son expansion', in *Cahiers de Fanjeaux* 2, 'Vaudois languedociens et pauvres catholiques' (1967), pp. 132–3. Selge believes that Alain testifies to a radicalization of certain groups in Waldensianism. He may also demonstrate an intellectual's readiness to run ahead of the people whom he describes, in pursuit of the argument.

teacher, the *Liber Antiheresis* or 'Book against the [Cathar] Heresy' of Durand of Osca.[26] Durand was certainly the most learned theologian ever to write from within the Waldensian movement; he was to be won over to Catholicism by Pope Innocent III and to continue his theological career within the Church after 1208.[27] The *Liber Antiheresis* was mainly written to defend orthodox Christian belief against the teachings of the Cathars, and as such will be analysed later. However, it also makes some vital points about how the early Waldenses perceived their relationship with the Roman clergy.

In his prologue, Durand described how God had chosen 'Lord Valdesius' to fulfil the apostolic task of preaching against error, when Christ saw that the prelates 'were dedicated to greed, simony, pride, avarice, feasting, . . . lechery, and other disgraceful acts' and so not able to do their duty.[28] This sounds quite Donatist; however, the body of the work does not really develop the rhetoric. When discussing the sacrament of ordination, Durand affirmed that he and his group upheld the orders of bishop, priest, deacon and so forth, though they did not receive them themselves. Jesus Christ was the Waldenses' true bishop, but so also were the prelates, in so far as they upheld the faith and the sacraments, and not otherwise. If the prelates commanded anything which was contrary to the word of God, the Waldenses were bound, not only by scripture, but also by canon law, to disobey. In so far as the bishops commanded things which were pleasing to God and according to scripture, however, the Waldenses felt bound to obey them and respect their commands, even though they were bad people.[29] Again, later on in the work Durand confirmed that Valdesius had received the word of God from the bishops

---

26 For whether the name 'Osca' should be taken to refer to Osques in the Rouergue or Huesca in Aragon, see the discussions in J. Gonnet and A. Molnar, *Les Vaudois au moyen âge* (Turin, 1974), pp. 107–9, with references, and in Wakefield and Evans, *Heresies*, p. 715. I incline to accept Gonnet's arguments on this point and have used the Latin form 'Osca', which is authentic, if not geographically decisive. However, given that there is evidence of some Poor Catholic activity in Aragon, the issue of the toponym is neither closed nor vastly important.

27 See below, section 5, and chapter 4.

28 Selge, *Die ersten Waldenser*, vol. 2, pp. 6–9, and esp. p. 8: 'Set suum non ex toto deserens populum, videns praelatorum opera summi patris filius cupiditati, simonie, superbie, philargie, cenodoxie, castrimargie, pellicatui, aliisque flagiciis intenta, et etiam divina misteria ob eorum pessima opera naucipendi, sicut in sue predicationis inicio piscatores sine litteris, te, domne valdesi, eligens in apostolico aporismate, ut per te tuosque comites, quod inposti non poterant, renitatur allegavit erroribus'. This highly intricate sentence is typical of Durand. For an alternative edition of the prologue (including punctuation to clarify the syntax) see C. Thouzellier, *Hérésie et hérétiques* (Rome, 1969), pp. 72–4.

29 Selge, *Die ersten Waldenser*, vol. 2, pp. 59–62, esp. p. 61: 'Et quamvis mali sint, nos tamen eis hac auctoritate, si, que deo placuerint et sanctis scripturis precepta sunt, vel iusserint vel docuerint – sin aliter, minime – parere conabimur'.

and priests; notwithstanding their bad lives, they were to be listened to whenever they taught anything which was good.[30]

This approach is not strictly Donatist. It says that priests, even bad priests, have a spiritual role; but if they command something wrong, they may be disobeyed. Clearly 'something wrong', for Durand and his associates, included forbidding the Waldenses to teach and preach. The significance of the clergy's sins was that lazy, ineffectual priests needed Valdesius and his followers to make up for their deficiencies in the mission field – not that sinful priests lost their ritual powers. This subtle theological distinction had vital practical consequences. A thoroughgoing Donatist position would, in principle, have implied that sacramental services, such as baptism, the eucharist, or other rites performed by sinful priests were invalid, and would have needed to be repeated. If the argument that 'merit conferred spiritual authority' were taken to its conclusion, then the 'meritorious' Waldensian preachers would have felt authorized to perform all the sacraments themselves, as laymen. Though this issue was to cause vehement debate, the outcome was that neither in earlier nor in later Waldensianism did the Waldenses consistently reject the sacraments of Catholic priests because of their sins. Primitive Waldensianism, as represented by Durand, was not Donatist in theory; most later Waldensianism would not be thoroughly Donatist in practice.[31]

2.2 The Assault on Catharism

The *Liber Antiheresis* is so impressive that it is easy to assume that it represents the main thrust of the Waldensian mission in the period *c*.1185–1205. This may well be true for the Languedoc and the Pyrenees, the region where Durand worked after and presumably before his conversion. In the Languedoc the Waldensian society's principal self-appointed task was to preach against the Cathar dualists, whose overt anti-clericalism, and rather more covert dualist mythology, had proved so remarkably seductive to all classes in the region.[32]

The prologue to the *Liber Antiheresis* attributed to Valdesius and his followers the primary task of refuting the 'heretics', the Cathars, and the secondary one of resisting 'others who spoke ill of them', that is, hostile Catholic opponents. Durand wrote, with more than a little false modesty,

30 Ibid., pp. 93–9, esp. pp. 95–6.
31 See the arguments proposed below, in chapter 5, notes 28, 105, 130; chapter 6, notes 29, 140, 262; chapter 7, note 36; and the conclusion.
32 On Catharism in the Languedoc, see esp. M. Lambert, *The Cathars* (Oxford, 1998), pp. 60–81, 98–107, 131–70 and references.

that he had prepared the work 'not presumptuously, as though regarding myself as more learned' than the other Waldenses, but because there was a shortage of suitable books for arming oneself in controversy of this kind; he offered the Waldensian preachers 'the sword of the spirit and theological arrows' to resist the audacity of the Cathars.[33] Most of the body of the first recension of the work, and nearly all of the later chapters, could have been written by a contemporary Catholic. The Trinity, the divine calling of John the Baptist, the full humanity and full divinity of Christ, were all buttressed by scriptural references and arguments.[34] The unity of the one Church and the seven traditional sacraments were upheld. Rain and storms came from God, not the devil. There were many ways to holiness, not the one way of the Cathar *perfecti*. Meat-eating was licit, while usury, condoned by the Cathars, was not. The Final Judgement to come would weigh the merits of each individual soul; transmigration of dead souls into other bodies was rejected.[35] Later on in the work, Durand defended the origins and tradition of the Catholic Church against Cathar critics. He rounded on the Cathars themselves with some erudition, tracing their errors to Manichaeans, Gnostics, other early heretics and even the ancient Pythagoreans.[36] The second part of the work, which consisted of smaller numbers of longer, fuller chapters, attacked Catharism even more exclusively. There was one God, not two; the one God created everything, not just the spiritual world. The angels who fell from heaven were irredeemably damned, and could not be restored to heaven through human lives as some Cathars claimed. The Law of Moses was holy and good, not a creation of the devils. At the general resurrection every individual would rise in their own flesh and none other.[37]

Both the style and the arguments of Durand's work were highly sophisticated. His dexterity in reasoning and ability to deploy scriptural, patristic and canonical authorities should have made him a formidable opponent in debate. The only potential problem with the work lies in its very sophistication. Durand wrote not just in Latin, but in a highly complex, recherché Latin. His word order was sometimes gratuitously

---

33 Selge, *Die ersten Waldenser*, vol. 2, pp. 8–9: 'opere precium contuens digestim capto utilia edere, non presumptive, quasi me diserciorem vobis autumans . . . set quia deest librorum copia, et distedet aporibus in tot altercationibus persepe tot volumina legere, perlibuit dei filio, sine quo nil possumus, per me ex agiografis vestre utilitati edecumare compendium. Gladium spiritus sagitasque theologicas habetote conterminatas ad debellandum predictorum virulentam eorumque complicum audaciam.'
34 Ibid., pp. 12–39.
35 Ibid., pp. 39–77.
36 Ibid., pp. 93–9.
37 Ibid, pp. 110–99, 202–47.

tortuous and obscure; his vocabulary bristles with words adapted from the Greek, with which the average clerk might have had some difficulty.[38] One cannot tell whether or not this feature of Durand's work limited his impact in any way, because there is little or no evidence concerning the disputes between Waldenses and Cathars in the Languedoc of his time. The Catholic preaching campaigns of Dominic and Diego, Bishop of Osma are better documented.[39] A few decades later, the Waldensian and Cathar preachers, whose appearance and itinerant habits made them appear somewhat similar despite the fundamental differences in their teaching, seem to have been regarded more or less equally by lay people in southern France.[40]

2.3 The Way of Life of the Travelling Preachers

For most of the people who saw the Waldensian preachers at work, their doctrine – which was in any case mostly that of the official Church – would have been less distinctive and less memorable than their way of life. In the generation before the mendicant friars, travelling poor preachers would have made as much of an impression by their conduct as their message. First and foremost, Valdesius and his society marked themselves out by travelling around, in pairs or small groups, having no fixed homes, no possessions and, above all, no work besides the teaching of the gospel. These features of their life-style were implicit in the *propositum vitae* submitted by Valdesius as early as the Council of 1180/1.[41] To 'renounce the world', give property to the poor and 'take no thought for the morrow' meant that fixed homes might not be owned, and regular work, bringing a wage, might not be undertaken. Valdesius's insistence on the renunciation of bodily work was to sour relations between him and his movement's Italian wing.[42] Not only that: the decision to 'live of the Gospel', that is, to perform no

38 As remarked by A. Patschovsky, 'The Literacy of Waldensianism from Valdes to *c*.1400', in Peter Biller and Anne Hudson (eds), *Heresy and Literacy, 1000–1530* (Cambridge, 1994), p. 119 and n. 22.

39 For these see, for example, Pierre de Vaux-Cernay, *Petrum Vallium Sarnaii Hystoria albigensis*, ed. P. Guébin and E. Lyon, 3 vols (Paris, 1926–39); Guillaume de Puylaurens, *Historia Albigensium*, ed. J. Beyssier, in Université de Paris, Bibliothèque de la Faculté des Lettres (Mélanges d'histoire du moyen âge) 18 (Paris, 1904).

40 See the comments on the book of sentences of the inquisitor Pierre Seila, as in H. C. Lea, *History of the Inquisition of the Middle Ages*, 3 vols (London, 1888), vol. 2, p. 579: 'The sects [Catharism and Waldensianism] were perfectly distinct, but frequently the people, in their antagonism to the established Church, looked favourably on both, and considered them equally as 'boni homines.'

41 See above, chapter 1 and note 37.

42 See chapter 3.4.

work other than preaching, quickly exposed the first Waldenses to the sneers of their clerical opponents. Alain of Lille agreed that preachers might receive the necessaries of life from their 'subjects', but the Waldenses, he said, 'are pseudo-preachers, and cheat their food out of the simple people, so that they may live in idleness'.[43] Somewhat later, Ebrardus of Béthune denounced the heretics for sitting around all day in the sun, eating the bread of others, meddling in other people's affairs and insinuating errors amidst a basically Catholic message.[44] On this point Durand of Osca was understandably sensitive, as both Cathars and Catholics criticized his colleagues because of it. Christ, he argued, called the apostles away from manual work to concentrate wholly on preaching. Work, he felt, led to worry about material things, and greed. Paul, who worked to avoid charging his congregations, could not be cited as a counter-example, because no modern apostle could emulate his energy and discipline. Spiritual labour was superior to earthly work.[45]

Several authorities claimed that the travelling groups of Waldensian preachers included women as well as men. Bernard de Fontcaude and Alain of Lille both pounced upon this apparent defiance of Paul's instruction that women keep silence in Church.[46] Burchard of Ursperg, writing in the early 1210s, remarked in even more shocked tones that among them men and women travelled together, stayed in the same house, even in the same bed.[47] Throughout the middle ages, religious single women tended to be more strictly enclosed than men; there was no accepted role-model for the single, undomesticated woman, let alone one who taught in public.[48] The presence of female as well as male preachers among the early Waldensian societies stimulated predictable accusations of sexual disorder, justified or not.[49] The extreme Cathar abhorrence of sexuality and procreation, and the ensuing avoidance of female contact, in due course had an effect on the Waldenses in Languedoc. Women would remain members of the society for a few decades

---

43 Migne, *Patrologiae*, vol. 210, cols 399–400.
44 See text in Gonnet, *Enchiridion*, vol. 1, pp. 144–52.
45 Selge, *Die ersten Waldenser*, vol. 2, pp. 77–88.
46 Migne, *Patrologiae*, vol. 204, cols 825–8; ibid., vol. 210, cols 379–80.
47 Burchard of Ursperg's text is in *MGH Scriptores rerum Germanicarum in usu scholarum*, vol. 16, 2nd edn, ed. O. Holder-Egger and H. von Simson (Hanover and Leipzig, 1916), pp. 107–8; see also the translation in Wakefield and Evans, *Heresies*, pp. 228–30.
48 On the position of women in medieval ethics and the restrictions upon their religious roles, see for example Eileen Power, *Medieval Women*, ed. M. M. Postan (Cambridge, 1975).
49 See, for example, Alain of Lille, in Migne, *Patrologiae*, vol. 210, col. 380; cf. Gonnet, *Enchiridion*, vol. 1, pp. 155–7.

into the thirteenth century, but ceased to act as preachers well before 1300.[50]

In another respect this early, public phase of Waldensian preaching led the poor preachers to adopt a unique custom. Presumably in imitation of the sandals worn by the apostles, they cut away the upper part of their shoes, leaving only strips and creating the impression of travelling almost barefoot. Numerous authorities remarked upon this custom. Ebrardus of Béthune noted how they crucified their shoes rather than their bodies, crowning their footwear but not their heads (that is, not adopting the tonsure).[51] Intriguingly, the first Waldenses to be formally reconciled to the Church, the followers of Durand of Osca, promised to use a different form of cut-away to their shoes to that of the heretics, but when they seem to have made no change, Innocent III admonished them to abandon distinctive footwear altogether, and made the same requirement of later groups who were reconciled.[52] Once the Church began to persecute the Waldenses in earnest, of course, the wearing of anything so distinctive as a special form of footwear was abandoned, and no mention of it appears in the later evidence. According to one source, these early preachers adopted a form of hood similar to that of monks, but this does not appear to have been widespread.[53] Plain, ordinary clothing, avoiding all rich material or bright colouring, seems to have been the norm.

Unlike some later commentators, the sources for early Waldensian preaching do not record the kinds of inducements or approaches used by the travelling preachers when they sought to attract hearers. Bernard de Fontcaude claimed that they spoke first to women 'and effeminate men', the weak-willed and ignorant, and via such people sought to convert the rest. He alleged that they were very slippery in disputation: if detected in any error, 'they rush, leap even, into some shadow of a reason, lest they might seem to be beaten'.[54] The moralizing tone and

50   For further discussion of the roles of women in Waldensian practice, see below, chapter 5, note 46 and references; chapter 8, note 17. It should be noted that the women found ministering in early sixteenth-century Alpine Waldensianism were sedentary, and do not appear to have fulfilled a public teaching role.

51   On Waldensian attitudes to footwear, see Walter Map, as in Gonnet, *Enchiridion*, vol. 1, p. 124, and in Wakefield and Evans, *Heresies*, p. 204; Ebrard of Béthune in Gonnet, *Enchiridion*, vol. 1, p. 144; Pierre de Vaux-Cernay in Gonnet, *Enchiridion*, vol. 1, p. 126; and especially Burchard of Ursperg in *MGH Scriptores*, vol. 16, p. 107: 'calceos desuper pedem precidebant et quasi nudis pedibus ambulabant'. Anselm of Alessandria, as trans. in Wakefield and Evans, *Heresies*, p. 371, refers to 'sandal-wearers'.

52   See the letters of Innocent III in Migne, *Patrologiae*, vol. 215, cols 1,510–13; vol. 216, cols 75–7, 648–50.

53   See note 47 above.

54   Migne, *Patrologiae*, vol. 204, cols 821–4.

scriptural imagery of his description, however, makes this testimony difficult to interpret. Later, unrelated observers, would remark on how heretic preachers insinuated their ideas gently and subtly into the minds of those who listened.

2.4 More Radical Opposition to Church Teachings

The core of the Waldensian message in the first generation seems to have been quite simple. The poor preachers believed that they had a mission to teach the Catholic gospel to the laity, since a morally deficient priesthood had shown itself incompetent. That same clergy and hierarchy, they thought, had no right to tell them to stop. The preachers 'renounced the world' not in order to escape from the world to a cloister, but to travel among ordinary people, unhindered by concern for goods. They felt justified in receiving material support from their hearers, in return for preaching.[55]

However, even in this very earliest phase there is clear evidence that other beliefs, and other rejections of official belief, were creeping in. First, there are signs of doubt concerning the Catholic belief about the purgation of souls after death, and therefore the value of offerings for the dead. Bernard de Fontcaude appended three further chapters to his treatise attacking those who denied purgatory and the value of religious offerings for the dead, although it is not clear that these chapters were specifically directed against the Waldenses.[56] However, in another treatise attributed to Ermengaud of Béziers (a former Waldensian preacher and companion of Durand of Osca) the Waldenses are specifically said to have denied the worth of such offerings.[57] More serious, and potentially more radical, was the idea that some Waldenses denied all value to priestly ordination, and therefore thought that they themselves, men and women alike, might administer such sacraments as baptism or the eucharist. The same text attributed to Ermengaud of Béziers claimed that the Waldenses baptized the children of their followers; though a later source, probably from the mid-thirteenth century, implies that this was only done exceptionally.[58] The Ermengaud text also states that the preachers 'had the right' to consecrate the eucharist. Pierre de Vaux-Cernay, the Catholic historian of the Albigenses, likewise said that Waldenses claimed they could consecrate 'in cases of necessity'.[59]

55 See the summary in Selge, 'Caractéristiques', pp. 120–7.
56 Migne, *Patrologiae*, vol. 204, cols 828–35.
57 Wakefield and Evans, *Heresies*, p. 235.
58 Ibid., p. 234; also Gonnet, *Enchiridion*, vol. 1, pp. 155–7.
59 Gonnet, *Enchiridion*, vol. 1, p. 168; Wakefield and Evans, *Heresies*, p. 241.

Some taboos properly originating with other heresies[60] seem to have seeped into the teaching of some Waldenses towards the end of this first phase of their history. Several sources claim that the Waldenses regarded the taking of oaths as absolutely forbidden in all circumstances; those same sources allege that they regarded all killing, including judicial execution, as wrong.[61] One text, the literary one written by Alain of Lille, alleged that the Waldenses regarded every lie as a mortal sin.[62] In the light of these claims, it is highly interesting that Durand of Osca chose to defend the doctrine of purgatory and the value of prayers and offerings for the dead in one of the last chapters of the first part of the *Liber Antiheresis*, citing canon law texts and Peter Lombard's *Sentences* in support.[63] Moreover, in one manuscript of his work there are also two chapters which respectively defend the formal, judicial oath as lawful, and assert that judicial execution is not forbidden.[64] It may be that Durand found himself trying to sustain a basically Catholic line against impulses from within the movement to broaden the range of its protest.[65]

Of these more radical dissenting beliefs, some would establish themselves as normal teachings of the Waldensian poor and some would not. Most later medieval Waldensian pastors made no attempt to consecrate the eucharist, and there is almost no further mention of baptism or rebaptism. On the other hand, rejection of oaths and judicial execution would appear again and again as 'core' Waldensian tenets in later generations. At this stage, however, they were clearly extraneous to the beliefs of the first generation of Waldenses.

2.5 The Disputation at Pamiers and the Conversion of Durand

In the autumn of 1207 the Waldensian movement suffered the first of what, down the centuries, would be a series of major and disabling defections from its ranks. Bishop Diego of Osma, one of the leaders of the Catholic preaching campaign against heresy, arrived in Pamiers in the Languedoc on his way back to his see. There a disputation was held

---

60 Both the swearing of oaths and the taking of human life under any circumstances had previously been forbidden by the Cathars. See the sources ed. and trans. in Wakefield and Evans, *Heresies*, pp. 173, 191, 193, 199, 361, 382.
61 Alain of Lille, in Migne, *Patrologiae*, vol. 210, cols 392–9; Ermengaud of Béziers, as in Wakefield and Evans, *Heresies*, p. 234; Pierre de Vaux-Cernay in Gonnet, *Enchiridion*, vol. 1, p. 126.
62 Migne, *Patrologiae*, vol. 210, cols 390–2.
63 Selge, *Die ersten Waldenser*, vol. 2, pp. 100–4 and references.
64 Ibid., pp. 248–57. These chapters are also found in Ermengaud's *Contra haereticos*, in Migne, *Patrologiae*, vol. 204, cols 1269ff.
65 Selge, *Die ersten Waldenser*, vol. 1, pp. 150ff. and esp. pp. 153–6.

between Catholics and Waldenses under the presidency of Arnaldus de Campranhano,[66] a secular priest whom one source reports as favouring the Waldenses. Two chroniclers report that the Waldenses were convinced by the Catholics in this encounter; that they abjured their heresy, and resolved to live as Catholics thereafter. The leader of the Waldenses thus converted was their most accomplished theologian and apologist, Durand of Osca.[67]

No report of the conversion process has come down to us from Durand or his companions, though their interesting history after 1208 is set out below, in chapter 4. It seems reasonable to suppose, though it is only supposition, that there was some link between the conversion of Durand to Catholic obedience and the growing trend towards more radical rejection of Church authority and ministries which appears in the sources around this time. One possibility is that Durand was so alarmed by the Waldenses' drift towards radical anti-Catholic beliefs that he could no longer stay with them. Alternatively, the reverse may be true: Valdesius probably died some time after 1205,[68] and with Durand's defection there may no longer have been the restraining force which had hitherto kept the Waldensian preachers from embracing clearly heretical teachings. More outright heresy may have been the cause, or the result, of Durand's decision. Moreover, the state of affairs in the Languedoc on the eve of the Albigensian crusade may have convinced Durand that the anti-Cathar forces could no longer remain divided and opposed. He may even have been impressed by the moral and intellectual qualities of Bishop Diego and Dominic, whose aims and ideals were so close to his own.[69] These are speculations, however. The essential fact is that during 1207–8 Durand made his peace with Rome and managed, as will be seen, to preserve not only his mission but also the group identity of his society. With him the Occitan Waldensian movement lost its major, if not its only, intellectual heavyweight. This loss came upon it just as it was struggling to maintain relations with its allies and fellow-members in Lombardy, who must now be considered.

66 Usually rendered as Arnaud de Crampagna.
67 Sources in Gonnet, *Enchiridion*, vol. 1, pp. 126–8.
68 See below, chapter 3, notes 13–15.
69 For the preaching campaigns of Bishop Diego and Dominic, see Lambert, *The Cathars*, pp. 100–2.

3

The Lombard 'Poor in Spirit', c.1205–c.1240

One of the most startling aspects of the early Waldensian movement is the speed with which it seemed to spread to other regions of Europe outside central and southern France. It is as well to say 'seemed to', for two reasons. First, the earliest chroniclers made the point that the followers of Valdesius 'mingled with other heretics',[1] which implies that other movements already existed to which the Waldensian protest could attach itself, and with which it could become confused. Second, the origins, paternity and description of many of the heretical groups identified before the days of inquisitorial registers – and even after – may never be clear. Valdesius did not hold a patent on the idea of laymen reading scripture or preaching spontaneously.[2]

Some of these problems become evident when one examines the first major region outside France to which the Waldensian protest spread, the towns of Lombardy in northern Italy. One may be absolutely sure that Valdesius and his associates were directly involved with these people, but whether he created the group, as it were out of nothing, is less certain. The 'Lombard Poor' were a distinct group from the very moment that we first hear of them. For studying the ways and attitudes of this group, there survive, fortunately, two exceptionally valuable sets of documents: first, the letters concerning the group of Lombard Poor who were reconciled to the Church shortly after the conversion of Durand of Osca; second, the long and complex letter written by the Lombards following a conference at Bergamo in 1218 between themselves and the representatives of the 'ultramontane' or francophone Waldenses, com-

---

1   See, for instance, Étienne de Bourbon's reference to the followers of Valdesius 'mingling with other heretics' in Provence and Lombardy: A. Patschovsky and K.-V. Selge (eds), *Quellen zur Geschichte der Waldenser*, Texte zur Kirchen- und Theologiegeschichte, 18 (Gütersloh, 1973), p. 17.
2   Compare the group of Bible translators at Metz, as described in the Register of Innocent III, in J.-P. Migne, *Patrologiae Cursus Completus*, Series Latina, vol. 214, cols 695–9.

monly known as the 'Reply of the Leading Heretics' or *Rescriptum Heresiarcharum.*[3]

3.1   A Milieu Saturated with Anti-clerical Dissent

Any account of the Waldenses of northern Italy must take account of the long history of anti-clerical sentiment in the region. In the second half of the eleventh century the Patarene movement at Milan had campaigned for the clergy to become truly celibate and free from simony. This was by no means a heresy, in as much as it enjoyed support and patronage from the controversial Pope Gregory VII. In his campaign to secure jurisdictional independence for the clerical estate the Patarenes were, to say the least, convenient and useful allies.[4] However, this movement could easily lapse into Donatist heresy, and some among its members may have done so. The Patarenes are but one example of a more widely observed phenomenon: that lay people's zeal for moral and disciplinary reform, often aroused and maintained by reforming clergy, could lapse into formal heresy when such initiatives for reform were frustrated.[5] A hundred years later the term 'Patarene' was generally used to describe the various groups of Cathars, for instance in the polemical *Dialogue between a Catholic and a Paterene heretic.*[6] In the late 1130s and mid-

---

3   Editions of this text are found in the following: W. Preger, *Beiträge zur Geschichte der Waldesier in Mittelalter* (Munich, 1875), pp. 56–63; J. J. Ignaz von Döllinger (ed.), *Beiträge zur Sektengeschichte des Mittelaters*, 2 vols (Munich, 1890), vol. 2 (*Dokumente vornehmlich zur Geschichte der Valdesier und Katharer*), pp. 42–52; G. Gonnet (ed.), *Enchiridion fontium valdensium (Recueil critique des sources concernant les Vaudois au moyen âge) du IIIe Concile de Latran au Synode de Chanforan (1179–1532)*, vol. 1 (Torre Pellice, 1958), pp. 169–83; G. Gonnet, *Le Confessioni di fede valdesi prima della riforma* (Turin, 1967), pp. 41–51; Patschovsky and Selge, *Quellen*, pp. 20–43, with the fullest critical apparatus; translation in W. L. Wakefield and A. P. Evans (eds), *Heresies of the High Middle Ages: Selected Sources Translated and Annotated* (New York and London, 1969), pp. 278–89, which needs to be read in conjunction with Patschovsky's notes. The title of the document 'Reply of the leading heretics of Lombardy to the Leonists in Germany' was of course added by a later, Catholic, copyist and the words 'in Germany' are missing in one manuscript. See Patschovsky and Selge, *Quellen*, p. 20, n. 1a.
4   On the Pataria or Patarenes, see M. Lambert, *Medieval Heresy: Popular Movements from the Gregorian Reform to the Reformation*, 2nd edn (Oxford, 1992), pp. 36–7; H. E. J. Cowdrey, 'The Papacy, the Patarenes and the Church of Milan', in *Transactions of the Royal Historical Society*, 5th series, vol. 18 (1968), pp. 25–48; R. I. Moore, *The Origins of European Dissent* (London, 1977), pp. 55–63.
5   Lambert, *Medieval Heresy*, p. 37; Moore, *Origins*, p. 60. See above, chapter 1, note 42.
6   The text is in E. Martene and U. Durand (eds), *Thesaurus Novus Anecdotorum V* (Paris, 1717), cols 1,703–53; compare Wakefield and Evans, *Heresies*, p. 289 and references.

1140s the cleric Arnaldo of Brescia (executed 1155) taught a message of violent anti-clericalism in Lombardy, Paris and Rome, denouncing especially the avarice and political power of prelates. He probably inspired a group of followers known as Arnoldists, who taught that the sinfulness of a priest destroyed the value of sacraments which he administered, and advocated that Christians confess to one another rather than to priests.[7] Hugo Speroni of Piacenza, a lay lawyer, by 1177 became committed to a vehement hostility to the priesthood and to the value of the sacraments. He, too, seems to have inspired a small sect of followers.[8]

More or less contemporary with the early mission of Valdesius was the movement of penitential poor working people or Humiliati, who had sought papal approval in 1179 and been excommunicated in 1184, to be partly reconciled to the Church c.1210.[9] Their combination of labour and the religious vocation may well explain one of the major controversies between Valdesius and the Italians. Some of the imprecision and diversity involved in defining religious movements then is shown by two letters of Innocent III to the Podestà and council of Faenza in 1206. In March of that year the pope exhorted the authorities at Faenza to drive out the 'heretics called Poor of Lyon, or also Patarenes, or other schismatics of whatever sect', seize their goods, and demolish their houses or assign them to the Church. In December he asked the same authorities to copy the example of Florence in expelling the '*Humiliati* Poor of Lyon, or whatsoever followers of heresy'.[10] Lastly, the late twelfth century saw the sudden rise of Italian Catharism, fissile, disputatious and temporarily fertile in a brittle but spectacular intellectual virtuosity.[11] The Italian Cathars played no part in the Waldensian story, except perhaps as opponents;[12] their presence did, however, both demonstrate and aggravate the weakness and political confusion within which the Catholic Church worked at this time.

3.2 'Lombards' and 'Leonists'

By *c.*1205 there appear already to have existed two groups of 'Poor', known to the Italian writers of the early thirteenth century as the 'Poor

7   On Arnold see Moore, *Origins*, pp. 115–36; Lambert, *Medieval Heresy*, pp. 52–4; sources in Wakefield and Evans, *Heresies*, pp. 146–50 and references.
8   Wakefield and Evans, *Heresies*, pp. 152–8.
9   See Wakefield and Evans, *Heresies*, pp. 158–9.
10   Migne, *Patrologiae*, vol. 215, cols 819–20, 1,042–3.
11   See Lorenzo Paolini, 'Italian Catharism and Written Culture' in Peter Biller and Anne Hudson (eds), *Heresy and Literacy, 1000–1530* (Cambridge, 1994), pp. 83–103; M. Lambert, *The Cathars* (Oxford, 1998), pp. 171–214; C. Lansing, *Power and Purity: Cathar Heresy in Medieval Italy* (Oxford, 1998).
12   But compare the interpenetration of dualist and ostensibly Waldensian ideas discussed below, chapter 7.3.

Leonists' (*Pauperes Leonistae*) and the 'Poor Lombards' (*Pauperes Lombardi*).[13] For the origins of these two related groups of 'poor' we depend on two Catholic accounts written by the anti-Cathar polemicist Salvo Burci of Piacenza and the *Summa contra Hereticos* attributed to the patron saint of inquisitors, Peter of Verona, also known as St Peter Martyr (*c.*1200–52). Salvo Burci, writing in 1235, reported that the Poor Leonists originated with 'Valdexius', who was within the Church until about sixty years previously; the Poor Lombards had broken off from the Poor Leonists some thirty years before, i.e. around 1205. The 'elder' of the Poor Lombards was one called Johannes de Ronco, 'an ignorant man without education'.[14] In a later apostrophe, Burci told how the Poor Lombards

> belonged to the Church of Rome, but because that displeased you, you joined yourselves to the Poor Leonists, and were some time under their rule; but afterwards you chose another leader who was displeasing to 'Gualdensis' and the Poor Leonists, called Johannes de Roncho, whom I saw, and for some years you preached the same things as the Poor Leonists, saying that you were not against them, but now there is the greatest disagreement between you.

Peter of Verona confirms the gist of this story. He likewise dated the separation of the Waldenses from the Church to about 1175, but stated that they split (without specifying a date) into the 'ultramontane poor' and the Poor Lombards, the latter led by 'Johannes de Runcharola', a native of Piacenza.[15]

Salvo Burci's account contains some inconsistency, due both to the somewhat incoherent way in which his text, entitled the *Suprastella*, was composed, and also his polemical line of argument. He sought to prove that all heretical sects had split off from the Catholic Church at some stage in the relatively recent past, and that they all disagreed with each other; and by comparison between the sects and the one, durable, true Church to bring doubting readers back to Catholicism.[16] The problem is that he can be read as saying either that the Poor Lombards arose as a schism among the followers of Valdesius, or that they were a pre-existent group who aligned themselves with the Waldenses but later split off again to form a separate and increasingly estranged sect. We can never, then, be certain how far the Lombard Poor

---

13 These are the terms used by Salvo Burci, Peter Martyr of Verona and Moneta of Cremona, as cited below.

14 The original Latin is 'idiota absque literis'.

15 Döllinger, *Beiträge*, vol. 2, pp. 64, 74; Wakefield and Evans, *Heresies*, pp. 269–78 and references.

16 See especially Burci's remarks about the origins of heretics in Wakefield and Evans, *Heresies*, pp. 271–2.

existed before the missions of Valdesius's followers.[17] Of Johannes de Ronco, surnamed 'the Good' according to a later inquisitor,[18] little else seems to be known: he did not appear at the Bergamo conference in 1218, so was presumably dead before that date. The destiny of his soul was not discussed with the same fervour as was that of Valdesius's on that occasion.[19]

The Lombard Schism seems to have affected the towns of northern Italy above all. While there seem to have been ultramontanes in Italy,[20] there is no corresponding sign that there were Lombards in the Languedoc. Thereafter, thirteenth-century writers such as Moneta of Cremona or Anselm of Alessandria took for granted the presence of two branches of the Poor in northern Italy, the ultramontanes who owed allegiance to the traditions of Valdesius, and the Lombards derived from Johannes de Ronco (though as we shall see, attempts to distinguish their doctrines sometimes lacked clarity). How long these two groups maintained their separate identities is hard to tell. However, by the later middle ages these distinctions were forgotten, and all Waldenses were described simply as Waldenses. The term 'Runcari', which suggests followers of Johannes de Ronco, appeared from the mid-thirteenth century in descriptions of heretics in Germany, but it seems to be less than clear just what kind of heretics it denoted.[21]

3.3 Organization of the Poor in Lombardy

In this early, public phase of the Waldensian story, when the threat from ecclesiastical authority was relatively feeble, it was possible for heretical groups to spring up with public meeting-places, a form of educational system, and an administrative structure parallel to that of the official Church. The Cathars of northern Italy were noted for their 'schools', their orders of ministry, and other trappings of public, institutional

17   On the historiography of the debate over the origins of the Poor Lombards, see J. Gonnet and A. Molnar, *Les Vaudois au moyen âge* (Turin, 1974), pp. 85–90 and references.
18   See Wakefield and Evans, *Heresies*, p. 370.
19   Compare below, section 3.5.
20   This may be inferred from the reference by Anselm of Alessandria in Wakefield and Evans, *Heresies*, p. 370, possibly also the reference to an ultramontane text being handled by a 'Massarius' at Verona, according to the *Rescriptum*, as in Patschovsky and Selge, *Quellen*, p. 23. However, the text here is extremely obscure.
21   The term 'Runcari' as used in Germany appears to refer to quasi-Cathar dualists, as for example in the texts in J. Gretser, *Lucae Tudensis episcopi scriptores aliquot succedanei contra Sectam Waldensium ...*, in M. de la Bigne (ed.), *Magna Bibliotheca Veterum Patrum*, 15 vols (Cologne, 1618–22), vol. 13, pp. 301, 315; Döllinger, *Beiträge*, vol. 2, p. 301.

existence.[22] The Lombard Poor seem to have emulated this development to some degree. One should beware of references in later inquisitorial writers to 'bishops' and 'priests' among them; however, one is on safer ground with evidence dating from before 1220. Some time before April 1209, Durand of Osca reported to Innocent III that about a hundred Waldenses in Milan wished to be reconciled to the Church, if only the Archbishop of Milan would return to them a piece of open ground ('quoddam pratum') 'where they had had a school where they used to gather and exhort their brethren and friends', and which the previous archbishop had caused to be demolished.[23] By July 1212 Pope Innocent had received from the followers of Bernardus Primus, the second group of reconciled Poor who made their peace in 1210, a proposal of a way of life which referred to communal reading in their quasi-monastic houses 'of which we have more than eight'. It seems unlikely that the Lombards would have acquired these buildings only after their reconciliation, therefore they must already have been acquiring schools and religious buildings in the period before 1210. This is startling, for it implies a much more structured, sedentary life-style than that of the travelling Poor of the Languedoc at the same period.

Reasonably enough, the evolution of a quasi-monastic order among the Lombards tended to divide the community of Waldensian supporters into those who were fully committed to the life of poverty, preaching and teaching, and those lay people who remained on the margins as supporters. These lay associates are specifically mentioned in the proposal of Bernardus Primus;[24] elsewhere, in the letters of Durand and the so-called *Rescriptum*, they are implicit in the phrase 'brethren and friends', which seems to refer respectively to the fully committed members of the community, and those living as lay people who supported and heard them.[25] In the later middle ages a rather different distinction would exist between the travelling clandestine preachers ('brethren') and the lay people who received them and heard them in secret ('believers', known by various names). At this early stage, however, the issue was not one of secrecy or itinerancy, but of varying degrees of commitment to a nascent, sedentary, quasi-monastic community. It is also evident from the *Rescriptum* that the Lombard Poor had acquired a form of hierarchy among their members before 1218. The document is headed with the name of

---

22   See Paolini, 'Italian Catharism'.
23   Migne, *Patrologiae*, vol. 216, cols 29–30.
24   In the 'proposal' of Bernardus Primus it is stated that any of 'their laymen followers' who have gained anything by deceit will be obliged to make restitution to those whom they have cheated. See Migne, *Patrologiae*, vol. 216, cols 648–50.
25   See Gonnet and Molnar, *Vaudois au moyen âge*, pp. 185–93, and for this text, p. 188, n. 291.

Otto de Ramezello,[26] described as the '*confrater* of the Poor in Spirit'. On the occasion of the conference, the Lombard group managed to convince the ultramontanes, against what seem to have been the wishes and tradition of the now deceased Valdesius, to approve the communal election of 'provosts' or 'rectors', and likewise to ordain 'ministers' to deal with the affairs of recent converts or 'friends'.[27]

3.4 Manual Labour among the Lombard Poor

According to the *Rescriptum* Valdesius was alleged to have said before his death that 'the Italian brethren . . . could have no peace with him unless they separated themselves from the "congregations of labourers" who were then in Italy'.[28] Two generations later, the inquisitor Anselm of Alessandria would note as a point of difference between the Lombards and ultramontanes that 'the Lombard works' whereas 'the ultramontane neither works for himself nor for wages from others, nor does he practice a trade or profession'; and later, 'the question of labour was the cause of the division among them'.[29]

It seems likely that the influence of the Humiliati may have led the Lombards, in the early days of their association, to copy the former's idea of combining physical work with religious devotion. The undertaking to carry on physical work alongside teaching persisted among the reconciled Poor of Bernardus Primus's group.[30] In the light of Durand's resolute defence of the Languedocien brethren's custom of 'living of the Gospel',[31] one might have expected conflict between the ultramontanes and the Lombards over this issue to continue. In the event, at the Bergamo conference the ultramontanes seem to have withdrawn their objection to manual labour as part of the negotiations.[32] On the other hand, by the mid-century Anselm of Alessandria could report that the 'sandal-wearer' among the Lombards did not work for pay but was cared for by others.[33]

26 Possibly Remedello near Brescia.
27 Alternatively, the text may refer to electing 'ministers' *from* 'those recently converted or from friends remaining in the affairs [of the world]': see Patschovsky and Selge, *Quellen*, pp. 23–4, with some important emendations of the reading in note 42. The text is both ambiguous and obscure; however, the ambiguity does not affect the point being made here.
28 Patschovsky and Selge, *Quellen*, p. 24.
29 Wakefield and Evans, *Heresies*, pp. 369–70; however, neither Salvo Burci nor Peter of Verona mentions the issue.
30 Migne, *Patrologiae*, vol. 216, cols 289–93, 648–50; Gonnet, *Enchiridion*, vol. 1, p. 139; this element is present, but in a lower key, in the *propositum* of Durand.
31 See above, chapter 2, notes 41–2.
32 See below, section 3.5.
33 Wakefield and Evans, *Heresies*, p. 371.

The issue of manual labour seems to have been symbolic. It represented one of the many tensions between the pristine legacy of Valdesius and the constantly inventive adaptation by the Lombards to different circumstances and influences. Like so many of the issues of this early stage, it would not remain a significant question for long. By the time that Waldensian preachers had to travel around in secret, they would have to assume some trade or business, as physicians or pedlars, simply for concealment.[34]

3.5 The Conference of Bergamo

The letter describing the discussions held at Bergamo in May 1218, known as the *Rescriptum*, gives a unique insight into the way in which the Waldenses in Lombardy handled their affairs in the first quarter of the thirteenth century.[35] Nevertheless, the letter appears to testify to a failure. The very structure of the piece presupposes the rift between ultramontanes and Lombards described earlier: two delegations were present at the conference, each of six men representing each of the two groups.[36] The conference seems to have been called to discover as much common ground as possible between the two groups; the letter does in fact summarize agreements reached between them on most of the issues under debate. Nevertheless, the letter ends by reporting unresolved conflict over two issues, one symbolic and one highly theological; and it appends an array of arguments and proof-texts with which the authors attempted to convince their 'brothers, sisters and friends beyond the Alps' of the rightness of the Lombard stance. From this, and the universal agreement of later writers that Lombard and ultramontane Poor remained divided, one must conclude that the conference failed in its purpose.

According to the report, the Lombard ('Italian') delegation pressed the ultramontanes over a number of issues where the traditions of Valdesius conflicted with the practices of the Lombards. Valdesius had preferred not to appoint a chief or 'prepositus' for the society in his lifetime; the ultramontane delegation at Bergamo included two men 'charged with the affairs' of the group for that year only.[37] Valdesius appears not to have envisaged an order of 'ministers' within it; and he disapproved, as noted earlier, of the 'associations of labourers'. On each of these three points the ultramontanes cited a tract produced by one

---

34 See below, for example chapter 5, note 109; chapter 6, note 56.
35 For locations of the manuscripts see Patschovsky and Selge, *Quellen*, pp. 12, 20. The fact that the manuscripts now exist in German archives does not of itself prove that the text was sent to Germany at the time of its composition.
36 Ibid., pp. 27–9.
37 Ibid., pp. 22, 28.

Massarius in Verona which, they claimed, authorized them to agree with the Lombards over the election of a superior, whether permanent or temporary, the ordaining of ministers, and the approval of working communities.[38]

The ultramontanes conceded to the Italians that baptism in water was necessary for salvation, that marriages might not be dissolved without mutual consent, and that allegedly criminous brothers might justify themselves to the society. They also agreed not to try to force the Lombards to adopt any custom or belief which did not have scriptural authority.[39] Thus far the letter reads like a list of capitulations by the ultramontanes' representatives to Lombard demands. However, matters came to a crisis over two further points. The ultramontanes demanded that the Lombards agree that Valdesius, and an otherwise unknown companion of his called Vivetus, were certainly in paradise. The Lombards would only accept that they would be in heaven if they had made amends for their sins before death. This was, in effect, to place Valdesius on the same plane as any other Christian believer, and therefore to deny him the sort of 'sainthood' which the ultramontanes claimed for him.[40]

Another issue was more complex. The Italians challenged the ultramontanes about their views on the Mass, and who might rightly and effectively consecrate. They attributed a range of different beliefs to the ultramontanes, from the idea that transubstantiation took place by the power of the words of consecration alone, to the idea that any lay person might consecrate (though the latter belief was disowned by the ultramontanes). Through the tortuous dogmatic language of the document it emerges that the issue was not really consecration as such, but the spiritual power of a priest who was in a state of sin. The Italians insisted that priests whose sins made them unworthy of their orders would not have their prayers heard by God, and their orders would be invalid. They buttressed this insistence with a range of authorities, biblical, patristic and canonical.[41] The ultramontane Waldenses had insisted that a lawfully ordained priest, sinner or not, who carried out the consecration of the eucharist with the approval of his church, would bring about the transubstantiation of the eucharistic elements.[42] The Italians explicitly declared that they would not be bound to their earlier statements on the subject and even cited against the followers of Valdesius the classic text

---

38 Ibid., pp. 23–5.
39 Ibid., pp. 25–7.
40 Ibid., pp. 27–9.
41 Ibid., pp. 31–42, and compare pp. 44–6 for a further collection of patristic and other proof-texts on this point. The heaping up of authorities shows how sensitive a point of division the Donatist argument was.
42 Ibid., pp. 29–30.

that they 'must obey God rather than men'.[43] Though the letter ended with pious fraternal greetings, the overall tone was one of insistence that the ultramontanes were wrong. In short, the Lombards had taken an explicitly Donatist stand where priestly consecrations were concerned; the ultramontanes just as explicitly refused to assent to it.

3.6   Lombard Beliefs and Teachings

It will already be clear that the Lombard Poor showed a fertile inventiveness in expressing their religious calling. In contrast to the restrained orthodoxy and modest teaching mission of the Waldenses in Languedoc, the Lombards acquired buildings and schools, created institutional structures, held religious debates. This inventiveness cannot have failed to express itself in the sphere of beliefs and teachings as well. Unfortunately, our evidence for the beliefs of the Lombard Poor, apart from the *Rescriptum*, comes only from Catholic sources. Except for the documents of the conversion of Bernardus Primus in 1210, these are literary in origin and date from *c.*1235–70. There will have been some development and elaboration, as there certainly were schisms and disagreements, within the period covered by this evidence.

The most distinctive feature of the early Waldenses in Lombardy was that they seem, in the years before Bergamo, to have celebrated their own form of eucharist. According to Peter of Verona, Johannes de Ronco had consecrated some wine in a goblet, which a fowl then knocked over. This episode scandalized some of those present, who claimed that only an ordained priest could consecrate. In horror at Johannes de Ronco's irregular consecration, a splinter called the Poor 'of the meadow' ('de prato') was formed but later disappeared.[44] One might be tempted to dismiss this tale, but for the fact that Bernardus Primus acknowledged how his group had been notorious 'regarding the breaking of bread'. They apologized for this: they said that they had never performed such rites out of presumption or contempt for the priestly Mass, but only to offer some semblance of the eucharist to those people who otherwise, living among Cathars, would have received none and become 'hardened'.[45] The attitudes reported of Johannes de Ronco and by Bernardus Primus are contrary to those of the Lombards who, in 1218, insisted that only priests in a state of grace could consecrate.[46] So these irregular con-

---

43   Ibid., pp. 42–3.
44   Wakefield and Evans, *Heresies*, p. 277. Peter of Verona's authorship of the text is not absolutely certain.
45   Migne, *Patrologiae*, vol. 216, col. 291.
46   See note 41 above.

secrations may have been a temporary measure, an attempt to associate some ritual with anti-Cathar evangelizing. By later in the thirteenth century, however, reports of irregular consecrations recur in the notebook of the inquisitor Anselm of Alessandria, though this time attributed to the 'Poor of Lyon' rather than Lombards.[47]

Some of the more radical rejections of common Catholic teaching and practice, based on literal reading of the New Testament, were attributed to the Lombards as they were to the earlier Waldenses by Alain of Lille. They allegedly taught that since the coming of Christ, all oaths were utterly forbidden.[48] They apparently entertained the same doubts about judicial execution as the Cathars.[49] Disbelief in purgatory is attributed to them by at least one source.[50] More unusual and more interesting is the claim that the Lombards believed that human souls were not generated by a unique act of creation, but naturally in the process of generation, the belief known as traducianism. This is intriguing, not only for the possibility of Cathar influence, but also because it implies a level of metaphysical speculation not normally found in Waldensian teaching.[51]

By far the most important body of teachings, historically and doctrinally, were those by which the Lombards attempted to define their position vis-à-vis the Roman Church. Bernardus Primus admitted that his group had been accused of believing that 'the Roman Church is not the Church of God'.[52] The Dominicans Moneta of Cremona and Anselm of Alessandria reported the Waldenses as teaching that the true Church had ceased to be since the time of Sylvester I, the pope on whom the Emperor Constantine had reputedly conferred great secular authority and estates for the Church to keep.[53] This belief that the 'poison' of worldly goods

47 Wakefield and Evans, Heresies, pp. 372–3; compare also the text, possibly from thirteenth-century Italy, found in Martene and Durand, Thesaurus Novus Anecdotorum V, cols 1,754–6.
48 Migne, Patrologiae, vol. 216, col. 292; Salvo Burci, in Döllinger, Beiträge, vol. 2, p. 83; Moneta of Cremona, Adversus Catharos et Valdenses libri v, ed. T. A. Ricchinius (Rome, 1743), pp. 462–75; Anselm of Alessandria in Wakefield and Evans, Heresies, pp. 371–2.
49 Burci, in Döllinger, Beiträge, vol. 2, pp. 69, 71, 75ff.; Moneta, Adversus Catharos et Valdenses, pp. 508ff.; also Anselm, in Wakefield and Evans, Heresies, pp. 371–2.
50 Anselm, in Wakefield and Evans, Heresies, pp. 371–2.
51 Burci, in Döllinger, Beiträge, vol. 2, p. 74, also p. 84; Anselm, in Wakefield and Evans, Heresies, p. 372; see also Martene and Durand, Thesaurus Novus Anecdotorum V, cols 1,754–6; on traducianism in general, see F. L. Cross and E. A. Livingstone (eds), The Oxford Dictionary of the Christian Church, 3rd edn (Oxford, 1997), art. 'traducianism', p. 1,636 and references.
52 Migne, Patrologiae, vol. 216, col. 292.
53 Moneta, Adversus Catharos et Valdenses, p. 412; Anselm, in Wakefield and Evans, Heresies, pp. 371–2.

had afflicted the Church since Sylvester was by no means unique either to the Waldenses or to heretics in general. It was in the Waldenses' later attempts to recreate their own history, however, that it would receive one of its most elaborate recensions.[54] According to Moneta, a 'perverse doctor of the Lombards' named Thomas (one of the delegates at Bergamo) argued that Valdesius derived his authority not from Rome, whose pope had forfeited the authority of Peter, but from the brethren themselves: they conferred on him their own spiritual right to self-government, and thereby made him a legal 'pontiff'.[55] This startling anticipation of the common priesthood of all believers, however, was not destined to take root in the later movement.

If the Roman Church was not the valid Church, then its rules, regulations and rites might be ignored, as possessing no abiding spiritual authority or worth. Its claim to regulate lawful marriage by establishing new laws was rejected.[56] Its fasts, pilgrimages, indulgences and so forth could be denied any spiritual value.[57] The essential question, however, remained the same as it had been at Bergamo: what sacramental power, if any, did a sinful priest have? Bernardus Primus admitted that he had been accused of teaching 'that of men only righteous ones should be obeyed' and that 'a bad priest is of no value and his prayers and masses are worthless'.[58] Later authorities would identify as one of the principal markers separating the Lombard from the ultramontane Waldenses that the Lombards rejected the sacraments and offices of a sinful priest. The Lombards denied that 'an evil priest or prelate fulfils his office', according to Peter of Verona.[59] Cathars and Poor Lombards alike, said Moneta, taught that bad prelates were like the tasteless salt[60] which could not salt anything else: so their prelacy was worthless, and their sacraments void. In contrast, the ultramontanes believed that the Roman Church held the priesthood, and they sought its sacraments.[61] According to Anselm of Alessandria, Lombards said that evil priests could not consecrate, but could 'give good advice'.[62]

Donatism was clearly embedded in the teaching of the Lombard Poor by the first decades of the thirteenth century. It accompanied a more

---

54   See below, chapter 6.4.
55   Moneta, *Adversus Catharos et Valdenses*, p. 403.
56   Ibid., pp. 443–6.
57   Anselm, in Wakefield and Evans, *Heresies*, p. 370.
58   Migne, *Patrologiae*, vol. 216, col. 292.
59   Peter of Verona, in Wakefield and Evans, *Heresies*, p. 277.
60   Matthew 5:13.
61   Moneta, *Adversus Catharos et Valdenses*, pp. 433–4; compare also p. 406: 'Valdensibus ultramontanis, qui concedunt quod Ecclesia Romana habet septem sacramenta, et quod a nobis ea reciperent, si dare vellemus, et credunt nos conficere.'
62   Wakefield and Evans, *Heresies*, p. 372; cf. pp. 369, 370.

general anti-clerical doubt and disbelief: a readiness to criticize any and every claim to sacral value made by the Church for its ministrations. This sort of scepticism would transmit itself, especially, to the mid-thirteenth century German Waldenses and also to the inquisitorial literature on the subject. However, two points need to be noted at this stage.

First, Donatism was a recipe for theoretical and practical confusion in later medieval Europe. While the Cathars did sustain a form of 'anti-Church' for some decades, the more orthodox Waldenses never did offer a comprehensive non-Catholic sacramental service. As the Lombards 'de prato' showed, there was a stubborn distaste among many people for unordained laymen claiming to consecrate the Mass. Neither was it practical to trace back the 'rightness' of the ordinations of a given group of priests to see whether they had, in fact, been duly ordained by a righteous bishop. So, at least as far as baptism and the eucharist were concerned, Donatist Lombards would find their practice and their beliefs at odds.

Second, Donatist belief did not originate with the followers of Valdesius. Multiple sources, including the *Rescriptum* itself, agree that the ultramontanes *did* accept the value of Catholic priests' ministries. From the early thirteenth century onwards, then, there seem to have been two strands of 'Waldensian' thought: one based on the followers of Valdesius in Languedoc, which was essentially a mission of committed lay people to preach where the clergy did not bother; and another, based on the Lombard Poor, which was much more vehemently opposed to the status and pretensions of the Church.

This distinction between less and more anti-clerical tendencies in Waldensian teaching should be kept in mind, however much events may have fogged and confused it after 1218. It may help to explain some of the startling differences in emphasis between the reports of later Waldensian preaching originating from different parts of Europe.

4

The Reconciliations with Rome, 1208–1212

From the evidence so far considered, it seems clear that the earliest Waldensian preachers, especially those in the Languedoc, did not seek to oppose the Roman Church simply for the sake of it. They wished to preach and teach, and rejected the Church's prohibitions. If the Church changed its mind about the prohibition, there was nothing in principle to stop some, at least, of the Waldensian preachers from making their peace with the Church. This took place in the wake of the dispute at Pamiers in 1207 described earlier.[1]

The key to the story of the reconciliations, and the source of most of our information, is the pontificate of Innocent III, one of the most accomplished and astute politicians and most able managers of ecclesiastical affairs in the whole history of the medieval papacy. His treatment of the reconciled Waldenses must be set alongside his reconciliation of some of the Humiliati; his endorsement and acceptance of Francis as well as Dominic, and the orders of friars which they founded; his preaching of the Albigensian crusade; and the formulation of a public body of Catholic doctrine and practice at the Fourth Lateran Council of 1215.[2] He clearly saw the big picture – defeating the Cathars, whom he detested, and winning back southern France and northern Italy for orthodoxy – as more important than sustaining the prestige and *amour propre* of local prelates. So the nervous clerical jealousy which had characterized the Church's response to Valdesius in 1179–84 was, in effect, reversed. This reversal was a personal policy of the pope, which seems to have suited him as well as it suited the one whom he patronized, Durand of Osca.

1 See above, chapter 2.5.
2 On Innocent III in general see C. Morris, *The Papal Monarchy: The Western Church from 1050 to 1250* (Oxford, 1989), pp. 417–51; Brenda Bolton (ed.), *Innocent III: Selected Documents on the Pontificate 1198–1216* (Manchester, 1999); on his responses to heresy see M. Lambert, *Medieval Heresy: Popular Movements from the Gregorian Reform to the Reformation*, 2nd edn (Oxford, 1992), pp. 91ff.; M. Lambert, *The Cathars* (Oxford, 1998), pp. 92ff.

4.1 Durand of Osca and his *Propositum Vitae*

On 18 December 1208 the pope was able to report to local prelates that a group of 'brethren' led by Durand of Osca, Johannes of Narbonne, Ermengaud of Béziers and Bernard of Béziers had come to the apostolic see and been received by him as good Catholics. Durand and the others had, first of all, subscribed to a confession of faith designed to resolve doubts about their Catholicity. Their confession was a slightly adapted and extended version of the one which had been subscribed by Valdesius himself at Lyon in 1180/1.[3] Apart from minor changes in wording, some significant additions were made to the original confession which reflected the particular circumstances of early Waldensian teaching. In this document Durand and the rest affirmed that the evil character of the priest in no way impeded the value of baptism or the eucharist; that only duly ordained priests, using the right form of words and having the right intention, might properly consecrate the eucharist; that oaths might lawfully be taken; and that preaching, especially against the heretics, was laudable, but only when authorized by the pope or prelates.[4]

The inclusion of these statements does not imply that Durand and his followers had been Donatists, had consecrated irregularly or refused oaths. Indeed, had they done so one might expect the confession to have contained some more explicit, penitential abjuration. The confession does imply, however, that the Waldenses had been *accused* of believing such things, and that some of them may in fact have held some or all of these heresies. This second implication is entirely consistent both with Catholic testimony and certain chapters of the *Liber Antiheresis*. Durand's readiness to make peace with Rome may even, as suggested earlier, have been precipitated by such a growth of more extreme heretical beliefs among some Occitan preachers.[5]

Like the profession of Valdesius, that of Durand contained a 'proposal for a way of life', but this time the details were far more specific. This proposal was in essence a form of monastic rule. The Poor had 'renounced the world' like Valdesius, but for a different, more corporate lifestyle. They

---

3   See above, chapter 1.3.

4   G. Gonnet (ed.), *Enchiridion fontium valdensium (Recueil critique des sources concernant les Vaudois au moyen âge) du IIIe Concile de Latran au Synode de Chanforan (1179–1532)*, vol. 1 (Torre Pellice, 1958), pp. 131–2 and references. The whole document is included in full in the Register of Innocent III, in J.-P. Migne, *Patrologiae Cursus Completus*, Series Latina, vol. 215, cols 1,510–13; in abridged form in Gonnet, *Enchiridion*, vol. 1, pp. 130–4, with apparatus; and trans. in W. L. Wakefield and A. P. Evans (eds), *Heresies of the High Middle Ages: Selected Sources Translated and Annotated* (New York and London, 1969), pp. 222–6.

5   For the suggestion that Durand may have been offended by radicalizing trends in the movement, see above, chapter 2.5.

would say the canonical hours, praying the traditional prayers seven times a day. 'Since they were mostly clerks, and nearly all were learned', i.e. competent in reading and writing in Latin,[6] they had resolved to devote themselves to reading, exhorting, teaching and disputing against the heretics. They would hold disputations under the guidance of the most learned and approved among them, so that enemies of the faith might be confounded. They would observe chastity, the ecclesiastical Lenten seasons and fasts, and wear a 'religious and modest habit'. They would wear their shoes cut away in a different fashion, so as to make it clear that they were separated from the Lyonnais unless they returned to Catholicism. Sacraments would be taken from the local clergy, to whom due obedience was to be shown. Provision was made for lay people to live with the group 'religiously and orderly', working with their hands and paying their dues, being members of the society 'except for those things relating to disputing with heretics'.[7] In the letter which accompanied the copy of this confession and proposed rule sent to Durand and his companions, they were referred to as 'Poor Catholics', which clearly implied a formal title, appropriate to a nascent religious order.[8]

Who were the Poor Catholics? From their confession we learn that they were mostly educated, some highly so, and that they were in a position to embrace monastic celibacy. From this and later correspondence it emerges that they included clergy in holy orders as well as laymen. The 'seculars' described in the final clause of the proposal suggest a lower class of uneducated lay participants, akin to third orders of mendicants.[9] Besides those already named, the society included Guillaume of St-

6 The term *litterati* can at this period be taken as meaning able to read Latin (though by later in the middle ages it came to mean more than mere literacy). See H. Grundmann, '*Litteratus-illitteratus*: Der Wandel einer Bildungsnorm vom Altertum zum Mittelalter', in *Archiv für Kulturgeschichte*, vol. 40 (1958), pp. 1–65; A. Murray, *Reason and Society in the Middle Ages* (Oxford, 1978), pp. 299–300.

7 The original clause reads: 'Si qui vero saecularium in nostro voluerint concilio permanere, consulimus ut exceptis idoneis ad exhortandum et contra haereticos disputandum, caeteri in domibus religiose et ordinate vivendo permaneant . . .' The meaning of 'saeculares' is disputed: Gonnet, *Enchiridion*, takes it to mean secular clergy, while Wakefield and Evans, *Heresies*, read it simply as 'laymen'.

8 See Migne, *Patrologiae*, vol. 215, col. 1,514: 'Durando de osca eiusque fratribus, qui pauperes catholici nuncupantur'. Perhaps not quite an order: H. Grundmann, *Religiöse Bewegungen im Mittelalter: Untersuchungen über die geschichtlichen Zusammenhange zwischen der Ketzerei, den Bettelorden und der religiöse Frauenbewegung im 12. und 13. Jahrhundert und über die geschichtlichen Grundlagen der deutschen Mystik*, 2nd edn (Hildesheim, 1961), pp. 100–18, in his discussion of the Poor Catholics, comments of the *propositum*: 'Dieses *Propositum* ist keine eigentliche Ordensregel, und die Genossenschaft der "Katholischen Armen" . . . ist nicht als religiöser Orden zu bezeichnen.'

9 On third orders see F. L. Cross and E. A. Livingstone (eds), *The Oxford Dictionary of the Christian Church*, 3rd edn (Oxford, 1997), art. 'Third Orders', p. 1,610.

Antonin, Durand de Najac, Raymond de St-Paul, and one 'Ebrinus'. All of the place-names given as surnames for Poor Catholics are from the Languedoc, which implies that the society was primarily Occitan in membership, and that Durand's surname 'of Osca' may more likely refer to Osques in the Rouergue rather than Huesca in Aragon.[10] The letters relating to the society were mostly directed to the archbishops of Narbonne and Tarragona; later letters reached the bishops of Marseilles, Barcelona and Huesca. In addition, some of the later correspondence was sent to the archbishops of Genoa and Milan, where Durand was also encouraging conversions.[11] The Poor Catholics were presumably active principally if not exclusively within these provinces and dioceses. Guillaume of Puylaurens related later how they lived for some years in 'a certain part of Catalonia'.[12] One cannot assess their numbers, nor whether or not they represented a majority or a minority of the Poor brethren at the time; it is clear only that they did not comprise all the Waldensian preachers in the Languedoc.

Over the next two years Innocent III, and probably Durand as well, had to play a delicate balancing game. To require the Poor Catholic brethren suddenly to abandon all their former ways might have driven some back into heresy; while to allow them free rein would have antagonized the local clergy, especially the bishops, and even compromised orthodoxy. In a separate letter also dated 18 December 1208, the pope gave conditional permission to 'those of the brethren remaining in the world' that they might not be compelled to go to war against other Christians, nor to offer oaths on secular matters, as far as this was practical and with their lords' permission.[13] Relations between the Poor Catholics and the prelates of Languedoc and Catalonia remained fraught for the next two years. By July 1209 a row had broken out between the Poor Catholics and the Archbishop of Narbonne. The latter accused Durand and his followers of being insolent to the bishops, relying on papal favour. They had brought unreconciled Waldenses to church and taken the eucharist with them. They had kept runaway monks in their society. They had in no way varied their previous form of dress. The sermons which they gave to their 'brethren and friends' in the schools had drawn ordinary people away from attending church services. Even clerics in holy orders among them had not been saying the offices. Some, allegedly, had persisted in the belief that no sentence of judicial execution might be passed without mortal sin.[14]

---

10   See the references in Wakefield and Evans, *Heresies*, p. 715, n. 2.
11   Migne, *Patrologiae*, vol. 215, col. 1,510; vol. 216, cols 29, 73–4, 256, 274, 607–8.
12   Gonnet, *Enchiridion*, vol. 1, p. 127.
13   Migne, *Patrologiae*, vol. 215, col. 1,514, letter 198.
14   Ibid., vol. 216, cols 75–7; trans. (not wholly accurately) in Wakefield and Evans, *Heresies*, pp. 226–8.

Innocent III's response to this outburst of mingled jealousy and zeal was statesmanlike. Writing to the prelates of the Archbishopric of Narbonne, he suggested that Durand might be using these tactics more easily to win over other heretics; he might be 'burying the old ways with honour', that is, gradually abandoning the Waldensian life-style. He warned the bishops not to act too harshly, or to insult the Poor Catholics' way of life.[15] To Durand and his brethren he was more severe: they should shun excommunicates, exclude apostate monks and change their habits as promised. They should not insist on wearing 'sandals', but should attend church and ensure that their clerics said the hours. The lawful character of judicial execution was to be upheld. In preaching against the Cathars they should associate with proven Catholic preachers, to avoid suspicion.[16]

Innocent III did not repeat these reproaches, so presumably Durand and his society behaved themselves thereafter. Nevertheless, they seem to have had constant trouble with the local hierarchy. A succession of papal letters called on the prelates to respect their way of life, and so to encourage them that others might be moved to follow their example.[17] Another letter gave Durand and his companions a veto over the appointment of any 'provost' made over them.[18]

4.2   The Penitents of Elne Diocese

Less than four years after their reconciliation Innocent III gave further proof of his trust in the Poor Catholics. Durand went to see the pope and asked permission for his society to act as guardians and pastoral visitors of a community of penitents which it was proposed to set up within the diocese of Elne, near Perpignan in Roussillon. One of the penitents planned to build a house on his own land, comprising two lodgings for men and women respectively, a 'guest house' and a chapel. There they wished to live communally and in celibacy, to abstain from 'lies and unlawful oaths', to wear white or grey habits, and to submit to a range of ascetic disciplines concerning their living conditions and diet. They would pray seven times a day, and clerics among them would say the hours; but they would also gather for 'exhortation' on Sundays. They would work for the poor, care for poor people, the sick, foundlings and poor women in childbirth within their guest house, and provide clothing for the poor at the onset of each winter. The founder of this community intended to provide bedding sufficient for fifty members.

15   Migne, *Patrologiae*, vol. 216, cols 73–4.
16   Ibid., cols 75–7.
17   Ibid., cols 256, 274–5.
18   Ibid., col. 274.

The pope asked the Bishop of Elne to check on the truth of the intentions of this group of penitents, and to approve its foundation on his behalf if everything was in order. He warned that the meetings for 'exhortation' must not threaten either faith or discipline, and that access between the men's and women's houses must be regulated.[19] It does not seem to be recorded whether the bishop approved, or whether the community was indeed founded: there was no need for further papal involvement once matters had been passed to the diocesan authorities. If there had been any trouble, one may infer that Durand would have made his way once more to Rome. This episode is, however, significant. It is not stated that the penitents were former heretics (either Waldenses or even Cathars), but this is quite possible. Under such circumstances the Poor Catholics might have seemed an appropriate and sympathetic order to guide their restoration to an approved, Catholic ascetic life-style. It is a striking testimony to the rapport which seems to have grown up between Durand and Innocent III that such a trust was placed in the Poor Catholics so soon after their own acceptance as a Catholic society by Rome.

4.3 Papal Protection and Disappearance

In other respects the year 1212 saw the pope struggle repeatedly to win recognition and acceptance for the Poor Catholics. The bishops of Marseilles, Barcelona and Huesca were told that Durand of Osca, 'acolyte' (the only reference to Durand holding any clerical order) and his companions were reconciled to the Church, and must not be molested on account of their previous reputation.[20] Similar missives reached the King of Aragon, the papal legates in southern France and the Archbishop of Genoa.[21] Meanwhile, Durand was told to report any misdemeanours by any of his brethren to the bishop.[22] Finally, Innocent placed the Poor Catholics and their 'special friends remaining in the faith' and all their property under papal protection.[23]

In the years that followed, the Poor Catholics continued to fulfil their original aim of disputing against the Cathars. The arguments developed in the later parts of the *Liber Antiheresis* were reworked in two further pieces almost certainly written by Durand, the *Opusculum contra hereticos et eorum errores* and the *Liber Contra Manichaeos*. The latter work is

---

19   Ibid., cols 601–2.
20   Ibid., col 607.
21   Ibid., cols 608–9.
22   Ibid., cols 607–8.
23   Ibid., col. 609.

dated to the early 1220s: it preserves substantial segments of a piece by an Albigensian heretic written into the text for the purposes of refutation, and is thus a major source for Occitan Catharism.[24] One of the original companions of Durand, Ermengaud of Béziers, also wrote a treatise *Contra Haereticos* against the Cathars, of which substantial parts have survived.[25] There may have been other writings which are now entirely lost.

Despite papal protection and their literary efforts against Catharism, the Poor Catholics were not destined to survive as an order. Continuing suspicion of their historic links with the Waldensian preachers who still travelled across Languedoc and occupied inquisitors in the 1230s and 1240s[26] cannot have helped. By 1247 they had been forbidden to preach in Narbonne.[27] Just as serious, one may conjecture, would have been the difficulty of attracting new recruits in the age of the newly founded mendicant friars. No one who had not previously been a heretic would have seen any advantage to joining an order which was linked with heresy in the past, rather than the irreproachable Franciscans or Dominicans. Eventually the supply of moderate, ex-Waldensian preachers who like Durand only wished to oppose Catharism, not Rome, must have dried up. Some forty to fifty years after their foundation, the Poor Catholics seem to have drifted quietly into obscurity, their members either dead or absorbed within other religious orders.[28]

4.4 Bernardus Primus: The 'Reconciled Poor' Working Religious

In the spring of 1209 Durand had tried to extend his movement of Waldensian reconciliation to Lombardy. He told the pope that about a hundred Waldenses in Milan wished to be reconciled to the Church, on condition that the piece of open ground ('quoddam pratum') where they had held their school, and which the previous archbishop had demolished, were returned to them. Innocent III replied that he would not, in effect, bribe men back to Catholicism for material reward. However, if they went to the archbishop and asked to return to the faith freely,

---

24 Wakefield and Evans, *Heresies*, pp. 634–5 and references.
25 See the edition in J.-P. Migne, *Patrologiae*, vol. 204, cols 1,235–72; vol. 178, cols 1,823–46; discussion in C. Thouzellier, 'Le "Liber antiheresis" de Durand de Huesca et la "Contra haereticos" d'Ermengaud de Béziers', in *Revue d'Histoire Ecclésiastique*, vol. 55 (1960), pp. 130–41.
26 See below, chapter 5.1.
27 Wakefield and Evans, *Heresies*, p. 221; Grundmann, *Religiöse Bewegungen*, p. 117 and n. 93. The former Poor Catholics in Narbonne were required to enter recognized religious orders.
28 See Wakefield and Evans, *Heresies*, pp. 221, 277, and 716, nn. 12–13.

then he might choose to give them the 'pratum' or any other suitable place to gather and teach.[29]

This incident recalls the story in Peter of Verona's *Summa Contra Hereticos* about the Lombards' 'de prato' who broke from Johannes de Ronco over eucharists said by those not duly ordained: several historians have pointed out the connection.[30] If this were correct, then the Lombards who wished to be reconciled to Rome would have been those *opposed* to the custom of laymen celebrating their own eucharists. Had they gone through with their reconciliation, one would expect them to have joined the order of Poor Catholics under Durand's obedience.

In actual fact it appears to have been a different group, one which *did* celebrate lay eucharists, which reconciled itself to Innocent III's obedience shortly before 14 June 1210. On that date the pope issued open letters announcing their conversion. Some Waldensian preachers led by two men named Bernardus Primus and Willelmus Arnaldi had approached the pope, and subscribed a confession of faith based on that already subscribed by Valdesius and Durand. However, in this case the confession contained substantial important additions. In these, a whole list of erroneous beliefs and practices were listed, in which the group either admitted having erred, or was accused of heresy by others. The new converts excused their 'breaking of bread' as a necessary ministry to those who had been used to living among Cathars, but they renounced it for the future. They accepted the need for judicial execution of criminals and the civil oath. They abjured the belief that only good people should be obeyed, that only good priests could consecrate, and that good lay people were entitled to preach without permission, consecrate the eucharist or absolve penitents. They were required by the pope, on their obedience, to desist from disrespectful attacks on the persons of the clergy, which had caused scandal. Those who promised on oath to observe all these points, the letter concluded, were to be reconciled, proclaimed as true Catholics, and protected from disgrace.[31] Here the penitent quality of the former Waldenses was much more clearly identified than in the case of Durand; the heresies to be renounced were both more specific and much more radical. According to Peter of Verona, these 'Reconciled Poor', as they were called, were drawn from both the ultramontane and Lombard wings of the Italian Waldenses; however, the scope of the heresies renounced in the confession has more in common with the Lombards' enthusiasm for heterodoxy.[32]

29 Migne, *Patrologiae*, vol. 216, cols 29–30, as noted above, chapter 3, note 23.
30 Wakefield and Evans, *Heresies*, p. 277 and reference as above; ibid., p. 715, n. 7 and references.
31 The letter is in Migne, *Patrologiae*, vol. 216, cols 289–93; and in abridged form in Gonnet, *Enchiridion*, vol. 1, pp. 136–40.
32 Compare Wakefield and Evans, *Heresies*, p. 277.

More than two years later, on 23 July 1212, Innocent III forwarded to Bernardus Primus and his brethren an official copy of the *Propositum Vitae* which had been approved for them. They undertook, in language very similar to that of the Poor Catholics, to live in common and in poverty, and 'since they were mostly clerks' to work against the heretics by writing and teaching as the associates of Durand did. There were various interesting alterations made here, as in the original confession and oath. They undertook to work with their hands, even though their main task was preaching. They proposed to have regular reading at the meals in their houses 'of which they [had] more than eight'. They would eat in silence, unless to expound the text which had been read. They would wear a religious habit, but would also wear ordinary shoes with no distinctive design.[33]

The distinctive features of Bernardus Primus and his group seem to be their more sophisticated monastic structure, with houses, readings and so forth; and their continued commitment to manual labour for all the brethren, not just for the 'secular' brethren on the margins, as in the case of the Poor Catholics. The omission of patterned shoes suggests a predictable response from the pope to the early troubles surrounding the Poor Catholics and their footwear. A few weeks after sending the copy of the *Propositum*, Innocent III wrote to the Bishop of Cremona, assuring him that he had examined Bernard and his companions and given them apostolic letters as a testimonial, and requiring the bishop to show them the same level of favour and support.[34] There definite information concerning the Reconciled Poor more or less gives out. Peter of Verona reported that, later on, they entered other religious orders on the advice of the pope. Of those still surviving when the *Summa Contra Hereticos* was written, some were apparently living within the Dominican order.[35] Once again, one can only conclude that the Reconciled Poor was a movement of one generation only: potential new recruits to the order had no reason to choose its rule, rather than that of the burgeoning orders of friars.

4.5 Some Unanswered Questions

There is a range of questions concerning the early Waldenses to which one would dearly like to have answers, but where the evidence simply does not exist. Quite a lot may be deduced or conjectured about the reasons for their protest, the beliefs of the different groups, and the response of the Church towards them. One can observe the gradual

---

33 Migne, *Patrologiae*, vol. 216, cols 648–50.
34 Ibid., col. 668.
35 Wakefield and Evans, *Heresies*, p. 277.

insinuation among them of such peripheral Cathar teachings as the avoidance of all oaths or the disapproval of judicial execution. Their geographical spread to southern France and the eastern Pyrenees, and across into Lombardy, is relatively clear: evidence of their early penetration into other regions is more doubtful and will be considered later.[36] The response of different elements within the Church, and especially among theologians and prelates, can be charted.

On the other hand, in this early phase there is very little known about the numbers or social context either of the preachers or their hearers. How many Waldensian preachers were there? There were enough for the defection of only one splinter-group at Milan to comprise a hundred people; enough for the Bergamo conference to have met with six representative delegates from each side; enough that the eight known Poor Catholic leaders were only a fraction of the order as a whole.[37]

Their educational levels varied from the sophisticated Latin scholasticism of Durand of Osca to one conventionally (and perhaps misleadingly) described as an 'ignorant man without education' like Johannes de Ronco. If the reconciled brethren really were 'mostly clerks', then either there were many other 'clerks' within the movement from its outset, or after 1210 the proportion of educated men may have dropped somewhat with the loss of so many to the Church. However, the *Rescriptum* and its associated list of proof-texts, both composed in Latin, show that there was still a very significant level of learning, both linguistic and biblical, among its authors.[38] Not until the 1360s in Germany will one see such clear evidence of the educational attainments of the brethren.[39]

In the light of the later evidence, perhaps the most frustrating lacuna concerns the hearers or 'friends' of the travelling preachers. When the movement was still largely a public affair, all sorts of hearers would attend and listen, not just the tight-knit, secretive communities of later decades. Were these listeners predominantly from the towns or the countryside? It seems more likely that they were urban, especially in Lombardy, which marks them off from later Waldensian 'believers';[40] but one cannot be sure. Did they come from any particular social group? There is nothing to suggest that these followers were engaged in any form of social protest;[41] on the contrary, we do learn from one source that the wife and

36   See below, chapter 6.1.
37   See above, chapter 3.5 and chapter 4.1.
38   See above, chapter 3, notes 3, 41.
39   See below, chapter 6.4.
40   Compare the social background of those Waldenses discussed in part 2, especially chapter 7.
41   See K.-V. Selge, 'Caractéristiques du premier mouvement vaudois et crises au cours de son expansion', in *Cahiers de Fanjeaux*, vol. 2, 'Vaudois languedociens et pauvres catholiques' (1967), p. 125.

one of the sisters of the Albigensian Raymond-Roger, Count of Foix, were followers of the Waldenses.[42] However, the long lists of 'believers and receivers', often with age, marital status and occupation, which later inquisitors would compile, are entirely lacking for the first half-century or so of the movement.

In the era of inquisitorial registers one can learn quite a lot about the manner of worship used and the relationships which were formed when travelling preachers met their recognized followers: the shared prayers, the confessions, the expositions of scripture. Of this there is nothing certain in the first generation, apart from the evidence that some more radical preachers occasionally and controversially celebrated illicit baptisms or eucharists. In the main, these early Waldenses seem to have been preachers: their work was to teach in public, to gather and 'exhort' their members and associated 'friends'. With time, other more elaborate group rituals would grow up; by the 1240s these are already visible in the Languedoc.[43]

The most important lesson of the first phase of the Waldensian story is that it was a minimally unorthodox movement, stubborn only in its insistence on unrestrained lay preaching, which was driven into permanent, structured heresy by a jealous and distrustful *local* church hierarchy. The papacy did its best, on several occasions, to retain or reclaim Valdesius and his followers, in the shape of papal legate Henri de Marcy of Clairvaux in 1180/1 and Innocent III in 1208–12. The sticking-point seems to have been local bishops and archbishops who, faced with the constant pressure of the Cathar churches at the same period, felt they could not risk allowing undisciplined preachers among Catholic believers as well.

Yet the movement of Valdesius may have been peculiar to that particular stage in Church history. The creation of the mendicant orders, itinerant, and in the case of the Dominicans well-educated and articulate preachers, performed roughly the same task as the Waldenses, only with rather greater success. It is striking how many Dominican inquisitors such as Peter of Verona or Rainier Sacchoni were, in fact, converted heretics won over by the new preaching movements. The creation of a new order, the changing face of Roman Catholicism, had evidently filled the intellectual and moral vacuum which led so many into exotic heresy in the later twelfth century.

Yet not everyone was satisfied. Waldensian preachers did persist: radically anti-clerical and Donatist critics of the Church in Lombardy, and a more muted preaching movement, less Donatist but disbelieving in pur-

---

42 The source for this detail is Pierre de Vaux-Cernay, as edited in Gonnet, *Enchiridion*, vol. 1, pp. 126–7.
43 See below, chapter 5.1–2.

gatory, rejecting oaths and the judicial sword like the Lombards, in southern France. Why did it continue? Possibly, the world of the travelling lay preachers had become a counter-culture, a movement whose *raison d'être* was to vindicate its spiritual authority, its religious mission, against the Rome which claimed the power of the keys for itself. Some such reason must explain why a movement called into being, at least partly to oppose Cathar heresy, long outlived the Cathars whom it opposed.

Part II

The Age of Inquisition, Thirteenth to Fifteenth Centuries

Introduction

The Impact of Organized Inquisitorial Activity

From the 1230s onwards the life of religious movements deemed heretical was increasingly dominated by the fact of ecclesiastical inquisition. This procedure, adopted sooner or later in all the areas where the Waldenses were active, changed the relationship between the Church and the popular movement, the nature of the evidence which that relationship threw up, and in due course changed Waldensian behaviour itself. Inquisition was the solution devised in the aftermath of the Fourth Lateran Council and the Albigensian crusade to deal systematically with the massive challenge presented primarily by Catharism in southern France, northern Italy and elsewhere, and secondarily by other heresies. Essentially, it is defined by the investigative procedure used, and the legal devices which it provided to extract from unwilling and often mendacious suspects the admission of wrong, or rather illegal, religious belief. In some respects inquisition was modelled on that other great institution of thirteenth-century Catholicism, auricular confession. In confession, a penitent was called upon to recall all and every mortal sin committed; he or she was then probed further by the confessor, so that a full, complete confession could be elicited, and the greatest possible authentic sorrow for sin ('contrition') stirred up within the penitent's soul. Absolution, which reintegrated the penitent into the society of good Christians, was given when sufficient evidence of sorrow for sin, sufficiently authentic detestation of the old ways, was forthcoming.[1]

The analogies with sacramental confession found in inquisitorial procedure are quite striking, and surely deliberate. Those who were presented, or presented themselves, before an inquisitor, would already have

1 On confession, see the classic work by Henry Charles Lea, *A History of Auricular Confession and Indulgences in the Latin Church*, 3 vols (Philadelphia, 1896); also T. N. Tentler, *Sin and Confession on the Eve of the Reformation* (Princeton, NJ, 1977); the provisions for confession are spelled out in the decree *Omnes utriusque sexus* of the Fourth Lateran Council, 1215, as in G. Alberigo (ed.), *Conciliorum Oecumenicorum Decreta: The Decrees of the Ecumenical Councils*, 2 vols, trans. N. P. Tanner (London and Washington, DC, 1990), p. 245 and n. 4.

given sufficient evidence that they were heretics, either by their own admission or on the evidence gleaned by witnesses. Great emphasis was laid upon the summons to heretics to come 'spontaneously' to confess, and special leniency was granted to those who appeared without the use or threat of force against them.[2] Confronted with a suspected heretic, an inquisitor, like a confessor, strove to extract the fullest possible confession, and to arouse the deepest sense of abhorrence for past sins. The 'fullest possible' confession tended to mean that which conformed closest to the inquisitor's own perception of the heresy. Many of the otherwise peculiar and abhorrent features of inquisitorial procedure derive from this search for sincere 'repentance'. The guilt of the interrogated person was, generally speaking, assumed, as were the sins of an ordinary Christian on Shrove Tuesday. Nevertheless, scrupulous inquisitors knew quite well when to stop, if confronted by someone genuinely ignorant and innocent of their supposed error.[3] A first-time offender, who wished to be reintegrated into the Church, had to reveal his or her accomplices (since they would no longer be allies or friends), and to promise to detect, pursue and persecute all such heretics who might be encountered in the future.[4] Numerous, often humiliating, expensive or dangerous penances, such as penitential garments, or long pilgrimages, were imposed on penitent heretics. In some senses these resembled the penances imposed on ordinary Christians for serious sins, but they had the additional effect of imposing a probationary period in which the former heretic must display exemplary loyalty, subservience and zeal towards the Church.[5]

2 See the judicial opinion on this and other points from Avignon, c.1235, in A. Patschovsky and K.-V. Selge (eds), *Quellen zur Geschichte der Waldenser*, Texte zur Kirchen- und Theologiegeschichte, 18 (Gütersloh, 1973), p. 53.

3 For instances where an inquisitor refrained from asking detailed questions about doctrine from those who could not understand them, see D. Kurze (ed.), *Quellen zur Ketzergeschichte Brandenburgs und Pommerns*, Veröffentlichungen der historischen Kommission zu Berlin, Bd. 45, Quellenwerke Bd. 6 (Berlin, 1975), pp. 240, 245.

4 Outside Waldensianism, an instance of this requirement to name accomplices is found in the abjuration of the Lollard Thomas Moon of Loddon, 21 August 1430: 'Yf I knowe ony heretikes or of heresie ony persons suspect or of thaym fautours, confortours or defensours, or of ony persones makyng prive conventicules or assembles, or holdyng of ony divers or synguler opinions from the commune doctrine of the Churche, Y shal late you, worshipful fadir, or your vicar general in your absence or the diocesanes of suche persones have soon and redy knowyng. So help me God . . .'. See N. P. Tanner (ed.), *Heresy Trials in the Diocese of Norwich, 1428–1431*, Royal Historical Society, Camden 4th Series, vol. 20 (London, 1977), p. 180.

5 Examples of the requirement to make pilgrimages are afforded in the Book of Sentences of the inquisitors of Toulouse (early fourteenth century), as printed in Philippus van Limborch, *Historia Inquisitionis. Cui Subjungitur Liber sententiarum inquisitionis Tholosanae ab anno Christi MCCCVII ad annum MCCCXXIII* (Amsterdam, 1692), in a separately paginated appendix, p. 341. In one case a group of penitents was required to visit 17 shrines across southern France and obtain certificates from each. See also Pierre Seila's sentences, as in note 15 below.

Those who were obstinate, who refused to renounce or 'abjure' their heresy, rejected re-integration into the Church, and therefore were cut off from its membership, passed to the 'secular arm', that is the lay court for punishment, usually by burning. Heretics who were detected in a second offence were deemed by the Church to have been insincere and cynical in their first repentance, and therefore ran the risk of receiving the same treatment as the obstinate and impenitent.

Inquisition was a peculiar style of thought-policing. It embodied the legal presumption that all baptized Christians had made a lifelong commitment to live according to the laws and teachings of the Church, and that by following a heresy they had reneged on a binding religious and moral obligation. It contrived to combine the formal wish to ensure that all Catholic Christians really were fully committed and loyal, with savage physical penalties for those who rejected that commitment. To work effectively, inquisition required that the majority of lay people, and all those vested with secular authority, share the inquisitors' assumption that Christian obedience was unconditionally binding, and provide whatever political, military or judicial assistance was called for. It therefore channelled a hatred of heresy which might otherwise have found its outlet in lynchings or pogroms, or in the widespread destruction of the Albigensian crusade. It provided a ritual framework by which the penitent heretic, displaying exemplary piety and wearing the penitential cross on his or her outer clothing, could be gradually and progressively reintegrated into society.[6] In other words, inquisition belonged to that stage in the fight against heresy when the Church was to some extent already confident of ultimate victory. It could only be used to its fullest extent in areas where heresy was already a minority belief: when faced with whole valleys where the Waldenses had subverted communal authority, late medieval persecutors would have recourse once again to crude force.[7]

A somewhat unproductive debate has flourished over recent years as to whether the term 'inquisition' should be applied not only to an ecclesiastical procedure (the 'inquisitio de fide') but also to an ecclesiastical institution, 'the medieval Inquisition'. The issues raised by this debate tend to boil down to rather technical questions concerning the legal instruments by which inquisitors were appointed, and are not of great interest to historians of heresy itself.[8] It is clear, though, that only in the Spanish and Roman Offices of the Inquisition, founded from 1478

6   On the penal and reformatory policies used in inquisition, see B. Hamilton, *The Medieval Inquisition* (London, 1981), pp. 49–52.
7   For the final episodes of this kind, see below, chapter 7.5–6.
8   On the debate over a medieval 'Inquisition', see R. Kieckhefer, *Repression of Heresy in Medieval Germany* (Liverpool, 1979), pp. 1–10.

onwards[9] and 1542 respectively,[10] does one find a recognizably modern bureaucracy, directing its thought-control activities from a central hub. In the middle ages, 'inquisition' denoted above all a procedure, a legal formula for investigating and punishing heretics and other deviant Christians. This procedure was used, at various times, by bishops, by other diocesan officials and penitentiaries, by other secular clergy with special commissions, and especially by members of the mendicant orders, Franciscans and more often Dominicans.[11] Second, there were named individuals who were appointed as 'inquisitors of heretical pravity', usually by papal authority, and usually from either of the two main orders of mendicant friars (though one of the greatest German inquisitors, Peter Zwicker, was a Celestine).[12] Many of these appointments are preserved in the bullaries of the two orders. Dominicans predominated; though significantly for late medieval Waldensianism, the Alpine regions to the west of the passes, in the Dauphiné, were most commonly surveyed by Franciscan inquisitors. These were colloquially known by the fourteenth century as the 'inquisitors of the [friars] minor'.[13] Papally appointed inquisitors usually held commissions over large areas of territory. They had either to move very swiftly, trawling through large numbers of cases in a short time; or they had to become specialists in a smaller region within their commission; or, finally, they might have to work in concert, with good or ill grace, with the resident local hierarchies. There were, then, different patterns in the behaviour of inquisitors, as there were to the records which they left behind.[14]

The continuous threat and intermittent assault of inquisition changed the nature of Waldensian social and religious behaviour. In the early years of the movement, it expressed itself in public preaching, against Cathar heresy and in disobedience to the Church's prohibition. Though illegal, Waldensian activity was not clandestine, and neither was it consistently or regularly persecuted. Given the poor pastoral state of the contemporary Church, it is fairly certain that many of those lay people who listened to Waldensian preachers before c.1220–30 did not realize that they

9   On the Spanish inquisition, see Henry Kamen, *The Spanish Inquisition* (London, 1965); revd edn, *The Spanish Inquisition: An Historical Revision* (London, 1998).
10   On the Roman inquisition, founded by papal bull in 1542, see B. J. Kidd (ed.), *Documents Illustrative of the Continental Reformation* (Oxford, 1911), pp. 346–50.
11   Examples of all these different sorts of inquisitors can be found in chapter 7 below.
12   For Peter Zwicker's membership of the Celestine order, a Benedictine congregation first established in 1259 (and of which he was the Provincial), see Kurze, *Quellen*, pp. 5ff., 73.
13   G. Amati, 'Processus Contra Valdenses in Lombardia Superiori, Anno 1387', in *Archivio Storico Italiano*, series 3, vol. 1, pt 2 (1865), pp. 32–3, 35.
14   See the introduction to this volume, pp. 3ff.

were 'criminals' in the eyes of the hierarchy.[15] During the middle of the thirteenth century, preaching friars (including inquisitors) and other churchmen gradually made ordinary people aware that the Waldenses were a lawless movement; where they did not do so by explicit preaching, the seizure, trial and condemnation of captured heretics had the same educating effect.

Paradoxically, to turn the Waldensian preachers into criminals may actually have *increased* the numbers of people consciously involved in Waldensian activity. While the Waldenses consisted solely of a body of travelling poor preachers, those poor preachers *were* the Waldenses. Their hearers and supporters would not have been a distinct body; they would simply have been whoever among the local Catholic population was willing to listen.[16] Once Waldensian preaching was criminalized, those who continued to support it became an identifiable group, the 'believers' or 'friends' of the preachers. An 'outer ring' of supporters, who unlike the preachers were sedentary, married lay people living visibly in ordinary society, came into being for the first time. These people supported the preachers, received them in their homes, and concealed their now clandestine activities. Those who share a secret of this kind become, necessarily, a tight-knit group.[17] In some instances the 'friends' acquired, by the end of the middle ages, a collective legal and political existence more obvious and more effective than that of the preachers themselves.[18] Because of their sedentary, visible lives, they also vastly outnumber the preachers in the lists of those interrogated in medieval inquisitions.

The category of 'favourer, receiver, and believer' occupied, moreover, a distinct niche in inquisitors' jurisprudence, due doubtless to the early

15 For examples of this attitude (which may not have been entirely insincere), see Pierre Seila's sentences, as in H. C. Lea, *History of the Inquisition of the Middle Ages*, 3 vols (London, 1888), vol. 2, p. 582: 'Jacobus Carbonel . . . credidit quod Valdenses erant boni homines usque ad tempus quo ecclesia condemnavit eos . . . P. Austorcs . . . credidit quod essent boni homines . . . postquam audivit quod ecclesia condemnaverat eos non dilexit eos.'
16 The process by which the Waldenses moved from being public preachers to secretive missionaries and supporters of a minority group is discussed in G. Audisio, *Les 'Vaudois': naissance, vie et mort d'une dissidence (xiie–xve siècles)* (Turin, 1989), pp. 31–3.
17 Note the attempts made by such groups to control the flow of information to inquisitors and the clergy generally; see below, chapter 6 especially.
18 On the organization of lay Waldensianism, see E. Cameron, *The Reformation of the Heretics: The Waldenses of the Alps, 1480–1580* (Oxford, 1984), pp. 15–24; P. Paravy, 'Waldensians in the Dauphiné (1400–1530): From Dissidence in Texts to Dissidence in Practice', in Peter Biller and Anne Hudson (eds), *Heresy and Literacy, 1000–1530* (Cambridge, 1994), pp. 165–7; P. Paravy, *De la Chrétienté romaine à la réforme en Dauphiné*, Collection de l'École Française de Rome, 183, 2 vols (Rome, 1993–4), pp. 1,015–31.

emphasis on tackling Catharism. The Cathar preachers, by their particular dietary abstinences and other taboos, found it absolutely essential to have a class of 'believers' who were not yet fully initiated into the way of life of the 'perfect', from whom they received lodgings, food and support. Cathar society was intrinsically a two-tier affair.[19] There was no such intrinsic need in the Waldensian movement, except in the obvious sense that preachers need someone to preach to. But for systematic persecution, Waldensian preaching would doubtless have continued to be cast far and wide, as was the preaching of the friars themselves. Nevertheless, records of the early inquisitions often carry over the term 'perfect one' ('perfectus'), which properly describes a 'hereticated' Cathar, to denote a Waldensian travelling preacher, and use the term 'believer' ('credens') to describe their sedentary lay hearer or 'friend'.[20] Inquisitors made an intellectual assumption about the structure of Waldensian life; their activities ensured that this assumption was fulfilled in practice, as the only means by which the movement could sustain itself.

The rise of a two-tier membership was not the only major change wrought by persecution on Waldensian religious life. The case of Durand of Osca showed how membership of an illegal group could be most unattractive to aspiring clerical intellectuals. When the chance of papal rehabilitation and recognition beckoned, the more learned in the movement tended to desert the uncomfortable life of the itinerant heretic.[21] The conversions among the more learned of the movement in 1208–12 were not unique. In the late 1360s and again in the 1390s the widespread and powerful German Waldensian movement would lose large numbers of its best-educated preachers to the Catholic Church, with all but fatal consequences for the movement in Germany. From the 1530s Waldensian preachers in the southwestern Alps would enter negotiations with another respectable religious movement, though this time it was the nascent churches of the Protestant Reformation which attracted them.[22] Intermittent losses of the more learned leaders led to intellectual proletarianization. It also made the maintenance of any sense of continuity within these movements very difficult. Waldenses had continually to reinvent themselves and their past.[23] Moreover, Waldensian pastors could not defend their flocks; indeed, they had to take flight at the first approach

---

19   See, for example, M. Lambert, *The Cathars* (Oxford, 1998), pp. 141–58.

20   The phrase 'friends and believers' ('amici et credentes') is used, for example, in Limborch, *Liber sententiarum inquisitionis Tholosanae*, p. 222, in contrast to the itinerant 'brethren' who ministered to them. Cf. also E. Martene and U. Durand (eds), *Thesaurus Novus Anecdotorum V* (Paris, 1717), col. 1,781.

21   See above, chapter 4.

22   See below, chapters 6.4, 6.6, 8 and 9.

23   For the problems with the Waldenses' perceptions of their past, see chapter 6.4 below, and chapter 6, notes 117–28.

of an inquisitor, as some of the latter were not slow to point out.[24] Neither could they protect them against the gradual erosion of support by preachers and, again, the better class of inquisitor. Inquisitors who took advantage of the procedure to re-educate and re-orient their penitents could at times achieve spectacular results.[25] Against such a background, the survival of one of the last branches of the movement, the Waldenses of the southwestern Alps, may be explained by the exceptionally strong internal cohesion of the 'believer' communities, their relatively inaccessible locations, and the remarkably crass way in which the Catholic hierarchy handled them.[26] Inquisition, in short, took a heavy toll on the Waldenses. Nevertheless, it achieved its results so slowly that remnants of the movement survived into the early modern period. In its long history it generated exceptionally diverse source material about the Waldenses, which must now be analysed.

24 See, for instance, the remark found in J. Gretser, *Lucae Tudensis episcopi scriptores aliquot succedanei contra sectam Waldensium*, in M. de la Bigne (ed.), *Magna Bibliotheca Veterum Patrum*, 15 vols (Cologne, 1618–22), vol. 13, p. 316: 'semper fugis, et pauperes simplices in suis tribulationibus relinquis'.
25 Ibid., pp. 315–16: Peter Zwicker claimed to have converted more than 1,000 in Saxony and Bohemia, and hoped for similar success in Austria and Hungary.
26 See below, chapter 8.

5

Waldenses in Occitan France, c.1220–1320

At the end of chapter 4 it was suggested that the Waldensian preachers in southern France[1] held a markedly less anti-clerical, less Donatist attitude towards the Roman clergy than their counterparts in northern Italy. This conclusion seems to be required by the rhetoric of the so called *Rescriptum*, and is consistent with the other evidence.[2] In this chapter the activities of the ultramontane brethren and their successors will be identified, with this distinction in mind. It seems fairly certain that in the years following Bergamo the Poor preachers continued in their mission to the laity of Languedoc and Provence. Their behaviour, as itinerant preachers, resembled that of the Cathar 'good men' with whom they disputed but were sometimes confused. Their teachings, on the other hand, differed very little from those of the Catholic priests. It took a few decades before ordinary lay people appreciated that there was a serious disagreement between the official Church and the Waldenses. With time, divisions between the two hardened and became clearer, and the activities of the preachers grew more furtive and cautious, restricted to their known spiritual (and sometimes biological) kin. Although there are signs that anti-clerical sentiment hardened among some French Waldensian teachers around 1300, this anti-clericalism seems always to have been a disadvantage rather than a help in attracting converts. French followers of the Waldenses seem, for no very clear reason, to have been less keen to join a fiercely Donatist movement of resistance against their clergy than their Italian, or in due course their German, counterparts. This attitude may ultimately explain their disappearance into obscurity in the middle of the fourteenth century.

---

1 'France' as used in this sense refers to approximately the modern frontiers of the country, not, of course, to the medieval kingdom of France, whose boundaries were much more labile and in some respects disputed.
2 See above, especially the conclusion to chapter 3.

5.1 Southern France in the Mid-thirteenth Century

From the second quarter of the thirteenth century onwards, fragmentary evidence starts to emerge of the way in which the travelling Waldensian preachers and teachers of the Languedoc and Provence went about their business. Evidence survives of their presence across a wide swath of the south, from Durand's territory of Narbonne and Pyrenean France, up through Toulouse and Montauban into Quercy, across the south through Montpellier and Nîmes towards Avignon and Provence, and northwards into the kingdom of Burgundy.[3] The preachers in their travels may have ranged even further afield than this, though later evidence suggests that they did not always make converts in every region where they travelled.[4]

The Waldensian preachers continued the same simple ministry which they had begun in the twelfth century, with few of the embellishments of either the Lombards or the Poor Catholics. They travelled around preaching their beliefs to those who would listen. They taught their followers the epistles and gospels, sometimes by rote. In the years before inquisitors began their work in earnest, the Occitan Waldenses practised their form of religion in public. In 1241–2, the inquisitor Pierre Seila investigated and sentenced a large and well-organized group of Waldenses centred on Montauban; there were also significant numbers in Gourdon and Montcucq, and scattered references to others at Beaucaire, Sauveterre, Moissac and Castelnau. One witness described in 1241–2 how he had 'frequently come to the schools of the Waldenses and read with them'. The Waldensian community is also reported to have possessed a hospital and a cemetery. This level of organized activity could only have been sustained before the Waldenses had been 'criminalized' in the minds of ordinary Catholics.[5] In the period before inquisition took hold, three testimonies referred to the Waldenses preaching publicly in the streets or in the squares.[6] At the start of this period, some were reported to have been seen 'reading and singing with the clerics in church', though it has been plausibly suggested that this testimony may

---

3 The 'kingdom of Burgundy' (also known as the kingdom of Arles or the Arelate) reached south into Provence, but there is also evidence of Waldensian activity from Burgundian heartlands of the Saone.
4 See below, section 5.3.
5 'Jacobus Carbonel dixit quod frequenter venit ad scholas Valdensium et legebat cum eis.' H. C. Lea, *History of the Inquisition of the Middle Ages*, 3 vols (London, 1888), vol. 2, p. 582. On the Montauban community see ibid., pp. 145–7; J. Gonnet and A. Molnar, *Les Vaudois au moyen âge* (Turin, 1974), p. 159 and references.
6 'P. Austorcs audivit multociens predicationem Valdensium dum predicarent publice in viis . . . A. Capra . . . dixit se audivisse predicationem eorum in platea multociens'. Lea, *Inquisition*, vol. 2, pp. 582–3.

have referred to Poor Catholics, who were visually indistinguishable from Waldenses at first.[7]

One important new trait appears, however. The Waldenses are already reported, by this early date, to have taken up the custom of hearing the confessions of their followers and assigning penances.[8] Auricular confession had a special significance in the decades immediately after the Fourth Lateran Council of 1215. Constitution 21 of that Council had for the first time required all Catholic faithful to confess their sins in the sacrament of penance at least annually, usually during Lent.[9] This particular form of an ancient ritual act, with its theological implications, proved to be one of the defining habits of late medieval western Christianity.[10] If the Waldenses adopted it almost immediately, this suggests that they wished to be seen to perform no less of a pastoral function than the parish priests, or in due course the friars. In their hands, however, it became a very useful tool for sustaining a persecuted movement. The ordinary faithful were used to private consultations with a priest or friar; so a private consultation with a heretic pastor seemed in no way strange. Confession provided the ideal forum in which moral exhortation might be given. From a rarely mentioned, perhaps peripheral activity in the early thirteenth century, it would become a basic rite for later medieval Waldenses.[11] It was not, of course, exclusive. The 'believers' still confessed to their parish priests as well; so, in all likelihood, did some of the teachers. Yet because they rarely, if ever, confessed their heretical associations in their Catholic Lenten confession, the latter remained partial, the submission to the priest incomplete.[12] Even their regular Catholic

---

7　'Quia ecclesia sustinebat tunc dictos Valdenses et erant cum clericis in ipsa ecclesia cantantes et legentes et credebat eos esse bonos homines.' C. Thouzellier, *Catharisme et valdéisme en Languedoc à la fin du xiie et au début du xiiie siècle* (Paris, 1966), p. 294 and n. 99.

8　A. Patschovsky and K.-V. Selge (eds), *Quellen zur Geschichte der Waldenser*, Texte zur Kirchen- und Theologiegeschichte, 18 (Gütersloh, 1973), p. 51; Lea, *Inquisition*, vol. 2, p. 582: 'Domina de Coutas . . . confessa fuit Valdensi cuidam peccata sua, et accepit penitentiam a Valdense.' See also G. Gonnet (ed.), *Enchiridion fontium valdensium (Recueil critique des sources concernant les Vaudois au moyen âge) du IIIe Concile de Latran au Synode de Chanforan (1179–1532)*, vol. 1 (Torre Pellice, 1958), pp. 155–7.

9　G. Alberigo (ed.), *Conciliorum Oecumenicorum Decreta: The Decrees of the Ecumenical Councils*, 2 vols, trans. N. P. Tanner (London and Washington, DC, 1990), p. 245.

10　See above, part 2 introduction, note 1.

11　See below, chapter 6 and especially chapter 7.

12　Cases where Waldenses admitted their Waldensianism in their Lenten (Catholic) confession are so rare as to arouse special notice: see D. Kurze (ed.), *Quellen zur Ketzergeschichte Brandenburgs und Pommerns*, Veröffentlichungen der historischen Kommission zu Berlin, Bd. 45, Quellenwerke Bd. 6 (Berlin, 1975), pp. 189–90, involving one Peter Rutling of Klein-Wubiser on 19 February 1393.

practice would have reminded them of their secret differences with the rest of society.

Although one source describes these preachers as the 'sandalled ones' ('sandaliati'), one may conjecture that increasing persecution would soon have required the abandonment of anything so distinctive as special footwear.[13] These Waldenses were 'received' by their followers; that is, they stayed in the houses of those who supported them and lived off them for short periods, as Durand had urged they should do.[14] On the other hand, the travelling teachers had already begun to acquire one attribute of secrecy. They performed other work, of a kind which would justify their travelling around in the eyes of a sceptical onlooker. Most commonly, they acted as travelling healers. At least five witnesses from the Montauban region called on their medical services for themselves or their families. On the other hand, on one occasion they re-hooped a barrel for one of their friends.[15]

The bulk of the evidence suggests that the Waldensian teachers formed a simple travelling society, without any elaborate administrative hierarchy, and with quite simple teachings and few rituals.[16] One source, however, which appears to derive from abjurations made by 'Johannes de Montel', 'Elias' and 'B. de Fiac' before the Bishop of Valence at this period, depicts a rather more sophisticated structure. These three converts painted a scandalous and libellous picture of the movement which they had left. They reported that the Waldenses conducted irregular eucharists, confessed to each other, elected their own bishops, allowed even the illiterate of both sexes to preach, and conducted a campaign of vitriolic hatred against the Church, despising the altar and the eucharist, baptizing or re-baptizing themselves and their followers, rejecting both

13   Around 1240 the title of 'sandaliati' was still being used: Patschovsky and Selge, *Quellen*, p. 66. One of the fullest descriptions of the Waldensian brethren (and sisters) as 'sandaliati', with repeated references to the cutting away of their shoe uppers, is found in the controversial text, of uncertain date and provenance, entitled 'De vita et actibus, de fide et erroribus haereticorum, qui se dicunt Pauperes Christi seu Pauperes de Lugduno', as edited (for example) in J. J. Ignaz von Döllinger (ed.), *Beiträge zur Sektengeschichte des Mittelaters*, 2 vols (Munich, 1890), vol. 2, pp. 92–7. The multiple references to the wearing of perforated footwear, and its assumption that the brethren lived partly sedentary lives in 'hospitia', which are found in this text, suggest a date no later than the middle of the thirteenth century.

14   For Durand's defence of 'living off the Gospel', see K.-V. Selge, *Die ersten Waldenser mit Edition des Liber antiheresis des Durandus von Osca*, 2 vols (Berlin, 1967), vol. 2, pp. 77–88. Compare Patschovsky and Selge, *Quellen*, p. 52: followers and supporters of the Waldenses 'visited [them], listened to them, received them, or otherwise conferred benefits on them'.

15   Lea, *Inquisition*, vol. 2, pp. 582–3. On healing, see also P. Biller, '*Curate infirmos*: The Medieval Waldensian Practice of Medicine', in *Studies in Church History* 19 (1982), pp. 55–77.

16   Thouzellier, *Catharisme et valdéisme*, p. 296.

the Lenten fast and the traditional creeds. They also accused their former associates of teaching abstinence from swearing but repeatedly swearing themselves; and of professing chastity but many times breaking their vows. One 'Maria de Narbona' they accused of sexual relations with no less than four of the preachers.[17] Given the evident spleen behind this document, one is entitled to doubt its picture of a much more radicalized anti-clerical society, which in any case cannot have lasted very long.

In one respect, however, the accusations of Johannes de Montel hold good for the movement as a whole at this period. The earliest travelling preachers had reputedly included women, as noted earlier.[18] Sources from the 1240s also report that women continued a teaching role in the movement. 'Geralda the Waldensian' was entertained by one of her followers near Montauban; Raymunda de Balinis and Alazais Calosa were detected in the diocese of Narbonne, and the house where they had stayed was razed. Arnalda and Bona Domina were captured near Castres in 1239: one converted and the other was burned.[19] Itinerant, visible women teachers must nevertheless have posed a problem for a movement lapsing into semi-secrecy. There were sufficient pretexts on which men might keep up a life of constant travelling; women were expected to be sedentary. As soon as concealment became necessary, one would expect Waldensian women to cease travelling. It may even be that women's propensity to travel around and teach publicly, in the early stages of the movement, was exaggerated by hostile critics for polemical reasons. By the 1300s, as will be seen later, women were rigidly excluded from any ministry among the Waldenses of the Languedoc (if the sources for that period are to be believed). Much later on, they would be found keeping house for novice preachers in a sort of beguine-style existence, but never again as travelling teachers.[20]

17 Gonnet, *Enchiridion*, vol. 1, pp. 155–7.
18 See above, chapter 2 and notes 46–50.
19 Lea, *Inquisition*, vol. 2, p. 580; Patschovsky and Selge, *Quellen*, pp. 58–9; Thouzellier, *Catharisme et valdéisme*, p. 295, n. 106.
20 See below, chapter 8.1. For a different view of the role of women in Waldensianism, see P. Biller, 'The Preaching of the Waldensian Sisters', in *La Prédication sur un mode dissident: laics, femmes, hérétiques . . .* , in *Heresis* 30 (1999), pp. 137–68; also P. Biller, 'The Waldenses 1300–1500', in *Revue de l'histoire des religions*, vol. 217, fasc. 1 (2000), pp. 89–91. Dr Biller notes the reference to sisters in the text 'De vita et actibus' (above, n. 13) but assigns to this a later date than seems consistent with the contents of the document. He also points to the admission of women to the Waldensian society in Strasbourg *c.*1400. Compare Shannon McSheffrey, *Gender and Heresy: Women and Men in Lollard Communities 1420–1530* (Philadelphia, 1995), *passim*, but esp. pp. 109–24, 137ff., who finds that Lollard heresy offered less to women than Catholicism, and gave few women preponderant roles. There is no *a priori* reason to suppose that heresy was less restrictive towards women than was Catholicism in the middle ages.

It is quite possible that most of the instruction given by these Waldensian teachers comprised nothing out of the ordinary in terms of doctrine. They probably continued to teach, as they had done before, mainstream Christian beliefs, especially in controversy with Cathars. Several of the testimonies recorded by the inquisitor Pierre Seila in the Quercy region in 1241–2 refer to the Waldenses holding public disputations with the 'heretics', the name by which the Cathars were always described.[21] One B. Remon told how he had gone to listen to the Waldenses and Cathars in turn, to choose which were the better; he decided in favour of the Cathars, and thereafter supported them in discussions with others.[22] In these circumstances it is likely that typical Waldensian teaching, like most of the *Liber Antiheresis*, would have defended beliefs shared by Catholics and Waldenses alike.

However, inquisitors took little interest in Waldensian teachings, except in so far as these deviated from Catholic norms. Most sources from this period concur in identifying three or four areas of consistent disagreement with orthodoxy. First, the Waldenses, like the Cathars, discouraged their followers from swearing under any circumstances, as the Cathars did. Second, they taught that to sentence someone to death and to execute them was sinful and forbidden: again they shared this trait with the Cathars, though perhaps for different reasons.[23] Third, a female follower admitted to inquisitors in the 1230s that she had heard the 'pestiferous advice' against belief in purgatory, and prayers for the dead. Two preachers seized in the diocese of Carpentras around 1240 likewise denied that purgatory existed, or that prayers for the dead served any purpose.[24] Waldenses would later justify the rejection of civil oaths and execution by strictly literal interpretation of certain biblical texts.[25] That they rejected purgatory is interesting, not least because some have questioned whether belief in purgatory impinged at all on the popular mind in the high middle ages.[26] The doctrine of purgatory presupposed that unconfessed venial sins, and mortal sins for which absolution had been given, must receive their due punishment or 'penalty' somewhere, for

---

21 Lea, *Inquisition*, vol. 2, pp. 582ff.
22 Ibid., p. 583.
23 Patschovsky and Selge, *Quellen*, pp. 61, 63, 66–8; Thouzellier, *Catharisme et valdéisme*, p. 295, nn. 100, 105.
24 Patschovsky and Selge, *Quellen*, pp. 61, 67.
25 The principal text cited against swearing was Matthew 5:33–7, but note the use also of Ecclesiasticus 23:9 and 11; the prohibition on killing even in execution or warfare appears to be based on a literalist reading of Exodus 20:13.
26 Compare the claim made by H. A. F. Kamen, in his *The Phoenix and the Flame: Catalonia and the Counter Reformation* (New Haven, Conn., 1993), that the doctrine of purgatory did not penetrate the popular mind before the Counter-Reformation.

strict justice to be observed: if the last-minute penitent entered heaven as quickly and easily as the ascetic, it was thought that divine justice would lack consistency.[27] The belief, however, inevitably enhanced the objective value of the Catholic rites which were believed to reduce time spent in purgatory, or release those trapped there. It therefore threatened to increase the importance of Catholic penitential exercises at the expense of Waldensian ones; it also appeared to lack convincing scriptural foundation.[28]

Most of the evidence for early Waldensian teaching includes nothing more than these distinctive elements, and one may assume that they represent a base-line of typical teaching. However, some authorities report a far more radical range of beliefs and disbeliefs. The inquisitor Étienne de Bourbon, writing around 1250, based his report of Waldensian teaching on his past career, which seems to have included participating in the interrogation of a Burgundian heretic who had learned his Waldensian beliefs among the Lombards at Milan.[29] Étienne agreed that they rejected oaths, execution and purgatory. He went much further, however: he claimed that they believed that the soul of every good person partook of the Holy Spirit, and that any good person was the son of God in the same way that Christ was. There was only one divine soul in heaven, into which the souls of the elect were absorbed. Thus, he claimed, they believed in the life of Christ only as an analogue of the spiritual life of a righteous person, and in the Trinity only as an analogue of the conversion process: the Father as the one converting, the Son as the one converted, the Spirit as the means of conversion.[30] They denied any spiritual worth whatever to the acts of an evil priest, and made sweeping claims for the spiritual powers of a good lay person; they rejected many of the rites and consecrations of the Church, and were rabidly anti-clerical.[31] Étienne's report of virulent anti-clerical feeling among the Waldenses whom he had met matches with the abjuration of Johannes de Montel and his friends, though in other respects the testimonies are different.[32] Had the Waldenses of Languedoc taught such inflammatory beliefs, it is

27 See in general J. Le Goff, *The Birth of Purgatory*, trans. A. Goldhammer (London, 1984), esp. pp. 237ff.; compare the detailed interrogation of Raimond de Sainte-Foy on this issue, in J. Duvernoy (ed.), *Le Registre d'inquisition de Jacques Fournier, évêque de Pamiers (1318–1325)*, 3 vols (Toulouse, 1965), vol. 1, pp. 92ff.
28 The standard text claimed by the defenders of the doctrine of purgatory is the apocryphal 2 Maccabees 12:43–5, though claims have also been made to prove the doctrine by Matthew 5:25–6 and 1 Corinthians 3:13.
29 Patschovsky and Selge, *Quellen*, pp. 47–8.
30 W. L. Wakefield and A. P. Evans (eds), *Heresies of the High Middle Ages: Selected Sources Translated and Annotated* (New York and London, 1969), pp. 346ff.
31 Ibid.; cf. E. Martene and U. Durand (eds), *Thesaurus Novus Anecdotorum V* (Paris, 1717), col. 1,755.
32 See above, note 17.

hard to imagine that other inquisitors besides Étienne de Bourbon would have failed to notice them. It is possible that Étienne had tried to 'reconstruct' the framework of belief among those whom he interrogated, or that particularly loquacious victims of the inquisition had elaborated their beliefs at his prompting. It is also possible that Milanese influence, given the greater fecundity of the Italian heresies, and their longer-standing anti-clerical sentiment, may account for the extremism described by Étienne de Bourbon.[33] Nevertheless, later heretics found in Burgundy would teach much more moderate ideas.[34] The problem defies satisfactory solution.

The Occitan Waldenses had one special rite of their own, which is found nowhere else in the history of the movement. Several testimonies describe how the Waldenses blessed bread and fish, which they then consumed ritually 'on the day of the supper', presumably Maundy Thursday.[35] Those interrogated by Pierre Seila likewise referred to the blessed bread, fish and wine.[36] The descriptions of this rite do suggest a ceremonial occasion when these blessed elements were distributed to the followers, in the manner of a ritual meal. This was not, as some clerics alleged, an alternative eucharist; rather, it was closer to some of the blessings of bread or herbs distributed as *sacramentalia* in popular Catholicism.[37] The analogy is heightened by the fact that the bread was not only consumed at a gathering, but also taken home and eaten by the followers.[38] The blessing of bread and fish would survive in the Languedoc into the 1300s, by which time it had become a secret rite, for the preachers or 'brethren' alone.[39]

The believers or followers of the Waldenses were far easier for inquisitors to apprehend than the mobile, fugitive preachers. Consequently, the early inquisitorial data is dominated by the need to define, categorize and punish the 'friends and supporters', and much is said about their relationships with the preachers. The preachers gave their friends a 'kiss of peace'.[40] The friends supported the preachers by receiving them in their

---

33 On the history of heresy in Milan, see above, chapter 3.1.
34 See below, section 5.2.
35 Patschovsky and Selge, *Quellen*, pp. 52 and nn. 14, 69; Lea, *Inquisition*, vol. 2, p. 584: 'B. Clavelz . . . cenavit cum eis in die Jovis cene'.
36 Lea, *Inquisition*, vol. 2, pp. 581–2; cf. also Thouzellier, *Catharisme et valdéisme*, p. 295, n. 105.
37 For *sacramentalia*, see esp. R. W. Scribner, 'Ritual and Popular Belief in Catholic Germany at the Time of the Reformation', *Journal of Ecclesiastical History* 35 (1984), pp. 47–77.
38 Patschovsky and Selge, *Quellen*, p. 61; Lea, *Inquisition*, vol. 2, p. 582.
39 See below, note 100.
40 Patschovsky and Selge, *Quellen*, p. 52 and n. 17; Thouzellier, *Catharisme et valdéisme*, p. 295, n. 105.

houses for several days at a time, and by giving them gifts of food, money or clothing. They would then naturally eat with the travelling preachers. Sharing a table with them not only provided legal proof of close support; it also made possible informal teaching and evangelizing, as later evidence will show. Believer hosts might at times help to conceal heretics, or look after their property.[41] While the rite known as 'adoration' seems chiefly or only to have been given to Cathar *perfecti* by their believers, it was reported of one 'Pana' that she loved Petrus de Vallibus, the leading Waldensian, 'as an angel of God'.[42] On the other hand, one need not assume that the Occitan supporters of the Waldenses quickly or readily embraced a religion of illegal resistance. Several of those interrogated claimed that they supported the Waldenses because they thought the Church approved of them, or at least did not persecute them, and that they changed their minds when news of their condemnation emerged.[43] To claim that one had not realized the Waldenses were condemned as heretics was, of course, a convenient excuse to use before an inquisitor; for all that, it may have been perfectly genuine, especially in the years before *c*.1230.

The Languedoc would experience a series of energetic campaigns by inquisitors up to the 1320s. By the early fourteenth century, however, the inquisitors of Toulouse would find that nearly all the Waldenses whom they apprehended were migrants from Burgundy, or their children and descendants. The indigenous heretic 'followers' interrogated by Pierre Seila in 1241–2, or by Bernard of Caux and Jean de St-Pierre in 1245–6, seem to have disappeared by the later thirteenth century.

5.2 The 'Brethren' in Burgundy and the Languedoc, *c*.1280–1320

Around 1310, inquisitors based in the city of Toulouse ordered the arrest and imprisonment, as suspected Waldensian heretics, of large numbers of inhabitants of Gascony who had migrated there from Burgundy several decades earlier.[44] Over the following ten years or so, dozens of inhabitants of the villages around Auch, to the west of Toulouse, and a smaller number from Alzon in Rouergue, in the diocese of Rodez, were

41 Patschovsky and Selge, *Quellen*, pp. 52, 56, 59, 61, 63, 68–9; also throughout the Seila register in Lea, *Inquisition*, vol. 2, pp. 579ff.
42 Lea, *Inquisition*, vol. 2, p. 580.
43 Patschovsky and Selge, *Quellen*, p. 56; Thouzellier, *Catharisme et valdéisme*, p. 294, n 99; also Lea, *Inquisition*, as above, part 2 introduction, note 15.
44 Philippus van Limborch, *Historia Inquisitionis. Cui Subjungitur Liber sententiarum inquisitionis Tholosanae ab anno Christi MCCCVII ad annum MCCCXXIII* (Amsterdam, 1692), pp. 216–17, 225, 368, 375.

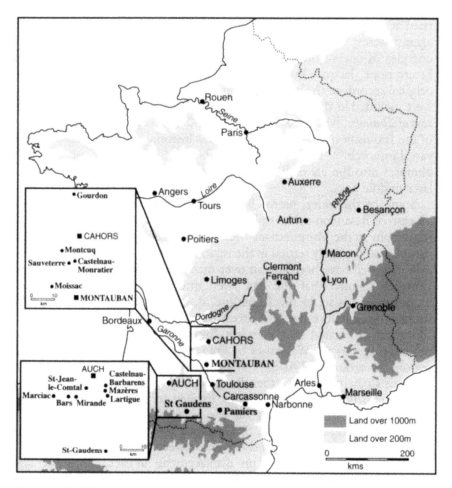

Map I   The Waldensian settlements in the Languedoc in the thirteenth century.

tried at Toulouse. These trials formed only a part of the great campaign against heresy which extended into the 1320s, and which occupied the energies of one of the most celebrated inquisitors, Bernard Gui, and a future pope, Jacques Fournier, then Bishop of Pamiers.[45] Although the original records of the interrogations are lost, detailed extracts from these were included in the digest known as the *Book of Sentences of the Inquisitors of Toulouse*, which was printed in 1692 as an appendix to the history of the Inquisition by the Dutch religious historian and polemicist Philips van Limborch.[46] This text affords the first of many close, detailed glimpses into the life of Waldensian preachers and their followers in the later middle ages.

Some of the older, native Burgundians gave various villages in the diocese of Besançon as their place of birth. However, by the time of the trials many of the 'Burgundians' were second-generation Gascons, whose parents had probably settled in the region around 1280–90.[47] The migration may well have been spread over many years. An old woman named Ermenio claimed that she had been interrogated under oath by an inquisitor at Najac, in the Rouergue, during her father's lifetime, presumably long before her final arrest. On the other hand, several of the 'Burgundians' stated that they left Burgundy during the persecutions mounted against the Waldenses by Fra Guy de Reims, inquisitor for that region, in around 1290–5.[48] Virtually all those who were tried for Waldensian heresy were either Burgundians by descent, or related by marriage to those who were. They formed in many cases quite close endogamous groups, centred on the villages of Mazères, Castelnau-Barbarens, Lartigue, Marciac, St-Gaudens, Mirande, Bars and St-Jean-le-Comtal in Auch diocese, and Alzon, between Millau and Montpellier, in the diocese of Rodez.[49] This displacement, in fact, offers the first example of collective migration by groups of Waldensian followers to escape persecution, even if their choice of the Toulousain as a place of

45 On Bernard Gui see F. L. Cross and E. A. Livingstone (eds), *The Oxford Dictionary of the Christian Church*, 3rd edn (Oxford, 1997), art. 'Gui, Bernard', p. 721; for Jacques Fournier, see below, note 86.
46 See above, part 2 introduction, note 5. Despite the statement in Wakefield and Evans, *Heresies*, p. 374, that the original Book of Sentences was lost, it survives as British Library, Ms. Add. 4697, having been presented to the British Museum on 21 August 1756. References to the Limborch edition are given here, for ease of access to the original text.
47 Limborch, *Liber sententiarum inquisitionis Tholosanae*, pp. 230, 262, 264, 352: Perrin Fabri came originally from 'Cortena', Jean Chanoat from 'Mulsia' near Orgelet, Perrin de Vincendat from 'Crancerum', and Pierre Aymon from 'Torum' (Dole), all in the diocese of Besançon.
48 Ibid., pp. 230–1, 253, 264, 352, 354.
49 Ibid., pp. 216–17, 223–4, 227, 235, 239, 339–41, 343.

refuge was most unfortunate. In later years similar migrations would transfer Alpine heretics to Provence and the Comtat Venaissin, and Provençal heretics to Apulia and Calabria.[50]

In contrast to the restricted origins of the followers, the preachers who ministered Waldensian religion to them were a much more heterogeneous group. One of their earliest leaders seems to have been Jean de Grandvaux, almost certainly a Burgundian, whom one follower first received in his house as early as 1275.[51] Other Burgundians included Étienne Porchier from Lons-le-Saulnier, and the barber Étienne Bordet.[52] However, a later leader of the group was Cristinus, described by one witness as 'a great big fat man' and by another as 'a simple illiterate', whose surname 'Maynes' may indicate that he came from Maine.[53] Other preachers were described as originating from Provence, the Albigeois, Vienne, Champagne, Cahors and the Toulousain.[54] It does not follow, however, that because one Waldensian travelling preacher came from a given region, then such a region necessarily had a thriving and undetected Waldensian community. Those recruited as preachers, regardless of their origins, may have met up with Waldensian teachers on their travels, and have done nothing to foster their beliefs in their country of origin.

The descriptions given of the preachers at this stage in the story still suggest a very simple association, without any complex hierarchy, though a long-term leader is identified. These Waldenses, by the testimony of many witnesses, called themselves 'the brethren'.[55] Most interestingly, it was the outsiders, the 'gentiles', that is, the clergy, who called them 'Poor of Lyon' or 'Waldenses'.[56] 'Poor of Lyon' had become an ecclesiastical title: it would mean nothing either to these Waldenses or to others also called by the same name. It may be assumed, given other contemporary evidence, that these preachers were celibate travellers, and that the

---

50   See below, chapter 7.6.
51   Limborch, *Liber sententiarum inquisitionis Tholosanae*, p. 352.
52   Ibid., pp. 200, 344, 359, 367.
53   Ibid., pp. 231, 346, 377–8; Duvernoy, *Registre d'inquisition*, vol. 1, pp. 99ff.
54   Limborch, *Liber sententiarum inquisitionis Tholosanae*, pp. 201, 216, 225, 230, 233, 345, 352, 367; compare Martin Schneider, *Europäisches Waldensertum im 13. und 14. Jahrhundert*, Arbeiten zur Kirchengeschichte, 51 (Berlin, 1981), p. 31.
55   Limborch, *Liber sententiarum inquisitionis Tholosanae*, pp. 216–17, 222–4, 226, 234, 354, 356, 359, and esp. 366: 'et vocabant se illi qui erant de illa societate fratres'.
56   Ibid., p. 351: 'si scirentur caperentur per dominum quia gentes vocabant eos pauperes de Lugduno'; p. 357: 'alii vocabant eos pauperes de Lugduno'; p. 367: 'gentes persequebantur eos, et vocabant eos Valdenses, et reputabant eos hereticos'; also p. 369 similarly; but cf. p. 354, which appears to give the opposite impression.

description of Jean Chanoat, husband of Agnes, as 'Valdensis perfectus' arose from a misunderstanding.[57] Although one testimony mentions a solitary woman, Raymonde of Castres, as a Waldensian, active preachers by this time seem to have been exclusively male.[58]

Since the time of the *Rescriptum* no evidence about the levels of learning of the Waldensian teachers had been forthcoming. In the *Book of Sentences*, however, several witnesses described, sometimes consistently, a few of the preachers as clerks ('clerici'). The term is ambiguous, because social conditions in the later middle ages were ambiguous. A literate person usually knew Latin, the language of religion and the liturgy. He was entitled to the legal status of clerk and to be tried in a spiritual court. He might, or he might not, be in minor or holy orders.[59] So, when twelve separate witnesses described Perrin Vaudry of St-Gaudens as 'clericus', one may take it that his learning was self-evident to ordinary lay people: that he could read Latin and the vernacular, possibly carried books with him, or in some other way showed visible trappings of education.[60] Besides Perrin Vaudry, only three others merited the description of clerk and only a handful of times each. Evidently, the presence of a reasonably educated man among the Burgundian preachers made him stand out. Such a person was therefore in a small minority among the two dozen or so preachers whose names we know from this period. In this respect the Burgundians of *c*.1300 were surely less educated than the Poor Catholics, described as 'mostly clerks', or even the authors of the 1218 *Rescriptum*.[61]

They were, it seems, nearly all laymen. The rather pathetic story of the exceptional one who was actually a priest, Jean Philibert of St-Sauveur in Burgundy, proves the rule. Around 1283 he was sent from Burgundy to Gascony to search for a fugitive Waldensian. While there he evidently made friends with the Waldenses: after a brief return to Burgundy he settled again in Auch diocese, where eventually Cristinus persuaded him to become a Waldensian preacher, saying 'it would be better for you to be a swineherd than to celebrate mass, for you are in mortal sin'. Around 1298 he was interrogated by the inquisitor Guy de Reims, and on refus-

---

57 Ibid., p. 241; but cf. p. 262, where the sentence of Jean Chanoat treats him like any other follower or believer. Note Raymond de Sainte-Foy's comments on the brethren's celibacy below, section 5.3.
58 Ibid., p. 201: 'quedam mulier que vocabatur Raymunda de Castris, que erat ejusdem secte'.
59 For the double significance of the term 'clericus' as both 'of the clergy' and 'educated' at this period, see A. Murray, *Reason and Society in the Middle Ages* (Oxford, 1978), pp. 263–70.
60 Limborch, *Liber sententiarum inquisitionis Tholosanae*, pp. 224–6, 231, 239, 253, 351, 366–7, 377.
61 See above, chapters 3.5, 4.1.

ing to swear was imprisoned for a time at St-Laurent-en-Grandvaux, near Besançon. After later taking the oath, abjuring heresy, and being released, he returned to Gascony and led a double life, administering the Catholic sacraments but still associating with the Waldenses. He was captured and led to face the inquisitors at Toulouse in 1311, where degradation and condemnation awaited him eight years later.[62]

Whereas the mid-thirteenth century followers mentioned confessing their sins to the Waldenses quite rarely, those interrogated around 1300 routinely confessed their sins to their heretic pastors and received a form of sacramental penance from them, sometimes on more than one occasion. The majority of the 'Burgundians' admitted to having confessed their sins in this fashion. Where the number of occasions was specified, the norm was for the follower to have confessed twice or perhaps three times over a period between five to fifteen years before their arrest by the inquisitors.[63] At one extreme, Pierrette 'la Crestiana', widow of Huguet the Burgundian, of Lartigue, had confessed five or six times over a fourteen-year period.[64] At the other, Pierre Aymon of Alzon confessed in August 1320 to meetings with Waldensian brethren going back forty-five years, but at no point said that he had confessed his sins to them.[65] However, even at this stage it seems that only the most senior and respected of the brethren heard the confessions of their followers. The same Pierrette who admitted five or six heretic confessions also mentioned by name twelve separate Waldensian pastors whom she had met. The brethren did not automatically ask to hear a confession of sins from every follower they met, as the first routine means of instruction, as would be the case with some other groups later in the middle ages. Sacramental confession was something of a special occasion. It was also, of course, rarer than the annual Catholic confession for the laity. Helyas Garin of Alzon, whose brother Huguet was of one of the travelling pastors, commented that when he confessed to his priest he concealed what he knew of the Waldenses and his relations with them. The brethren administered penances to their followers in keeping with their general pious practice: fasting on Fridays, and the repetition of a certain number of paternosters.[66]

The Burgundian Waldenses had another distinctive form of ritual behaviour which was visible to everyone. Routinely, after they had taken a meal in the house of one of their followers, they knelt down leaning

62   Limborch, *Liber sententiarum inquisitionis Tholosanae*, pp. 252–5, 274–7.
63   Ibid.: these are impressionistic figures, but given that the number of confessions is not specified in all cases, attempting to offer precise statistics would be misleading.
64   Ibid., p. 236 (actually mis-numbered as p. 234 (*bis*) in the Limborch edition).
65   Ibid., pp. 352–3.
66   Ibid.; e.g. pp. 241–2, 356–8.

on a bench, or sometimes a box, and prayed for long periods, while their hosts did the same. Most witnesses reported that while praying in this posture they said the paternoster many times.[67] One said that they repeated it ten times; on another case prayer lasted long enough, apparently, to repeat the Lord's Prayer eighty to a hundred times over.[68] None of the testimonies in the *Book of Sentences* suggest that the Lord's Prayer was said in the vernacular, although they do specify that the epistles and gospels were expounded in the common language. On the contrary, one Waldensian pastor interrogated by Jacques Fournier at this period approved of people going to church, because they 'could learn their paternoster better'.[69] The clear implication is that the Lord's Prayer was repeated in Latin among the Waldensian brethren; that their most visible religious act, in the sight of their followers, was lengthy repetition of the most standard of all prayers in the language of the official Church.

Besides repetitive prayer, the Waldensian teachers also expounded the 'epistles and gospels' to their followers after meals, in the vernacular.[70] This description of scripture passages implies the specific passages of the Bible set aside for reading at Mass, which were brief enough to be learned by heart. The same phrase had been used in an inquisitors' memorandum of 1235, where lay people had learned 'epistles and gospels' from the Waldenses; Étienne de Bourbon told the story of a cowherd who learned in a year 'forty gospels for Sundays (excepting festival ones)'.[71] It would not have been essential, in such circumstances, for all the preachers to be literate, or to carry translations with them, with all their attendant risks. If they relied on rote memory of short passages of scripture used in the liturgy, then ordinary, unlettered pastors could discharge their function while carrying no tell-tale evidence of their work about them.

In practice, most of the followers remembered the moral instruction of the brethren much better than their scriptural exegesis. Here a distinction emerges, not exactly between the brethren and the believers, but rather between those on the periphery of the movement and those close to its centre (which might include some believers as well as the travelling pastors). The beliefs as taught and apprehended by the ordinary believing lay adherents were quite simple. First of all, they were taught that it was wrong to swear; sometimes the prohibition was combined

67 Ibid., pp. 353–4, 356–8, 367, 369, 375–6, 378.
68 Ibid., pp. 368, 355. There is an interesting parallel between this practice and the prayer of the Bogomils and Cathars. All these groups restricted prayer to frequent, regular repetition of the Lord's Prayer in very large numbers at a time. See M. Lambert, *The Cathars* (Oxford, 1998), p. 29.
69 Duvernoy, *Registre d'inquisition*, vol. 1, p. 80.
70 Limborch, *Liber sententiarum inquisitionis Tholosanae*, pp. 254, 264, 353.
71 Patschovsky and Selge, *Quellen*, pp. 48, 52.

with forbidding one to 'say evil' or to lie; but most showed a clear awareness that every oath, including those taken in civil contexts such as swearing in court to tell the truth, was wrong and a sin. One reported that
penance would be imposed for taking an oath, and another that one
should confess taking an oath as though it were a mortal sin.[72] Second,
several of the believers had learned that a judgement by which a person
was condemned to death was a sin.[73] Several, though only a minority of
the sample, had learned to disbelieve in purgatory; one explicitly denied
the value of indulgences.[74] These rejections of official teaching and practice correspond exactly to what was reported in the middle of the thirteenth century in southern France.[75]

A handful of Waldenses, brethren and believers alike, affirmed these
positions with much greater intensity, and added some other ones.
Several of those who were brought before the inquisitors steadfastly and
absolutely refused to take the oath to tell the truth, while perfectly aware
that such a refusal of itself exposed them to the penalties for obstinate
heresy. Jean Philibert the priest had been told rather to allow himself to
be killed than to take an oath, and earned a spell of imprisonment
through his refusal.[76] It was not enough, for 'core members' of the movement, to take an oath and regret it: they felt they had to refuse and take
the consequences. Further, certain of those at the heart of the heresy
repudiated the authority of the prelates and hierarchy of the Roman
Church, along with its indulgences.[77] Jacqueta the weaver of Combe-
Rotgier, widow of Philipot the Burgundian, related the pastors' teaching
that the clergy knowingly kept the scriptures and the divine law from the
people, to ensure their dominion over them; that if they expounded the
scriptures they would be less wealthy.[78]

The Waldenses evidently harboured resentment against the clergy,
especially the hierarchy which persecuted them. It would have been
astonishing if they had not objected, in principle, to the authority of a
Church whose prohibitions they defied in practice. In this light, it is
remarkable how little anti-clerical sentiment the Waldenses and their
friends expressed. It was the *authority* of a persecuting Church, not its
moral stature or its sacramental services, which the heretics denied.
Waldensian heresy in France around 1300 was not Donatist in its atti-

---

72 Limborch, *Liber sententiarum inquisitionis Tholosanae*, e.g. pp. 201, 207, 231,
233, and in many other places in the same document.
73 Ibid., pp. 201, 207, 353–4, 369–70, 374.
74 Ibid., pp. 201, 208, 235, 240–1, 247, 374, 377.
75 See above, section 5.1.
76 Limborch, *Liber sententiarum inquisitionis Tholosanae*, pp. 207, 253–4, 263,
265, 379–80.
77 Ibid., pp. 201, 207, 263–5, 369.
78 Ibid., p. 377.

tude to the Roman Church; in this respect it was the heir of the ultra-montane moderates and the associates of Durand of Osca. As will be seen below, some associates of the Burgundians were about as far from Donatism as any heretic could conceivably be.[79] The Waldenses kept what anti-clerical feelings they did have muted before some of their followers, who remained only partially aware that they were opposed to and condemned by the Church. Agnes 'de na Bernarda' associated with the brethren for some seven years until she heard that Huguet Garin of Alzon had been burned as a heretic, after which she abandoned them.[80] Gerald son of Formont the Burgundian claimed that he no longer thought the Waldenses were good men, once he heard that they were hunted by the inquisitors.[81] Modern historians, like contemporary inquisitors, may prefer to doubt the sincerity of such statements; but there remains a distinct relative lack of evidence for strong anti-clerical feeling, compared to that expressed by other Waldenses at the same or at other times, in thirteenth-century Germany or the fourteenth- and fifteenth-century Italian Alps.

One final trait about the 'Burgundians' deserves a mention. Many of the brethren evangelized followers who were their own blood relations; several of them were related to each other. They relied upon friends and relations to make the first contact with prospective, sometimes sceptical adherents. Pierre Carrot refused to keep the nocturnal appointment made to meet Barthélemi de Cajarc, and was reproached for this by Helys Garin, the mother of Barthélemi's novice Huguet. Perrin Vaudry came up to Gerald son of Formont and asked him if he was Formont's son: presumably Gerald had been pointed out to him. Perrin then told him he should not do or say evil, and not lie or swear, and asked Gerald to confess his sins to him, 'since he [Gerald] did not know if he would be alive tomorrow'. Mystified by the request, Gerald answered that he held no one else's property and had not stolen anything, and so left him.[82] Establishing trust between brethren and followers took time. Once the relationship was secure, the believers would receive the brethren in their homes, feed them and eat with them, give them gifts of money, and accept from them small gifts or tokens, possession of which may have helped to disguise the brethren as pedlars: gloves, needles or knives.[83] Huguet Garin of Alzon was brought up by his parents Guillaume and

---

79 See the next section below.
80 Limborch, *Liber sententiarum inquisitionis Tholosanae*, p. 359.
81 Ibid., p. 378.
82 Ibid., pp. 368, 377.
83 For staying in followers' homes, see for example ibid., pp. 216, 222–3, 354–5, 357, 365; for the giving of gifts, pp. 233, 240–1, 354. Needles would also be a regular gift given by Waldensian pastors in the Alps in the fifteenth century.

Helys with the specific intention that he should be trained as a member of the Waldensian brotherhood. He travelled round with Barthélemi de Cajarc, and seems to have been largely responsible for converting his relatives and friends in Alzon. His capture and execution in the papal palace at Avignon led to the arrest of nearly all the Burgundians of Alzon and their trial at Toulouse.[84] Even after the heretics were imprisoned, their followers continued to go to some lengths and considerable risks to support them and send them surreptitious gifts of clothing.[85]

'Burgundian' Waldensianism, like its predecessor movement in Occitan France, left little evidence of its passage after the inquisitors at Toulouse had done their work. Yet this was not because the heretics had been physically eliminated: most of the penitent believers were sentenced to arbitrary penances, the wearing of crosses, or other humiliations; sentences of 'perpetual' imprisonment were often reduced to conditional release with a penance after a few years. Most of the brethren seem not to have been caught at all. Despite the limited impact of the inquisitors' campaign, this particular strand of Waldensian religion seems to have died out before the end of the middle ages. Its stance in regard to the Church was perhaps too nuanced, too close to orthodoxy, for it to keep an independent position for long. The same problem may well have beset the final branch of French Waldensianism now to be considered.

5.3 The 'Poor of Christ' at Pamiers: Raymond de Sainte-Foy and Jean de Lorraine

Jacques Fournier, Bishop of Pamiers, has earned himself a special place in social history as the author of the inquisitorial register on which *Montaillou* was based.[86] Near the start of his inquisition, which ran from 1318 to 1325, Fournier interrogated a curious figure called Raymond de Sainte-Foy, from La Côte-St-André in the Isère, who had

---

84 Ibid., pp. 345–6, 355, 359, 365.
85 Ibid., pp. 232, 254, 264.
86 The register itself survives as MS Vatican Lat. 4030; the standard edition is J. Duvernoy (ed.), *Le Registre d'inquisition de Jacques Fournier, évêque de Pamiers (1318–1325)*, 3 vols (Toulouse, 1965); a French translation by Duvernoy, with a preface by E. Le Roy Ladurie, was published in 3 volumes (Paris, 1978). References here are to the original Latin edition only. Part of the material is explored in E. Le Roy Ladurie, *Montaillou: village occitan de 1294 à 1324* (Paris, 1975; revd edn 1982), and translated in abridged form as *Montaillou: Cathars and Catholics in a French Village, 1294–1324*, trans. B. Bray (London, 1978). On Jacques Fournier (d. 1342, Bishop of Pamiers 1317–26, and pope as Benedict XII from 1334) see J. M. Vidal, 'Notice sur les oeuvres du Pape Benoît XII', *Revue d'histoire ecclésiastique* 6 (1905), pp. 557–65, 785–810; Cross and Livingstone, *The Oxford Dictionary of the Christian Church*, art. 'Benedict XII', p. 184.

been captured along with his nurse, Agnes Francou, and a couple, Jean 'Fustier' and Huguette de Vienne, at Pamiers.[87] Raymond de Sainte-Foy was about 40 years old, and at the start of his interrogation claimed to be in deacon's orders, though it later emerged that these were not Catholic orders. He was not only literate, but possessed a considerable level of theological knowledge. Under interrogation he gave unique details about the inner organization and spiritual life of the celibate, itinerant community to which he belonged. He was even captured with some liturgical writings in his possession. Jacques Fournier investigated his beliefs with typically meticulous attention to detail, though often rather to trap his victim in a contradiction than to elucidate his precise beliefs. In the light of its detail, Raymond de Sainte-Foy's confession tantalizes the historian: much of what he says overlaps with other evidence; some is unique; some actually contradicts what is said in other sources.

Raymond described a hierarchical, graded community ruled by an elected, ordained superior called at various times a major, majoralis or minister. He claimed to have been associated with this group from about 1293 onwards, and to have been ordained a deacon by the then majoralis, Jean de Lorraine, around 1300.[88] His society contained three grades of dignity: the lowest was that of deacon, above that was the rank of priest, and above the priests the majoralis or minister. The deacons were there to provide for the bodily needs of the priests, and to discharge no other religious function; the majoralis presided over the society and could ordain the deacons and priests.[89] No one belonged to this society unless they had the rank of deacon. The society or order was called the 'Poor of Christ' ('Pauperes Christi'). They were bound to poverty, but were allowed to keep movable goods in common to sustain themselves. They were committed to strict celibacy: married men, or even widowers with living children, were not admitted to their number. Women were not allowed so much as to kiss their hands, or to sleep in the same room; women could not enter any of their orders.[90] Their association was neither wholly 'clerks' nor wholly illiterate, so they used the vernacular in their instruction; Raymond himself was literate, able to read Latin, and carried books with him.[91]

---

87   The trials of Raymond's companions are recorded in Duvernoy, *Registre d'inquisition*, vol. 1, pp. 123ff; vol. 2, pp. 508ff., 519ff.; the sentences of two of them are also found in Limborch, *Liber sententiarum inquisitionis Tholosanae*, pp. 289–91.
88   Duvernoy, *Registre d'inquisition*, vol. 1, pp. 48–9, 99–102; cf. Limborch, *Liber sententiarum inquisitionis Tholosanae*, pp. 289, 291.
89   Duvernoy, *Registre d'inquisition*, vol. 1, pp. 57–62, 68–72; cf. Limborch, *Liber sententiarum inquisitionis Tholosanae*, p. 290.
90   Duvernoy, *Registre d'inquisition*, vol. 1, pp. 96–9, 72–6.
91   Ibid., pp. 48, 80ff., 102–5.

The greater emphasis on rank and dignity within this order gives a different impression to that conveyed by those of the Waldensian brethren who were interrogated at Toulouse, such as Étienne Porchier and Jean Brayssan.[92] Nevertheless, there can be no doubt that Raymond's group was tangentially connected to, if not actually the same as, the brotherhood described by the 'Burgundians'. The majoralis Jean de Lorraine may possibly be the same as either Jean de Châlon, or Jean de Grandvaux.[93] Raymond knew 'Christianus' (Cristinus), who was the majoralis after Jean; he also knew Barthélemi de Cajarc and Jean Moran, while his companion Huguette de Vienne mentioned Gerard de Provence and Jean de Cernon. All four appeared in the testimonies from Toulouse.[94] Yet why did he say that Barthélemi de Cajarc was only a deacon (therefore, on his account, not permitted to hear confessions) when several believers said that they had confessed to him?[95] Who was 'Michel the Italian', whom none of the other sources mention?[96] Why did Raymond call his society the 'Poor of Christ' and not the brethren? Why did no-one in contemporary Waldensianism speak of priests and deacons in their society, besides Raymond and his companions?

Of many unique features in Raymond's evidence, the most striking is his detailed description of the rituals by which members of his order were ordained. The majoralis was elected by a conference of the priests and deacons which discussed his virtues and invited him to assume the headship; in traditional ecclesiastical manner he protested his unworthiness, but was urged to accept the dignity. He was then ordained by laying-on of hands by either the majoralis who was already in post, or the oldest of the priests if the previous majoralis had died.[97] Deacons lived in the society as probationers for five or six years or more; after living satisfactorily for that time, a meeting of the group might agree to ordain them. To perform this rite, the majoralis would lay hands on the ordinand. Meanwhile, the brotherhood prayed that the ordinand might receive the Holy Spirit, and then said the paternoster and the Ave Maria. This diaconate involved the taking of vows of poverty, chastity and obedience. Satisfactory deacons were available to be elected priests.

92 Compare Limborch, *Liber sententiarum inquisitionis Tholosanae*, pp. 200–1, 207–8.
93 For Jean de Châlon, see Limborch, *Liber sententiarum inquisitionis Tholosanae*, p. 201, and for Jean de Grandvaux, ibid., pp. 352, 365: these may well have been the same person.
94 Duvernoy, *Registre d'inquisition*, vol. 1, pp. 99–102; Limborch, *Liber sententiarum inquisitionis Tholosanae*, p. 290. For these pastors in the other records, see above, notes 82–4.
95 Duvernoy, *Registre d'inquisition*, vol. 1, pp. 101–2, and cf. pp. 70ff. For Barthélemi hearing confessions see above, note 82.
96 Ibid., pp. 99ff.
97 Ibid., pp. 54–7.

An equivalent ritual was followed for the ordination of priests, except that the other priests as well as the majoralis laid hands on the ordinand's head.[98]

Ironically, the highly sacerdotal and ritualistic language in which Raymond described the ordination of priests and deacons was not matched by a similarly wide-ranging liturgical practice. First, although the majoralis and the priests administered sacramental confession, of a kind, they did not use the traditional formula of absolution as used by Catholic priests.[99] Second, only the majoralis performed anything resembling a Mass. On Maundy Thursday each year the majoralis washed the feet of his companions and blessed bread, fish and wine, not as a sacrifice but as a memorial. In contrast to the mid-thirteenth century Waldenses who had distributed the blessed bread and fish to all their followers, the Maundy Thursday rite described by Raymond was reserved to the members of the order itself, and kept secret from their followers.[100]

Raymond's group, he claimed, kept a version of the canonical hours: at his interrogation he quoted a sort of shortened breviary, sufficiently simple to be remembered by heart. It was also claimed that the group observed the Church's seasons of fast and feast days. Raymond also gave details of various prayers, in Latin, said by the majoralis when he blessed the meal-table in the presence of others of the brotherhood. At other times, according to Raymond, members of the order would kneel down and say at least fifty paternosters before meal-time and a similar number afterwards.[101] This custom of repetitious prayer confirms the other evidence, save in one respect: Raymond was most insistent that the Ave Maria was said, as well as the paternoster, in his group's worship. The Ave Maria, the basic Marian prayer, hovered on the edge of Waldensian custom through the later middle ages. Hardline opponents of the cult of saints, or even rigid scripturalists, allegedly would not use it; but it is mentioned here, and was learned in other forms of Waldensianism less orthodox than this one.[102]

Raymond avowed holding the usual Waldensian taboo against swearing an oath, and with some tergiversation admitted to disbelieving in purgatory.[103] However, he went to extraordinary lengths to try to prove that the priesthood of the Roman Church, and his own order's ministry, were branches of the same thing, and that each was valid in its own sphere.

98   Ibid., pp. 57ff., 68ff., 96–9.
99   Ibid., pp. 60–2, 68ff.
100 Ibid., pp. 60–1, 66–8.
101 Ibid., pp. 102ff.
102 See the use of the Ave Maria attested below, chapter 7.4, esp. note 168.
103 Duvernoy, *Registre d'inquisition*, vol. 1, pp. 40–3, 49–51, 63–4, 92ff.; cf. Limborch, *Liber sententiarum inquisitionis Tholosanae*, pp. 289–91.

He steered well clear of anything resembling an anti-clerical attack on the Church, let alone a Donatist rejection of its sacraments. On two separate occasions he insisted that the value of a sacrament did not depend on the moral status of the person administering it. He steadfastly refused, though pressed hard by Fournier to do so, to admit to thinking that the Roman Church's 'error' over oath-taking meant that its sacraments were invalid.[104] This affirmation of orthodoxy, of a kind, in no way saved Raymond from the inquisitor's condemnation, and one may take it as sincere. He argued that the power of a *majoralis* to consecrate was essentially the same as that of a bishop, and that 'priests' had the same powers, whether they were ordained by Catholics or heretics: nevertheless, these correspondences remained entirely theoretical. It was quite sufficient for the Poor of Christ to receive most of the sacraments from the Catholic priesthood.[105] The Catholic Church he regarded as somewhat in error ('but not seriously', as he put it) over oaths and purgatory; it was still the Church.

In many other respects Raymond de Sainte-Foy affirmed Catholic orthodoxy without any guidance from Fournier, during a close theological interrogation which did not allow for 'yes' or 'no' answers. He upheld traditional teaching on the Trinity, the Incarnation, the resurrection and the Last Judgement, also on the number of the seven sacraments (though he got into a tangle over confirmation). He endorsed the belief in saints and their relics, the use of Latin and church buildings in worship, marriage and the prohibited degrees of affinity.[106] He even, on several occasions, affirmed that the use of capital punishment on criminals was valid and right, though he considered the condemnation of members of his order to death for heresy to be a mortal sin. In accepting the use of the sword in justice, he went further to meet orthodoxy than his companions had done.[107] On the theology of penance, he was able to handle questioning on contrition, and the difference between 'fault' and 'penalty' ('culpa' and 'pena') with some dexterity and assurance. Raymond's knowledge of theology, however, is more likely explained by his having attended theological lectures (as he admitted) in the Franciscan *studium* at Montpellier, where he had stayed for a year to learn grammar.[108] He cannot be cited to prove an autonomous theological tradition among the Waldenses; on the contrary, he shows how Catholic training could attenuate and moderate the implications of the Waldensian protest.

104 Duvernoy, *Registre d'inquisition*, vol. 1, pp. 62–3, 68ff., 83–5.
105 Ibid., pp. 59–60, 62, 76–80, 84.
106 Ibid., pp. 43–8, 65–6, 80ff., 88–90, 94–6.
107 Ibid., pp. 43–4, 50–1, 74–6; cf. Limborch, *Liber sententiarum inquisitionis Tholosanae*, p. 289.
108 Duvernoy, *Registre d'inquisition*, vol. 1, pp. 61–3, 101–2.

In the light of Raymond's cultured and in some respects 'Catholicized' Waldensian outlook, one may perhaps explain some of the oddities of his confession as an attempt to bridge the gap between Catholic theory and heretic practice. In practice, the Burgundian brethren had a master or superior, senior 'brothers' who heard confessions, and more junior ones who accompanied them and learned their calling. It may have been Raymond's own invention to call these three ranks bishop, priest and deacon, given that even he did not claim they purveyed a full range of prelatical or priestly rites. Nevertheless, he seems to have lived at arms-length from the 'Burgundians': none of those from Auch or Rodez dioceses mentioned him or his companions. He *may* therefore represent a sub-group of French Waldensianism whose traditions had developed along different, more 'clerical' lines. He offers a glimpse of the different ways in which low-key French Waldensian religious practice persisted and adapted to the conditions of the century after the conference at Bergamo.

5.4   The Inquisitor Bernard Gui and the Waldenses

Bernard Gui OP (*c.*1261–1331) was the most celebrated of the inquisitors based at Toulouse. In a career which stretched from 1307 to 1324 he would have encountered personally many of the 'Burgundian' Waldenses described above. In his *Pratica Inquisitionis Heretice Pravitatis*, compiled during his time at Toulouse, he included a substantial chapter devoted to the Waldenses.[109] Gui's work is one of the earliest contributions to a late medieval genre: the inquisitorial treatise where literary traditions and empirical forensic evidence are subtly, sometimes almost invisibly intermingled. In some respects he offers unique evidence about the behaviour of Waldenses in the Toulousain; yet his information cannot always be taken at face value.

In many respects Gui reports faithfully details of the Occitan Waldenses which can be corroborated from the *Book of Sentences* and the other records. He relates their vehement objections to oath-taking and judgements of death, their claim to hear confessions, their repudiation of indulgences and their disbelief in purgatory. He recalls the threefold order of bishops, priests and deacons described by Raymond and his asso-

---

109   Bernard Gui, *Manuel de l'inquisiteur*, abridged ed. and trans. G. Mollat and G. Drioux, 2 vols (Paris, 1964), vol. 1, pp. 34–83. The work also appears as Bernardus Guidonis, *Practica inquisitionis heretice pravitatis*, ed. *c.*Douais (Paris, 1886). The chapter on the Waldenses is translated in Wakefield and Evans, *Heresies*, pp. 386–404. On Gui himself, see 'Bernard Gui et son monde', *Cahiers de Fanjeaux* 16 (1981).

ciates, with their majoralis. From the Burgundians' evidence, he describes their repeated praying of the Lord's Prayer at meal-times, and the description of the preachers as 'brethren' as well as 'Poor of Christ'.[110]

However, Gui believed with good reason, as was seen above, that those most closely initiated into the belief held more, and more extreme, views than were revealed to the majority of their friends and supporters.[111] This knowledge seems to have led him to import into his description of Waldensian belief and practice other, more radical elements. He claimed that they thought a sinful priest could not validly consecrate the eucharist, but a good lay person could; and he gave a description of one of their irregular consecrations. Both the Donatist belief and the rite were derived from two separate thirteenth-century texts. Sections of these were transcribed verbally into Gui's manual, although they found no echo in the trial records, at least those which survive.[112] He attributed to the brethren a systematic disbelief in saints and their miracles, and a refusal to keep saints' days, on the basis of the thirteenth-century German text *De Inquisitione hereticorum*; again, this was despite the lack of any local evidence to this effect. Towards the end of his account Bernard described how difficult the Waldenses were to interrogate, and how they would equivocate under pressure, affirming belief in an orthodox doctrine, but inwardly understanding it differently. In these sections, despite seeming to describe his own experience, he quoted many paragraphs bodily from *De Inquisitione hereticorum* and from the *Seven Gifts of the Holy Spirit* of Étienne de Bourbon.[113]

It is not necessary to assume that Bernard Gui deliberately falsified his account to make the Waldenses appear more radical than those in France actually were. His victims may well have wriggled and equivocated under interrogation: Raymond de Sainte-Foy certainly did. Faced with the frustration which this evidently caused,[114] Gui may have assumed in perfect honesty that there was a larger body of heretical teaching under the surface than the evidence actually revealed. In particular, he seems to have assumed that 'the Waldenses' must be a single group. If his victims did not overtly express a Donatist attitude towards sinful priests, or reject the cult of saints, they must have been concealing their opinions. Gui was well enough aware that 'at other times they held other heresies', by which he may have had in mind the extreme and eccentric beliefs

110 Gui, *Manuel*, vol. 1, pp. 46–59.
111 Ibid., pp. 46–7, 78–9.
112 Ibid., pp. 40–3: the allegation of Donatism appears to be transcribed from the 'Doctrina de modo procedendi contra hereticos' as edited in Martene and Durand, *Thesaurus Novus Anecdotorum V*, col. 1,800; the manner of consecrating Mass from 'Disputatio inter Catholicum et Paterinum haereticum', also in ibid., cols 1,754–5.
113 Ibid., pp. 46–7, 64–75.
114 Ibid., pp. 74–7.

reported by Étienne de Bourbon, whom he had read.[115] Nevertheless, he still believed that evidence from one part of Europe ought to hold good for another.

Careful textual criticism has teased out of Gui's account the numerous quotations from earlier ecclesiastical descriptions of heresy. There remains an intriguing residue of uncorroborated information, which seems not to derive from any other written authority. He described the brethren holding one or two 'chapters-general' each year in some town, where they would gather as though they were travelling merchants, meet their leader, and render accounts of the collections made in the previous months before being assigned their mission-field for the next period.[116] He reported that they had a sort of compendium of orthodox teachings on faith, the commandments, and the works of mercy, which they knew by heart.[117] This summary resembles the sort of mnemonics which were popular in Catholic circles at the same time, as prelates struggled to impart consistent teaching to their secular clergy.[118] He asserted, in a way which is difficult to prove, that when the Waldenses fasted on Fridays and in Lent, or when they took communion, they were acting purely from dissimulation, conforming to a rite in whose value they disbelieved.[119]

For a further two centuries or so, inquisitors great and small would continue to describe Waldensian belief and practice with the aid of a similar intellectual technique. Such fusion of one's own experience with the literary tradition founded by one's elders was, after all, the norm for almost all academic writing in the schools of the epoch.[120] With the passage of time, however, Waldenses adopted various strategies by which to accommodate the Catholic sensibilities of their neighbours, most of which entailed a dilution or diminution of the radicalism implicit in their earlier beliefs. At the very least, they became used to teaching one thing

115 Ibid., p. 38; for Étienne, see above, notes 29–31.
116 Gui, *Manuel*, vol. 1, pp. 50–3.
117 Ibid., pp. 54–5.
118 An equivalent Catholic example would be the decree *Ignorantia sacerdotum* issued by Archbishop John Pecham of Canterbury in 1281, which compressed contemporary orthodoxy into just over 1,500 words of Latin, and which was then digested into William Lyndwood's *Provinciale* in the 1440s. See W. Lyndwood, *Lyndwood's Provinciale*, ed. J. V. Bullard and H. *c*.Bell (London, 1929), and E. Duffy, *The Stripping of the Altars: Traditional Religion in England, 1400–1580* (New Haven, Conn., and London, 1992), pp. 53–4 and nn.
119 Gui, *Manuel*, vol. 1, pp. 50–1.
120 The same trend can be seen, for example, in the numerous medieval authors on superstition, who invariably merged literary traditions with their own observed data: see D. Harmening, *Superstitio: Ueberlieferungs- und theoriegeschichtliche Untersuchungen zur kirchlich-theologischen Aberglaubensliteratur des Mittelalters* (Berlin, 1979), *passim*.

and practising another. A greater and greater gulf opened up between the thirteenth-century founding traditions of inquisitorial lore, and the Waldensian outlook as it was received and professed, above all by its believers who remained in ordinary society. Some inquisitors bridged this gulf with great intellectual dexterity and subtlety; others showed a depressing willingness to ignore the nuances of what emerged before their eyes.[121]

There is general agreement, even among those who take the most optimistic view of the spread and durability of heresy, that Waldensianism in the Languedoc declined into invisibility well before the end of the middle ages.[122] It may be that this disappearance can be explained solely by the pressure of inquisition, despite the fact that it appears to have been sporadic, patchy in its effects, and laborious in its procedures: possibly the *fear* of inquisitors may have deterred the continuance of heresy. However, it seems likely that the movement also suffered from its own internal contradictions, such as emerge with special clarity in Raymond de Sainte-Foy's evidence. The Occitan Waldenses were not Donatists: indeed, as Durand's writings and the Bergamo *Rescriptum* had shown, they never had been. They rejected the jurisdiction of the clergy, and especially of the inquisitors, over themselves and their mission, but they continued to send their faithful to the priests for the sacraments, including penance, even though that was 'duplicated' by the heretics. Once it became widely known that the Waldenses were outlawed, the laity of Languedoc seem to have shown little enthusiasm to learn a religious counter-culture. If Gui's reports of the gradual and careful way in which the brethren insinuated their teachings give an accurate picture, winning adherents was a delicate process. Hence, their last flowering was among a self-supporting migrant group, the 'Burgundians' in Gascony and Rouergue. It seems likely that as such migrant groups were assimilated into the rest of society, their beliefs would likewise have been reduced to conventional local norms.

121   Compare, for example, Peter Zwicker (below, chapter 6.5–6) with Alberto Cattaneo (below, chapter 7.5).
122   See M. Lambert, *Medieval Heresy: Popular Movements from the Gregorian Reform to the Reformation*, 2nd edn (Oxford, 1992), pp. 160–2.

6

Germany and Eastern Europe

The Waldensian movements in the middle ages show all sorts of different curves of growth and decline. The heretical groups in urban Italy, so hard to trace after *c.*1250, seem to have exploded on to the scene in the early thirteenth century with a flurry of new foundations and buildings, and a scarcely less fertile diversity of opinions. Those of France and the Languedoc rose up in little waves, overlapping each other in the same territory, but refounded and extinguished within a few generations of each other. The Alpine heretics, discussed below, proved close-knit and extraordinarily tenacious and durable. The German-speaking Waldensian heretics followed yet another pattern. Their origins are obscure, made even more so by the extravagant and credulous imaginations of some thirteenth-century chroniclers. Yet by the middle of the thirteenth century they had gained enormous, indeed intimidating strength in the Danube valley in the southeastern corner of the Holy Roman Empire. Between the late thirteenth and early fourteenth centuries they spread northwards into the German communities in the towns of Bohemia and Moravia, and even further north to the Baltic coast. Then, by the middle of the fourteenth century, the movement began to decline. Several times within some thirty or forty years it suffered catastrophic defections by some of its most educated and articulate leaders. It entered the fifteenth century irreversibly weakened and shrunken, yet did not disappear entirely. Rather, its tattered remnants seem to have merged with elements of the Bohemian heresy, Hussitism; ultimately, the name of 'Waldensian brethren', though little else besides the name, would be transferred to Czech dissenters who survived into the sixteenth century. German Waldensianism therefore presents the historian with a problem peculiar to that section of the movement. Why did it spread with such phenomenal success in the thirteenth century, yet all but collapse in the later fourteenth? The fate of Waldensian sentiment in late medieval Germany must, moreover, be linked to the wider development of religious belief in the later middle ages. Waldensian heresy was not a pure entity of itself, but a reaction to certain trends in medieval Catholicism: as that developed, the nature of the heresy changed also.

6.1 The Earliest Evidence from Germany

Evidence of Waldensian activity in German lands around 1200 is extremely sparse. At Metz, near the linguistic frontier, the bishop wrote to Pope Innocent III in 1199 to report that certain people had been reading and discussing the gospels and Pauline epistles, the Psalms, Job, Gregory the Great's *Moralia* and other works in the vernacular. Innocent gave a typically balanced response: he approved of the people's zeal for scripture but warned against private meetings. He urged first the bishop, then (in a later letter) three Cistercian abbots, to investigate the translations.[1] Some of the abbots reportedly later burned these translations.[2] According to Caesarius of Heisterbach, the Bishop of Metz also denounced some leaders of an illicit preaching movement around this time from the pulpit. Local hostility against him prevented him from taking any further action.[3] It is likely that both the reading and the preaching were led by the same people, and that they were (as the bishop is reported to have claimed) Waldenses from the Languedoc. However, nothing further seems to be known about these people, and they certainly did not found any lasting movement.

Within Germany proper there are fragmentary mentions of heresy before the 1230s. Tantalizing evidence survives regarding some heretics discovered at Strasbourg in 1212. According to a lost manuscript by the Strassburger Daniel Specklin (d. 1589), evidence had emerged in a text from St Arbogast's monastery about a group of heretics, supposedly Waldenses, whom the local bishop discovered were governed by three leaders. One, the superior, was at Milan; a second was a priest in Strasbourg; a third was in Bohemia. However, long ago Specklin's

---

1 These are described in the Register of Innocent III, in J.-P. Migne, *Patrologiae Cursus Completus*, Series Latina, vol. 214, cols 695–9, 793.
2 *Chronica Albrici Monachi Trium Fontium*, ed. P. Scheffer-Boichorst, in *Monumenta Germaniae Historica*, Scriptores 23 (1874), p. 878; W. L. Wakefield and A. P. Evans (eds), *Heresies of the High Middle Ages: Selected Sources Translated and Annotated* (New York and London, 1969), p. 729.
3 Wakefield and Evans (eds), *Heresies*, pp. 257–8 and references; H. Haupt, 'Waldenserthum und Inquisition im südöstlichen Deutschland bis zur Mitte des 14. Jahrhunderts', *Deutsche Zeitschrift für Geschichtswissenschaft* 1 (1889), pp. 285–6 and notes. On the Metz episode see also H. Grundmann, *Religiöse Bewegungen im Mittelalter: Untersuchungen über die geschichtlichen Zusammenhänge zwischen der Ketzerei, den Bettelorden und der religiöse Frauenbewegung im 12. und 13. Jahrhundert und über die geschichtlichen Grundlagen der deutschen Mystik*, 2nd edn (Hildesheim, 1961), pp. 97–100.

account was shown to have contained a number of anachronisms and historical impossibilities, and it cannot be regarded as conclusive. As will be seen, sixteenth-century commentators had reasons of their own to 'improve', and sometimes to invent outright, documents relating to early Waldensianism.[4] It used to be thought that the title appended to the *Rescriptum* of the Bergamo conference demonstrated a Waldensian presence in Germany in 1218. Some surviving manuscript copies of the *Rescriptum* are headed 'The Reply of the Heresiarchs of Lombardy to the Leonists in Germany'. The manuscripts themselves are now in libraries in Munich, Vienna and Erfurt.[5] Nevertheless, the use of the term 'heresiarchs' leaves no doubt that the title derives from a Catholic copyist; so does the term 'Leonist', a characteristic expression of mid-thirteenth century ecclesiastical writers. The text addresses itself to 'brothers and sisters, and friends living across the Alps'; but this is far more likely to refer to southern France rather than Germany.[6] All that is certain is that by the time the manuscript was copied, Waldensianism had become a serious enough concern for German churchmen to collect manuscripts about it.

Heresy certainly was a serious problem in central Germany, especially the Rhineland, by the early 1230s. Unfortunately, the surviving evidence for heresy in this period consists of Gregory IX's notorious letter *Vox in Rama*, from 13 June 1233, and a handful of entries in contemporary chronicles. The chroniclers, and indeed the pope, focused on the most spectacular and sensational of the heretics' alleged activities, which clouds the evidence considerably. The story of German heresy-hunting at this period is bound up with the figure of Conrad of Marburg (*c.*1180–1233). Conrad had begun his career as a preacher of crusade some twenty years earlier, and rose to prominence as a visitor to monasteries and confessor to Elizabeth, wife of Ludwig IV of Thuringia. On 11 October 1231 he received the first ever papal appointment as inquisitor to Germany.[7] Conrad was reportedly abetted by two converted former heretics called Tors and Johannes: the three, with the zeal sometimes associated with converts, set about the heretics in Germany with unbridled ferocity.

4   The source is analysed in Haupt, 'Waldenserthum und Inquisition', pp. 320–2.
5   See above, chapter 3, note 3, esp. the details regarding the manuscripts in A. Patschovsky and K.-V. Selge (eds), *Quellen zur Geschichte der Waldenser*, Texte zur Kirchen- und Theologiegeschichte, 18 (Gütersloh, 1973), p. 12.
6   G. G. Merlo, 'Le Mouvement vaudois des origines à la fin du xiiie siècle', in G. Audisio (ed.), *Les Vaudois des origines à leur fin (xiie–xvie siècles): Colloque international... Aix-en-Provence, 8–10 avril 1988* (Turin, 1990), pp. 21–33, discusses Bergamo with reference only to the 'Italians' and the 'Ultramontanes', i.e. the French.
7   On Conrad, see R. Kieckhefer, *Repression of Heresy in Medieval Germany* (Liverpool, 1979), pp. 14–15; also Malcolm Lambert, *The Cathars* (Oxford, 1998), pp. 118–22 and references.

Conrad took for granted the guilt of all those who fell into his hands: the choice for these people was either to confess to heresy and to have their head shaved as a humiliating penance, or to suffer burning as obstinate heretics. Conrad over-reached himself, however, when he accused Henry II, Count of Sayn, of heresy. When Siegfried III, Archbishop of Mainz, told Conrad to restrain himself, he refused to listen; shortly thereafter he was murdered by some heretics near Marburg on 30 July 1233. Following investigations by the archbishops, the Count of Sayn and other nobles who had been accused were fully vindicated and rehabilitated on 2 April 1234.[8]

Conrad's fate was not particularly unusual for inquisitors, who down the centuries would repeatedly show an appalling zeal which forced their superiors to investigate and sometimes to undo their prosecutions.[9] In these later instances, one further characteristic would appear very starkly: inquisitors who wished to blacken all their victims would often resort to accusations, not of plausible Christian heresy, but of outrageous demonic magic or apostasy. Conrad of Marburg's case is the first of a long sequence of such 'demonizing' episodes. Conrad showed himself remarkably credulous in listening to witnesses: Siegfried of Mainz complained of how he listened over-much to a woman named Aleydis, who caused many innocent people to be executed.[10] At Trier, however, a woman named Lucardis seems to have grieved publicly over Lucifer's exclusion from heaven.[11] It may have been from her evidence that the story of the 'Luciferans' arose: heretics were accused of worshipping and kissing the devil in the form of a toad, a cat, or a pale, cold man. This story was then given papal sanction in Gregory IX's *Vox in Rama* letter.[12] These fantasies, which often include miraculous and magical elements, can in all probability be put down to clerical imagination and Conrad's desire to blacken his victims. Even contemporary commentators were sceptical. However, they afford the first instances of a trend which would repeat itself again and again through the later middle ages. Because heretical assemblies were both secret and opposed to the official Church, it was tempting to apply the rhetoric of opposites and extremes to them: to infer that they must, literally, invert or pervert everything associated with

8 *Gesta Treverorum Continuatio IV*, ed. G. Waitz, in *MGH Scriptores* 24 (1879), pp. 400–2; *Chronica Albrici Monachi Trium Fontium*, *MGH Scriptores* 23 (1874), pp. 931–2; *Cronica S. Petri Erfordensis Moderna*, ed. O. Holder-Egger, in *MGH Scriptores* 30, pt 1 (1896), p. 391.
9 Compare below, chapter 7, notes 131, 202, 218.
10 *Chronica Albrici*, p. 931.
11 *Gesta Treverorum Continuatio*, p. 401.
12 The Letter of Gregory IX entitled 'Vox in Rama', of 13 June 1233, is in *MGH Epistolae Saeculi XIII Selectae* I (Berlin, 1883), no. 537, pp. 432–5; echoes are found in *Chronica Albrici*, p. 932, and in *Gesta Treverorum Continuatio*, p. 401, esp. n. 2.

Christian worship.[13] The specific allegation that there was a sect of Luciferans would persist long into the fourteenth century. It resurfaced in the inquiries of even so sober an investigator as Peter Zwicker.[14] The belief that heretics indulged in promiscuous and perverted sexual excess at their meetings would recur in the Alps in the fifteenth century.[15]

Conrad's techniques did not lend themselves to the sort of careful analysis of heretic teachings which is possible for France or northern Italy in the same period. Some features of the German heretics do stand out from the chronicles, however. They were manifold and widespread. They had access to the scriptures through German translations. They were vehemently opposed to the spiritual claims and ministrations of the clergy. Some rejected the real presence in the eucharist, or denied that evil priests could consecrate it. Others entertained doubts about other sacraments, or offerings for the dead.[16] The impression conveyed by the chronicles is of an explosion of anti-clerical and anti-sacerdotal dissent: this impression would be confirmed by the more circumstantial documents of the 1260s and after. If this movement is to be derived from other Waldensian movements elsewhere, it shows more affinities with Lombard Waldensianism than with the French groups. Indeed, one source claimed that the heretics in Germany 'sent an annual tax to Milan, where the leadership of various heresies and errors was run'.[17] However, one should probably not emphasize the role of Italian influence: another chronicle spoke of a local heretics' hierarchy, with a rival archbishop called Dietrich (like the Catholic one at the same time). What the commentators most stressed was that the German heretics formed multiple and diverse groups, which reacted in various ways against the disciplinary culture of the Catholic Church in the decades after the Fourth Lateran

---

13 For the instinct to see the demonic as inversion, compare Stuart Clark, *Thinking with Demons: The Idea of Witchcraft in Early Modern Europe* (Oxford, 1997), pp. 14–21, 69–79.

14 W. Preger, *Der Tractat des David von Augsburg über die Waldesier*, Abhandlungen der historischen Classe der königlich Bayerischen Akademie der Wissenschaften, 14, pt 2 (1879), p. 211; M. Nickson, 'The "Pseudo-Reinerius" Treatise, the Final Stage of a Thirteenth-Century Work on Heresy from the Diocese of Passau', in *Archives d'Histoire Doctrinale et Littéraire du Moyen-Age* 34 (1967), pp. 304–5. For a late fourteenth-century description of 'Luciferans' see the text in J. Gretser, *Lucae Tudensis Episcopi Scriptores aliquot succedanei contra Sectam Waldensium*, in M. de la Bigne (ed.), *Magna Bibliotheca Veterum Patrum*, 15 vols (Cologne, 1618–22), vol. 13, p. 341; also D. Kurze (ed.), *Quellen zur Ketzergeschichte Brandenburgs und Pommerns*, Veröffentlichungen der historischen Kommission zu Berlin, Bd. 45, Quellenwerke Bd. 6 (Berlin, 1975), pp. 61–2; for Zwicker's investigations, see Kurze, *Quellen*, pp. 88, 91, 132, and for subsequent evidence, ibid., pp. 270–2.

15 See below, chapter 7, notes 120, 192–4.

16 *Gesta Treverorum Continuatio*, p. 401.

17 *Annales Marbacenses*, ed. R. Wilmans, in *MGH Scriptores* 17 (1861), p. 176.

Council. Diversity and extremism would remain the hallmarks of thirteenth-century German Waldensian protest.

6.2   The Austrian Waldenses, *c.*1265–1315

The frantic diversity of heretical activity in German lands seems to have calmed down and crystallized somewhat over the next thirty years. A source from the middle 1260s claimed that whereas there used to be more than seventy different sects, now there were only, in effect, 'Manichaeans' (Cathars) and Waldenses.[18] What they lost in diversity they made up for in numbers, concentration and cohesion. From the middle 1260s to *c.*1315 a series of mostly anonymous authors described a powerful, indeed threatening Waldensian movement concentrated in the valley of the Danube between Passau and Vienna.[19] Over the following decades traces of this movement would be found just north of the Danube, into Bohemia and Moravia, and much further north into Brandenburg and Pomerania. There is little doubt that this crucible of heretical activity represents the most powerful, and nearly the most durable, of the Waldensian movements of the later middle ages.[20] We are told almost nothing of how it began. It seems likely that Lombard rather than Occitan influence provided the initial stimulus to this aggressively anticlerical heresy. There are even references to collections being made in Germany 'for the brethren in Lombardy' and pilgrimages being made to 'their bishops in Lombardy'.[21] However, sources and origins matter much less than the fact that the native movement rapidly acquired sufficient strength in one area, to leave the local ecclesiastical authorities

---

18   The Passauer Anonymous, as ed. in Gretser, *Lucae Tudensis* . . . , in *Magna Bibliotheca*, vol. 13, p. 299: 'De quarto nota, quod sectae haereticorum fuerunt plures quam lxx, quae omnes, per Dei gratiam deletae sunt, praeter sectas Manichaeorum, Arianorum, Runcariorum et Leonistarum, quae Alemanniam infecerunt. Inter omnes has sectas, quae adhuc sunt vel fuerunt, non est perniciosior ecclesiae, quam *Leonistarum* . . .'. The first three names are in reality all names of species of Cathar. On the text of the Passauer Anonymous, see the exhaustive diplomatic description of the source in A. Patschovsky, *Der Passauer Anonymus: Ein Sammelwerk über Ketzer, Juden, Antichrist aus der Mitte des 13. Jahrhunderts*, Schriften der MGH, Deutsches Institut für Erforschung des Mittelalters, Bd. 22 (Stuttgart, 1968).
19   The fullest monographic treatment of this episode is in P. Segl, *Ketzer in Österreich: Untersuchungen über Häresie und Inquisition im Herzogtum Österreich im 13. und beginnenden 14. Jahrhundert*, Quellen und Forschungen aus dem Gebiet der Geschichte, Neue Folge, Heft 5 (Paderborn, 1984).
20   On the importance of Germany in the Waldensian story, see the comments of Martin Schneider, *Europäisches Waldensertum im 13. und 14. Jahrhundert*, Arbeiten zur Kirchengeschichte, 51 (Berlin, 1981), p. 98.
21   Nickson, ' "Pseudo-Reinerius" Treatise', p. 302; Gretser, *Lucae Tudensis* . . . , in *Magna Bibliotheca*, vol. 13, p. 308.

unable to cope; inquisitors were left beleaguered and bewildered by the scale of the problem.

The first fact about Waldensianism in mid-thirteenth-century Austria is its breadth and depth of support among the laity. A list compiled in the mid-1260s, of which many copies survive, reported that the heretics had 'infected' over forty parishes in Austria. Many of these were in Upper Austria, in the Traunkreis around Steyr, or in the Hausruckviertel; but some were in the environs of Vienna. Several of these places, Einzinspach, St Peter an der Au, Steyr, Kammer, and especially Kematen, were listed as having 'schools' of heresy, which suggests sufficient numbers of heretics to meet regularly, perhaps even publicly.[22] This impression of the scale of the heresy is supported by a range of other evidence. A heretic leader called Neumeister, before his execution at Vienna in the early four-teenth century, claimed that he had been 'bishop and master' of the Waldenses for fifty years; that there were 80,000 of them in Austria, but an 'infinite' number in Bohemia and Moravia.[23] The figure ought not to be taken seriously, but it certainly alarmed the cleric who reported it.[24] From this period onwards one reads occasionally of shows of defiance and force mounted by the Waldenses against the Church and clergy. In Kematen in the Traunkreis, where there were reportedly ten 'schools' of heresy, the local heretics killed their parish priest some time before c.1266, and his murderers went unpunished.[25] A Waldensian from Grafenschlag reportedly said that if his faith had only lasted a few years longer, it would have been sufficiently strong to be preached publicly and defended by force.[26] Waldensianism appears to have been almost on the threshold of a public revolt like that mounted by the Hussites over a century later: almost, but not quite.

The power and aggression of this Waldensian movement was matched by the fierceness of its teachings against the Roman Church. The main sources for this period roughly concur in attributing to the Waldenses a far-reaching rejection of and contempt for the ministry and pretensions of the sacral Church and its priesthood. The earliest surviving list of heresies held by the Austrian Waldenses, written in the 1260s by an anonymous churchman in Passau diocese, begins by attributing to the

22 Versions of this list are found in Nickson, ' "Pseudo-Reinerius" Treatise', pp. 294–5, 308–9, 314, and in W. Preger, *Beiträge zur Geschichte der Waldesier in Mit-telalter*, Abhandlungen der historischen Classe der königlich Bayerischen Akademie der Wissenschaften, 13, pt 2 (Munich, 1875), pp. 241–2.
23 Nickson, ' "Pseudo-Reinerius" Treatise', p. 307.
24 Compare the discussion below, section 6.3, of the possible statistics in Alexan-der Patschovsky (ed.), *Quellen zur böhmischen Inquisition im 14. Jahrhundert*, MGH Quellen zur Geistesgeschichte des Mittelalters, vol. 2 (Weimar, 1979), pp. 21–2.
25 Nickson, ' "Pseudo-Reinerius" Treatise', p. 294.
26 Ibid., pp. 308, 313.

Waldenses a complete rejection of the Roman Church. It was not the Church of Christ but the Whore of the Apocalypse; it had forfeited spiritual authority, just as the clergy had lost the exclusive right to minister. All the sacraments of the Church, so the Anonymous alleged, the heretics in some way rejected or despised. Good lay people could consecrate the Mass, but sinful priests could not; the same was true of the power to absolve. Confirmation, unction and ordination were deemed to be of no consequence. The Waldenses also disdained the spiritual jurisdiction of the clergy. They ignored excommunications and interdicts, objected to tithes, and criticized the range of ministrations, such as indulgences or the dedications of churches, which appeared only to serve for raising money. They refused to ascribe any special holiness to consecrated objects or ecclesiastical ornaments, disbelieved in relics or miracles, denied the existence of purgatory, and objected to judicial execution and formal oaths.[27] These long lists of 'errors', though they appear complex, resolve themselves into a few major themes. Undoubtedly the most important, at least in the eyes of the clerical commentators of the time, was that the Waldenses refused to hold the sacred institutions of the Church, its priesthood and its cult in the required degree of respect.[28] Their quasi-Donatist denial of spiritual power to the priesthood flowed from this source (though they show little sign of having actually distinguished between 'bad' and 'good' priests). So did their rejection of purgatory, as the place where the souls of the departed supposedly required the ministries of the priesthood.[29]

The most striking thing about the earliest of these lists of Waldensian errors is not its content but the reasons which the author supplied for their prevalence. The Anonymous of Passau asserted with great candour that the reason for the success of Waldensian heresy was the way in which the rites of the thirteenth-century Church were being mismanaged. The laws of the Church became discredited because they were so numerous, while Christ's were so few. The sacraments fell into disrepute through the lack of reverence with which the clergy themselves administered them. Priests, who in baptism asked incomprehensible questions in Latin of the godparents, or baptized candles or images, brought baptism into discredit.[30] Belief in the real presence was made difficult when the eucharist was clumsily handled and the elements scattered, when it was made with the wrong materials (such as vinegar) or when it was ministered by the wrong grade of cleric: 'Goth the heresiarch' claimed

27 Patschovsky and Selge, *Quellen*, pp. 77–103.
28 Compare Nickson, '"Pseudo-Reinerius" Treatise', pp. 296–303, and also 304ff., 311ff.; E. Martene and U. Durand (eds), *Thesaurus Novus Anecdotorum V* (Paris, 1717), cols 1,777ff.; Preger, *Tractat des David von Augsburg*, pp. 206–9.
29 Compare above, chapter 2, notes 52–3.
30 Patschovsky and Selge, *Quellen*, pp. 78–9, 81; Preger, *Beiträge*, p. 243.

that a deacon had spent all night in a tavern and then celebrated the eucharist the following morning.[31] A whole range of errors was reported in the administration of penance: besides the predictable gossiping of priests about what their penitents had reported, Czech priests sometimes heard the confessions of German penitents, and neither understood the other.[32] The Passauer Anonymous admitted that there were too many festivals, too frequent and casual use of excommunication, too many false relics and spurious miracles, too many dubious or uncanonized saints.[33] While the critiques in this text may have owed something to a learned regular's contempt for ill-disciplined secular clerics, the complaints ring true. They suggest strongly that Waldensianism prospered in Austria because the Catholic Church asked its layfolk to ascribe a degree of holiness to the acts of their priests which common sense and the evidence of their own eyes made it difficult to concede.

The religious credibility of the Austrian Waldenses rested on their claims to superior knowledge of scripture, and superior moral conduct. The sources expanded on both of these claims. The Passauer Anonymous claimed that many knew the entire New Testament by heart. He also cited gross mistranslations to prove the heretics' illiteracy: they supposedly confused 'sui', 'his own', with 'sues', 'swine', and therefore rendered John 1:11, 'his own received him not', as 'the swine received him not'.[34] Two separate sources claimed that it was 'rare to find among them a person of either sex who cannot recite the text of the New Testament by heart in the vernacular'.[35] A more negative image was conveyed by another late thirteenth-century text, formerly misattributed to David of Augsburg. This claimed that the Waldenses rejected the Old Testament and only accepted the authority of the gospels, though it added that they used abbreviated extracts from several early Fathers for controversial purposes.[36] The same author condemned their false pride in knowing parts of the 'gospels and epistles' by heart, alleging that they did not really understand them.[37]

These undoubtedly hostile sources showed no hesitation in reporting that the Austrian Waldenses were temperate, modest and generally well-behaved. The Passauer Anonymous commented that it was the very appearance of piety on the part of the 'Leonists' that made them so dan-

---

31 Patschovsky and Selge, *Quellen*, pp. 83–4; Preger, *Beiträge*, p. 243.
32 Patschovsky and Selge, *Quellen*, pp. 86–7; Preger, *Beiträge*, pp. 243–4.
33 Patschovsky and Selge, *Quellen*, pp. 91–100; Preger, *Beiträge*, pp. 244–5.
34 Patschovsky and Selge, *Quellen*, p. 71; Nickson, '"Pseudo-Reinerius" Treatise', p. 292.
35 Patschovsky and Selge, *Quellen*, p. 76; Nickson, '"Pseudo-Reinerius" Treatise', p. 313.
36 Preger, *Tractat des David von Augsburg*, p. 209.
37 Ibid., p. 212.

gerous: apart from their anti-clericalism, they set a good example before the world.[38] Their dress was neither sumptuously rich, nor affectedly or spectacularly miserable. They avoided business dealings and worked as artisans. Pseudo-David remarked that their behaviour was restrained, virtuous and religious.[39] A later Protestant editor of that text would remark that it was a wretched age in which virtuous and restrained behaviour was taken as a sign of heretical deviance.[40] Yet the conduct and behaviour of the Waldenses made them stand out in other ways. Several writers observed their distinctive jargon. They used particular code-words to describe the Church and the clergy, rarely referring to them by their usual names, in a language elsewhere described as covert and oblique, designed to avoid detection.[41] They apparently used unusual greetings among themselves; they had a coded form of enquiry, by which one asked another whether any non-heretics were present in a gathering: they asked if any 'bent wood' was present.[42] It is easy to explain these peculiar traits of behaviour and speech as ploys to avoid detection, like the 'language of Canaan' used by French Protestants some centuries later.[43] However, it seems that they had more or less the opposite effect to what was intended. These sober, restrained individuals, with their own distinctive traits of speech, their avoidance of verbal or sartorial extravagance, would have stood out from the crowd as starkly as Puritans or Jansenists in later eras. Their behaviour was almost as much an act of social defiance as of concealment.

One particular piece of verbal defiance stood out, namely the Waldensian refusal to swear in affirmation of the truth. From the Passauer Anonymous to the later fourteenth-century trial registers, one learns that Germanic Waldenses would refuse even to say 'truly', 'indeed' ('treuen', 'warlich') to emphasize the truth of any statement, since they thought these were oaths.[44] Far less would they consent to utter any more

---

38 Patschovsky and Selge, *Quellen*, p. 73; Gretser, *Lucae Tudensis...*, in *Magna Bibliotheca*, vol. 13, p. 299.

39 Preger, *Tractat des David von Augsburg*, pp. 216–17.

40 See M. Flacius Illyricus, *Catalogus Testium Veritatis qui ante nostram aetatem reclamarunt papae* (Basel, 1556), pp. 723ff., and esp. J. Ussher, *Gravissimae Quaestionis, de Christianarum Ecclesiarum... continua successione et statu, Historica Explicatio* (London, 1613), pp. 151–4, quoting M. Freherus, *Rerum Bohemicarum antiqui scriptores* (Hanoviae, 1602), p. 231 (a post-Reformation edition of the Pseudo-Reinerius treatise).

41 Patschovsky and Selge, *Quellen*, p. 71; Preger, *Tractat des David von Augsburg*, p. 212; Nickson, '"Pseudo-Reinerius" Treatise', p. 293.

42 Patschovsky and Selge, *Quellen*, p. 71; Nickson, '"Pseudo-Reinerius" Treatise', p. 307.

43 See, for example, the allusion to this in P. Chaunu (ed.), *The Reformation* (Gloucester, 1989), p. 286.

44 Patschovsky and Selge, *Quellen*, p. 74; Gretser, *Lucae Tudensis...*, in *Magna Bibliotheca*, vol. 13, p. 307. For the reluctance to say 'treuen', see also below, section 6.5.

profane oath. They would only utter the 'yes, yes' or 'no, no' recommended by Jesus in Matthew 5:37. This rejection of profanity on the part of the German Waldenses led to a curious story being told of them in the early fifteenth century. Johannes Nider, in book 4, chapter 1 of his *Formicarius*, written in the 1430s, remarked on the evil of repeated blasphemy among the ordinary German people of his time:

> This bad habit, I think, took root in the German people from a misunderstanding of one article of the heresy of the Waldenses, which is, that in no circumstance is it permitted to take an oath. However, in the German language, which lacks for many specific words, it is one and the same word to 'swear' and to blaspheme. And so that no one might be marked out as a Waldensian, from the levity and sinfulness of actors it came about that blasphemies in words, by the limbs of Christ true or imagined, honourable or dishonourable, are far too commonly found on the lips of many people.[45]

Of course, the rejection of the *forensic* oath had been a distinctively and recognizably 'Lombard' heresy.[46] As far as refusal to swear in court was concerned, however, the pressures of inquisition were already taking their toll by the middle of the thirteenth century. While the earliest version of the Passauer Anonymous simply relates that the Waldenses regarded it as a mortal sin to swear any oath,[47] later versions of the same text reported that the 'perfect' among them would die rather than swear, whereas the 'imperfect' would swear under pressure, in order to keep the secrets of the sect.[48] Elsewhere, the text suggested a technique for inquisitors to use on this point:

> Let the judge ask: 'Do you wish to abjure heresy?' If he is one of the perfect, he will answer, 'I shall not swear, because Christ forbad swearing'. Thus he is convicted by his own confession. If, however, he is imperfect, he will answer 'If I ought to swear, I shall swear'. Or 'If an order is given to me to swear, I shall swear'. Then the judge should say, 'I do not command you to swear; but if you wish us to believe you, swear'. If the heretic says 'I do not know how to make an oath, or how to swear; teach me a formula for swearing'. He has all sorts of similar tergiversations, so as to convince his own conscience that he is not swearing, but merely reporting the judge's oath.[49]

---

45   J. Nider, *Formicarius*, consulted in the edition entitled *De Visionibus ac revelationibus . . .* (Helmstedt, 1692), bk 4, ch. 1, p. 425.

46   See above, chapter 2, notes 61–2; chapter 3, note 48.

47   Patschovsky and Selge, *Quellen*, p. 103.

48   Nickson, ' "Pseudo-Reinerius" Treatise', p. 303.

49   Gretser, *Lucae Tudensis . . .* , in *Magna Bibliotheca*, vol. 13, p. 308: 'Et quaret Iudex; vis haeresim abiurare? Si perfectus est, respondebit; non iurabo; quia Christus prohibuit iurare. Et tunc est convictus et confessus. Si autem est imperfectus, tunc

Another text, formerly misattributed to David of Augsburg, similarly reported that the followers of the heretics would wriggle around when asked to swear, trying to oblige the inquisitor while salving their consciences. Whereas they all used not to swear at all, and by this means were easily captured, by *c*.1270 they had become more wary, and to save themselves they denied, swore and perjured themselves; except for some of the more obstinate, 'regarded as "perfect" amongst them and regarded as masters': but they took great care that these should not be captured, to prevent their accomplices from being identified.[50] Fourteenth-century inquisitors would experiment with the techniques proposed by their forebears, with interesting results.[51] At the opposite extreme, an inquisitor from Krems claimed that the Waldenses despised all oaths as insignificant, and would readily perjure themselves, quoting a vernacular proverb to this effect.[52] This same inquisitor made various other sensational allegations against the Waldenses, such as that they joined full siblings in marriage, and thought that sins of the flesh went unnoticed by God so long as they were committed below ground level. This implies either that his testimony is suspect, or that he encountered Waldenses whose contempt for the clergy caused them deliberately to try to shock their interrogators.[53]

How were the Austrian Waldenses organized, and how did they teach? It would be easy to assume that, for all sorts of reasons, they followed the same two-fold structure of itinerant, celibate teachers and sedentary, married laity found in nearly all Waldensian communities in the later middle ages. This was undoubtedly the pattern by the middle of the fourteenth century, if not before. However, in the earliest sources one glimpses a different style to their religious life. Teaching of heresy was, apparently, the task of everyone in the sect without distinction: 'one who has only been a pupil for seven days already looks for someone else to teach'.[54] The list of towns in Austria which contained 'schools' of heresy suggests that instruction took place more or less permanently in these places. Their teachers were, according to this same source, weavers and shoemakers. In contrast to the clergy, who were sexually incontinent and

---

respondebit; si debeo iurare, iurabo: Vel dicet; si iubetur me iurare, jurabo. Tunc iudex dicat; non iubeo te iurare; sed si vis ut credamus tibi, iura. Si dixerit haereticus; nescio iuramentum facere, vel iurare; docete me formam iuramenti. Has omnes et similes tergiversationes habet, ut formet sibi conscientiam, quod non sit iurans, sed tantum recitator iuramenti iudicis.'

50 Preger, *Tractat des David von Augsburg*, pp. 215, 221.
51 See below, section 6.3, notes 102–5.
52 Nickson, ' "Pseudo-Reinerius" Treatise', p. 307.
53 Ibid., p. 306.
54 Patschovsky and Selge, *Quellen*, p. 70–1; Nickson, ' "Pseudo-Reinerius" Treatise', p. 292.

idle, the heretics lived chastely in marriage, and worked with their hands. Both men and women taught, as several commentators agreed.[55]

While this description suggests a sort of religious co-operative run by its members, the nearly contemporary account of Pseudo-David of Augsburg describes a much more familiar two-tier structure. The 'perfect', who were only received as such after a long period within the heresy, had no homes or property, and renounced wives if they had them. They regarded themselves as successors to the apostles, masters and confessors, and relied on the followers whom they visited to provide for their needs. They travelled around in secret, sometimes disguised as pedlars.[56] When seeking to make converts, they were cautious and gradual: they insinuated heretical teachings very slowly into a mass of other uncontroversial religious material.[57] They sought to win over the powerful, especially powerful women, for their protection.[58] It is curious to find two descriptions of Waldensian instruction, so different in their emphases, from virtually contemporary documents. If the two-tier structure of Austrian Waldensianism did, in fact, emerge in the middle of the thirteenth century, following after some period of fruitful anarchy and semi-public profession, then the reasons are clear enough. Not only was the pressure of inquisition starting to weigh heavily on the movement: the rise of the mendicant friars offered a parallel example for the heretics to follow.[59] Pragmatism and imitation would account for the adoption of this model, even without any influence from parallel movements elsewhere in Europe. By the early fourteenth century their secrecy would become almost obsessive.[60]

On the other hand, the references to 'bishops' of the Waldenses, which had first appeared as early as the 1230s, are puzzling. At Einzinspach there was apparently not only a 'school', but a 'bishop'. Philipp of Pöchlarn OP, of Krems, reported in 1315 that they had a bishop called Herword, who assigned penances. Another 'bishop and leader' called Neumeister had been burned at Vienna. He also claimed that their hierarchy comprised a bishop, then a 'greater son', beneath him a 'lesser son' and beneath him a deacon.[61] It is possible that there was some confusion here,

55 Nickson, '"Pseudo-Reinerius" Treatise', pp. 294–5; Patschovsky and Selge, *Quellen*, p. 76; Preger, *Tractat des David von Augsburg*, p. 209.
56 Preger, *Tractat des David von Augsburg*, pp. 209–11.
57 Ibid., pp. 213–15.
58 Patschovsky and Selge, *Quellen*, p. 75; Preger, *Tractat des David von Augsburg*, p. 218.
59 The resemblance between itinerant Waldensian pastors and friars is pointed out in Peter Biller, '*Multum jejunantes et se castigantes*: Medieval Waldensian Asceticism', in *Studies in Church History* 22 (Oxford, 1985), pp. 215–28.
60 Below, note 98.
61 Nickson, '"Pseudo-Reinerius" Treatise', pp. 306–8, 310. For bishop, 'greater son' and 'lesser son' as titles among the Cathars, see Lambert, *The Cathars*, pp. 33, 157–8.

given that the German Cathars are reported to have had bishops, whereas the Waldenses were supposed to have despised the pomp associated with the title.[62] Most likely the term 'bishop' was applied imprecisely to any leading heretic by ecclesiastical writers. There is the suggestion, though, that certain figures emerged as leaders from within the German movement, and wielded moral authority over their colleagues and followers.

This talk of bishops and teachers should not mislead. Even at the height of its numerical success and influence, when the Church's instruments of repression were still rudimentary, the Waldenses did not offer a comprehensive religious service, nor did they absent themselves from Catholic worship. They attended church, made offerings, confessed their sins to priests, took communion and attended sermons. They also observed the fasts and feasts of the Church calendar.[63] This conduct appeared paradoxical to inquisitors, who could not see why heretics who disbelieved so aggressively in the sacral nature of the Church could continue to partake of its ministrations. The inquisitorial writers all stated that the Waldenses attended church in pretence, to conceal their heresy and escape detection. One of the early fourteenth-century texts insisted that when the Waldenses entered church, they said to themselves quietly that all that was sung, said and done was a lie.[64] This insistence that Waldensian participation in church worship was only a pretence would be repeated down the decades. Some witnesses observed the heretics failing, for instance, to gaze at the consecrated host.[65] The explanation of dissimulation does, however, have its problems. The most serious is that it simply did not work. The heretics did not conceal their presence by attendance at church; indeed, other aspects of their behaviour made them stand out rather than the opposite. The inquisitorial authors seem to have had some difficulty reconciling the heretics' virulent anti-clericalism with their apparent readiness to attend common worship. Yet, in the light of the later middle ages, this is actually less surprising. Many anti-clericals were also conventionally devout,[66] and Austrian Waldensianism was, essentially, an exaggerated form of anti-clericalism. Pseudo-David of Augsburg noted how the Waldenses exploited general anti-clericalism in order to attract people to their way of thinking.[67] In

---

62 Nickson, ' "Pseudo-Reinerius" Treatise', p. 297; the 'making of a bishop' is described in another part of the Anonymous of Passau, in Gretser, *Lucae Tudensis...*, in *Magna Bibliotheca*, vol. 13, pp. 306–7.
63 Patschovsky and Selge, *Quellen*, p. 74; Preger, *Tractat des David von Augsburg*, p. 212.
64 Nickson, ' "Pseudo-Reinerius" Treatise', pp. 312–13.
65 See below, notes 108, 194.
66 On the complex coexistence of anti-clericalism and devotion in late medieval Europe, see E. Cameron, *The European Reformation* (Oxford, 1991), pp. 91–3. See also above, chapter 3.
67 Preger, *Tractat des David von Augsburg*, p. 219.

times of interdict the heretics rejoiced because of the increase in their own numbers.[68]

The real objects of the heretics' anger were, predictably, the inquisitors and preachers against heresy themselves. Although they may have kept their heresy secret, Waldenses did not hide themselves from the rest of the congregation. As one ecclesiastical author remarked, 'If [a cleric] tries to preach against heresy, they stir up the people against him, saying that he is defaming the people, since no heretic has ever been found there, and makes the people indignant at the insult; the heretics intimidate those around them so that no one dares to speak of their reputation for heresy.'[69] The same author bemoaned the difficult life of an inquisitor in the late thirteenth century. Heretics were so difficult to get hold of or win over, that one despaired of exterminating them. Zealous inquisitors were few and far between; most people were willing to let them continue as long as they did not rise up openly, for the sake of peace. Few people knew how to deal with them properly: either they didn't understand their deviousness, or they let them go away, thinking that they were genuinely penitent when they had made a fictitious abjuration from fear of death only. It was hard to get evidence on which to excommunicate them, because once they saw that two or three concordant witnesses were needed, they took care to teach only one person at a time, save among those about whom they felt secure.[70] The life of an inquisitor was full of worries: he feared that he might condemn the innocent; but also that he might release the devious heretic, and that lay people might be scandalized and the whole business left unfinished. The faith would be weakened when lay people saw that learned men had been deceived by crude common people.[71]

Clearly, a balanced judgement is called for here. The Austrian Waldenses were not so strong in the late thirteenth century that they could defy the Church openly. Among the general population, the accusation of heresy still carried some weight and aroused some shame. On the other hand, there may well have been many lay people who would turn a blind eye to a moderate form of religious deviance which did not outrage shared values. Inquisitors could in certain circumstances seem as extreme as those whom they attacked. Waldensian heresy did not exactly flourish between the end of the thirteenth and the middle of the fourteenth century;[72] on the other hand, it had achieved the nearest thing to a means of survival and continuity.

68 Patschovsky and Selge, *Quellen*, p. 91; Nickson, ' "Pseudo-Reinerius" Treatise', p. 302.
69 Preger, *Tractat des David von Augsburg*, p. 218.
70 Ibid., pp. 219–20.
71 Ibid., pp. 231–3.
72 Despite what is suggested in Kieckhefer, *Repression*, p. 16.

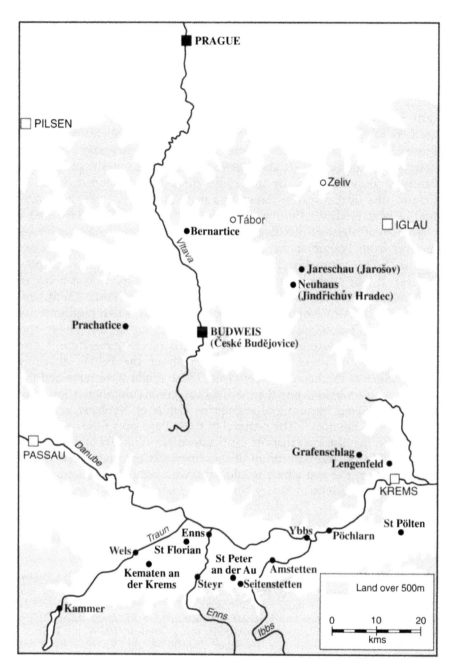

Map II The Waldensian presence in Austria, Bohemia and Moravia, 13th–14th centuries.

6.3   The German Waldenses in Bohemia and Moravia in the Early Fourteenth Century

It is a very short distance indeed – less than fifty miles – north of the Danube valley to the southern reaches of Bohemia and Moravia. By the early fourteenth century there had long been settlements of German-speakers in the towns of these predominantly Czech-speaking regions. From Austria there came not only the German language, but also heterodox religious beliefs and practices. So serious was the problem of heresy in Bohemia, that by the 1330s there had developed, based in Prague, one of the nearest things to a permanent office of the Inquisition in later medieval Europe, with its own building, its library, and a collection of registers.[73] A large and well-known inquisitors' handbook survives from Prague at this period, available since 1975 in a modern edition.[74] This manual is extremely informative on the inquisitors' procedures. It tells us the names of the most important inquisitors active in Bohemia, notably Colda of Colditz OP, Hartmann of Pilsen OFM, and above all Gallus of Neuhaus OP, one of the most active inquisitors of the period.[75] Traces appear of the conflict between secular clergy and mendicant friars during 1334 over the status of the inquisition.[76] The handbook is not particularly informative about the beliefs, practices and conduct of the heretics themselves. These might have remained the subject of speculation, but for the discovery of six numbered leaves of the dismembered inquisitorial register of Gallus of Neuhaus, scattered across several libraries.[77] The retrieval of these fragments offers a salutary warning to the historian that the capricious survival or loss of documents can easily distort our perception of movements at the grassroots. It also helps to fill in the gap which would otherwise occur in our knowledge of Germanic Waldensian heresy between the late thirteenth and the late fourteenth centuries. For the first time in the history of the Germanic movements, it allows us to see beyond the literary images of embattled inquisitors to named individuals, securely located in their contexts.

---

73   A. Patschovsky, *Die Anfänge einer Ständigen Inquisition in Böhmen; Ein Prager Inquisitoren-Handbuch aus der ersten Hälfte des 14. Jahrhunderts*, Beiträge zur Geschichte und Quellenkunde des Mittelalters, Bd. 3 (Berlin, 1975); see also A. Patschovsky (ed.), *Quellen zur böhmischen Inquisition im 14. Jahrhundert*, MGH Quellen zur Geistesgeschichte des Mittelalters, vol. 2 (Weimar, 1979), pp. 115ff.

74   Patschovsky, *Anfänge einer Ständigen Inquisition*, pp. 93–231, based on Wolfenbüttel, Herzog-August-Bibliothek, MS. 311 Helmst.

75   Patschovsky, *Anfänge einer Ständigen Inquisition*, pp. 15–29.

76   Ibid., pp. 58–9.

77   Four fragments consist of two double parchment leaves from Heiligenkreuz; a fifth was found at Gottweig, and a sixth at Brno. For full descriptions see Patschovsky, *Quellen zur böhmischen Inquisition*, pp. 11–18.

Around 1315 Neumeister, 'bishop and master' of the Waldenses for fifty years, claimed before his execution that besides the 80,000 Austrian Waldenses, there was an 'infinite' number in Bohemia and Moravia.[78] This supposedly immense number was certainly an exaggeration. Modern estimates of the population of the kingdom of Bohemia suggest that there were perhaps 100,000 Germans there in the early fourteenth century, and it was almost exclusively among the Germans that the heretics were found.[79] Yet by no means all of those were Waldenses: indeed, Germans figured as largely as witnesses against their neighbours, as they did among the accused. Other forms of heresy surfaced, including beghards and beguines, and an unusual intellectual heretic, Ricciardino of Pavia.[80] The surviving fragments of Gallus's register list some 180 suspected Waldenses and mention the burning of 15 people for heresy. Extrapolation for the missing remainder of the register – a most unsafe procedure, but unavoidable in the circumstances – yields potentially over 2,600 Waldenses among those caught in the toils of Gallus's inquisitions, and possibly over 200 people burned.[81] These estimates are sufficient to make the Bohemian inquisitions rank with the roughly contemporary activity of Bernard Gui and his colleagues at Toulouse; however, they do not lift them into a different order of magnitude from what is seen elsewhere. For some twenty years between the mid-1330s and the mid-1350s, somewhere in Bohemia and Moravia, Gallus of Neuhaus would have been conducting an inquisition. He forced the Waldenses of the region to move around, conceal themselves or otherwise try to escape the consequences.[82] The glimpse of German-speaking Waldenses in Bohemia shows us a movement under serious pressure, exposed as rarely before or after to the glare of sustained ecclesiastical scrutiny.

It is fairly certain that the Waldenses of Bohemia were in contact with, and probably derived from, those in the Danube valley, which is mentioned several times in the Bohemian register.[83] They lived in a range of towns across the region, including Budweis, Jareschau (near Neuhaus), Königgrätz, Namesz, Olesna (interestingly divided into 'German Olesna' and 'Czech Olesna'), Prachactice, Wilhelmsdorf, Zahlenicz and Znojmo.[84] Given that these Waldenses were town-dwellers, it is not surprising that they engaged in a variety of artisan crafts, like their Austrian

---

78 Nickson, ' "Pseudo-Reinerius" Treatise', p. 307.
79 Patschovsky, *Quellen zur böhmischen Inquisition*, pp. 21–2.
80 Ibid., p. 37; Patschovsky, *Anfänge einer Ständigen Inquisition*, pp. 30–46.
81 Patschovsky, *Quellen zur böhmischen Inquisition*, p. 20.
82 Ibid., pp. 22–4.
83 Patschovsky, *Anfänge einer Ständigen Inquisition*, pp. 72–3 and notes.
84 Patschovsky, *Quellen zur böhmischen Inquisition*, pp. 181–2, 188ff., 193ff., 201–2.

counterparts. Many were involved in the cloth industry, as weavers, shear-men or in other crafts. Several were hatters and some were innkeepers. There is a tantalizing mention of schoolmasters in some records.[85] Several implicated in the inquisitions acted as local magistrates. The 'judge of Zliv' figured in multiple testimonies.[86] We are clearly not dealing here with marginal figures in society. Ulrich 'the rich' of Budweis, and his brother Dytlin the judge of Olesna, reportedly visited each other for a fortnight on each occasion, travelling 'in great pomp' to stay in each other's ample homes.[87] It is striking that in Bohemia, but seldom else-where in the period, one reads of special buildings being constructed to receive the pastors and hold meetings, as at Budweis or Jareschau; or of a capacious hidden chamber in a secret passage in a house at Bernharcz.[88] Merthlin, the clothier of Budweis, had a 'marvellous cellar'.[89] Nor were these scattered, isolated communities: the surviving testimonies show multiple links by consanguinity and marriage between the various centres. When the inquisitors turned up in one town, the Waldenses reportedly moved to another to avoid them.[90] These societies of locally powerful and influential artisans are reminiscent, for example, of the Lollard communities in East Anglia or the Chilterns in the fifteenth and early sixteenth centuries.[91] However tempting it may be to envisage rising town-dwelling artisans emancipating themselves from the rural folk-religion of those around them – especially when the country-dwellers were of a different language group – the temptation should be resisted. Throughout the later middle ages Waldensian heresy took root among different sorts of people, from urban artisans via entrepreneurial farmers to mountain-dwelling peasants. No particular identification can be made between heresy and any one life-style.

In contrast to the very public and notorious lay heretics were the pastors. In keeping with the usual pattern for such secretive movements, these were celibate itinerants, who visited their flocks at intervals in ones and twos. They were known by Christian names (sometimes in the diminutive forms favoured in the area), as Albrecht, Gottfried, Johannes, Peter and Ulrich of Donaudorf near Krems.[92] 'Henzlin the knife-maker',

85 Ibid., pp. 175, 181–2, 231–3.
86 Ibid., pp. 177, 183.
87 Ibid., pp. 197–8.
88 Ibid., pp. 197, 232, 238.
89 Ibid., pp. 182–3; cf. p. 234.
90 Ibid., p. 181.
91 Compare the communities described in J. A. F. Thomson, *The Later Lollards 1414–1520* (Oxford, 1965), and in N. P. Tanner (ed.), *Heresy Trials in the Diocese of Norwich, 1428–1431*, Royal Historical Society, Camden 4th Series, vol. 20 (London, 1977), *passim*.
92 Patschovsky, *Quellen zur böhmischen Inquisition*, pp. 189, 192, 202, 210, 235, 238.

who may have been a pastor and is known through his brother's reluctant testimony, is the only one alleged to have practised a craft.[93] Of the pastors' leader Rudlin, we learn from his brother Heinrich that he was introduced to the sect some time in the mid-1290s. He had been an innkeeper and was a lifelong celibate: because of the latter he was received into the 'mastership' of the sect. He remained a pupil for 12 years and then was made a master, presumably towards the end of the first decade of the fourteenth century.[94]

The pastors provided more or less the same services to their followers as in other areas of late medieval Waldensianism, though there were some peculiarities. Typically, they were received at their followers' homes several times in the year.[95] There they heard confessions of sins, sometimes from those whom other lay adherents had induced to confess, and often at night.[96] They held meetings at the houses of the more wealthy followers, and presumably preached their doctrines. Sometimes they met in cellars.[97] By the middle of the 1340s even this furtive religious activity was, apparently, fraught with danger. Heinrich, a smith from Vohenstrauss in the Palatinate, who was in c.1345 living at Jareschau near Neuhaus, when asked about the itinerary of Ulrich of Donaudorf, told the inquisitor how the pastors' visits had become even more secretive than they used to be:

> Now I tell you: it is not the way it was before, because now they arrive most secretly and leave secretly, such that one person, no matter how close a friend he is, does not allow another to know about the arrival of the said confessors; hence, when they enter or leave a house, they leave and enter secretly and hidden, allowing no one to know where they are going or where they come from. Thus I know nothing about their arrival and departure.[98]

Of their teaching, all that is recorded is their denial of purgatory and their advice to their followers not to swear.[99] A unique testimony, however, refers to the Waldensian pastor Albrecht conducting a form of marriage at Hedreinsdorf near Neunburch in Austria, between Heynczlin (Heinrich) Zaumer and his wife Elizabeth, who later settled at Olesna.[100] Likewise, there is one mention from the environs of Neuhaus of a Waldensian pastor offering some sort of last rites to a sick

93   Ibid., pp. 212–13.
94   Ibid., p. 250.
95   Ibid., pp. 189, 199, 205–6, 209–10, 235.
96   Ibid., pp. 205ff.
97   Ibid., p. 234.
98   Ibid., p. 211.
99   Ibid., pp. 204, 243; cf. p. 26.
100   Ibid., pp. 191–2.

woman of the sect – though since the sole witness was not actually present, one cannot infer anything about what actually happened.[101]

Though hard pressed by an experienced and resident inquisitor, the Bohemian Waldenses could not help getting themselves into difficulties over oaths. It was remarked that several of them would not even say 'treuen'.[102] Gallus exploited their overwhelming distaste for forensic oaths to cause them as much discomfort as possible. Margaretha, wife of Hertlin the tailor of Budweis, claimed she was entirely innocent of heresy. When asked if she wished to swear to tell the truth, the following conversation occurred:

Margaretha	'I shall swear willingly, just as you direct.'
Inquisitor	'I do not command you to swear, but ask whether you wish to.'
Margaretha	'I readily wish to, but don't know how to.'
Inquisitor	'Swear whatever way you know.'

Then the inquisitor several times offered her a form of oath. Eventually she swore, 'with considerable difficulty'. On two further occasions in that interrogation she was invited to swear an oath to confirm her denials. When asked whether she was related to Conrad the furrier who had been burned at Budweis for heresy, she said no, but she had known him in Prague. Asked if she was willing to swear that he was not a relative, she answered: 'How much and how often must I swear? Have I not already sworn three times?'[103] Even less prudent was Katherina, wife of Heinczlin the shearman, who when told that she was not compelled to swear to tell the truth, but should do so out of obedience, 'departed as though contemptuously'.[104] Avoidance of oaths seems to have become almost a mental block among confirmed heretics. A woman named Zertla, on the margins of the group, reportedly 'said to the women whose husbands had been captured, that if they were in captivity, they should swear to what they said; this would be easy for her because she was used to swearing; but difficult for them, because they were unused to it.'[105]

It was not only the compulsive avoidance of oaths which marked off the Waldenses from their neighbours. Like their antecedents, they adopted distinctive forms of speech: Heynczlin the hatter, Pezold the painter and Johlin the tailor, suspected heretics, had 'a peculiar way of living and a special *conversacio* amongst themselves'.[106] Gruczczo the

---

101   Ibid., pp. 235–6; compare the Alpine 'last rites', below, chapter 7, note 164.
102   Ibid., pp. 217, 230.
103   Ibid., pp. 184–6.
104   Ibid., p. 233.
105   Ibid., p. 189.
106   Ibid., pp. 177–8.

furrier of Budweis was long suspected of heresy because he was not 'common' with people, but 'singular'.[107] Several witnesses claimed that the heretics of Budweis, when the host was elevated during Mass, refused to look at the body of Christ but instead stared around the church.[108] One called Herbord reputedly avoided keeping church feasts, discouraged almsgiving to the Church and showed public dislike for the clergy.[109] The same paradox appears here as earlier: the Waldenses would keep their pastors hidden with obsessive secrecy, but their own social conduct was the very reverse of clandestine.

In the thirteenth century it might have been possible to stir up the populace as a whole against the clergy in general and the inquisitors in particular. The fourteenth-century Bohemian heretics tried something similar. Heynlin the younger, consul of Budweis, said among the consuls when the inquisitor first came to the town: 'You lords, we must all speak with one voice before the inquisitor, saying: we know no one here who is a heretic; if you wish to do this, say so to me'.[110] This attempt at a conspiracy of silence did not work, as the very fact of its being reported in the trial registers shows all too clearly. Around 1338 the sons of Hermann of Neuhof allegedly plotted to murder Gallus of Neuhaus when he was on his way to Iglau. According to the same witness, another heretic called Schomberger had said that 'if they had known in advance for how long they were to be bound in penance, it would have been better to have been burned'.[111] This is a rare and early instance of public penance being regarded as a shame and an irritant to the heretics.

The Waldenses in Bohemia were clearly placed under severe pressure by the inquisitions of the early fourteenth century. The readiness of many lay people to testify to the distinctive behaviour of the suspected heretics reveals both the efficiency of the Church's repression and the growing isolation – despite their substantial wealth and their numerous interconnections across Bohemia and Moravia – of the heretics from the rest of Catholic society, German and Czech alike. Did this trend continue? No similarly abundant evidence survives for the activities of inquisitors in Bohemia after c.1355, if indeed there was any in those decades of plague and dislocation. Yet within a decade or so of the end of Gallus's career, Bohemia would be swept up, first in the ecclesiastical reform movements associated with the Prague city preachers and the university masters, and then from c.1420 onwards by the Hussite movement.[112] When Hussitism fragmented into a range of different movements, its rural and revolu-

107 Ibid., p. 182.
108 Ibid., pp. 175–6, 181.
109 Ibid., p. 176.
110 Ibid., pp. 176–7.
111 Ibid., pp. 192–3.
112 See below, section 6.7, note 267.

tionary branch, Taboritism, would take root in substantially the same areas, southern Bohemia and Moravia, where the German Waldenses had been most abundant.[113] This coincidence has produced a long and largely inconclusive debate between scholars as to whether Waldensian heresy can in any sense be regarded as the 'forebear' or the 'source' of social Hussitism.[114] The arrival of Hussitism would overlay and all but obliterate Bohemian Waldensianism. At the very least, one must conclude that Gallus von Neuhaus's endeavours left the Waldenses in poor shape to preserve their identity when confronted with a new, intellectually fecund and politically vibrant movement of dissent.

6.4 The Austrian Brethren and their Defectors, 1368

In this section and in section 6.6 below one witnesses what has been called the 'crisis' of the late medieval German Waldenses.[115] The expression is well justified by the sequence of losses and betrayals which the movement suffered between 1360 and 1400. At this period one gains a unique insight into a vigorous intellectual debate over the validity of the Waldensian protest as it manifested itself in the German lands. Since the 1230s the German Waldensian masters, especially in the southeast, had sustained a confident and vehement polemic against the spiritual claims of the ordained Catholic clergy. From the 1360s to the 1390s those claims were placed in the spotlight not only by inquisitors, but also by defectors from within the ranks of the masters of the sect. Some of those masters reveal themselves as having possessed considerable scriptural knowledge and a quite impressive grasp of ecclesiastical Latin. Yet that very education seems to have brought their downfall as members of the Waldensian movement. Its claims could not bear the glare of those trained in the syllogistic logic of the schools. This phase also sees nearly unique evidence of contact between the Italian and German wings of the movement.

The evidence consists in the first place of two documents originating in Italy. First there is the 'Book of the Elect', a Latin summary of around 1,000 words which describes the supposed origin of the Waldensian movement in the remote past and its history up to that time. Then there is the so called 'Letter of the Italian Brethren', an open letter of over 5,000 words which defends the conduct of the Waldensian pastors against the accusations which had been made by converts to Catholicism from within their own ranks; answers some objections evidently raised against

---

113 Patschovsky, *Quellen zur böhmischen Inquisition*, pp. 121–2.
114 See below, note 269.
115 Kieckhefer, *Repression*, pp. 53–73.

the 'Book of the Elect'; and exhorts the remainder of the German pastors to stand firm. From the other side of the argument, there survive three substantial pieces written by the convert pastors in Austria themselves. The first, dated within the text to 1368, appears to be a reply by the convert Johannes Leser to an earlier, lost letter attacking his conduct and motives, presumably written by the same group which wrote the 'Letter of the Italian Brethren'. The second is a relatively short (*c*.3,500 words) rebuttal of the claims made by the Italian brethren about their history and authority in the 'Book of the Elect', written by an otherwise unknown ex-Waldensian master named Seyfridus, who also seems to have received a lost letter criticizing his actions. The third is again by Johannes Leser and appears to be a short, possibly unfinished treatise which contrasts the continuity and certainty of the Roman Church with the uncertainty and unreliability of the Waldensian position. It dismembers the first few claims of the 'Book of the Elect' in considerable detail, but does not complete the analysis. All these documents survive in German archives, though an adaptation of the 'Book of the Elect' is also found in a manuscript originating from northern Italy or Provence. All are in Latin; and the Latin is in places highly ornate, liberally sprinkled with quotations not only from the scriptures, but from the Fathers and canon law.[116]

The confrontation can be best appreciated if one analyses all these documents together by themes and deals with the arguments raised by each of them in turn. First, all the disputants were very concerned with these questions: where did the Waldenses come from? What was the source of authority for their ministry? At a popular level in Germany, as will be shown later, the question of authority was answered by an extraordinary supernatural legend which would certainly not have commended itself to the writers of these letters.[117] The 'Book of the Elect' explained Waldensian origins by a dexterous and individual adaptation of a familiar medieval legend. It claimed that for the first three centuries the Church was holy, pure and above all *poor*, until the time of the Emperor Constantine. Constantine, suffering from leprosy, called on Pope Sylvester I to baptize him and was cured of his leprosy. As a reward,

---

116   The fullest modern critical edition of this correspondence is Peter Biller, 'Aspects of the Waldenses in the Fourteenth Century Including an Edition of their Correspondence' (Oxford University D.Phil. thesis, 1977). Some key texts are in J. J. Ignaz von Döllinger (ed.), *Beiträge zur Sektengeschichte des Mittelaters*, 2 vols (Munich, 1890); vol. 2: *Dokumente vornehmlich zur Geschichte der Valdesier und Katharer*, pp. 351–62. The locations of most of the manuscripts are supplied in J. Gonnet and A. Molnar, *Les Vaudois au moyen âge* (Turin, 1974), pp. 448–50. A dialect version or adaptation of the 'Book of the Elect' is in Cambridge University Library, MS. Dd.XV.29, fos 230ff., as discussed below, chapter 8.2.
117   See Nickson, '"Pseudo-Reinerius" Treatise', p. 305; Kurze, *Quellen*, p. 208; as discussed below, notes 167–70.

Constantine gave Sylvester power and authority over the western Empire, and himself left for the east to found Constantinople. Sylvester accepted the proffered wealth; but (and here the Waldensian account differed from the traditional story) a companion or companions[118] of his broke away from the now wealthy and decaying Church, and remained in their former state of poverty. Eight hundred years after Constantine there arose someone called Petrus Waldis,[119] a good rich man. He read, or heard read, the gospel precepts on poverty, sold his goods and gave to the poor, gathered disciples and confronted the 'heresiarch' (the pope) at Rome. Despite the support of an Apulian cardinal, he was eventually expelled and excommunicated. He travelled throughout Italy and he and his successors gathered many supporters: sometimes as many as 700 or 1,000 gathered at once. For two hundred years they were able to preach in public. Thereafter persecutions arose which had continued to the present time.[120]

The version of Waldensian history in the 'Book of the Elect' is fascinating, not only for what it includes but for what it omits. It claims ancient origins for the Waldensian movement by incorporating the story, well known in Catholic circles, that the gift of temporal wealth and property to Pope Sylvester 'poured poison into the Church'.[121] It leaps the eight centuries from Sylvester to Valdesius by a general claim that the true Church subsisted in those days as a minority movement. It knows of Valdesius (Waldis), but adds the name 'Peter', and is quite unaware of his origins in Lyon, though this was stated in several chronicles. In the 'Letter of the Italian Brethren', 'Petrus de Walle' is given a companion, 'Johannes Ludinesis', who was the source of the name 'Pauperes Ludinenses' also given to the movement.[122] This tradition located the early Waldensian movement entirely within Italy, and claimed for it a surprisingly long period of immunity from persecution. Rather strikingly, the Italians gave reasons why their account of their own history lacked precision:

> The reason why we cannot answer, or give proof, as positively as it is written or proved in other chronicles . . . is two-fold. The first is because of the absence of witnesses: for there is no one today who has heard or

118 The texts disagree as to whether the companion was singular or plural. See Biller, 'Aspects', pp. 264–5, 283–5.
119 This appears to be the first occasion on which Valdesius was re-christened by the addition of 'Peter' to his name.
120 Biller, 'Aspects', pp. 264–7.
121 The fullest account of the legend of Pope Sylvester I and the Donation of Constantine is W. Levison, 'Konstantinische Schenkung und Silvester-Legende', in *Miscellanea Francesco Ehrle*, 2 (*Studi e Testi*, 38, 1924), pp. 159–247. The Waldensian version of the story exhibits certain unique features.
122 Biller, 'Aspects', pp. 286–7.

seen the true origins of the matter, because a long time has passed. The second and more important reason is because of the innumerable persecutions which we have suffered, through which many times our books have been reduced as it were to nothing, such that we could barely preserve the sacred page.[123]

The German converts mercilessly pointed out the implausibilities in these accounts on grounds both theological and historical. The companion or companions of Sylvester who deserted him were unnamed, whereas many known bishops joined the pope in the anti-Arian councils after Constantine's conversion.[124] No mention of the Waldenses' early history could be traced in the accounts of other heresies.[125] Leser contrasted the utter silence about eight hundred years of their history with the unbroken succession of popes down to Gregory XI.[126] If they claimed that they used to meet by the thousand, and now had dwindled to a hundred, that showed that they were a sect, not the true Church.[127] Their claim of two centuries of public preaching after the time of Petrus Waldis could not be true, since this would bring the time of public witness up to the early fourteenth century, well within the memory of those alive, who could remember no such thing. 'Therefore desist, we ask you, from such fables because of the disgrace they will bring upon you.'[128]

A further dispute arose over the claim that the Waldensian pastorate derived its authority from priestly orders, supposedly given to Petrus Waldis and then passed on to others. Both sides in the argument seem to have accepted the idea that some sort of apostolic succession, if not the usual one, was needed to vindicate the claims of the Waldensian pastorate to spiritual authority. The Italian brethren, in their long letter, elaborated on this point. If 'Petrus called Waldensis' had by any chance not received authority from the true Church descended from the companions of Sylvester, then surely he and his companion John, who were (they claimed) priests in holy orders, confirmed by their Apulian cardinal, could have laid hands on the brethren and so given them priestly status.[129] The Italian brethren then reported the names of various alleged heretic leaders who were supposedly priests: Johannes of Burgundy (a real heretic mentioned in a mid-thirteenth-century inquisitors' handbook),[130] dignified in this source with the title of 'brother'; two unnamed

123   Ibid., p. 289.
124   Ibid., p. 347.
125   Ibid., pp. 328–9.
126   Ibid., p. 349.
127   Ibid., p. 317.
128   Ibid., pp. 317–18.
129   Ibid., p. 290.
130   Patschovsky and Selge, *Quellen*, pp. 56–8.

friars; and a 'bishop of Lescar', probably Raymond de Benac, recorded as investigated 'for transgressing the faith' in 1218.[131] None of these proved the point, since none was definitely both a priest *and* a Waldensian heretic. However, they testify to an oral tradition, however imprecise, about the fate of previous heretics stretching over more than a century.

This claim that Petrus Waldensis was in truth an ordained priest, which is entirely absent from the evidence of the early chronicles, stirred up a host of problems. Even if Petrus were accepted as a priest – and the German converts neither conceded nor refuted the claim – then he had heaped up irregularities by his actions. As a simple priest rather than a bishop, he could not consecrate other priests. Once excommunicated by the Church, he could not perform any priestly functions at all. By preaching while under ban, he became an illicit preacher and schismatic.[132] The Italians had conceded the vital point: by accepting *any* validity to priestly orders, they yielded *ipso facto* to the sacerdotal claims of the Roman hierarchy.

The competing claims of the priesthood and the Waldensian masters came into sharp focus in the rest of the correspondence. There were, essentially, two questions: were the Waldensian masters as good as they claimed to be and were the Catholic priests as bad as they were alleged to be? A whole range of charges was alleged against the Waldenses by their detractors and those who departed their ranks, tending all in the same direction, to the effect that they were insufficient spiritual guides and protectors of their followers. One charge was that they lacked sufficient learning for their task. Compared with many parish priests, of course, some Waldensian leaders would have seemed more than adequate. In the 'Letter of the Italian Brethren' it was the Waldenses themselves who raised the question of their own learning, precisely in order to demolish it with a display of religious erudition and not a little sententious false modesty. The letter was liberally sprinkled with citations not only from the Vulgate Bible, but also from Augustine, Jerome, Bernard, Peter Lombard, the *Opus Imperfectum in Matthaeum* (then attributed to John Chrysostom) and even the poet Horace. Some of these quotations may have been taken from collections: many of the passages from Augustine could have come from Gratian's *Decretum* or Prosper of Aquitaine's *Sententiae*.[133] Nevertheless, the authors of the letter were clearly out to make a point. Once again, however, they made their point by tacitly accepting the standards and criteria of their Catholic adversaries.

131   References for these are supplied in Biller, 'Aspects', p. 290 and notes.
132   Ibid., pp. 325–6, 351.
133   See the notes to ibid., pp. 277–97.

The German converts did not press the charge of ignorance. They were much more concerned with the inadequacy of the spiritual service which the heretic pastors offered to their people. Everything hinged on whether, as the 'Book of the Elect' claimed, the Waldenses were indeed the true Church. If they were the true Church, why did they not administer the sacraments? All three convert critics focused on this objection. On their failure to deliver the eucharist, Leser remarked: 'woe to those who wish or presume to be physicians, and do not have the medicines to cure wounds'.[134] Seyfridus observed how the Waldenses offered only half a sacrament, their inadequate form of confession; for the rest they sent people to the papal Church, which offered all seven sacraments and much more.[135] As Johannes Leser later put it:

> Why do your people not then receive the faith in the same place that they receive the sacraments? It is quite improper to imagine that Christ, who loved the Church, would have denied to his faithful people the administration of the sacraments, and entrusted it to strangers and infidels. This would be like limbs of the body receiving nourishment from parts which were separated from the body: it is impossible in a natural body, and forbidden in a spiritual one.[136]

The Italians answered that their ministry was like that of St Paul, to evangelize and preach rather than to baptize or minister ceremonies: not everyone could undertake all spiritual tasks equally. Confronted with the charge that they did not give the sacraments to the dying, and therefore many died without communion, they answered (quoting copiously from Augustine) that true communion consisted in spiritual unity with the true Church, that is, the minority Church. In an earlier or a later age, this reply might have been sufficient, but in the fourteenth and fifteenth centuries, at the very apogee of sacramental, cultic worship in the west, it must have sounded somewhat lame. Certainly the pastors had no answer to the charge of self-contradiction: how could one deny the holiness of a Church, while accepting its sacraments and urging one's followers to do so too?

Even more damaging charges, in terms of their effects on the German masters' morale, arose out of the clandestine nature of Waldensian preaching and teaching. If they were the 'true shepherds', why did they desert their people as soon as persecution threatened, in effect 'leaving them to the wolves' as the letter-writers put it? If they preached the true gospel, why were they so secretive about it, concealing the content of their message as far as possible from all but the most trusted? It was no

134   Ibid., p. 305.
135   Ibid., pp. 326–7.
136   Ibid., pp. 338–9.

answer to say that such behaviour was made necessary by persecution: the issue was whether the Waldenses were the true Church or not, and therefore whether they behaved like true pastors. Phrased in such idealized terms these charges were unanswerable, and the Italian brethren did not even attempt to address them. They seem to have accused the converts of deserting their flocks and of perfidiously breaking their vows, which provoked Seyfridus to retort that whoever took flight when his friend was persecuted was no friend; yet when persecutors attacked the flock the Waldensian pastors fled and left their sheep in the wilds, like the hireling shepherds spoken of in the New Testament.[137] Both the convert masters made much of the fact that the Waldenses kept their message secret. If their faith were true, the pastors would proclaim it publicly and stay with their people under persecution. While one might conceal oneself for a time, the faith must always be made entirely public. To conceal the faith was to mock past generations of confessors and martyrs.[138] The truth, argued Seyfridus, did not seek to hide itself in corners, but the opposite.[139]

Eventually, the debate resolved itself into moralistic comparisons between the lives of the Waldensian pastors and the Catholic clergy. Here the Donatist attitude which the German Waldenses had inherited from their Lombard forebears ran up against reality as well as the Church's sacramental teaching. Both the convert ex-Waldenses pointed out that it was impossible to blacken *all* the Catholic clergy with the sins of a few. While everyone agreed there were some bad priests around, that did not justify separation from the entire Church. Everyone knew that the priests spent all their time denouncing vices and exhorting to virtues.[140] If the clergy's possession of lands was such a terrible offence against the principle of apostolic poverty, then the Waldenses were (so two of the German converts claimed) themselves guilty of hypocrisy, since they professed poverty but kept hidden treasures of gold and silver.[141]

The correspondence of 1368 gives us a glimpse into the mental and spiritual world of the Italian and German Waldensian pastors. It is, unfortunately, unique in several respects. It offers the only substantial evidence of contact between the Italian and German movements in the later middle ages; while it demonstrates contact between these at a time of crisis, it cannot be used to prove more regular interchange across the Alps.[142] It shows the level of Latinity and erudition of which some

137   Ibid., p. 321.
138   Ibid., pp. 306–7, 312–13, 315–16.
139   Ibid., pp. 330–1.
140   Ibid., pp. 310–12, 333–5, 351–3.
141   Ibid., pp. 329, 332, 349.
142   G. Audisio, *Les 'Vaudois': naissance, vie et mort d'une dissidence (xiie-xve siècles)* (Turin, 1989), pp. 75–6, observes that the Germanic and Meridional Waldensian

heretics were capable, but also shows that their reading was entirely dependent on the shared, western Catholic religious literature. There was, as the Italian brethren themselves explained, no surviving literary tradition within Waldensianism itself.[143] It proves that the Waldenses knew less about their own supposed origins than earlier Catholic chroniclers. Most of all, it bears witness to the climate of the later fourteenth century, in which many of the Waldensian masters would be offered, and would accept, the chance to make their peace with the Catholic Church. The following decades would deal German Waldensianism a serious blow.

6.5 The Waldenses Before the Great Conversions of the 1390s

At the very end of the fourteenth century the German Waldenses fell under the scrutiny of some exceptionally dedicated, intelligent and (by the standards of inquisitors) merciful and sympathetic opponents. As the previous section showed, the more educated of the Waldensian leadership was already being thrown into some confusion by the internal contradictions of the heretics' traditional attitude towards the Church. These contradictions were ruthlessly exposed by a series of critics, especially the Provincial of the Celestine Order, Peter Zwicker, who displayed consummate skill in winning over the leaders as well as the followers of the heresy. Zwicker was out to make converts, not martyrs. As a result of his and others' efforts, German-speaking Waldensianism would, by the early fifteenth century, have diminished to a shadow of its earlier strength. In the course of his investigations, Zwicker and the others compiled a body of subtle and credible evidence, much of it still extant, which depicts late medieval Waldensianism in a detail not so far seen. For the first time one can distinguish between the characteristic religiosity of the masters, the 'brethren' as they called themselves[144] on one hand, and their lay followers on the other. One can see how the followers tried to reconcile the two conflicting modes of religious instruction which they received from their priests and the heretics' masters. The conflicts at local level caused by the arrival of the surprisingly seductive inquisitor, Zwicker, also appear through the inquisitorial records which he compiled.

The inquisitions revealed that the heretics had, by this time, well-established groups of followers scattered across nearly all of eastern Germany, from the Danube to the Baltic, though these were for the most part in isolated village pockets. They were found in their old heartlands of Austria, but also north into Saxony and Brandenburg. One of

communities grew apart to such an extent over time that contacts between them occurred only at times of exceptional stress.

143   See above, note 123.

144   For the title of 'brethren' see, for example, Kurze, *Quellen*, p. 204.

Zwicker's most effective and detailed investigations uncovered communities of over 400 Waldenses in the diocese of Cammin, in the Uckermark between Berlin and Stettin.[145] In the southwest of Germany and in Switzerland other groups of Waldenses were found in towns rather than the countryside: in Mainz in 1390, in Augsburg in 1393, and in Strasbourg, Bern and Freiburg im Uechtland (Fribourg) in 1399. Although these groups were apparently visited by travelling preachers from the same 'circuit' as those in the east, they appear to have been short-lived and somewhat isolated.[146] The key to holding the scattered communities of Waldensian followers together was the ministry of the 'masters' or 'brethren'. These travelled around over great distances to visit their followers at quite long intervals; their visits were critical to sustaining the movement.

The names of some two dozen of the brethren are known, and they reflect the geographical spread of the movement at the time: Johannes and Nicolaus of Vienna, Hans of the Steiermark, Hanns of Enns and Hans Simmler of Steiermark all came from the earliest heartlands in the southeast. Several came from the region of Saxony: Nicolaus of Plauen, Conrad of Erfurt and Conrad of Thuringia (the last two may well be the same person). Yet others came from the far northeast, above all Nicolaus Gottschalck of Königsberg in Brandenburg Neumark (modern-day Chojna, in western Poland), often known as 'Claus of Brandenburg'. It is suggestive to find some names, all of them German, but associated with places much further afield: Conrad of [Schwäbisch] Gmünd, Jakob of Buda, Gottfried of Hungary, Peter of the Siebenbürgen (in German Transylvania), Nicolaus and Johannes of Poland, and especially Nicolaus of Solothurn in Switzerland.[147] However, like the far-flung names used by the leaders of Burgundian Waldensianism in the late thirteenth century[148] these cannot definitely

145   Ibid., esp. p. 235, and in general pp. 77–261 passim, based on the inquisition protocols of Peter Zwicker from the Stettin district 1392-4, in Wolfenbüttel, Herzog-August-Bibliothek, Cod. Helmst. 403, fols 21–125 and Novi 348.

146   For the trials at Mainz and Augsburg, see Döllinger, Beiträge, vol. 2, pp. 363–4, 620–1. For the trials in Strasbourg, Bern and Freiburg, see Kathrin Utz Tremp, 'Les Vaudois de Fribourg (1399–1430): état de la recherche', in Revue de l'histoire des religions, vol. 217, fasc. 1 (2000), pp. 124–5, 136–7. The trial records from Strasbourg await a modern edition, which is in preparation by Georg Modestin of Bern.

147   These lists are found in Döllinger, Beiträge, vol. 2, pp. 330–1; Kurze, Quellen, pp. 81, 89, 100, 138, 147, 172; see also D. Kurze, 'Zur Ketzergeschichte der mark Brandenburg und Pommerns vornehmlich im 14. Jahrhundert, Luziferaner, Putzkeller und Waldenser', in Jahrbuch für die Geschichte Mittel- und Ostdeutschlands 16/17 (1968), pp. 50–94, for a discussion of names and origins of heresiarchs listed here.

148   See above, chapter 5, notes 79–80.

prove Waldensian centres in these places. They may only prove that travelling people were especially susceptible to the allure of joining the heretic masters.

If the Catholic sources are to be believed, the Waldensian masters of the 1390s were significantly less educated than their predecessors a generation earlier. Many of them were reputedly the sons of artisans, or had been artisans themselves before they took up the travelling pastorate. Nicolaus of Vienna and Johannes of Mainz had been tailors; Conrad of Erfurt, Ulrich of Hardeck and Gottfried of Hungary were shoemakers; Hans of Enns and Hermann of Mistelgen in Bavaria were smiths. Hans Simmler, Conrad of Gmünd and Johannes of Poland, on the other hand, were sons of peasants.[149] Witnesses gave conflicting evidence of their learning: one said 'some were shoemakers and some were learned';[150] another presumed they were priests because they were 'well learned';[151] another claimed he had 'never known them to read anything unless recently'.[152] Catholic critics like Stephan Bodecker, Bishop of Brandenburg, claimed that most were illiterate and relied on knowing their scriptural texts by heart.[153] Another critic pointed out that as they had few or no books of their own to show, they disparaged those written by the Fathers of the Church out of envy.[154]

The ritual by which men were admitted to the pastorate reflected the simplicity of their origins. A young chaste man whom the seniors thought fit to become a master was sent to accompany one of them on his travels for a year or two. Thereafter, at one of their meetings, which for the sake of concealment took place in towns when there was a great gathering of people, the initiate was presented to the 'council' and asked if he wished to become one of their number. He then made confession of his sins and was asked about a simple creed in seven articles. On assenting to this he was bound to perpetual chastity; to live from alms alone and not by manual labour; not to swear falsely to escape trouble if captured; and to go wherever he was sent. He was then 'ordained' by the laying-on of hands by the brethren, though it would be some years before he was allowed to hear confessions. One source claimed that masters were regularly moved from one 'circuit' of visits to another, to avoid being recognized by Catholics in their regions of activity.[155]

149 Döllinger, *Beiträge*, vol. 2, pp. 330–1.
150 Kurze, *Quellen*, p. 164.
151 Ibid., p. 111.
152 Ibid., p. 214.
153 Ibid., p. 280.
154 Döllinger, *Beiträge*, vol. 2, pp. 304, 345.
155 Ibid., pp. 368–9; Kurze, *Quellen*, p. 281. Although these details come from Catholic sources, they are plausible, given the large numbers of masters who defected to the Church around this time and may have supplied the information.

The ministry of the travelling brethren relied heavily on the support of their regular adherents in the communities which they visited. Some of the more trusted supporters escorted them round from place to place.[156] The laity gave them modest amounts of money,[157] though they seemed mystified when asked about the 'hidden treasure' which the converts of the 1360s claimed had existed.[158] Moreover, the support of the laity was needed even to identify potential converts: the brethren did not approach people on their own. Peter Zwicker described their way of dealing with a new lay follower:

> While you hide in a corner or wander about the world, old women and girls are your servants, and are accustomed to pour into others the poison which they have drawn from you. And when, after you have come back, they wish to lead the new lamb to you, you make excessive qualifications, and introduce doubts: 'look carefully to see whether that man is well disposed, otherwise I shall not admit him'. Hence it once happened, that when a certain woman did not wish to agree to make a confession, the heresiarch said to those who had brought her, 'you have brought not Rachel but Leah to me'. Peter and Paul did not do this . . .[159]

Something like this happened to Katherina Fricze when she was living in the house of 'old Heyne Vilter' at Prenzlau in the Uckermark. She fell into conversation with one of the heretic masters, but evidently did not know what she ought to say. After a brief conversation, he said 'you are a dissolute woman, go away'; though it later appeared that he heard her confession after all.[160]

Apart from their dealings with their followers, the masters seem to have led a life of simple religiosity. They reputedly fasted four times a week and prayed in an informal way seven times a day (though they are supposed to have denounced the saying of the canonical hours themselves). Like the Burgundians of the 1280s–1320s, they took pride in saying the paternoster over and over again, without the Ave Maria or the creed, as their main form of devotion.[161] There is some evidence that a few masters were seeking to celebrate a form of eucharist at this period. One source reported that at Easter one of them placed a piece of unleavened bread on a plate and some water on a spoon, blessed these and gave it to the others, then throwing the plate and spoon in the fire.[162] Zwicker

156 Kurze, *Quellen*, pp. 156, 171, 174, 228.
157 Ibid., pp. 86, 157, 162, 172, 191, 221.
158 Ibid., p. 172; cf. above, note 141.
159 Gretser, *Lucae Tudensis . . .* , in *Magna Bibliotheca*, vol. 13, pp. 314–15.
160 Kurze, *Quellen*, pp. 129–31.
161 Gretser, *Lucae Tudensis . . .* , in *Magna Bibliotheca*, vol. 13, p. 340; Döllinger, *Beiträge*, vol. 2, pp. 367–8; Kurze, *Quellen*, p. 280.
162 Gretser, *Lucae Tudensis . . .* , in *Magna Bibliotheca*, vol. 13, p. 340; Döllinger, *Beiträge*, vol. 2, p. 339.

himself was aware of some such activity, but claimed the other heresiarchs strongly disapproved of the practice.[163] Normally the masters preferred to take communion, when they took it at all, from the Catholic priesthood.[164]

One final point should be noted about the German masters, before one considers their followers. In the previous section they were shown in contact, by letter, with their counterparts in Italy.[165] Nevertheless, the brethren mentioned in the evidence from the 1390s were all German. There is no suggestion even in the fullest of the Catholic discussions that they formed part of a larger international conspiracy against the Church. Indeed, the very divisions between the different Waldensian pastorates were used in Catholic propaganda to prove that they could not be the true Church: 'these Waldenses create a monster in nature, who say that they comprise one body and yet have three heads; for some of their heresiarchs are called Romans, others Piedmontese, others Germans, nor does any of these receive authority or jurisdiction from any other, nor confess himself subject to any other.'[166]

What of the Waldensian laity? Under investigation they revealed all sorts of facets to their beliefs and practices which differed slightly from the pastors', even as they discussed their dealings with them. First of all, they explained the authority of the brethren quite differently to the 'Book of the Elect'. At least nineteen of those interrogated by Peter Zwicker in Brandenburg thought that their teachers and confessors gained authority by a direct visit to paradise. In the fullest testimony about this belief, Aleyd Takken of Baumgarten reported on 12 March 1394 that

> She had heard from a certain woman and believed, that two of these apostolic and heresiarch brethren went to hell, and heard the pitiable cries and saw the devils attacking the souls in hell and saying 'that one was an adulterer, that one a usurer, that one a tavern-haunter', and so on of all the other sorts of vice-laden souls; and afterwards they came to paradise and heard the voice of the Lord God giving them wisdom and learning, with which they were to instruct the people committed to their care on earth.[167]

Others added further details: these visits took place every seven years[168] or, one witness claimed, once a year;[169] the apostles, or an angel, or God himself, instructed them and gave them the authority to hear confessions.

163 Gretser, *Lucae Tudensis . . .* , in *Magna Bibliotheca*, vol. 13, pp. 312–13.
164 Ibid., pp. 325–6; Döllinger, *Beiträge*, vol. 2, p. 364.
165 See above, section 6.4.
166 Döllinger, *Beiträge*, vol. 2, pp. 304, 344–5.
167 Kurze, *Quellen*, p. 241.
168 Ibid., pp. 223–6, 229–32.
169 Ibid., p. 208.

This legend which circulated in Brandenburg had also been picked up by the Dominicans of Krems as early as 1315. They had learned that two Waldenses supposedly entered paradise each year to receive from Elias and Enoch the authority to bind and loose; having received this they then returned and shared this authority with their followers.[170]

The Waldenses confessed their sins to the brethren, at most once or twice a year,[171] and more commonly, for the more devout, once every one or two years.[172] In some cases lay people confessed to holding Waldensian beliefs for many decades but had confessed at intervals several years apart.[173] The youngest had begun to do so at the age of five or six,[174] but a more normal age was in adolescence, or indeed in adulthood. The pastors heard private confessions from the laity, apparently in much the same way as the priests, and assigned penances: so many days on bread and water, or bread and beer (sometimes small beer), and many times saying the paternoster (evidently in Latin).[175] One follower claimed that the penances were so heavy that he was put off the sect.[176] For the majority, however, confession seems to have been a supportive experience. Five witnesses claimed that someone who confessed to one of the heretic masters could not be damned if they should happen to die within that year.[177] This superstition offers a most interesting equivalent to the widespread popular Catholic belief that those who saw the eucharistic host could not die suddenly, i.e. without confession and absolution, within the same day; or that those who undertook 'Lady Fasts' would be safe from sudden death for the rest of their lives.[178] The brethren also preached to their followers, though the need for concealment made it difficult for numbers to attend,[179] and some confessed sins more often than they heard preachings.[180] Cecilia Bukeman of Tramburch had been

170   Nickson, ' "Pseudo-Reinerius" Treatise', p. 305.
171   Kurze, *Quellen*, pp. 79, 81–2, 85.
172   Ibid., pp. 86, 95, 97–8, 109, 135, 172.
173   Ibid., pp. 128, 185, 238–9. Heyne Melkaw (p. 185) said that for the past 16 years he had preferred going to drink beer to going to confess to the heretics.
174   Ibid., p. 162.
175   Ibid., pp. 79–80, 89 (this penance included saying the paternoster 200 times on ordinary days and 400 times on festival days), 113, 119, 130, 134, 155, 165, 176, 186, 192, 212, 219, 238, 241, 253, 256.
176   Ibid., p. 251.
177   Ibid., pp. 200, 237, 238, 247–8.
178   On techniques used to avoid sudden death, see for example E. Duffy, *The Stripping of the Altars: Traditional Religion in England, 1400–1580* (New Haven. Conn., and London, 1992), p. 100, where seeing the consecrated host at Mass gives this, and many other blessings. On Lady Fasts, regarded as 'new-fangled' in the 1400s, see P. H. Barnum (ed.), *Dives and Pauper*, vol. 1, pts 1–2, Early English Text Society, Old Series, 275, 280 (Oxford, 1976–80), pp. 172–4.
179   Kurze, *Quellen*, p. 172.
180   Ibid., pp. 79–80.

a Waldensian believer for 40 years but had not heard the pastors preach.[181]

German Waldensian heresy upheld, in theory, a rigid distinction between those who were of the sect and those who were not. As multiple witnesses reported, the Germans divided humankind into those who were 'known' of the sect, 'Die Kunden', and the rest, the unknown, 'the strangers', 'Die Fremden'.[182] The implication was that only the known were saved, and the rest were damned, as several witnesses admitted they believed. However, for at least a dozen of the Uckermark Waldenses, this stricture was too rigorous. While most continued to call Catholics 'the strangers',[183] they refused to assert that all were damned: they believed instead that Waldenses and Catholics alike would be dealt with in the hereafter according to their deeds in life.[184] So to condemn the rest of humankind went against instinct and common sense, especially given that the German Waldenses were not, unlike those in the remoter Alps, exclusively endogamous.[185] Some wives were Waldensian followers while their husbands were not.[186] The reverse also happened, though more rarely.[187] In one case a wife was deeply involved in the heresy while her husband was on the margins.[188] Uckermark Waldensianism achieved a low-key approach to survival within a suspicious but essentially forbearing popular Catholicism. It is unimaginable that Catholic spouses remained entirely ignorant of their partners' religious proclivities; but their activities were so slight, so infrequent and so harmless that they aroused little objection. This must explain how some of the heretics of northeastern Germany had lived relatively undisturbed to great ages. Mette Doerynk of Fredewalde claimed in February 1393 to be 90 years old and had been initiated into the heresy aged 16, i.e. in 1319; her parents had also been followers. Several others in their seventies and eighties had been born in the sect; Heylewyg Fricz's father was, she claimed, himself born in the sect, presumably around 1280 or 1290.[189]

181   Ibid., p. 200.
182   Gretser, *Lucae Tudensis . . .* , in *Magna Bibliotheca*, vol. 13, pp. 315, 335, 341; Kurze, *Quellen*, pp. 113, 125, 129, 131, 165, 173–7, 182, 208. The expression 'the known' can be compared to the phrase 'known men' used to describe Lollards by their own membership.
183   Though not those whose statements are found in Kurze, *Quellen*, p. 169: 'abhorruit alios nominare dy vremden', also p. 242.
184   Ibid., pp. 106, 117, 120, 152, 166, 171, 184, 193, 241, 248, 256, 260. The last statement to this effect comes from the leading lay heretic, Sybert Curaw.
185   See below, chapter 7.4.
186   Kurze, *Quellen*, pp. 80–1, 102, 132–3, 203, 209, 210: 'nec maritum induxerit, nec aliquid dixerit de secta, et quod sit malus et iurator et eam dixerit hereticam'.
187   Ibid., pp. 175, 179, 251.
188   Ibid., p. 204.
189   Ibid., pp. 138, 154; cf. pp. 104, 143, 256.

Crucial to the religious life of the lay Waldensian followers was their relationship with the official, and the popular, Catholic cult. Most inquisitorial writers elaborated the traditional thirteenth-century litany of sacraments, sacramentals and consecrations in which the Waldenses (theoretically) disbelieved.[190] It was certainly possible, on interrogation, to elicit from accused Waldenses scepticism or disbelief about many Catholic cult-objects. What is more interesting is how they actually lived and how their religious lives achieved a *modus vivendi* with Catholicism as then practised. First of all, the norm was that the Waldensian followers took communion annually from the Catholic clergy at Easter like other lay people.[191] To take one's Easter communion required one to make sacramental confession in Lent. The Waldensian followers seem to have done so; ordinarily they would omit to mention their dealings with the heretics to their priest.[192] Peter Rutling of Klein-Wubiser, unusually, claimed he had confessed to the priest that he had also made his confession to the heretics. The priest apparently replied 'what use would it be then, to confess to him?' and said nothing more about it.[193] Waldenses were, in this sense, 'minimal conformists' with popular Catholicism. Yet minimal conformity was itself a statement. Contemporary piety expected and required of people much more than bare obedience. A range of ritual gestures was expected of good Catholics while in Church, for instance towards the host or to the crucifix. Peter Zwicker remarked how he had seen many former Waldenses enter churches 'as though they were blind and mute, deaf and obstinate, like asses lacking sense'; he ascribed this to their early training.[194]

Yet the minimal conformity of the Waldenses was, for a variety of reasons, diluted by partial acceptance of Catholic teaching or prescriptions. While Waldensian theory supposedly rejected confirmation as a waste of time, several of the Uckermark followers had in fact been confirmed by their bishop.[195] A whole range of ambiguities surrounded Waldensian attitudes to the cult of saints. Waldenses were supposed not to learn the Ave Maria, the other great lay person's prayer of the age.[196]

---

190   One of the most comprehensive of such lists is in Döllinger, *Beiträge*, vol. 2, pp. 305–11.
191   See, for example, Gretser, *Lucae Tudensis . . .*, in *Magna Bibliotheca*, vol. 13, pp. 340–1; Kurze, *Quellen*, pp. 89, 113, 130. Zwicker took pains to establish that Waldensian followers had received communion in a state of imperfect penitence, i.e. having failed to disclose their heretical activities to their priests at their Lenten confession.
192   See, for example, Kurze, *Quellen*, pp. 195, 219, besides the texts cited above.
193   Ibid., p. 190.
194   Gretser, *Lucae Tudensis . . .*, in *Magna Bibliotheca*, vol. 13, pp. 329–30.
195   Kurze, *Quellen*, pp. 113, 120, 158, 221, 228, 239, 242.
196   The 'index errorum' in Gretser, *Lucae Tudensis . . .*, in *Magna Bibliotheca*, vol. 13, p. 340, claimed that Waldensian brothers and their followers did not say the Ave Maria 'unless very rarely'.

Peter Zwicker actually asked several of those he interrogated about the Ave Maria. Some tried to repeat it in the mixture of Latin and German which was evidently the local version, and made rather a mess of it;[197] others apparently 'knew it well'.[198] Some learned it at the behest of the masters for the (surely futile) purpose of dissembling heresy,[199] while another said the prayer 'from habit' although the masters had not told her to.[200] In principle, Waldensian heretics disbelieved in the intercession of saints: the idea was that the saints were so absorbed in the joy of heaven that they could not be distracted by the prayers of mortals, and therefore prayer was to be directed only to God.[201] Yet in practice a significant number of confessed heretics actually prayed to saints, whether from habit or to appear more Catholic.[202] Some half-dozen suspected Waldenses claimed that they believed in the power of the Virgin Mary to intercede and prayed to her, but not to the other saints.[203] In late fourteenth-century Germany ordinary Christians were encouraged in the cult of saints by being assigned one of the apostles as a sort of personal patron saint, whose days the individual would celebrate with special devotion.[204] Waldenses were, logically enough, supposed to reject this custom.[205] Yet nearly twenty of those whom Zwicker questioned in c.1392–4 had chosen an apostle and could name him.[206] Some, it would seem, followed Catholic practice but *interpreted* it in a heterodox way: fasting and feasting on the saints' days, but 'in honour of God only'.[207] One woman actually believed that only her apostle St Bartholomew could pray for her, because she had chosen him before entering the sect.[208]

197 Kurze, *Quellen*, pp. 97, 99, 227. These stumbling versions are sometimes taken (e.g. Audisio, *Les 'Vaudois'*, pp. 110–11) as evidence that the Ave was learned purely for dissimulation rather than devotion. That inference assumes that all lay Catholics would have been able to repeat a prayer partly or wholly in Latin with exemplary accuracy.
198 Kurze, *Quellen*, pp. 237, 239.
199 Ibid., pp. 159, 241, 246.
200 Ibid., p. 134.
201 For example, ibid., pp. 80, 113, 117, 120, 130, 148, and elsewhere.
202 Ibid., pp. 82, 85, 169 (where the accused prayed to saints 'from habit'), 177, 195 (where the accused only believed her 'apostle' could pray for her), 199. Peter Beyer, ibid., pp. 172–3, disbelieved in the intercession of saints but fasted and feasted in their honour to avoid being conspicuous.
203 Ibid., pp. 124, 145, 159, 178, 226–7.
204 This seems to have been a regional variation of the cults of saints found everywhere in Catholic Europe; see B. Hamilton, *Religion in the Medieval West* (London, 1986), pp. 124–6.
205 Gretser, *Lucae Tudensis . . .*, in *Magna Bibliotheca*, vol. 13, p. 341, para. 36; Döllinger, *Beiträge*, vol. 2, p. 309. The first of these texts admits that the Waldenses followed the custom, but only as a pretence.
206 Kurze, *Quellen*, pp. 99 (where the apostle was assigned by the inquisitor), 113–14, 120, 148, 161, 169–71, 178, 183, 195, 199, 210, 212, 219, 238–40, 260.
207 For example, ibid., pp. 148, 161, 210.
208 Ibid., p. 212.

By the later fourteenth century popular Catholicism had become in certain respects more elaborate: more voluntary co-operation with the fashionable cults was expected of the Catholic faithful. Inquisitors' treatises and their formulae for interrogations all attest that the Waldenses' reluctance to become involved in this proliferation of (ostensibly voluntary) devotion marked them out from the majority more and more. They apparently showed contempt and derision for processions, like the ever more popular Corpus Christi processions, calling them ridiculous trifles.[209] An Austrian document from 1395 cited their disapproval of Corpus Christi and rogation-tide processions, together with all the flowers, clothing and candles used on these occasions. Similarly, they were said to despise the most fashionable relics of the era, the wood of the true cross and the other relics of the passion, the holy shroud, the holy places and the apostles' chains.[210] They were alleged to object to the congregational singing known as 'Den Leyse'.[211] It was the scope of popular Catholicism that had increased, not the depth of Waldensian hostility to it.

In some areas at least, however, the expansion of cult-objects available to the laity eroded the traditional scepticism of Waldensian followers. Holy water was dispensed by the Church as a means to wash away venial sins, and to confer blessings and exorcisms on people, places and things.[212] It also accrued around itself a wide range of superstitious beliefs and practices. Holy water was probably the most popular of an array of consecrated objects, including holy bread and salt, palms, candles and herbs, grouped under the name of sacramentals. These, because they were accessible to and regularly used by the laity, may actually have bulked larger in ordinary Catholics' religious and para-religious lives than the sacraments themselves.[213] The Waldenses of the Uckermark quite

209   Gretser, *Lucae Tudensis*..., in *Magna Bibliotheca*, vol. 13, p. 341, para. 15; compare M. Rubin, *Corpus Christi: The Eucharist in Late Medieval Culture* (Cambridge, 1991), pp. 243–71.
210   Döllinger, *Beiträge*, vol. 2, pp. 308–10, 333–4; compare C. Zika, 'Hosts, Processions and Pilgrimages: Controlling the Sacred in Fifteenth-century Germany', *Past and Present* 118 (1988), pp. 25–64.
211   Kurze, *Quellen*, pp. 156, 165, 198–9, 201, 206, 208, 212, 258; cf. Gretser, *Lucae Tudensis*..., in *Magna Bibliotheca*, vol. 13, pp. 326, 340; Döllinger, *Beiträge*, vol. 2, p. 338.
212   For a late medieval instance of the use of holy water, see for example J. Nider, *Formicarius*, bk. v, ed. as *De Maleficis et eorum deceptionibus* in H. Institoris and J. Sprenger, *Malleus Maleficarum* (Frankfurt, 1582), pp. 703, 725–6, 740, 775, where the use of holy water in exorcism is liberally documented.
213   The best recent discussion of *sacramentalia* is R. W. Scribner, 'Ritual and Popular Belief in Catholic Germany at the Time of the Reformation', *Journal of Ecclesiastical History* 35 (1984), pp. 47–77. A rich late medieval description of *sacramentalia* and their uses is offered by Martin Plantsch, *Opusculum de sagis maleficis* (Phorce, 1507), sigs f i^r–g i^v.

often admitted to using holy water, though a variety of reasons are given for this. Some said that they used it to avoid being remarked upon, denying it had any spiritual power.[214] Two accused said that they made more use of holy water in summer than in winter, to cool their faces rather than wash away sins: this statement has the ring of a defiant public utterance of disbelief, and may have been something Waldenses said to each other.[215] Most intriguingly, though, two otherwise well-informed Waldensian followers, who refused to believe in the power of holy water to wash away sins, nevertheless thought that the consecration it received must have made some difference, since (they said) holy water did not go stale as quickly as other water.[216] They would not believe the orthodox Catholic teaching, but they would subscribe to the popular superstition which encrusted it.[217] Some heretics were actually ready to combine two belief-systems, insisting that they believed in the power of sacramentals even though they knew that the leaders of the heresy taught otherwise.[218] As with holy water, sometimes popular practice proved more tenacious than orthodox teaching: the ancient Heylewyg Fricz of Prenzlau, after a long lifetime spent in Waldensian belief, denied the spiritual power of sacramentals, but put palms on the fire in bad weather 'like other people', presumably in the expectation that the smoke from consecrated palms would calm storms.[219]

On two issues some of the Uckermark Waldenses defied the advice of their heretic confessors and incorporated Catholic conduct into their lives for more than just concealment or public decency. Several people insisted that they had been on pilgrimages to shrines and earned indulgences there, despite the advice of the Waldensian leadership to the contrary.[220] Much more significant, in the light of contemporary preoccupations, was the attitude taken towards the cult of the dead. In principle, Waldenses disbelieved in purgatory and treated with derision

---

214   Kurze, *Quellen*, pp. 86, 157, 173, 210.
215   Ibid., pp. 92, 160; cf. also p. 169.
216   Ibid., pp. 120, 223.
217   The belief that holy water remained fresh for longer than ordinary water is not of the essence of Catholic teaching, though it was widely believed. See, for example, Franciscus de Osuna, *Flagellum Diaboli, oder Dess Teufels Gaisl, darin gar lustig und artlich gehandelt wird: Von der Macht uund Gewalt dess boesen Feindts: von den effecten und Wirckungen der Zauberer / Unholdter und Hexenmaister* . . . (Munich, 1602), f. 40ᵛ, which argues fulsomely in favour of holy water against Protestant sceptics, alleging its incorruptibility as one of the proofs.
218   Kurze, *Quellen*, pp. 155 (where the ancient Mette Doerynk argued for her right to hold two contradictory beliefs!), 161, 198.
219   Ibid., pp. 138–9.
220   Ibid., pp. 143, 209–10, but cf. p. 155, where it was claimed that pilgrimages were encouraged as a means of concealment. The sources are contradictory on this point.

the elaborate apparatus by which the Church offered service to God for the liberation of souls from pain: it was needless for the saved in heaven and useless for the damned in hell. There were only two ways out of this world, to paradise or hell.[221] Jakob Welsaw of Prenzlau said graphically in 1392 that praying for the dead was like putting food in front of a dead horse.[222] Yet when one collates the statements made about prayers for the dead in purgatory, the prevailing impression is that the Waldenses' denials produced in their followers a confused muddle of opinions. Katherina Huter could not accept the teaching that there was no purgatory, 'because those who were not fully good could not come to heaven'.[223] Two people testified that they prayed for their parents when the priests told them to, but not otherwise.[224] Cuene Gyrswalde and Gyrdrud Cremer both thought there were only two ways after death, but still prayed for God to take mercy on the departed.[225] Cuene Hutvilter made offerings for masses for the dead 'to benefit souls', claiming additionally that the heretic pastors encouraged this as a concealment.[226] Sybe and Mette Hutvilter of Bernwalde, while they believed in 'two ways', 'nevertheless hoped for purgatory', which suggests considerable ambiguity, or simply remembering the pastors' slogans without always accepting their implications.[227] Katherina Sachze dedicated her pilgrimage to Rome for the liberation of her father's soul, notwithstanding what the heretics had taught her about prayers for the dead.[228]

There is no doubt whatever about Waldensian teaching on this subject. The point, though, is that the message handed out by the heretic confessors ran up against the powerful instinct, sedulously cultivated in popular Catholicism, to do the best one could for one's departed relatives and family. The heretic followers who made these contradictory or confused statements were not marginal or ignorant members of the movement; on the contrary, their beliefs were explored by Zwicker in such detail precisely because they were thought to be especially important members of the heretical community. They exemplify, it is suggested, a phenomenon which was probably present in popular Waldensianism from the very first, but which is only detectable from the

221 For example, ibid., pp. 80, 98, 170, 186, 195.
222 Ibid., p. 96.
223 Ibid., p. 87.
224 Ibid., pp. 98, 113.
225 Ibid., pp. 128, 139.
226 Ibid., p. 148, and cf. p. 155.
227 Ibid., pp. 120, 166; cf. also p. 145: '. . . solum due vie essent, attamen crediderit purgatorium post mortem'.
228 Ibid., p. 210; on this subject see also p. 179, where Hennyng Fricze gave 8 marks to the Waldensian brethren from his deceased wife's property 'so that they might pray to God for her'. For further evidence of confusion see pp. 188, 196, 198, 239.

middle of the fourteenth century, when records of sufficient detail become available.[229] Lay followers of the Waldenses had, in effect, to *negotiate* within themselves a position *vis-à-vis* both Catholicism and heresy. With such intermittent contact between heretic confessors and their followers, religion became a matter of personal decision and instinct. While some followers accepted the confessors' 'negative faith' wholesale,[230] others might be resolutely ignorant of most of its teachings;[231] some would carve out for themselves a complex and internally contradictory hotchpotch of beliefs.[232] Some would even devise for themselves purely private theologies, significantly different from the characteristic teachings of the movement. Andreas Hesel, a heretic from the Austrian heartlands of Waldensianism tried by Peter Zwicker, disbelieved in baptism, because if it worked the recipient ought not to be harmed by wild beasts; disbelieved the real presence, because if it were true Christ's body would long since have been entirely eaten up by the faithful; and thought that monasticism was an error and it would please God if someone fathered a child on a nun.[233]

To think so hard about religious things as the Waldensian followers did, was not the mark of a careless or negligent conscience. The Waldenses maintained the high standards of morality and restraint for which they had been noted for over a century. Peter Zwicker, in his treatise *Cum Dormirent Homines* ('While men slept, the enemy came and sowed tares . . .'), attested to this in the most striking fashion. He blamed the heretic confessors and teachers for stealing away the best of Christians, instead of trying to reform the worst:

> When Christ said 'you are the light of the world' he said that your words and deeds should enlighten hearts across the world, which you Waldensian heretic do not do: you do not go out into the world, you do not preach to great sinners, to the litigious, fornicators, deceivers, thieves, robbers, drunkards, leaders of dances, usurers, rapists, and other criminals; you only draw to yourselves those whom you have heard are peaceful, quiet, silent, composed, who but for you would remain sons of the kingdom . . . [you are] like the wolf which commonly seizes the fattest sheep of the flock.[234]

Zwicker's frustration resonates through this passage. The Waldensian followers' religious zeal, if guided within orthodox channels, would have

229 Compare the equally nuanced and at times confusing evidence from the Alps, as below, chapter 7.4.
230 For example, Peter Beyer of Bernwalde, in Kurze, *Quellen*, pp. 171–4, or Sophia, in ibid., pp. 219–20.
231 Such as Heyne Melkaw, in ibid., p. 185, or Hans Kukeler, ibid., pp. 247–8.
232 Esp. Mette Doerynk, ibid., pp. 154–5 and Tylss Smet, ibid., p. 186.
233 Döllinger, *Beiträge*, vol. 2, pp. 343–4.
234 Gretser, *Lucae Tudensis . . .*, in *Magna Bibliotheca*, vol. 13, p. 314.

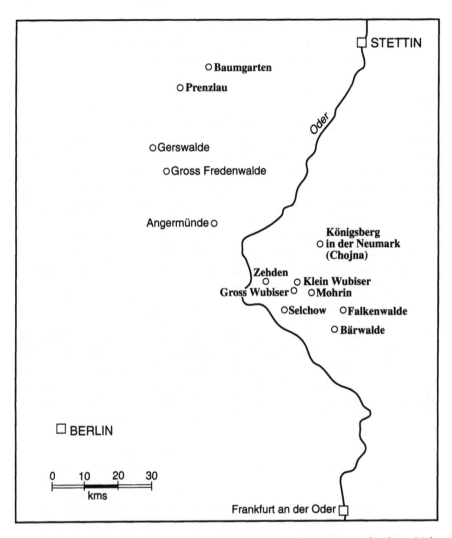

Map III Waldensian communities in northeastern Germany in the late 14th century.

gratified the wishes of the most ambitious reforming preacher. Yet because of their (often inherited) antipathy to the claims of the Church, they were criminalized. In this light Zwicker's zeal to make converts at all costs makes considerable sense.

The Waldenses, as Johannes Nider would remark a few decades later, still made themselves conspicuous by the purity of their language. Several repeated the long-standing refusal not only to swear an oath by the truth, but even to utter the word 'treuen' ('verily' or 'forsooth'!).[235] Some were becoming more relaxed, allowing 'treuen' to strengthen a true statement, or at least regarding it as a much lesser sin.[236] Nonetheless, 'swearers could not enter heaven';[237] 'one should not take a wife who swears'.[238] Given Nider's remarks on the habitual profanity of contemporary Catholics, this fastidiousness of utterance must have shouted out the presence of Waldenses to all around.

6.6   Prosecution and Persuasion:
The Late Fourteenth-century Inquisitions

The campaign against heresy in late fourteenth-century Germany was a complex affair, involving numerous officials acting under different juris-dictions. It is not possible, in the surviving state of the evidence, to es-tablish precise itineraries for the leading inquisitors of the period, Peter Zwicker, Martin of Amberg and Heinrich Angermeier. We know that Peter Zwicker was active in Erfurt in 1391, in Stettin during 1392–4, in Austria in 1395 and again in 1398, and further east around the turn of the century.[239] Around the same period there were trials in Mainz (1390) and Augsburg (1393).[240] Numerous heretics were certainly dealt with by local tribunals, though these may have relied on evidence supplied by specialist itinerant inquisitors.[241] What does seem clear from all the evidence is that the inquisitors who targeted Waldenses at this period were travelling investigative judges, who usually took care to obtain episcopal sanction for their actions but were not specifically invited to carry out their work by the local bishops.[242] For these men, converting

---

235   Ibid., p. 341; Kurze, *Quellen*, pp. 117, 131, 190, 198.
236   Ibid., pp. 120, 127, 177, and for regarding the word as a 'lesser sin', ibid., pp. 148. Peter Oestrycher (ibid., p. 251), often 'swore trwen' to avoid notice.
237   Ibid., p. 223.
238   Ibid., p. 228.
239   The evidence left by these can be seen for instance in Preger, *Beiträge*, pp. 246ff.; Döllinger, *Beiträge*, vol. 2, pp. 305ff., 330, 346ff.; Kieckhefer, *Repression*, p. 55.
240   Döllinger, *Beiträge*, vol. 2, pp. 620–1, 363–4.
241   Kieckhefer, *Repression*, pp. 55–7 and references.
242   On Zwicker in Poznan diocese, see Kurze, *Quellen*, pp. 235ff.

heretics seems to have been a personal passion and vocation: this emerges not only from the formal records, but even more clearly from their writings.

The sheer numbers of Waldensian masters and followers won over at this period testify to the extraordinary dedication and remarkable success of the inquisitors. Zwicker himself claimed in 1395 that 'within the space of two years, in Thuringia, the Mark [Brandenburg], Bohemia and Moravia, around a thousand Waldensian heretics were converted to the Catholic faith'. In Austria and Hungary it was hoped that more than a thousand of their followers would be 'taken from the jaws of Leviathan'.[243] Another treatise of the same period remarked that 'Brother Peter [Zwicker] within the space of one year called back to the faith around six hundred of these heretics'.[244] Some time in the 1390s a list was prepared of around twenty leading Waldenses, mostly brethren or masters of the movement, who had converted to Catholicism: their names, and in at least one case their conversion, can be corroborated by other documents.[245] These converts then, in turn, revealed the names of their followers in detail. In a specimen questionnaire, devised by the inquisitors for use with the friends and followers of the confessors, it was taken for granted that the person under interrogation had been identified by a convert: if the accused claimed to be ignorant as to why he or she was captured and interrogated, the inquisitor was to say that by the information 'of certain secret masters, to whom in your simplicity you have confided' he or she had erred from the faith.[246] So thoroughly were the convert masters trusted, that five of them, Johannes of Vienna, Nicolaus Gottschalck 'of Brandenburg', Friedrich of Hardeck, Heinrich of Engellstadt and Peter of the Siebenbürgen, were received into the Catholic priesthood: this was something which had not even happened to Durand of Osca.[247] In the case of Nicolaus Gottschalck from Königsberg we can date his conversion quite precisely. He was still hearing the confessions of Waldensian followers in the autumn of 1392;[248] by 10 December of that year he was referred to as 'the heresiarch now converted at Prague';[249] on the 23rd of the same month his sister Geze described him as 'now a Catholic priest living in Vienna'.[250] One must envisage Gottschalck's conversion as a major coup for Zwicker.

243   Gretser, *Lucae Tudensis* . . . , in *Magna Bibliotheca*, vol. 13, pp. 315–16; Kurze, *Quellen*, pp. 261–2.
244   Gretser, *Lucae Tudensis* . . . , in *Magna Bibliotheca*, vol. 13, p. 335.
245   Döllinger, *Beiträge*, vol. 2, pp. 330–1.
246   Gretser, *Lucae Tudensis* . . . , in *Magna Bibliotheca*, vol. 13, p. 341.
247   Döllinger, *Beiträge*, vol. 2, p. 330.
248   Kurze, *Quellen*, pp. 166, 192.
249   Ibid., p. 99.
250   Ibid., p. 109.

All the indications are that his information, as one of the masters who had most regularly visited the followers in the Uckermark, enabled Zwicker to gather them all in, despite their being scattered among many villages, with exceptional accuracy and efficiency.

How were the inquisitors, Zwicker especially, regarded by the followers, to whom no such blandishment as priestly ordination could be offered? Some of the heretic followers were evidently angered and horrified by the inquisitor's proceedings. When Fikke of Gross-Wubiser arrived in the village of Klein-Wubiser bearing a letter of summons to the parish priest on Zwicker's behalf, he was surrounded in threatening fashion by half-a-dozen of the leading Waldenses of the village. The local magistrate Jakob Hokman, whose attitude to heresy seems to have been oddly ambivalent, appointed the chief local heretic, Sybert Curaw, to look after the messenger, in effect suppressing the letters. He nevertheless ensured that the second set of letters of citation were duly read.[251] Some two years later the heretics of Steyr were even more threatening: they burned down the barn of the parish priest of Steyr, in punishment for his receiving an inquisitor, presumably Zwicker, to stay with him. They also attached some burned wood and a bleeding knife shaped out of wood to the town gates at Steyr, an obvious threat of further violence.[252]

Yet, quite unlike the events in the Alps a century later, there is little or no mention of actual violence between people during these inquisitions. The heretics' followers were scattered individuals and family groups rather than entire communities, so the use of extreme force from either side was not really appropriate. Quite extraordinarily, there is some evidence to suggest that Zwicker actually made some friends among the heretic communities. Gyrdrud Melsaw of Klein-Wubiser testified in February 1393 that Sybert Curaw and others were preventing most of the village from going to the inquisitor: he had sarcastically suggested that she should bear Zwicker a child. Notwithstanding, she said that she considered divorcing herself from her husband 'when he came back praising the inquisitor'.[253] Zwicker's methods divided the community; and some who went to see him early on were surprised to discover how lenient and gentle he was.

Zwicker's leniency went well beyond the bounds allowed by canon law. In principle, and usually in practice, heretics who were obstinate or repeated offenders were not supposed to receive mercy, but to be handed over to the secular arm for burning.[254] Yet a woman named Sophia had

---

251 Ibid., pp. 233–4; cf. pp. 170–1. The syntax of the records where this incident is described is somewhat confusing and unclear.
252 Döllinger, *Beiträge*, vol. 2, pp. 311, and cf. pp. 305–6.
253 Kurze, *Quellen*, pp. 167–8.
254 For the canonical rule that second offenders should be burned, see for example B. Hamilton, *The Medieval Inquisition* (London, 1981), pp. 54–6.

been inducted some fifty years previously by another woman who was burned for heresy. Sophia's husband Hans Myndeke had been burned in Angermünde; she herself only escaped burning because of her pregnancy. Notwithstanding all this Zwicker accepted her abjuration and absolved her on 9 February 1394.[255] In Austria during 1398 Zwicker dealt with three exceptionally stubborn heretics: one of them had perjured himself; another had been absolved under the earlier inquisitor Heinrich of Olmütz; later he had accepted a penitential cross but abandoned it, and prevaricated when asked to swear an oath; a third absolutely refused to swear before the inquisitor, opening herself to the charge of obstinacy. All of these received public and humiliating penances, but their lives were spared.[256]

Why, then, was Peter Zwicker so effective? Clearly, he did not achieve his ends by terrifying his victims into submission, as Bernard Gui may have done. The anti-Waldensian literature written at this time, especially Zwicker's own *Cum Dormirent*, suggests that he used persuasion and preaching. He integrated his arguments skilfully with those used by the convert masters of thirty years earlier, whose writings he clearly knew, so as to weaken the resolve of the masters first, and then their followers. Zwicker dissected the version of Waldensian history contained in the 'Book of the Elect'. The Waldenses claimed that eight hundred years after the Church lost its holiness through Pope Sylvester's acceptance of possessions, Petrus of Walden and Johannes from Lyon tried to renew the apostolic life. Yet they also claimed that Petrus Waldensis was a priest: if the Church had lost its holiness under Sylvester, who, by their reckoning, was left on earth to give Petrus the true priesthood?[257]

The supposedly apostolic quality of the heretic master's mission was attacked even more strongly for its secrecy and furtive quality. As another inquisitorial treatise commented, picking up the words of a convert master from the 1360s, the truth does not seek corners to hide in.[258] Yet the heretic masters, despite claiming that only their sect were saved, were careful not to reveal its contents to any of whose loyalty they had the slightest doubt. They imposed similar secrecy on their followers: 'sons hide it from their parents, sometimes parents from children, brother from brother, sister from sister, and such people you knowingly (according to your opinion) allow to be condemned. Therefore you are all damned.'[259] A third treatise from Zwicker's circle contrasted Jesus's teaching daily in

255 Kurze, *Quellen*, p. 220.
256 Döllinger, *Beiträge*, vol. 2, pp. 346–51.
257 Gretser, *Lucae Tudensis*..., in *Magna Bibliotheca*, vol. 13, pp. 312–13; cf. Biller, 'Aspects', pp. 286, 325.
258 Gretser, *Lucae Tudensis*..., in *Magna Bibliotheca*, vol. 13, p. 334; cf. Biller, 'Aspects', p. 331.
259 Gretser, *Lucae Tudensis*..., in *Magna Bibliotheca*, vol. 13, p. 315.

the temple, with the heretics teaching at night, in chambers, solars, granaries and store-rooms behind closed doors.[260] They did not stay with their flocks like good shepherds, but took to flight and left their followers to their troubles.[261]

Zwicker was also unafraid to engage the Waldenses in debate over their doctrines: the homely and graphic quality of his imagery suggests strongly that he may have done so from the pulpit as well as on paper. He confronted the Donatist argument that the priests' sins deprived them of spiritual authority. Even if priests were 'fornicators, usurers, and tavern-haunters' they were still priests: a pure layman, on the other hand, no matter how holy, would not dare to touch the body of Christ. What mattered was the holiness of the sacrament itself, rather than the holiness of the person administering it. 'A rose glows just as much in the hands of an emperor as of a polluted woman'; 'a pearl is as beautiful in the hands of a king or a peasant'. 'My servant cleans the stable just as well with a rusty iron fork as with one made of gold and studded with precious stones.' What was more, Zwicker argued, the Waldensian confessors when speaking to their followers habitually blackened the entire priesthood with the faults of one perverse priest. They said no good of good priests, though they said bad things about bad ones. They could not deny there were many good priests, and, for that matter, many criminous people among both their leaders and followers.[262] As another treatise pointed out, if the efficacy of the sacraments depended on the goodness of the priest, no one would even know whether he had been baptized: one could not be certain of one's own goodness, far less of anyone else's.[263]

A similarly homely set of arguments defended the Catholic doctrine of purgatory and all that it entailed. The Waldenses might say that there were 'two ways' and in a sense this was true: 'suppose that a king tells everyone with good eyesight to go to Jerusalem and everyone who is totally blind to go to Babylon; and those with slightly foggy eyesight to go to Rome and stay there until their eyes clear, and then to go to Jerusalem: in this there are three ways, but eventually only two end destinations, Jerusalem and Babylon.' It was false to argue that there were no such things as slight sins which needed expiation, and that all sins were mortal; one does not throw away a costly vessel because of a little flaw, or discard clothing which is slightly stained: one cleans and repairs it.[264]

260 Ibid., p. 335.
261 Ibid., pp. 315–16; cf. Biller, 'Aspects', p. 321.
262 Gretser, *Lucae Tudensis* . . . , in *Magna Bibliotheca*, vol. 13, p. 316.
263 Ibid., p. 335.
264 Ibid., pp. 320–1, 339–40.

The inquisitors were perhaps on strongest ground when they appealed to the contemporary culture which laid such stress on the cult of saints. It was an insult to the saints to claim that they were indifferent to the concerns of humankind: there was 'joy in heaven over the sinner who repented'. In particular, the inquisitors made a great deal of the Waldenses' neglect of the cult of the Virgin Mary:

> So oh you pitiful and wretched Waldensian heretics, who never say 'blessed and chaste mother of God' since you think she is unconscious and deaf; rather, as though she were unworthy, you do not bless her, though she herself said, 'all generations shall call me blessed'. It is clear therefore that you are not generations but corruptions, and the worst of corrupters.

If to take pity on us would make her wretched, how could she be a mother of mercy?[265]

There was much more to these arguments than homely imagery. Zwicker sprinkled his text with liberal citations from scripture, and familiar scholastic arguments, deployed with some erudition as well as rhetorical skill (though his defence of the legitimacy of swearing was somewhat sophistical).[266] He worked through all the characteristic Waldensian rejections of the Catholic cult in considerable detail. What is different from earlier treatises, however, is first, Zwicker's understanding of the heretics' own dilemmas, based on evident familiarity with the arguments ventilated in 1368; and second, the use of concrete imagery and everyday logic to persuade readers and, presumably, hearers. Had Waldensian heresy turned away from the assumptions behind 'Holy Church' more consistently, as Protestant theologians would later do, his arguments might not have held water so effectively. However, the Waldenses lived in the same world as the Catholics, characterized by ritual penance and mediated holiness. When an unusually clear-sighted and merciful opponent confronted their internal inconsistencies and offered them a way back to the Church, very large numbers of them took it.

6.7 The German Waldenses meet the Hussite Movement

Waldensian heresy by at least the fourteenth century had spread east into Bohemia and the Brandenburg Mark, with the settlements of German townspeople in the Slavic lands of Eastern Europe. In the first decades of the fifteenth century the old assumption, that there were German heretics living among Catholic Slavs, was abruptly turned on its head. In

265   Ibid., pp. 317–18, 337.
266   Ibid., pp. 331–2, and cf. Kurze, *Quellen*, pp. 282–5 for Stefan Bodecker's version of the argument.

Prague two movements coalesced to form what was first an academic and religious protest, and which then became a multifaceted national revolution, the Hussite movement. The two movements which shaped it at Prague were, first, the succession of moralistic reforming preachers who denounced the evils and excesses of the ecclesiastical hierarchy to a listening populace (as did many other such preachers, not least in the era of the Great Schism); and second, the intellectual protest in which Czech masters in the Carolinum university at Prague reacted against the prevailing German nominalist scholasticism by embracing a realist philosophy and concept of the Church, based at least in part on some of the writings of John Wyclif. These movements merged above all in the person of Jan Hus. The Fathers of the Council of Constance, in a desperate attempt to prove their own ecclesial orthodoxy in a very shaky legal situation, burned Hus as a heretic in 1415. In the wake of Hus's execution, movements of religious protest and reform sprang up in Prague and elsewhere in Bohemia. These varied from the socially and religiously conservative Utraquist party, to the social radicalism of the preacher Jan Zelivsky among the Prague artisans, and the rural, communal millenarianism which established itself at Tábor. These movements swept the Catholic hierarchy aside so effectively that the Czech Church remained in a unique, anomalous position up to the Reformation era and beyond.[267]

What does the story of the Hussite revolution have to do with that of the medieval Waldensian movements? The issue of their interrelation is complex and controversial, and must be approached from several angles, not all of which yield satisfactory conclusions. First, there has been a long and profoundly inconclusive debate as to how far the Waldensian presence in Bohemia influenced, or contributed to, the success of the Hussite movements and Taboritism in particular. It is best to dispose of this issue relatively briefly. After the inquisitions of Gallus von Neuhaus between the 1330s and the 1350s, there is very little evidence indeed of what happened to the German-speaking Waldenses in the towns of Bohemia and Moravia. It was, at any rate, among the German-speaking artisan townspeople that Waldensianism was most prevalent. It is in the highest degree improbable that Waldensianism in any way inspired the reform preaching of the Prague clergy; it is even more unlikely, if possible, that it contributed to the nationalistic Czech philosophical realism of the university masters, anxious as they were to establish both their orthodoxy and their

---

267 The most recent discussion of the Hussite movement in English is T. A. Fudge, *The Magnificent Ride: The First Reformation in Hussite Bohemia*, St Andrews Studies in Reformation History (Aldershot, 1998). Earlier studies include R. R. Betts, *Essays in Czech History* (London, 1969); H. Kaminsky, *A History of the Hussite Revolution* (Berkeley and Los Angeles, 1967); F. Šmahel, *La Révolution hussite, une anomalie historique* (Paris, 1985).

distinctness from the Germans.[268] Where Waldensian sentiments *may* have played a role is in the gathering of supporters for the communities at Tábor and elsewhere. This point can never be resolved satisfactorily one way or the other. However, it should be noted that the fervent expectation of the end of the world, the drastic revisions of liturgical practice and social expectations, which were features of Tábor, must have made anything like the memory of previous Waldensian heresy seem pallid and insignificant by comparison.[269]

There is a second way to look at the question. As Hussite theology developed, it had to confront the consequences and implications of its rejection of the claims to spiritual jurisdiction of the Roman hierarchy. In the circumstances of a furious critique of the wealth, pomp and ostentation of Catholic prelates such as the Hussites made, might not arguments drawn from the Waldensian tradition have proved useful? Amedeo Molnár has made something of the fact that a sermon preached by the Hussite theologian Jakoubek of Stribro in 1415 envisaged a Church which rejected the consequences of the supposed Donation of Constantine, in terms which seemed to recall those of the 'Book of the Elect' and the 'Letter of the Italian Brethren' sent to Austria in the late 1360s.[270] In truth, the legend of Constantine and Sylvester was part and parcel of medieval religious folklore, and short of very good textual or historical reasons for positing a connection, one should beware of drawing too much from it.[271]

Similarly doubtful is the thread which has been drawn between the Waldenses and the society of Nicolaus of Dresden and his friends. These were a group of students who moved from Saxony to Prague in 1411, and contributed a denial of purgatory and a refusal to take ceremonial oaths to the ferment of ideas in contemporary Bohemia. These German students worked at something of a tangent to the early Hussites. Nicolaus of Dresden disagreed with the Prague masters and returned to Germany, where he was captured and burned at Meissen in 1417. In the same year the Prague academics tried to flush out of southern Bohemia some radical religious reformism; in the wake of that assertion of author-

268 Even Gonnet and Molnar, *Vaudois au moyen âge*, pp. 211–13, which otherwise maximizes the links between Waldensianism and Hussitism, agrees with this point.
269 The issue of whether Waldensianism influenced popular Hussitism is discussed, with full bibliographical references, in Fudge, *Magnificent Ride*, pp. 37–41. Fudge notes how several protagonists in this debate have changed their views over time. On this topic see also the article by F. Šmahel, 'Crypto- et semi-vaudois dans la Bohême hussite', in *Revue de l'histoire des religions*, vol. 217, fasc. 1 (2000), pp. 101–20.
270 Gonnet and Molnar, *Vaudois au moyen âge*, pp. 218–20; on these texts see above, notes 116ff.
271 Compare also Gonnet and Molnar, *Vaudois au moyen âge*, pp. 234–5, on Chelcicky's use of the Sylvester legend.

ity others of Nicolaus of Dresden's group, notably Bartholomaeus Rautenstock and Johann Draendorf, left Bohemia for Germany. Rautenstock and Draendorf travelled around as itinerant preachers and were soon executed as heretics at Nuremberg and Heidelberg respectively.[272] Attempts have also been made to trace Waldensian elements in the thought of early Taborite theologians. In truth the Taborite movement was fecund in ideas of its own, some of which (like its apocalyptic expectations and desire to build the new Jerusalem by military victory) were both spectacular and far removed from the experience of the secretive Waldensian brotherhoods. Taboritism had little need to learn from the Waldenses; and such things as *did* resemble Waldensian teachings could as easily have been discovered independently, through a literalist reading of the Bible.[273]

The question of Waldensian and Hussite contacts acquires greater reality when one moves on beyond the heroic period of the revolution of the 1420s and the ensuing Hussite wars. A third means of contact between Waldenses and Hussites would have been the opposite of those considered so far, namely, that Waldensian preachers may have been 'drawn in' to the orbit of the Hussite movement at its peak of expansion, and acquired Hussite qualities. Here the lines of influence would run from the new heresy to the old, rather than the reverse. This appears to have happened in the case of the German Hussite leader Friedrich Reiser (*c*.1402–58). Reiser's life and career is known largely through the story which emerged when he was tried for heresy.[274] He was the son of Konrad Reiser, a Waldensian 'follower' and merchant of Donauwörth who had briefly known the English Wycliffite Peter Payne. Friedrich met Payne himself at Nuremberg in 1418; in the early 1420s he moved to Switzerland and worked as both a travelling merchant and an itinerant Waldensian pastor. In 1429 he moved to Prague, possibly working as a servant in an inn in the university district. He acquired a German Bible and became, in effect, a travelling Hussite missionary.

Concern about Hussite activity appears to have led to the persecution of the Waldensian communities of Freiburg im Uechtland (Fribourg) in Switzerland in 1429–30. An inquisitor had already tried unsuccessfully to bring these people to heel in 1399. On that occasion they denied all heresies and were released. In 1429–30 the inquisitor Ulric de Torrenté OP of Lausanne interrogated over seventy people. These were centred around a group of merchant families, especially the Praroman and Bonvisin, who received visits from German-speaking heretic pastors from the eastern fringes of the Germanic world, in the kingdom of Bohemia. The Freiburg Waldenses appear to have included some French-speakers,

272 Ibid., pp. 220–8.
273 Ibid., pp. 229–39.
274 The sources for this are found in ibid., pp. 239–53 and references.

who were not always comfortable with the German language of their pastors. Nevertheless, they had no links with the meridional Waldenses of the Dauphiné or Piedmont, though some knew of their existence. They denied the reality of purgatory, and left gifts to the poor in their wills rather than founding obit masses. Friedrich Reiser had visited Freiburg in 1420 and stayed with Mermet Hugo there. His contacts seem to have inspired a hope among the Freiburg Waldenses that a great uprising led by the Hussites would change their world and overthrow the Church.[275] Reiser's position as a Hussite missionary leader was established on some sort of formal basis in the early 1430s. In autumn 1431 the Taborite theologian Nicholas of Pelhrimov, named 'bishop' of the Taborites, consecrated Reiser and Johan of Wallachia as missionary priests. While on a visit to the Council of Basel in 1433, it is possible that Reiser was consecrated as a sort of bishop. He subsequently used the title of 'bishop of the faithful in the Roman Church who scorn the Donation of Constantine'. His key belief seems to have been that the Roman Church was irretrievably lapsed since its acceptance of worldly wealth and power, and a minority tradition must supplant it in preaching the pure gospel.

Subsequent to the defeat of the Taborites at the battle of Lipany in 1434, the Taborite movement lost much of its autonomy and was partly subsumed within orthodox Hussitism. Reiser was in a manner left high and dry. Nevertheless, in 1450 he revived his preaching ministry: he organized missions into German lands from a safe base in Bohemia, and provided for meetings of the leadership at three-year intervals. He is known to have laid hands on at least six followers, who continued his mission. He and his group visited heretic followers in the towns of Germany from the Alps to the Baltic. They travelled as merchants and thereby made their presence in the towns seem plausible, though it later emerged that commerce made these 'poor brethren' sometimes embarrassingly wealthy. Reiser and his followers discovered, whether from his Waldensian heritage or from simple expediency, many of the techniques of itinerant preachers of the past. They met clandestinely and at night; they

275   The traditional account of the Freiburg Waldenses is G. F. Ochsenbein, *Aus dem schweizerischen Volksleben des 15. Jahrhunderts. Der Inquisitionsprozess wider die Waldenser zu Freiburg i. A. [sic] im Jahre 1430 nach den Akten dargestellt* (Bern, 1881). A modern edition of the documents relating to this episode is forthcoming as Kathrin Utz Tremp (ed.), *Quellen zur Geschichte der Waldenser in Freiburg im Uechtland (1399–1439)*, Monumenta Germaniae Historica, Quellen zur Geistesgeschichte des Mittelalters, vol. 18 (Munich, 2000). Dr Tremp has also produced a biographical register of those involved, as Kathrin Utz Tremp, *Waldenser, Widergänger, Hexen und Rebellen: Biographen zu den Waldenserprozessen von Freiburg im Uechtland (1399 und 1430)* (Fribourg, 1999) (special number of the *Freiburger Geschichtsblätter*). See also Kathrin Utz Tremp, 'Les Vaudois de Fribourg (1399–1430): état de la recherche', in *Revue de l'histoire des religions*, vol. 217, fasc. 1 (2000), pp. 121–38.

preached in hidden places; they took care not to speak to all and sundry, but heard confessions of trusted followers. In some instances they revisited regions which had embraced Waldensian heresy somewhat earlier. Matthäus Hagen, a tailor of Selchow who was burned at Berlin in 1458, had visited the same Waldensian villages in the Brandenburg Uckermark as Nicholas Gottschalck in the 1390s.[276] However, there were two important differences between Reiser's followers and the earlier Waldensian missionaries. First, Reiser was something of a theologian, and the impact of the ideas of Nicholas Biskupec prevented this new movement from becoming as theologically impoverished as its predecessor. Second, the German Hussites, drawn as they were from the great eucharistic movement of the later middle ages, celebrated the eucharist and gave it in both kinds to their followers, as the Waldenses before them had emphatically *not* done. Reiser also ran a system for distributing clandestine vernacular Bibles and other literature to his followers.

There is no doubt that Friedrich Reiser's group represents a mediation of the Hussite message through to the German-speaking laity through the methods of the earlier Waldensian masters. There is just enough evidence to show that some of his followers were probably the same as those who heard the confessors in the 1390s, or at least were their descendants. However, the time Reiser spent in Prague, and his absorption of Hussite ideas, had interrupted the succession of Waldensian masters. There is no evidence that Reiser and his followers 'took over' in any face-to-face way from Nicholas Gottschalck's brotherhood, which had been so successfully swept bodily into Catholicism in the 1390s. Reiser's heretic ministry was, in effect, a new creation. Moreover, it was extremely short-lived. Reiser himself was captured at Strasbourg, interrogated, tortured and burned in March 1458. Before that time, despairing of sustaining his ministry over a vast area with few personnel, he had notoriously likened his cause to 'a flame going out'. Stefan of Basel, who inherited his mantle, was captured at Vienna and burned in August 1467.[277]

Reiser's fellowship forged some links with the quietist religious order of the Bohemian 'Unity of Brethren' which came into being in the late 1450s and 1460s. Gregory Krajcí, one of the founding members of the Unity, reported in 1471 that at their inception they had met Stefan of Basel and other preachers of the Reiser group. A planned union of the groups had not materialized; however, a follower of Reiser 'ordained' one the first priests of the Unity in 1467, to confer respectability on him

---

276   Gonnet and Molnar, *Vaudois au moyen âge*, p. 253, n. 195, and cf. above, note 145. The trial of Matthäus Hagen and several companions is in Kurze, *Quellen*, pp. 288–302.
277   Gonnet and Molnar, *Vaudois au moyen âge*, pp. 249–59.

among Reiser's lay adherents.[278] Thereafter, it would seem that those northeastern Germans who wished to find spiritual solace outside Catholicism took the route into Bohemia. Reiser's heirs, who were in any case Hussites rather than Waldenses, finally lost themselves into the pacifist wing of the Hussite movement. When Martin Luther briefly discussed the 'Waldenses' in his Lenten sermons of 1525, he seems only to have had the Bohemians in mind. Certainly, he betrayed no awareness that Nicolaus of Plauen had frequented the 'schools of heresy' at 'the house of Magaretha in Wittenberg' less than a century before Luther himself was born.[279]

---

278   Ibid., pp. 259–62.
279   Luther referred to the 'Waldenses', evidently meaning the Bohemian Brethren, in his Lent Postils for 1525; for Margaretha, see Döllinger, *Beiträge*, vol. 2, p. 331.

7

The Southwestern Alps

From the end of the thirteenth century onwards, Waldenses started to be discovered across quite a wide swath of mountainous territory in the southwest of the Alps. On what is now the French side, they were particularly densely packed in the valleys around the river Durance, in the Dauphiné between Gap and Briançon. They were also found on the western edge of the Vercors near Valence. Across the mountain passes, they spread from the Valle di Susa, on the principal route through Piedmont into Italy, southwards into a series of valleys which cut east–west into the Alps. The valleys of the Chisone and the Pellice were especially secure strongholds of the Waldenses, though they could appear even further south, into the marquisate of Saluzzo.[1] The heretics of these regions displayed exceptional tenacity when faced with the threat and the reality of persecution throughout the later middle ages. To a much greater degree than the Waldenses of southwestern France or eastern Germany, they resisted the pressures and blandishments of the Church to make them conform. The inquisitors who dealt with Waldensianism in these regions were less doggedly consistent than Bernard Gui, and much less skilful and persuasive than Peter Zwicker. Geography, politics and society in the region conspired to make the enforcement of orthodoxy abnormally difficult. One major attempt to extirpate heresy, in the Dauphiné in 1487–8, backfired on its perpetrators. Ultimately, the Waldenses of the Alps survived into the era of the Reformation, and allowed themselves to be subsumed into Genevan reformed or 'Calvinist' Protestantism. In one particular part of the Alps, the Piedmontese valleys of the Duchy of Savoy, the former Waldenses became the *only* significant group of Protestants within the state. As a result, they retained their distinct identity as 'Waldensian Protestants', reaffirmed it in a series of conflicts and tribulations, and continue to do so to this day.[2]

1 See map IV.
2 See below, chapters 8–10.

The survival of the Piedmontese Waldenses into the modern era, albeit as a Protestant Church rather than a heretical movement within Catholicism, creates a problem of perspective for the historian. The Alpine Waldenses have tended to some extent to be seen as *the* Waldenses of the later middle ages, though in truth they have no uniquely special claim to the name, any more than the many others who were so designated elsewhere in Europe. Discarding hindsight, one ought to treat the Waldenses of the Alps as just another of the multiple manifestations of the 'Waldensian' tendency to reject the sacral and sacerdotal Church which developed in thirteenth-century Europe. Their origins, and their relationship to the primitive Waldensian movement and to the other movements of the later middle ages, are uncertain. In the fourteenth century their identity was compromised by the presence of various groups with diverse leaders and a range of contradictory beliefs. For long periods of their existence we depend on very fragmentary records, so daunting to inquisitors was the prospect of taking them on in their mountain heartlands. What documentation survives from the heretics themselves – especially from the very end of the middle ages – raises as many questions as it answers.

Where did the Waldenses of the Alps 'come from'? In the thirteenth century there are scattered documents which refer to 'Waldenses' in the plain of the river Po, but these sources stubbornly resist any attempt to establish a firm connection with later heresy in the Alps.[3] The first evidence for prosecutions for Waldensianism on the edge of the Alpine valleys, in the Val Perosa, dates from the 1290s.[4] By the 1330s, as will be seen, support for the movement was well established in the Piedmontese valleys. From that point onwards one can prove that there was continuity – in the places affected and even some of the surnames of the leading pastors – up to the sixteenth century.[5] Early historians used to infer that at some time in the thirteenth century the survivors of the persecution of Waldenses in France or in Italy, or both, 'took refuge' in the Alpine valleys as a place to escape the unwanted attentions of ecclesiastics.[6] There is nothing intrinsically improbable in such an explanation. The 'Burgundians' who migrated from Burgundy into Rouergue and the Toulousain in the 1280s–90s represent just such a migration, though the

3   See G. G. Merlo, 'Su radici e origini della presenza eterodossa tra le Alpi occidentali', in G. G. Merlo, *Valdesi e valdismi medievali: itinerari e proposte di ricerca* (Turin, 1984), pp. 27–41.
4   Merlo, 'Su radici e origini', p. 42; F. Gabotto *Roghi e vendette: Contributo alla storia della dissidenza religiosa in Piemonte prima della riforma* (Pinerolo, 1898), pp. 13, 53.
5   See the long continuity of the Pastre dynasty, as below, note 18.
6   For the traditional interpretation, see for example E. Comba, *History of the Waldenses of Italy*, trans. T. E. Comba (London, 1889), pp. 81ff.

Languedoc was an ill-fated choice of destination.[7] However, the 'Burgundians' stood out precisely because they were migrants. There is no similar evidence to suggest that the Alpine Waldenses were 'migrants' from another part of France or Italy. Their names, their culture, their knowledge of the terrain, above all their language, suggest that they had firm roots in the Alpine valleys well before 1300. On the contrary, the Alps, relatively over-populated at the best of times, were places away from which people migrated, to Provence or to the extreme south of Italy, rather than places to which they moved for refuge.[8] It remains possible, however, that the ideals of the Waldensian protest were imported into the Alpine regions by missionaries from outside, and then adopted as their own by the indigenous peoples of the region. However, proving whether such an importation of ideas took place – or even discovering whether the transmission came from the French or the Italian side – is extraordinarily difficult. Mere parallels between ideas taught in one and another place are insufficient; indeed, there are beliefs taught in the Alps in the fourteenth century which have no parallels elsewhere in Waldensian heresy. Nor is there any clear tradition from the Alpine Waldenses as to the origins of their beliefs. In 1335 Peroneta, sister of Michael Plancha, related this account of the source of Waldensianism, which she claimed to have heard from her pastors:

> They also said that when Christ ascended to heaven he left twelve apostles in the world to preach his faith. Four of these kept his books; but the other eight went to make gardens and chanted from other books, not understanding them. However, the other four chanted from Christ's books and understood them all. Hearing this, the eight were stronger, and drove the four out of the Church. When the four had gone out into the square and chanted there, the eight were stronger and drove them out of the square. Then the four began to go about secretly and by night. The Waldenses added 'we keep to the way of the four to whom the books of Christ remained; the priests and clergy follow the way of the other eight who wished to keep to a life of indulgence.[9]

This clearly home-spun (and unbiblical) story has no parallel elsewhere in Europe. Moreover, it shows that the Waldenses themselves had no idea of their recent history. There does exist one piece of evidence which suggests a tentative link to other Waldensian groups elsewhere. At the very

7   See above, chapter 5.2.
8   For the seasonal migrations of the inhabitants of the Alps in search of work, see E. Cameron, *The Reformation of the Heretics: The Waldenses of the Alps 1480–1580* (Oxford, 1984), p. 12 and n. 29 and references. For permanent migrations see below, section 7.6.
9   G. G. Merlo, *Eretici e inquisitori nella società piemontese del trecento* (Turin, 1977), p. 220.

end of the middle ages, a version or adaptation of the 'Book of the Elect', written in the Franco-Provençal of the western Alps, would turn up among the manuscript literature of some of the Alpine heretic pastors.[10] The 'Book of the Elect', with its distinctive elaboration of the legend of Pope Sylvester I, derived from an Italian Waldensian group some time before 1368, though it is otherwise known only from manuscripts in German archives. There is nothing to link the Latin original – as opposed to the translation – with the Alpine pastorate; and the translation survives among manuscripts of very late date, comprising subject-matter largely of non-Waldensian origins.[11] It is more likely that the 'Book of the Elect' was imported into the Alpine milieu from outside, than that it was originally written in the Alps. It suggests contacts, but does not prove anything about the Alpine Waldenses' origins.

Within the Alpine region itself, some fragments of evidence suggest that heresy may have moved eastwards from the Dauphiné rather than westwards from Piedmont. Several of those interrogated in the region of Giaveno in 1335, the earliest for whom such interrogations survive, said that some of the heretics' teachers came from the region of Gap, in the Dauphiné.[12] In May 1373 it was reported that 'two brothers from Briançon' had been staying with Fina di Lanzo, a woman highly influential in Piedmontese heresy.[13] In 1387 a group of heretics from Valpute (later renamed Vallouise) north of Briançon, had settled at Barge near Pinerolo. This last migration, however, was to escape the activities of inquisitors in their home village.[14] If Waldensianism first took root in the Dauphiné in the late thirteenth century, one might tentatively ascribe its introduction to the same diaspora from Burgundy which produced the Waldensianism of the Languedoc in the 1280s and 1290s.[15] However, this is pure speculation. There was traffic in both directions across the Alps, and similar documents from the Dauphiné (had they existed) might have shown Piedmontese masters teaching there.

One final point must be made about the 'origins' of the Alpine Waldenses. Origins are chiefly relevant (1) if they help to define a group's self-consciousness and identity, and (2) if movements of ideas can be shown to need a tradition on which to build and continue. In fact, the self-consciousness of the Alpine Waldenses depended more on their myths and images of themselves, than on any explicit knowledge of their own history. Moreover, the heretics of fourteenth-century Piedmont

10   See above, chapter 6, note 116.
11   See the discussion of the Waldensian texts below, chapter 8.2–3.
12   Merlo, *Eretici e inquisitori*, pp. 167, 169.
13   Ibid., pp. 280, and cf. p. 282.
14   G. Amati, 'Processus Contra Valdenses in Lombardia Superiori, Anno 1387', in *Archivio Storico Italiano*, series 3 (1865), vol. 1, pt 2, p. 35.
15   See above, chapter 5.2.

were fecund and inventive in producing new movements of dissent. They could and did devise heterodox religious ideas for themselves, without requiring any known antecedents.

7.1 Piedmont: Martin Pastre and the 'Men of Recognition', c.1335

It is usual for the first evidence of heresy in any given region to tell of the earliest assaults of clergy and inquisitors upon them. Exceptionally and significantly, the first detailed evidence for the Piedmontese valleys tells of the exact opposite. A letter of Pope John XXII written on 8 July 1332 to Jean de Badis OFM, the inquisitor at Marseilles, tells of the first known act of defiance by Martin Pastre and the Waldenses of Luserna. Alberto di Castellario OP of Cuneo, inquisitor in Piedmont and Upper Lombardy, had reported that the heretics of the valleys of the Luserna and the Perosa had grown to such numbers and confidence that they gathered in groups as large as five hundred at a time. When Castellario was about to conduct an inquisition against them, the Waldenses in Angrogna, suspecting that their rector Guglielmo had reported them to the inquisitor, killed the rector after Mass in the square in Angrogna. They then besieged Alberto di Castellario in a castle, forcing him to abandon his intention of conducting an inquisition in those valleys. Jean de Badis, meanwhile, apparently held in prison 'Martin Pastre, otherwise called Peyre Martin, or Julian', who was described as the 'chief in the [heretics'] congregations, . . . a fugitive from the inquisitors in Piedmont for the past twenty years, and general preacher of heretical pravity'. Jean de Badis was directed to make it possible for Alberto di Castellario to interrogate Pastre; it is not recorded whether or not such an interrogation took place.[16]

Undeterred by his experience in Luserna, in January to February 1335 Alberto di Castellario conducted an inquisition in the castle of Giaveno, in the Alpine foothills of Piedmont, into the Waldenses of the district. The trial register which he compiled on this occasion is one of the earliest such documents to survive, albeit in damaged and incomplete form. It relates the interrogations of some forty accused Waldensian followers from the towns and villages of Giaveno, Coazze, Valgioie and their environs. It provides evidence from the period approximately a generation after the first forms of Waldensian sentiment had become thoroughly established in the region.

16 Marc'Aurelio Rorengo de' Conti di Lucerna, *Memorie Historiche dell'introduttione dell'heresie nelle valli di Lucerna, Marchesato di Saluzzo, e altre di Piemonte . . .* (Turin, 1649), pp. 16–17, citing an original document.

Plates 1 and 2 Traditional buildings near Bobbio, in the Waldensian heartland valley of the Pellice (formerly known as the Luserna). Traditional architecture in this region still follows a vernacular style which is centuries old. These views show how the Waldensian valleys are not only precipitous, but also densely wooded, which may help to account for their long and successful resistance to ecclesiastical justice. (Photographs by the author.)

Although the people interrogated were from a narrowly confined district, they received instruction from a group of heretic leaders and pastors who were based across most of the Piedmontese valleys affected with heresy. The leader of the Waldenses at this time had been the same Martin Pastre 'of Val Luserna', described in one testimony as 'an old foreign man' (though 'extraneus' might mean only that he came from outside

Plate 2

the Giaveno district).[17] Val Luserna (since renamed Val Pellice) is the most central of all the 'heartland' regions of the Waldenses of Piedmont; its chief town, Torre Pellice, is now the organizational centre of the Vaudois Church. It is striking to find that one of the earliest and oldest Piedmontese Waldensian leaders came from there. The surname 'Pastre' is equally significant: heretics of this name would figure in the leadership of the movement in the mid-fifteenth century and again in the mid-sixteenth, when two of that family became Protestant ministers.[18] The other leaders named in the confessions were likewise from the Piedmontese valleys. 'Francesco' from San Giòrio di Susa, and his regular companion 'Peyret' from Coazze, were near neighbours of the people to whom they ministered.[19] Johan Valencon of Usseaux, Martin or 'Martinet' of Laux, and Michel of Pragelato all came from the Val Chisone, just to the south and west of Giaveno.[20] There may have been other

17   Merlo, *Eretici e inquisitori*, p. 218, and cf. ibid., pp. 176, 184, 187, 189, 191, 198, 201–2, 206, 209, 211–13, 215, 220–1, 223, 225–6, 228–30, 232, 237.
18   For later Pastres, see Alessio, 'Luserna e l'interdetto di Giacomo Buronzo', *Bollettino storico-bibliografico subalpino*, vol. 8, no. 6 (1903), pp. 413–14; Cameron, *Reformation of the Heretics*, pp. 171–2 and refs.
19   Merlo, *Eretici e inquisitori*, pp. 234, 190, and elsewhere in the register.
20   Ibid., pp. 176–7, 198, 201, 204, 206, 230, 233.

teachers from further afield, but the heretic leaders best known to the people of Giaveno came from within some 30 kilometres' radius.

These 'Waldenses' gave themselves a range of names. One of the most distinctive was the 'men of recognition' ('gentes de recognoscencia'), which has affinities to the later English Lollards' nickname of 'known men'.[21] More durable and persistent would be the description of Waldensian heresy as 'our law', an expression which would resonate down the late middle ages.[22] At other times the heretics were known simply as the 'good people' or 'people of the apostles' or, on one occasion only, the 'poor of Christ'.[23] In the main, the impression given by the 1335 inquiries is that the pastors travelled around in pairs from village to village, and were escorted by particularly trusted lay sympathizers. For instance, Palmier Goytrat once escorted Francesco and Peyret of Coazze on a round trip from Giaveno to Avigliana, San Gillio, Orbassano and Cumiana, describing a circuit which took them dangerously close to Turin, to visit isolated followers.[24]

Thus far the Piedmontese Waldenses more or less conformed to the pattern of itinerant poor pastors ministering to sedentary lay followers, which has been seen elsewhere in Europe. However, there also appear to have been some 'leaders' of heresy among the sedentary village lay people. Palmier of Villelmeta, living at Buffa, was, according to one witness, a 'priest of the Waldenses' at whose house heretics' meetings took place.[25] Palmier Goytrat (who may have been the same person) 'taught the paternoster of the Waldenses'; he was the 'leader' of the Waldenses at Buffa. According to Bonet de Bonet, Palmier said that there was no one in Giaveno who had been appointed by the Waldenses to hear confessions and to give absolution save himself. The same Palmier received his confession and gave him a penance that he should fast for one day on bread and water.[26] This example of a resident 'lay' person administering the Waldensian quasi-sacrament of penance is unprecedented in the heretic movements so far studied, though sedentary lay leaders reappeared later in the century.[27] In the main, the hearing of con-

---

21 Ibid., pp. 178, 189, 210, 218, 232; on the designation 'known men' in Lollardy, see for example A. Hudson, *The Premature Reformation: Wycliffite Texts and Lollard History* (Oxford, 1988), pp. 143, 478, 482–3.

22 Merlo, *Eretici e inquisitori*, pp. 168, 184–5, 192–3, 195–6, 199; for Dauphiné Waldenses referring to Waldensianism as 'our law', see M. Fornier, *Histoire générale des Alpes maritimes ou cottiennes et . . . de leur métropolitan Embrun*, ed. J. Guillaume, 3 vols (Paris, 1890–2), vol. 2, p. 413.

23 Merlo, *Eretici e inquisitori*, pp. 169, 189 (good men), 190 (people of the apostles), 193 (Poor of Christ); cf. Fornier, *Histoire générale*, vol. 2, p. 180.

24 Merlo, *Eretici e inquisitori*, pp. 223–4, 236.

25 Ibid., p. 169.

26 Ibid., pp. 167–9, 224.

27 But see above, chapter 6.2, on the earliest German Waldensian teachers.

fessions appears to have been the work of the travelling pastors, though the Giaveno evidence says relatively little about its details. The more fully initiated followers confessed to the senior among the pastors, and were often given penances of prayers and a period of fasting.[28]

The teachings and beliefs of these earliest Alpine Waldenses were largely what might have been expected. They avoided swearing or lying, which seems to have made them more respected among their neighbours; supposedly, 'every oath was a mortal sin'.[29] Only one, however, Peroneta Plancha, known as 'Bruna', was suspected of Waldensianism 'because she never affirmed or denied anything',[30] which suggests an extreme aversion even to accidental lying. The same Bruna cited two rather unusual texts which she claimed the pastors had used to warn her against swearing: 'Do not accustom your mouth to oaths' and 'One who swears many oaths is full of iniquity'.[31] These texts from the Apocrypha appear to discourage profane or casual swearing, rather than the formal civil oath; this is an issue to which one will return. Certainly, in the presence of the inquisitor witnesses and suspects alike took judicial oaths with no recorded signs of reluctance, unlike those in Austria or Bohemia at the same time.

The Alpine Waldenses, like their counterparts elsewhere, rejected belief in purgatory and the cult of praying and offering services for the dead. In the next world there was only paradise or hell; purgatory existed only in this world. In a striking parallel to the later German evidence, numerous lay followers reported that there were 'only two ways', that is, paradise and hell.[32] However, the Alpine Waldenses added some colourful images unparalleled in other accounts. The 'two ways' were likened to 'the two tables of Moses, of which one was white and the other black'. This misunderstanding of the two tables of the law has no scriptural basis, but may reflect the use of deliberately contrasting imagery in teaching.[33] In the same way, works done before death were of more value than those done after, 'just as a light carried before a person is helpful, but one carried behind one is useless'.[34] One follower admitted to holding that 'pilgrimages were of no use other than to break shoes in'.[35] Relatively little was said about the priesthood: several witnesses

28 Merlo, *Eretici e inquisitori*, pp. 171, 177–8, 187, 189–91, 193–4, 196–7, 199–202, 204–8, 210–13, 215, 223.
29 Ibid., pp. 166–7, 170–1, 190, 193, 197–200, 214.
30 Ibid., p. 164.
31 Ecclesiasticus 23:9; 23:11; Merlo, *Eretici e inquisitori*, p. 220.
32 Merlo, *Eretici e inquisitori*, pp. 178, 188, 190–2, 198, 201, 203–4, 206–7, 209, 211, 214, 216, 218, 220, 225, 232; compare the German evidence as above, chapter 6, notes 221, 225, 227.
33 Merlo, *Eretici e inquisitori*, pp. 190, 203–4.
34 Ibid., pp. 198, 200.
35 Ibid., p. 207.

agreed that the heretic pastors kept God's law better than the priests
and could therefore absolve more effectively than the priests; but the
Donatist argument largely passed this group of people (or this inquisitor) by.[36]

In some respects the Piedmontese heretics went far beyond the opposition to the sacral church, the anti-sacerdotalism and anti-clericalism traditionally associated with heresies called 'Waldensian'. The letter of John
XXII referred to Martin Pastre 'particularly preaching against the presence of the body of Christ in the sacrament of the altar'.[37] Giovanni
Mathei of Giaveno reported that the Waldenses claimed that 'God did
not come down into that host which the priest elevates'.[38] On one occasion two people were travelling to Pinerolo, and one of them, Nicoleto
Bastardo, found the tip of a lance in the dust and elevated it, in mimicry
of the elevation of the host. His companion, Giovanni Castaygni, apparently answered that 'you would not do that if you were of our law'.[39]
Another witness reported hearing one heretic claim that the saints would
have enough to do to help themselves in the day of judgement, never
mind help others; he went to church, but not to pray to the saints painted
on the walls. The same heretic also claimed that the 'Great Father' would
not have so humiliated himself as to take on human flesh.[40] In the same
way, John XXII's letter claimed Pastre preached 'against the incarnation
of the Son of God'.[41]

However, these sketchy indications of spontaneous resistance to difficult doctrines of the orthodox Church, such as the real presence or the
Incarnation, remained fairly isolated comments. It is remarkable, though,
that John XXII's letter *only* referred to Pastre preaching against those
two major dogmas. The relatively restrained nature of most statements
recorded in 1335 contrasts with later in the century, when heretics would
become bolder, more sweeping, and more diverse in their rejections of
the Church and its apparatus.

7.2 The Waldenses in their 'Heartlands' from 1387 Onwards

In the intervening decades there is little evidence that the Waldenses of
the southwestern Alps were persecuted in any organized or effective way,
despite the presence of a number of active inquisitors – Tommasso di

36 Ibid., pp. 178, 203, 205.
37 Rorengo . . . di Lucerna, *Memorie Historiche*, pp. 16.
38 Merlo, *Eretici e inquisitori*, p. 166.
39 Ibid., pp. 168, 171.
40 Ibid., p. 166.
41 Rorengo . . . di Lucerna, *Memorie Historiche*, p. 16.

Casasco, Huguet Bergognini and others – from the 1370s onwards.[42] The lords of Luserna were ordered to hunt out heretics in their lands in 1354. There is no clear evidence of the results, though a memorandum from these gentry claims that they had tried to drive heresy out of Angrogna, Villar and Bobbio.[43] Whatever the behaviour of their lords, the heretics seem to have mounted a concerted, effective and sometimes bloody defence. Pietro di Ruffia, inquisitor in Piedmont, was murdered at Susa around this time. Antonio Pavò of Savigliano, a Dominican inquisitor who had also been active in the region, was murdered at Bricherasio shortly after Easter 1384 after preaching to the people. His murderers included Giovannino Gabrieli of Bricherasio, who died in 1386 before the inquisitors caught up with him. Another inquisitor, Bartolommeo da Cervere, suffered a similar fate around this time as he travelled from Brà to Cervere.[44]

In some cases the heretics appear to have found supporters among the local aristocracy. In the 1370s Pope Gregory XI several times complained to bishops and secular rulers alike about the abundance of Waldenses in the Alps. Most of his efforts were directed to the Dauphiné, but he also protested to Amadeus VII, Count of Savoy, that heretics in his dominions were being protected by the local nobles, and were frustrating the moves made by inquisitors against them.[45] In mid-December 1387 Antonio Settimo OP seems more or less to have abandoned his campaign against the Waldenses of the district of Val Perosa, on the eastern edge of the Waldensian valleys in Piedmont. It emerged that the people of the Val Perosa, on the advice of Giovanni de Brayda, chancellor to Count Amadeus VIII (1383–91) and Ysoard de Dominis of the Val San Martino (now the Val Germanasca), had negotiated with the Count's treasurer to pay him some 500 florins annually, on condition that he prevented the inquisitor from visiting their valleys to investigate their religious allegiances. Settimo left Pinerolo and returned to Turin in disgust, denouncing the contumacy of those who had blocked his work.[46]

---

42   See the references to these inquisitors in, for example, G. Boffito, 'Eretici in Piemonte al tempo del Gran Scisma', *Studi e Documenti di Storia e Diritto*, 18 (1897), p. 393; and Merlo, *Eretici e inquisitori*, pp. 259ff.
43   Rorengo ... di Lucerna, *Memorie Historiche*, pp. 17–18.
44   Amati, 'Processus Contra Valdenses', vol. 1, pt 2, pp. 23–4, 29–30; Rorengo ... di Lucerna, *Memorie Historiche*, p. 17, dates Pavò's murder to 1374, but it seems that he was still alive in 1384. See also Amati, 'Processus Contra Valdenses', vol. 1, pt 2, p. 15.
45   The sources for Gregory XI's moves are the letter collections of the mendicant orders: for analysis and references, see H. C. Lea, *History of the Inquisition of the Middle Ages*, 3 vols (London, 1888), vol. 2, pp. 153–6.
46   Amati, 'Processus Contra Valdenses', vol. 1, pt 2, p. 51.

In the light of this persistent obstruction, the register compiled by Antonio Settimo between March and May 1387 into some of the Waldenses of the Val Perosa offers a precious and rare insight into the Waldenses of the heartland valleys. The people of Perosa were significantly closer to the key valleys of the Pellice, the Angrogna and the Germanasca than those of Giaveno. Moreover, in the 1380s Piedmont served as a place of refuge for some of the Waldenses of the Dauphiné. The inquisition mounted over several years by the Franciscan François Borelli, based at Briançon, caused significant numbers of the Dauphiné communities to flee across the Alps.[47] With both Piedmontese and Dauphinois represented among the suspects, therefore, one may assume that this register documents the beliefs and practices of the 'core' Waldensian population of the southwestern Alps at this time.

So what do Antonio Settimo's interrogations reveal? For the most part, they confirm and continue the story so far. However, certain distinctive features of Piedmontese Waldensian dissent, which were embryonic in 1335, appear to have consolidated themselves as more consistent features by the last quarter of the fourteenth century. Teaching and ministry continued to be entrusted to a mixture of people, some of whom were local residents of fixed abode, while others, still local to the region, probably travelled around some of the time. The masters most frequently mentioned were natives of the region, who ministered over the whole area: Colet de Famolasco, based at Campiglione,[48] Guilhem Justin of Angrogna,[49] Peyre Pascal of Val San Martino[50] and Turin 'Rubeus' of Angrogna.[51] However, the arrival of refugees from the Dauphiné introduced at least one outsider. The brothers Guilhem and Johan Pruza, from Valpute but living at Barge, told how they had attended meetings at Barge where Johan Baridon, from Apulia, preached and led the meeting. The Pruzas spoke of a 'pope' of the Waldenses in Apulia who sent Baridon and other masters to them.[52] As early as 1353 it had been reported that some Vaudois of the Dauphiné had migrated to Apulia in search of peace and isolation. The interesting thing about Johan Baridon is his name. The Baridon family came from Freissinières in the Dauphiné, and figures largely in the story of its persecutions in the 1480s.[53] On the other hand,

47   Ibid., pp. 33, 35, 48–9.
48   Ibid., pp. 25, 36, 44–5.
49   Ibid., pp. 24, 44.
50   Ibid., pp. 34, 44.
51   Ibid., pp. 32, 44–5.
52   Ibid., pp. 39–40. An oddity of this admission is that in the one testimony Johan and Baridon appear as separate individuals, in another they are forename and surname of the same person. The second reading seems more likely.
53   See below, section 7.4. A member of the Baridon family was still living at Dourmillouse in the Val Freissinières in the mid-1980s.

some resident householders also led meetings and taught other follow-ers. Johan Moti held Waldensian preaching meetings in his own house at Sauze de Cesana.[54] Johan Freyria of Val San Martino, living at San Secondo di Pinerolo, also held meetings at his house where 'he preached those things which he had heard at other times from the Waldensian masters with whom he had many times confessed his sins'. Another time he held a meeting in his house and heard confessions as well.[55] The impli-cation of these and earlier instances is that, despite the intermittent pres-ence of travelling masters, lay Waldenses also taught others what they had in turn learned, allowing the spiritual control of the movement to become somewhat diffuse. This diffuseness may partly account for some of the diversity which started to appear in their teachings.

The beliefs and teachings as described by Settimo show some similari-ties to those recorded by Alberto di Castellario earlier in the century. When arguing against the belief in purgatory, Johan Borset of Lauset allegedly said that 'it is good for a man to place a light before him, that is, to do good in his lifetime, because after his death alms offered for him will not help him': this echoed a saying recorded in 1335, that good works done after death were as useless as a light carried behind a person.[56] Accordingly, several suspects admitted believing that pilgrimages and other offerings for the dead were futile.[57] However, two Waldensian fol-lowers, when asked about the destiny of baptized children who died in infancy, said that they thought they went to purgatory because of their parents' sins: this suggests a curiously garbled concept of original sin.[58] Yet again, Guilhem Pruza argued that one should not celebrate the feasts of saints, because, he claimed, not one saint's soul had yet entered paradise: they were waiting for the Day of Judgement.[59]

Even though the information culled by Antonio Settimo about Waldensian teachings was quite sparse, his interrogations yielded further

54 Amati, 'Processus Contra Valdenses', vol. 1, pt 2, p. 18.
55 Ibid., p. 22
56 Ibid., p. 46; compare Merlo, *Eretici e inquisitori*, pp. 198, 200; there are more commonplace denials of the existence of purgatory and the affirmation of 'two ways' after death in Amati, 'Processus Contra Valdenses', vol. 1, pt 2, pp. 18, 21, 23–4, 39–40, 46.
57 Ibid., pp. 21, 39–40, 46.
58 Ibid., pp. 20, 24. The fate of unbaptized children was a contentious issue at this period; the Augustinian theologian Gregory of Rimini (d. 1358) argued that the souls of unbaptized children must necessarily be damned, earning himself the title 'tortor infantium'. See F. L. Cross and E. A. Livingstone (eds), *The Oxford Dictionary of the Christian Church*, 3rd edn (Oxford, 1997), art. 'Gregory of Rimini', p. 713.
59 Amati, 'Processus Contra Valdenses', pp. 40–1. It should be noted that the Piedmontese argument for not praying to saints is quite different from the German argument, as above, chapter 6, note 201.

evidence of the increasing radicalism already hinted at in the 1330s.[60] Perrona de Famolasco of Fenile, described as a 'thoroughly evil Waldensian woman' by one witness, 'spoke ill of those who believed in the holy body of Christ': this offers another rare instance of disbelief in the eucharist.[61] Much more surprising is the evidence of heresies about the nature of Christ. Cardon de Lauset taught 'that one should believe in God the Father only, and that God did not have a son'. Johan Freyria was unclear over the Trinity; Johan Baridon allegedly preached 'that Christ was not true God; because God could not die as [Christ] died', and 'that they ought to believe in God the Father and not in Christ'.[62] These admittedly rare testimonies, supported by hints in the earlier evidence, show a Waldensian dissent which was not wholly confined to the traditional disbelief in the sacral church and priesthood,[63] but was starting to chafe at wholly orthodox teachings which strained the sceptical mind.[64]

These Waldenses also practised some unusual religious customs. Four separate testimonies refer to different masters at Waldensian meetings distributing to all those present 'the blessed bread which they called *consolamentum*'. This rite is puzzling. The term *consolamentum* had a specific set of meanings in Catharism. Originally it denoted the 'hereticating' or inducting of a believer into the ranks of the perfect; by *c*.1300 in the Languedoc, it usually referred to the form of last rites given to Cathar believers on the point of death.[65] However, only one witness, and a doubtful one at that, would subsequently link this Waldensian blessing of bread to preparation for death.[66] Here, on the contrary, it seems to mean a sort of substitute either for the eucharist or for the 'blessed bread' distributed in popular Catholicism.[67]

60　Merlo, *Eretici e inquisitori*, pp. 166–7, as discussed above, notes 40–1.
61　Amati, 'Processus Contra Valdenses', vol. 1, pt 2, p. 46; cf. Merlo, *Eretici e inquisitori*, p. 166.
62　Amati, 'Processus Contra Valdenses', vol. 1, pt 2, pp. 21, 23, 39–40.
63　On this theme see ibid., pp. 24, 35, 39. Statements about the priesthood are as rare in this dossier as in di Castellario's (above, note 36) and very inconsistent.
64　Predictably, the Waldenses of 1387 also registered their objections to swearing oaths: Amati, 'Processus Contra Valdenses', vol. 1, pt 2, p. 39; also to lies (ibid., pp. 23–4) and usury (ibid., p. 31).
65　On *consolamentum* among the Occitan Cathars, see Malcolm Lambert, *The Cathars* (Oxford, 1998), esp. pp. 141–58, 239–44.
66　G. Amati, 'Processus Contra Valdenses in Lombardia Superiori, Anno 1387', in *Archivio Storico Italiano*, series 3 (1865), vol. 2, pt 2, pp. 15–16.
67　Amati, 'Processus Contra Valdenses', vol. 1, pt 2, p. 22: 'comedit . . . pluries et post alia panem benedictum quem vocabant consolamentum'. Compare Lambert, *Cathars*, p. 245 and nn. On the custom of distributing 'blessed bread' (called *panis benedictus, panis lustratus, panis lustralis,* and now known in France as pain bénit, which has received a special benediction), see *New Catholic Encyclopedia* (New York, 1967–79), vol. 2, p. 779, art. 'Liturgical Use of Bread'.

Some statements about what heretics did pose larger problems. Should one believe Johan Freyria's admission that 'he worshipped the sun and the moon on bended knee, saying the paternoster and the Ave Maria'?[68] More significant, in the light of the later history of the Alpine Waldenses, is that Antonio Settimo was evidently sniffing around to find sexual scandals as early as 1387. Johan Fauvre of Sauze de Cesana confessed that after a meeting at the house of Johan Moti, Moti extinguished the light, saying 'let him who has, hold', after which Fauvre had intercourse with a young woman named Margaret.[69] The summary nature of this admission, and the fact that Settimo would later extract much fuller admissions of the same kind from Antonio Galosna, suggest that he already had an idea of what sorts of rumours he wished to see proved.[70] The theory was that the nocturnal meetings of the Waldenses were followed by a promiscuous act of sexual indulgence by those present. This rumour was probably nothing more than ill-natured gossip from Catholic neighbours, based on ignorance and suspicion: once planted in the inquisitors' mindset, however, it would persist for over a century. Johan Pruza admitted that the preacher said 'let him who has, hold' at the end of his sermon, but claimed that people then simply waited in the darkness a while, then left.[71]

For some sixty years or so after 1387, when Settimo abandoned his inquisitions in the Val Perosa, there is little clear evidence of what was happening to the Waldenses of the heartland valleys. It is safe to assume that they remained there, defiant as before. Despite their strength, however, Catholic worship continued to take place until early in 1448, when an armed rising in the valleys of the Luserna led the local clergy to flee the valleys completely. Giacomo Buronzo OP, inquisitor in Piedmont, was sent to confront them. In the middle of July of that year he met one of the heretics' leaders, Claude Pastre (presumably of the same family as Martin Pastre!), accompanied by three hundred armed supporters. Pastre offered to hold a disputation with the inquisitor in the square at Torre di Luserna (now Torre Pellice). The offer was rejected, and the churches of the region were placed under interdict. One might have expected the ending of formal Catholic services to be greeted with relief rather than regret by the heretics. On the contrary, it appears

---

68   Amati, 'Processus Contra Valdenses', vol. 1, pt 2, p. 22: 'adoravit solem et lunam genibus flexis, dicendo Pater Noster et Ave Maria'.
69   Ibid., p. 18.
70   Compare below, section 7.3; see also the mysterious statement in Merlo, *Eretici e inquisitori*, p. 168: 'multas personas vidit per stratas tenentes posteriora unus contra alium'.
71   Amati, 'Processus Contra Valdenses', vol. 1, pt 2, p. 40: 'in fine precipiebant extingui lumina dicendo: qui habeat teneat, et recedebant postmodum transacto aliquo spacio sine lumine'.

that they still wished Mass to be said, and the other ministrations to be provided for them. According to a breve of Pope Nicholas V of 16 July 1453, significant numbers of the inhabitants abjured their heresy and sought absolution and the lifting of the interdict, which the pope conceded.[72]

Buronzo's willingness to absolve persistent and relapsed heretics and restore them to their property turned out to be somewhat naive. Less than twenty-five years later it was clear that little had changed. An exchange of correspondence in the winter of 1475–6 showed how heresy still persisted. On 28 November 1475 Giovanni Andrea di Aquapendente, apostolic subdelegate and vicar for purposes of inquisition to Giovanni di Campesio, Bishop of Turin (1469–82), described in a letter how many of the people of the valleys of Luserna and thereabouts had relapsed into heresy after abjuring it before Giacomo Buronzo. To escape the attentions of the inquisitors, they were selling their property and moving to other jurisdictions. Accordingly, Aquapendente visited Luserna, and in the presence of the local lords and the podestà decreed that no convicted heretics or their heirs were to buy or sell goods over a florin in value, or to alienate, buy or sell any land without permission from the bishop or his vicar. The explicit intention was to allow the Church to confiscate heretics' property under canon law. Not surprisingly, the local podestà resisted this intervention by the Church into secular affairs and prevented publication of Aquapendente's letter. The dowager Duchess Yolande of Savoy then issued an order on 23 January 1476 ordering him to comply and to present himself before her council. The outcome of this exchange is not known; the heretics are reported to have risen against the lords of Luserna in 1483 or 1484, but details are scanty.[73]

While the Dauphiné was being ravaged by the great and bloody crusade of 1487–8,[74] inquisition in Piedmont appears to have been delayed. There is a report of an abjuration made by Waldensian deputies before Duke Philippe at Pinerolo in 1488.[75] In 1491, however, Pope Innocent VIII issued a bull to Angelo Carletti of Chivasso OFM, the great confessional theorist and theologian, and to the bishop of St-Jean de Maurienne, authorizing them to proceed against heresy in the

---

72   Alessio, 'Luserna e l'interdetto di Giacomo Buronzo', pp. 409–24; Rorengo . . . di Lucerna, *Memorie Historiche*, pp. 19–20. There also survives from this period one trial, that of Philippe Regis of Val San Martino, conducted in 1451: see Giacomo Weitzecker, 'Processo di un valdese nell'anno 1451', *Rivista Cristiana* 9 (1881), pp. 363–7, and summary in J. Gonnet and A. Molnar, *Les Vaudois au moyen âge* (Turin, 1974), pp. 265–6.
73   Rorengo . . . di Lucerna, *Memorie Historiche*, pp. 22–5; Fornier, *Histoire générale*, vol. 2, pp. 373–4; D. Carutti, *La Crociata valdese del 1488 e la maschera di ferro, con alcune appendice alla storia di Pinerolo* (Pinerolo, 1894), pp. 7–10.
74   See below, section 7.5.
75   Rorengo . . . di Lucerna, *Memorie Historiche*, p. 25.

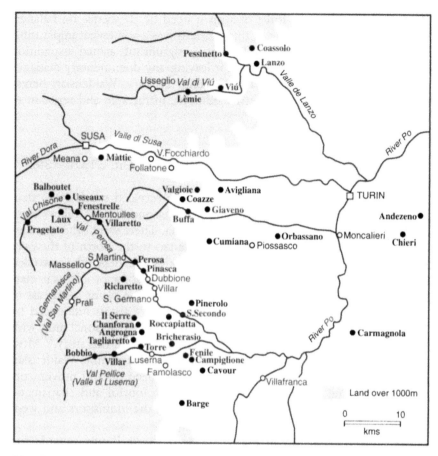

Map IV Centres of heresy in Piedmont, 14th–15th centuries.

Piedmontese valleys, by force of arms if need be. It seems, on balance, unlikely that anything came of this. Carletti was a somewhat implausible inquisitor and it is improbable that a significant armed expedition could have been mounted without it leaving any documentary evidence whatever. Certainly, by the early sixteenth century, Waldensian heresy was still in the valleys of western Piedmont, intractable and resistant as ever.[76]

7.3   Charismatic Individual Leaders in Piedmont, c.1370–1395

The inquiries of the Piedmontese inquisitors revealed much more than just the heartland Waldensian community, ensconced in its valleys from the Valle di Susa down to the Valle di Luserna. There were other groups, based on the Val di Viù and the Valle di Lanzo to the north of the river Dora; and there were some wayward religious leaders who travelled around the plain of Piedmont. These groups pose some problems in classifying them. In one centre of heresy, Chieri, in the plains southeast of Turin, the heretics were almost certainly Italian Cathars influenced by the Bogomil Church of Bosnia. But for their evident personal links with some of the other heretics, they would have no role in this story.[77] Most of the others, on the other hand, appear more to resemble Waldensian dissent than anything else. They seem to have been one-off movements of anti-sacerdotal protest, led by a range of colourful and charismatic leaders, several of whom fell into the hands of the inquisitors and were burned for heresy.

Do these have a part in the Waldensian story? If one regards the Waldensian movement as single self-conscious tradition, divided geographically into only a few strands in each of the main regions of Europe, then the fractional movements described in this section are peripheral to the story. However, one must remember that 'Waldensian' was a term used by inquisitors and churchmen, not by the heretics themselves. Contemporary churchmen would have defined Waldensian heresy simply as a regularly occurring group of credal and behavioural errors in religion, which all sorts of people might exhibit, whether they were conscious of each other's activities or not. It is later historians who have construed out of the Waldensian heresies a *tradition*, a continuous thread of self-reinforcing dissent linked by people and places, which survived to the

76   On the alleged post-1491 'crusade', see esp. M. Viora, 'Le persecuzioni contro i valdesi nel secolo xvº: a crociata di Filippo II', *Bulletin de la société d'histoire vaudoise* 47 (1925), pp. 5–19.
77   For the Piedmontese Cathars, see the sources in Amati, 'Processus Contra Valdenses', vol. 2, pt 1, pp. 50ff.; Boffito, 'Eretici in Piemonte', pp. 421–4; Lambert, *Cathars*, pp. 290–6.

Reformation and then redefined itself as a form of Protestantism. It is noteworthy that the historian who has studied these fourteenth-century movements most closely, Grado Merlo, habitually refers to 'medieval Waldensian*isms*' in the plural rather than the singular.[78] If only because they *do* raise the question of how one defines what was 'true' Waldensianism, the individual movements of dissent charted in this chapter certainly deserve detailed consideration.

The story of these movements appears to begin around the 1360s with a charismatic religious leader called Pietro Garigli. Around 1366 Garigli met the religious vagrant Giacomo Bech, while the latter was returning from Rome. Garigli claimed to be the Son of God, and was accompanied by ten others whom he called his apostles. He invited Bech to join their number and make up the full number of the true apostles. Bech declined and instead joined the Cathars of Chieri.[79] However, Garigli acquired many other followers on his travels. One of the most significant was Antonio Provana, often mentioned in the same breath as Garigli and presumably a contemporary.[80] Garigli acquired a group of lay followers in the Valle di Lanzo, in Lanzo and Pessinetto, several of whom recalled his ministry later on.[81] However, his mission was short-lived. By 1373, when the relatively mild inquisitor Tommasso di Casasco investigated the Lanzo heretics, Garigli and Provana had already been burned as heretics at Avignon. Garigli apparently promised to rise again three days after his execution.[82] Garigli's mantle passed to two, it would seem rather different, heretic leaders. One was Fra Angelo de la Marcha, who may possibly have been an early member of the Fraticelli.[83] He attracted an impressionable follower from Carmagnola called Giacomo Ristolas, who subsequently accepted Angelo's description of himself as Elijah. He appears to have been an itinerant, preaching in other people's homes.[84] Angelo described Garigli and Provana as martyrs because of the manner of their deaths; however, at least as far as 1395, Angelo de la Marcha appears to have escaped the same fate himself.[85]

The other leader who inherited Garigli's mission and adherents, about whom rather a lot of information survives, was Martinus de Presbitero or Martin Prestre, of the Piedmontese town of Viú, near the Valle di

---

78   See Merlo, *Valdesi e valdismi medievali, passim.*
79   Amati, 'Processus Contra Valdenses', vol. 2, pt 1, p. 50.
80   Merlo, *Eretici e inquisitori*, pp. 263, 267, 270; Amati, 'Processus Contra Valdenses', vol. 2, pt 1, p. 46.
81   Merlo, *Eretici e inquisitori*, pp. 263–4, 267, 270, 276–7, 279.
82   Ibid., pp. 265, 276, 279; Boffito, 'Eretici in Piemonte', pp. 393–4.
83   On the strength of the Fraticelli in the Marche, see D. L. Douie, *The Nature and Effect of the Heresy of the Fraticelli* (Manchester, 1932), pp. 243–5.
84   Amati, 'Processus Contra Valdenses', vol. 2, pt 1, pp. 5, 60; Boffito, 'Eretici in Piemonte', pp. 392–8.
85   Ibid., pp. 393–4.

Lanzo.[86] Unlike the others of this group, Prestre was of fairly sedentary habits. He was married and had a house at Viú which seems to have functioned both as a home and a religious retreat. According to one of his followers, Antonio Galosna, Prestre announced to a gathering in 1385 or 1386 that he and Giacomo Bech of Chieri intended 'to build here a chapel to carry out our prayers and disciplines'. Bech and Prestre spent one winter together at Viú 'doing penance and walking barefoot in the snow'.[87]

Martin Prestre led a conventicle of people from Viú and the surrounding villages of Lanzo, Pessinetto and Coassolo for several years. He attracted many followers, especially a woman called Fina who lived at Lanzo, who had previously been a pupil of Pietro Garigli.[88] His followers visited him at Viú and 'showed him reverence'. He taught groups of people 'often in his own house, or in the street, or in the pastures, wherever was convenient, more than 150 times'.[89] Not surprisingly, such a public display of heresy soon attracted notice. Some time before 1373 Martin was summoned to meet the inquisitor Huguet Bergognini at Avigliana. He raised problems, offering to meet the inquisitor in another town, and eventually seems to have obtained some form of absolution indirectly from the Bishop of Turin.[90] In the spring and early summer of 1373 Tommasso di Casasco caught up with Martin Prestre. He interrogated not only Prestre himself but a succession of his followers. At the end of the trial Prestre abjured his heresy and was given a penance of three years' imprisonment with fasting, prayers, rough clothing and a promise never to discuss religious teachings or expound scripture to others.[91] Nevertheless, by the mid-1380s at the latest Prestre was back to his old ways. He was leading religious discussion among his heterodox friends at Viú, possibly more privately than before, but with no sign of real conversion. At some time between 1388 and 1395 Prestre must have been subjected to a further trial. By 1395 he had been burned for heresy in the town of Avigliana.[92]

What did Martin Prestre teach and what were his links, if any, with Waldensian heresy in the heartland valleys of Piedmont further south?

86   Merlo, *Eretici e inquisitori*, p. 276.
87   Amati, 'Processus Contra Valdenses', vol. 2, pt 1, pp. 4–5.
88   Merlo, *Eretici e inquisitori*, pp. 263–5.
89   Ibid., pp. 264, 269, 280.
90   Ibid., p. 280.
91   Ibid., pp. 259–61.
92   Boffito, 'Eretici in Piemonte', pp. 391, 397, 400. Note that a marginal reference to the manuscript in Amati, 'Processus Contra Valdenses', vol. 2, pt 1, p. 8, refers to Prestre as having been burned in Avigliana. The main text, however, assumes he was still alive when Antonio Galosna was interrogated in 1388.

Some of Prestre's and his followers' teachings, as summarized at his 1373 trial, appear very Waldensian. He taught that there was no purgatory; that priests in mortal sin could not absolve penitents; and that the power of the keys had been removed from the priesthood because of the sins of the clergy. This anti-sacerdotal teaching reached back, it would seem, to Garigli and Provana.[93] In one sermon at Lèmie in the Val di Viú, Martin asserted that after Sylvester I there was no true pope or bishop.[94] Prestre added some points which, while not 'classically' Waldensian, are in keeping with the other Piedmontese heresies of the period. He taught that 'the substance of the body of Jesus Christ was not in the sacrament of the altar, but only the divinity';[95] he is reported to have made fun of his wife when she came back from Church saying 'that she had seen Christ consecrated on the altar'.[96] In his followers' hands this teaching became a simple denial of the real presence. Fina di Lanzo commented ironically that when the priest said the words of consecration, it was claimed that Christ was present in the Mass on the altar. However, just after the priest had elevated the consecrated host, he said 'Our Father, who art in heaven'. 'See how quickly', Fina had remarked, 'he makes a great leap!' At one moment Christ was on the altar, at the next in the heavens.[97] At other times the same denial could be tacked on to doubts about the clergy: a priest who was a sinner could not consecrate the Mass.[98] Like the Dauphinois heretic Guilhem Pruza, Prestre's group believed that the saints were not in Paradise until the Day of Judgement and therefore should not be prayed to.[99] Prestre also dissuaded his followers from showing reverence to the cross: 'the cross was not to be adored because a man was hanged on it'; and urged that no reverence be shown to religious images.[100] Some other slight links seem to tie in Prestre's group to the main Waldensian community: two 'brothers from Briançon' in the Waldensian lands of the Dauphiné stayed once with Fina di Lanzo.[101] More interesting still, in one interrogation it was reported that 'Petrus of Coazze', burned at Avignon for heresy, was revered as a martyr by Prestre's followers, along with Garigli and Provana. This may be the same as the 'Peyret of Coazze' who had been a (younger?) com-

93 Merlo, *Eretici e inquisitori*, pp. 263, 281; cf Amati, 'Processus Contra Valdenses', vol. 2, pt 1, p. 9.

94 Merlo, *Eretici e inquisitori*, p. 282. This marks the first appearance of the Sylvester legend in a trial dossier from Piedmont.

95 Ibid., pp. 259, 281.

96 Amati, 'Processus Contra Valdenses', vol. 2, pt 1, pp. 8–9.

97 Merlo, *Eretici e inquisitori*, p. 264; cf. p. 262.

98 Ibid., pp. 278–9, 283.

99 Ibid., p. 270.

100 Ibid., pp. 259, 282.

101 Ibid., p. 280.

panion of one of the senior Waldensian pastors in the Valle di Susa in the 1330s.[102]

However, Prestre also had links with the Cathar community of Chieri. The dualists of Chieri were a tight-knit group based around a few families, especially the Raneta and the Narro.[103] They taught and practised a religion very close to the classic absolute dualism of the Italian Cathars of the high middle ages. Their leaders practised the same ritual abstinences and received the same devotion and respect from their followers as in other Cathar communities.[104] They had contacts through correspondence and visits with the dualist Church in Bosnia.[105] Links were established between Martin Prestre's group and the Chieri group when one of Prestre's followers, a compulsive religious nomad named Giacomo Bech, migrated from the Garigli–Prestre orbit into that of the Chieri dualists. Bech had a long history of wandering from one religious dissenting community to another, punctuated by at least two trials for heresy. He was tried by Tommasso di Casasco around 1380, by which time he had already joined the Cathars;[106] Casasco spared him the worst penalties because he revealed the presence of other heretics. Antonio Settimo in 1388 discovered him to have relapsed and was not so merciful: Bech was burned at Turin.[107] By 1412 it would seem that Catharism had died out at Chieri: the inquisitor Giovanni di Susa of Rivoli condemned the leaders posthumously and confiscated their property, with certain exemptions.[108]

Because of his links through Bech, Prestre was interrogated about some Cathar beliefs, though he mostly denied holding these. Tommasso di Casasco asked if he believed that the souls of those who died impure passed into other bodies: he denied it.[109] Yet according to Antonio Galosna, Prestre once told him that the one who 'was stronger than anything else which could be found was the dragon which fights against God and rules over the whole world': such a statement is resonant with Cathar dualism. However, as Galosna attributed a nearly identical statement to Lorenzo di Lormea, a Cathar leader living at Andezeno near Chieri, one may suspect some confusion in his otherwise bewildered testimony.[110] Giacomo Bech later told how Martin Prestre used to write frequently to Bartolomeo Bocacio, one of the Chieri Cathars. Bocacio 'many times

102 Boffito, 'Eretici in Piemonte', pp. 396–7.
103 Amati, 'Processus Contra Valdenses', vol. 2, pt 1, pp. 52–6.
104 Ibid., pp. 50–2.
105 Ibid., p. 53.
106 Ibid., pp. 48–9, 52.
107 A fuller version of Bech's life story is found in Lambert, *Cathars*, pp. 291, 294–6.
108 Boffito, 'Eretici in Piemonte', pp. 421–9.
109 Merlo, *Eretici e inquisitori*, p. 281.
110 Amati, 'Processus Contra Valdenses', vol. 2, pt 1, pp. 5, 9, 15.

asked Martin Prestre to be entirely of their faith and sect along with his followers in the Valle di Lanzo; he many times wrote back to them that in some respects he wished to be with them and in other respects not.'[111] Prestre's group had its own identity, which precludes it from being regarded as purely an extension of either Waldensian or Cathar traditions. It taught various unusual prayers;[112] its followers looked to their resident leaders rather than to any wider fellowship of travelling teachers.

Martin Prestre showed striking inventiveness in his religious practices. If Antonio Galosna is to be believed, during a meal at his house he performed the following rite with a loaf of bread, calling it 'the first grace and the first sacrament, [which] exceeded all other sacraments':

> When the meal was ready, he took a loaf, placed it on his knee, then cut three mouthfuls of the said loaf; he gave one to brother Peter, one to brother Anthonius [Galosna] and the third to his wife. Then he made another two mouthfuls, and gave one to his servant-girl, and [took] one himself; then he signed the bread with the sign of the cross, and afterwards everyone ate the said mouthful on bended knee; then they all drank, one after another.[113]

It is possible, though by no means certain, that this ritual with the bread resembles the distribution of 'blessed bread' called the *consolamentum* described by the Waldenses in the Val Perosa whom Antonio Settimo investigated in 1387, although Prestre's followers had not recognized the use of the term when asked about it in 1373.[114] Galosna claimed to have imitated the ritual himself at other meetings in Màttie in the Valle di Susa and also in Avigliana.[115] He also reported the administering of bread to a dying Cathar woman at Andezeno, near Chieri, calling it a *consolamentum*.[116] Galosna reported other curious happenings at Prestre's table:

> While he was dining with the said Martinus de Presbitero, Petrus [of Sardinia] the priest and Fontanellus [of Viù], he saw a shadow over the door of Martinus's house which quite frightened him; . . . while they were dining Martinus kept by him a black rabbit as big as a lamb, and gave it to eat of the food which they were eating; and Martinus said that this rabbit was the best friend one could have in the world.[117]

111 Ibid., p. 56.
112 Merlo, *Eretici e inquisitori*, pp. 263, 275, 280.
113 Amati, 'Processus Contra Valdenses', vol. 2, pt 1, p. 4. There are Cathar parallels for this rite.
114 Merlo, *Eretici e inquisitori*, pp. 264, 276.
115 Amati, 'Processus Contra Valdenses', vol. 2, pt 1, pp. 6, 8.
116 Ibid., pp. 15–16.
117 Ibid., p. 5.

One suspects that Settimo may have been inquiring about the possibility that Prestre engaged in magical or demoniac practices; however, the interrogation was not followed up, and these curious details of the atmosphere were left to stand as they were. More conventionally, Prestre appears to have heard confessions of sins from his followers, and to have conferred this power on others as well. Fina di Lanzo confessed her sins with Garigli and others, as did Giacomo Borelli, the tailor of Viú; Giovanni Belleza of Coassolo had confessed to Martin Prestre.[118] Prestre may, moreover, have conferred the authority to hear confessions on Antonio Galosna. Asked about this 'ordination', he reported that 'he received it humbly on bended knee: Martinus signed him with the sign of the cross, just as any other priest would, and he gave him this power from year to year [i.e. annually]'. He claimed to have heard the confessions of seven people in the Lanzo district as a result of this commission.[119]

One serious problem afflicts the sources for Martin Prestre's group, which has already been touched upon. It affects the reliability of the testimony of Antonio Galosna, a significant though not unique source for these heretical societies, and to some extent the reliability of the inquisitor Antonio Settimo, who tried Galosna in 1388. Galosna reported a great many things in his testimony which seem inherently implausible, or at least to suggest that he was desperate to satisfy the inquisitor and improvised his story accordingly. After describing the ritual by which Martin Prestre 'ordained' him as a confessor, Galosna was asked about 'congregations' of the heretics in all the towns which he had visited. Some of the details of these meetings are superficially plausible. However, Settimo was clearly fishing for sexual scandals, as he had been with the Waldenses of Val Perosa in the previous year. As the interrogation progressed, it narrowed down to a description of towns visited, meetings attended with the accompanying sexual orgies, and lists of those present. Galosna was able to describe the people who attended, and gave their professions, residences and relationships to each other, but not their names, which is more or less the opposite of what might have been expected of a casual visitor. When speaking of the people of Chieri and its environs, he gave more details: indeed, he seems to have known quite a lot about the teachings of Lorenzo de Lormea, leader of the dualists of Andezeno. However, even here his testimony is contaminated with implausible tales:

> The leader among the women was 'Bilia la Castagna', now dead, who gave everyone drinks when they sat down at table. . . . She brought the drink in a phial, and that drink was foul to look at, and one who had drunk

118 Merlo, *Eretici e inquisitori*, pp. 264, 269, 276.
119 Amati, 'Processus Contra Valdenses', vol. 2, pt 1, p. 6.

enough of it swelled up, so much so that one person who drank a lot of it nearly died; and he and all the others took of such a drink as often as they began the said synagogue. It was, or ought to have been, of such efficacy that anyone who drank of it once was not able thereafter to leave the company of the said synagogue, and the rumour was that she kept a large toad under the bed which she fed on meat and bread and cheese.[120]

Some of the meetings which Galosna reported took place in traditional Waldensian territory, as for example in Giaveno, Coazze and Pinasca. The striking thing about these statements is that Galosna appears to attribute similar debased Cathar statements to all the heretics whom he claimed to have met, whether they were from the region of Chieri or elsewhere. The heresies taught at Giaveno allegedly included the denial that Mary was a virgin, or that Christ was conceived by the Holy Spirit, or that God took human flesh at all; all visible nature was created by the 'great dragon who fights against God'; and the soul died with the body.[121]

Galosna finally over-reached himself when interrogated about the heretics of Pinerolo. He claimed that synagogues took place at the house of 'Coleta the beguine', where Pietro Bermondi of Pragelato preached and distributed bread, and Bertino Franco of Coazze, called 'Basterio' distributed wine. Bermondi and Basterio were real people, who fervently denied any involvement in heresy whatever.[122] Moreover, they seem to have had the ear of the local nobility. When Galosna accused the two from Pinerolo, the Count of Savoy's chancellor and the local judge took him aside and offered to let him escape if he would withdraw his accusations against Bermondi and Basterio. When he refused to withdraw his claims, they tortured him in the great hall of the castle, by pinning him to the ground and pouring water through his nostrils. Finally he was brought before the Count of Savoy himself and threatened with the strappado if he would not retract his statements. Eventually he agreed to admit – so the inquisitor's account says – that his confessions were false. However, on Settimo's own showing the inquisitor himself had previously tortured him, to extract the confessions in the first place![123] It is impossible, with only one side of the evidence, to conclude how much of Galosna's testimony was true and how much invented, given that he was tortured both to confess and retract. All one can rely on is a reader's intuitive response to the text. Clearly, though, much is bizarre, some confused, and much of it barely consistent with other sources. It is not only

120 Ibid., pp. 6–13, and esp. pp. 12–13 for the quotation.
121 Ibid., p. 25.
122 Ibid., pp. 30–2, and cf. pp. 51–2 for the interrogations of Bermondi and Basterio.
123 Ibid., pp. 33–5.

the modern reader who feels some sympathy with the hapless Galosna. Ysoard de Dominis of the Val San Martino offered to let him escape on payment of some money. All was in the end to no avail: Galosna was burned as a heretic at Turin shortly afterwards.[124]

These in some ways eccentric religious individualists bulk larger in the record than their likely numbers deserve. Already by the late fourteenth century the Waldenses in the heartland valleys west of Pinerolo were sufficiently well ensconced to resist both the attacks and the curiosity of ecclesiastical justice. Over the next few centuries they would give further abundant proof of this tenacity. Consequently, inquisitors expended effort, ink and cruelty on Martin Prestre and his unfortunate followers: they were easier to reach, more loquacious and more vulnerable. However, these personalities can do more for the historian that just arouse sympathy, or curiosity as to the religious significance of Martin Prestre's pet rabbit. They show, beyond all doubt, that heresy did not need an ancient tradition, real or invented, to raise doubts about the difficult and challenging dogmas of contemporary Catholicism: it could be reinvented and rediscovered at will. They represent an apparently fresh and independent flowering of the 'Waldensian' style of religious dissent. One need not, therefore, assume that every previous expression of Waldensian beliefs and teachings was necessarily sprung from the same source.

7.4 The Dauphiné, 1360s–1487

While Waldensianism in Piedmont was proliferating into a diversity of syncretic and imaginative variants, a closely related but more homogeneous movement took root and established itself just across the Alpine passes in the semi-autonomous French-speaking principality of the Dauphiné. While it was found as far west as the Valentinois, its strongholds were in the valleys of the Gyronde and the Biaysse leading into the Durance, which flows from the Alps near Briançon past the little archiepiscopal city of Embrun into the Rhône. Two communities, Valpute and L'Argentière, would acquire notorious heretic minorities; one, Freissinières, would become almost totally heretic. Waldensianism would establish itself not only as a form of religious dissent, but also as a social organization. In this particular case, there grew up alongside the clandestine structures of the celibate pastorate, a structure of self-defence and collective action managed by the leaders of Alpine peasant society, which ultimately resisted ecclesiastical justice with unprecedented tenacity: therein lies much of the special interest of the Waldenses of the

---

124 Ibid., p. 35; Boffito, 'Eretici in Piemonte', p. 400.

Map V Waldensian communities in the region of Embrun and Briançon, 14th–15th centuries.

Dauphiné and their spectacular history from the fourteenth to the early sixteenth centuries.

As in Piedmont, so in the Dauphiné the story appears to begin with an attack on inquisitors. In 1321 two Franciscans from Saillans, emissaries of the inquisitor Jacques Bernard, were murdered by heretics who stormed into the priory of St-Jacques at Montélier where they were spending a night.[125] A little later, in 1335, there appears the first evidence of heretics in the valleys of the Durance around Briançon. By 1338 the accounts of the castellany of Valpute first recorded formal legal persecution of these people.[126] Even as early as the seventeenth century, when the archiepiscopal archive of Embrun was better preserved than it is now, no evidence showed Waldensian penetration of the region before this period.[127] Already in the latter half of the thirteenth century, a series of papal documents had, somewhat unusually, entrusted the function of inquisition in the Dauphiné to members of the Franciscan order, rather than the Dominican friars who usually acted as inquisitors elsewhere.[128]

Evidence about these early inquisitions is fragmentary. Around 1353, according to the Jesuit Marcellin Fornier (1591–1650), who had access to much of the Embrun archive, a mass sentence of heretics in 1353 saw 150 men and women reconciled to the Church with penances of cross-wearing, fines and pilgrimages.[129] The inquisitor was probably Petrus de Montis OFM, through whose work the local nobility had by September 1354 acquired a share, amounting to over 115 gold florins, of the property which he had confiscated.[130] Inquisition seems to have ceased during the archiepiscopate of Guillaume des Bordes at Embrun (1352–63). In 1369 François Borelli OFM was appointed as inquisitor for Arles, Aix, Embrun and Gap. He seems to have had difficulty in securing sufficient support in the region until Pope Gregory XI stepped in with the sending of an apostolic nuncio, Antonius, Bishop of Massa: shortly thereafter he captured so many heretics that problems were experienced in housing and feeding them. Despite papal encouragement, Borelli appears soon afterwards to have fallen foul of that distrust and scepticism in high places

125 J. Marx, *L'Inquisition en Dauphiné: Étude sur le développement et la répression de l'hérésie et de la sorcellerie du xvie siècle au début du regne de François Ier*, Bibliothèque de l'École des Hautes Études, Sciences Historiques et Philologiques, 206e fasc. (Paris, 1914), p. 17 and refs.

126 Marx, *L'Inquisition en Dauphiné*, p. 5 and notes; P. Paravy, *De la Chrétienté romaine à la réforme en Dauphiné*, Collection de l'École Française de Rome, 183, 2 vols (Rome, 1993–4), pp. 958–67.

127 Marx, *L'Inquisition en Dauphiné*, p. 9; Fornier, *Histoire générale*, vol. 2, pp. 175ff., which dates the persecution specifically from 1353.

128 Marx, *L'Inquisition en Dauphiné*, pp. 6–8.

129 Fornier, *Histoire générale*, vol. 2, pp. 211–14.

130 Marx, *L'Inquisition en Dauphiné*, pp. 201–2.

in the Church which (no doubt deservedly) haunted over-enthusiastic inquisitors. In August 1376 Gregory XI commanded the Abbot of St-André at Vienne to investigate his 'improper exactions and excesses'.[131] Notwithstanding, Borelli persisted, and soon afterwards recruited the Châtellain of Valpute, Antoine Ruchier, to help him in his work. After the Great Schism broke out in 1378, Borelli secured confirmation and extension of his powers from the Avignonese antipope Clement VII in 1380. From that point he concentrated on the environs of Valpute, which for the time being was the most notorious centre of heresy. By June 1381 Johan Lambert, 'master of the sect of the Waldenses', was a captive at Embrun. Borelli investigated and absolved some of his associates; but some fled, and others failed to perform penances assigned to them. In August 1383 he returned to Valpute and brought several dozen suspected heretics back to Embrun for interrogation. In November the castellan seized Estève Chabrelli of Valpute, a 'seriously relapsed' heretic; he was taken and imprisoned at Embrun and burned that December.

In September 1383 Borelli had made a brief foray into the Val Chisone, the valley east of the Alpine passes which fell, by a quirk of political geography, under the rule of the Dauphin. During this ten-day visit the inquisitor and the castellan of the Valpute were attacked by the inhabitants: both the castellan's thumbs were dislocated. Apparently stung by this experience, Borelli made a further expedition to the Val Chisone in May 1384; that October he decided to lead an armed punitive raid into the valley. Large numbers of heretics were captured and led to Oulx for sentencing. On this occasion Borelli used the help of the (Catholic) inhabitants of the valleys of the Queyras in his attack. In July 1385 the vice-castellan of the district was told to investigate rumours that the Queyras people had stolen property from the heretics and not declared it to the Dauphin's officials.[132] Although many dozens of heretics were caught up in Borelli's inquisitions, the figure of 150 heretics sentenced to death, claimed by one late source, probably exaggerates.[133] The vast majority of his trials, like those of all other late medieval inquisitors, ended in abjurations and penances. After his long inquiries in the mid-1380s only five men and two women were burned within Valpute itself.[134] Although it was claimed in the early seventeenth century that

131 J. P. Perrin, *Histoire des Vaudois, divisée en trois parties* (Geneva, 1618 and 1619), pp. 109–15; N. Chorier, *Histoire générale du Dauphiné*, 2 vols (Valence, 1878–9; repr. Grenoble, 1971), vol. 2, pp. 391–2; Lea, *Inquisition*, vol. 2, pp. 152–6; Marx, *L'Inquisition en Dauphiné*, pp. 145, 202–3.
132 Ibid., pp. 203, 205–13.
133 If this figure does not indeed represent a confusion with de Montis's large penitential sentence as above, note 129.
134 Ibid., pp. 212–13.

Borelli passed a great sentence against the Waldenses in 1393, he may have ceased activity rather earlier. In March 1393 Pierre Motet, a new castellan of Valpute, had been helping a new inquisitor, Antoine Aillaud OFM, in prosecutions of heresy at Embrun, Briançon, and St-Martin-de-Queyrières.[135]

For another hundred years or so the Franciscan inquisitors of the Dauphiné harassed the Waldenses among whom they lived, though none appears to have equalled Borelli's zeal in persecuting the Waldenses before c.1470. Partly, this may have reflected a reorientation in the interests of inquisitors towards new targets, especially demonic witchcraft. It was in the Dauphiné that some of the earliest stories of what would become the stereotype of the classic witch first emerged, in the 1420s.[136] Franciscan inquisitors based in the house of their order at Briançon nevertheless maintained a quiet campaign against heresy. In 1419 Pierre Fabri OFM (d. 1452) was appointed inquisitor to assist Pons Feugeron; notes of interrogations he made in 1429, 1432 and 1437 have survived.[137] After Fabri's death Glaude Martin OFM carried out some 'skirmishes' against the Waldenses in 1459–60; heretics interrogated in the 1480s remembered his inquiries.[138] In January 1472 Jean Veyleti of Apchier OFM succeeded to the post of principal inquisitor in the Briançonnais. Apparently made of sterner stuff than his immediate predecessors, he almost immediately began proceedings which led, in July 1473, to a mass sentencing of reconciled Waldenses to pilgrimages, fasts, penitential prayers and other penances. One relapsed heretic was burned. Within a few months, however, Veyleti was attacked and wounded while crossing the Montgenèvre pass with money for a trip to Rome. Most of his assailants escaped; two were tried and hanged for this assault by the local judge Oronce Émé, who would play a major role in persecutions thereafter. The Jesuit Fornier subsequently seized on the picturesque testimony that one of Veyleti's would-be murderers was unable to hold up his weapon when confronted with the sight of the

135 Perrin, *Histoire des Vaudois*, pp. 113–15; Chorier, *Histoire générale*, vol. 2, p. 392; Marx, *L'Inquisition en Dauphiné*, p. 204.
136 On the rise of the witch-myth in the Alps, see for example Robin Briggs, *Witches and Neighbours: The Social and Cultural Context of European Witchcraft* (London, 1996), p. 33; R. Kieckhefer, *European Witch Trials: Their Foundation in Popular and Learned Culture, 1300–1500* (London, 1976), pp. 20–1, 73–4; N. Cohn, *Europe's Inner Demons* (London, 1977), pp. 225–30.
137 Fornier, *Histoire générale*, vol. 2, pp. 326–30; E. Arnaud, 'Histoire des persecutions endurées par les Vaudois du Dauphiné aux xiiie, xive et xve siècles', *Bulletin de la société d'histoire vaudoise* 12 (1895), p. 64; Marx, *L'Inquisition en Dauphiné*, pp. 214–17; Cambridge, University Library, MS. Dd. 3. 26, sect.4, fo. 2r.
138 Fornier, *Histoire générale*, vol. 2, p. 358; Cambridge, University Library, MS. Dd. 3. 25, fo. 53v; Cambridge, University Library, MS. Dd. 3. 26, sect.4, fo. 5r.

inquisitor's face, but dropped it helplessly at his feet. Even inquisitors could work miracles.[139]

Veyleti's persecutions evoked a further response in the Waldenses of the Briançonnais, which would become a typical feature of this period. The local people appealed to royal justice to protect them from the inquisitors. Quite why Louis XI chose to intervene in favour of the suspected Waldensian heretics of the Dauphiné is unclear. He is known to have been at odds with the Archbishop of Embrun, Jehan Baile (1457–94), the son of a former *président* of the *parlement* of Grenoble, who had also (perhaps significantly) been *coseigneur* of the Vaudois village of Freissinières. From 1461 Archbishop Baile was absent from his diocese, and his activities against heresy only began in the dying months of Louis XI's reign, in 1483.[140] In any event, on 18 May 1478 Louis XI issued the first of what became some celebrated letters ordering the inquisitors to desist. The letters presumably incorporated some of the claims made in the original supplication from the people of Vallouise (as Valpute was now known), Freissinières and L'Argentière. They alleged that mendicant inquisitors had illegally extracted confessions of heresy from those who were and had always been good Catholics, and on that pretext had seized large amounts of their property in confiscations. Louis XI accordingly voided the entire legal processes against these people (though how he claimed jurisdiction in what was indubitably an ecclesiastical case was not clear). Any who were nonetheless obstinate heretics were not, of course, granted the benefit of this verdict.[141] Around this time (it was later alleged) the *vibailli* of Briançon, Oronce Émé or Aymé, and the *procureur-fiscal* of the Briançonnais, Jordanon Cordi (or Coeur), were arrested and imprisoned on the orders of the *Grand Conseil* for their excesses. They escaped prison and had their case referred to the Grenoble *parlement*, where it was stalled.[142]

From before 1480 until 1509 and beyond the case of the Waldenses of the valleys of the Briançonnais would become ensnared in the tangled mass of French royal and Delphinal justice. The demarcation between the two jurisdictions of Paris and Grenoble was a subject of perpetual contention, somewhat more troublesome and fruitful of delay, in this

---

139 Fornier, *Histoire générale*, vol. 2, pp. 367–73; D. Godefroy, *Histoire de Charles VIII* (Paris, 1684), p. 280. For Veyleti's trials see the references in Cambridge, University Library, MS. Dd. 3. 25, fos 53r, 116v–17r; Cambridge, University Library, MS. Dd. 3. 26, sect.4, fos 2r-v, 5r, 10r; Paris, Bibliothèque Nationale, Fonds Latin, MS. 3375, vol. 2, fos 445r–6v.
140 Fornier, *Histoire générale*, vol. 2, pp. 352–5, 371 n.
141 Cambridge, University Library, MS. Dd. 3. 25, fos 46–50; in Perrin, *Histoire des Vaudois*, pp. 118–24; see also Fornier, *Histoire générale*, vol. 2, pp. 409–10; Marx, *L'Inquisition en Dauphiné*, pp. 147–9.
142 Paris, Bibliothèque Nationale, Fonds Latin, MS. 3375, vol. 1, fos 381r–2v. On persecutions at this period, see also Paravy, *De la Chrétienté romaine*, pp. 975–7.

case, than the boundary between ecclesiastical and secular law. After over a century of humiliations and confiscations, the Waldenses of the Dauphiné had embarked on a dangerous strategy, based on the claim that they were utterly good Catholics, unfairly harassed by unscrupulous and selfish churchmen and lawyers. When examining their religious practices, there will appear more than a little evidence to lend support to the claim that the Waldenses did (at least) perform the minimum religious duties expected of Catholics. However, it is equally clear that they formed a close-knit, clearly identified group; and that their strategy of legal self-defence emerged (by an irony) out of their social cohesiveness as a dissenting minority in the population, whose religious practices differed significantly from those of the majority.

From April 1483 Archbishop Jehan Baile began to act against the Waldenses of his diocese on his own account. His inquiries conducted up to the start of the crusade of 1487–8 left a mass of testimonies which, unlike the records of earlier inquisitors, survive in profusion.[143] Between April and August 1483 Baile held a series of increasingly acrimonious meetings with representatives of the Waldensian villages, leadership of which had now passed to the syndics of Freissinières. Baile regarded himself as something between a pastor and an inquisitor, whose job was to guide the erring back to the Church. The Waldenses' representatives took the posture that they were litigants in an unresolved process in the king's *Grand Conseil*, pending a resolution of which the archbishop should leave them alone. Meanwhile the Catholic majority of Vallouise, led by the priest and the syndics, positively invited the bishop to clear up the mess and redeem their community's reputation by identifying and punishing the heretics. Jehan Baile then paused for nearly three years. In the autumn of 1486 he began some meticulous and prolonged interrogations of rather marginal Waldensian heretics whom he had seized.[144]

143   The distribution of the records of fifteenth-century Dauphiné Waldensianism deserves explanation. After the dispersal of the archive originally kept in the former archiepiscopal palace at Embrun in the Wars of Religion (see below, Epilogue), the records passed into the hands of the Lesdiguières family at Geneva, from which they were collected by the diplomat and historian Samuel Morland in the 1650s, and thence found their way to the University Library, Cambridge. Meanwhile, some original and some copied documents, gathered by James Ussher through correspondence with the Dauphinois historian Jean-Paul Perrin, were ultimately deposited in the library of Trinity College, Dublin. The records of the 1487–8 crusade, which were returned to the *Chambre des Comptes* of the Dauphiné when the crusaders' expenses were paid, were deposited in what became the Archives Départmentales de l'Isère at Grenoble. Those from the lawsuit leading to the rehabilitation of 1509 were lodged at Paris, finding their way to the Bibliothèque Nationale. Meanwhile, what remained of the Embrun archive was severely damaged during the French Revolution; some scraps ended up in the Archives Départmentales des Hautes-Alpes at Gap.

144   These long trials included that of Antoni Blazy of Angrogna, between 13 March and 14 September 1486 (Cambridge, University Library, MS. Dd. 3. 25, fos

Late in the same year he issued a mass excommunication of the people of Freissinières. On 5 February 1487 two representatives from that community formally appealed from the archbishop to the *legatus a latere*, the Archbishop of Vienne, before whom Baile refused to appear personally. Both parties then appealed to Rome and the process seemed destined to become bogged down in delay.[145] It was against this background that one of the most extraordinary dramas of the history of late medieval heresy was about to unfold, the Waldensian crusade of 1487–8.

The surviving evidence gathered just before and in the course of the crusade amounts to a widely dispersed dossier of unprecedented size and complexity in the history of medieval Waldensianism.[146] It supplies many circumstantial details and unusual pieces of information about the lives of the lay Waldensian communities of the last quarter of the fifteenth century. However, it is essential to use this Dauphiné evidence in a discriminating way, for it presents a number of challenges.

1   None of the locally based pastors of the Waldenses, known by this period as 'barbes', are known to have been captured and interrogated and to have left a record of their trial.[147] For this precise period, all

59r–77v); the trial in absence of Antoni Baridon (ibid., fos 81r–94r); and the trial of Odin Valoy, Cambridge, University Library, MS. Dd. 3. 26, sect.2.

145   The documents of this process are found in Cambridge, University Library, MS. Dd. 3. 25, fos 53r–6v, 57v, 78r–9v, 98v–9v; Dublin, Trinity College, MS. 265, fos 23r–9r, and MS. 266, fos 15r–18v; Paris, Bibliothèque Nationale, Fonds Latin, MS. 3375, vol. 2, fos 105–373; see also Marx, *L'Inquisition en Dauphiné*, pp. 149–58, 231–5; Fornier, *Histoire générale*, vol. 2, p. 427, and vol. 3, pp. 413ff.

146   The principal manuscripts are Cambridge, University Library, MSS. Dd. 3. 25 and 26 (materials from the archdiocese of Embrun itself); Dublin, Trinity College, MSS. 265, 266 (early modern copies of much of the Cambridge MSS.); Grenoble, Archives Départmentales de l'Isère, MSS. B 4350 and B 4351 (incomplete and damaged but substantial dossiers from the 1487–8 crusade); Paris, Bibliothèque Nationale, Fonds Latin, MS. 3375, 2 vols (the dossier of the lawsuit for the rehabilitation of the Waldenses).

147   Two *barbes*, Francesco di Girundino and Pietro di Jacopo, were captured and tried at the ecclesiastical court of Oulx, near the passes, in 1492: the dossiers survive as Cambridge, University Library, MSS. Dd. 3. 26, sect.6, fos 1r–8v, 9r–12r respectively; the trial of the first of these is edited with numerous misreadings in P. Allix, *Some remarks upon the Ecclesiastical History of the Ancient Churches of Piedmont* (London, 1690), pp. 307–17. In the (unedited) trial of Pietro di Jacopo, it is stated several times, esp. sect.6, fo. 9r, that he was one of the 'brethren of the opinion': 'in Italia inter se nominantur fratres de oppinione [*sic*]'. This phrase denoted a sect of the Fraticelli, not the Waldenses; and the two travellers came from Spoleto and the Marche, where the Fraticelli remained strong: see D. L. Douie, *The Nature and Effect of the Heresy of the Fraticelli* (Manchester, 1932), pp. 243–5. While one might argue about the precise affiliation of these two, they were not local to the Dauphiné and betrayed no special knowledge of local conditions. They certainly revealed nothing about the *barbes* comparable to what is discussed below, chapter 8.

that survives are the confessions of the followers, the supporters, receivers and friends of the heretic leaders.

2   Much of the evidence for the way of life and customs of the Waldensian followers comes from inquisitorial trial registers. Some are virtually verbatim records of the gradual process of interrogation, covering weeks, months or even years, during which Archbishop Baile teased out admissions from the accused.[148] Others are cursory, mechanical, repetitive statements taken down by the notaries after the crusade, when several dozen heretics might be interrogated and sentenced in a single day.[149] In these latter instances the accused can have done little more than assent, under some measure of threat, to a series of more or less leading questions: often the register recorded how a heretic had confessed to a given error in exactly the same words over and over again.[150] In such circumstances it would be misleading to draw hard conclusions from simple arithmetic: one cannot count up the appearances of a given statement in the trials and conclude that the most frequently mentioned elements were the most important. On the contrary, the occasional pieces of unusual testimony – details neither expected nor sought by the interrogator – may prove to be particularly revealing.

3   One dossier from the Dauphiné cannot be taken at face value as a statement of the beliefs and behaviour of the Waldenses. This is the register compiled from 1501 onwards during the process of rehabilitation.[151] In this case Waldenses and their neighbours alike took part in a grand conspiracy of silence to suppress any information about the heresies held by the people of Freissinières: suspected heretics insisted on their Catholic beliefs, and their neighbours, landlords and employers supported them. If nothing else, this flat contradiction of the other sources shows how a credulous, simplistic belief in the veracity of all the evidence cannot be correct.[152]

---

148   See references above, note 144.
149   For examples of mass interrogations, see Grenoble, AD Isère, MS. B 4351, fos 143v–73v, 220v–242v, 324r–40r.
150   An example of such a stereotyped phrase occurs in ibid., e.g. fo. 345v: 'quod solus deus est orandus sancti et sancte dei non sunt deprecandi nec ad eos preces porrigere debemus quia solus deus est qui potest nos iuvare'. In this case, after the stereotyped phrase, the accused affirmed that, nevertheless, she believed in the Virgin Mary.
151   See the discussion below.
152   Rival registers, taken down by different secretaries attending the same interrogations, are found in Cambridge, University Library, MSS. Dd. 3. 25, fos 25r–38v; Paris, Bibliothèque Nationale, Fonds Latin, MS. 3375, ii, fos 46r–95v. For comparisons between the two see Cameron, *Reformation of the Heretics*, pp. 53–5.

So how did the Waldenses of the Dauphiné live between the mid-fourteenth and the late fifteenth centuries? The pattern of their behaviour is what will be expected, given what has already been said about the Waldenses east of the Alps. Lay followers led their ordinary lives, practising an exterior observance of Catholic ritual in its compulsory and even some of its voluntary aspects. They attended Catholic churches, made confession and took communion. Some purchased Masses for the souls of their dead relatives.[153] They used holy water, and one at least went on pilgrimage to the local shrine at Embrun.[154] However, they showed certain distinctive habits in their behaviour and speech. They received, at widely spaced and irregular intervals, visits from the itinerant, celibate pastors of the sect. These were, as Jean Marx wrote in 1914, 'in general people of modest education and humble condition, who knew by heart certain parts of the Gospels and some quotations from the Fathers of the Church . . . some were natives of the Briançonnais valleys, some came from Piedmont.'[155] Many were known only by Christian names: '*barbe* Henri', '*barbe* Benoît' and so forth. A few had surnames which can confidently be matched with some of the families of the region: Antoni Porte, Johan Bret, Jame Ruffi, Johan and Antoni Brunet. Thomas Tercian of Meana di Susa was one of several Tercians known to have been *barbes*. References to '*barbe* Symunt' from the Valentinois, or '*barbe* Estève' from Luserna, testify to links with other parts of the same Waldensian community.[156] They served some of the religious needs of their followers by meeting them in secluded places, preaching to them, hearing their confessions and assigning penances. From them the followers acquired much of their grasp of Waldensian teachings – even though not all swallowed what they heard uncritically.

Though the Waldensian followers were by this time a minority in all their villages except Freissinières, they were tenaciously aware of themselves as a community. Years of legal pressure from inquisitors led the followers – quite distinctly from and independently of the *barbes* – to set up their own mechanisms for defending and sustaining their cause. As

153 Cambridge, University Library, MSS. Dd. 3. 25, fos 29r, 33r, 35v, 54v, 57r, 99r-v; Dd. 3. 26, sect.4, fo. 10v; Dublin, Trinity College, MS. 266, fo. 57; Grenoble, AD Isère, MS. B4351, fos 115v, 268v; Paris, Bibliothèque Nationale, Fonds Latin, MS. 3375, i. fos 246r, 250r-v, 257r, and ii, fos 58v, 70r, 78v.
154 Cambridge, University Library, MS. Dd. 3. 25, fos 53v, 54v, 57r, 66r-v, 112v.
155 Marx, *L'Inquisition en Dauphiné*, pp. 12–13.
156 Cambridge, University Library, MS. Dd. 3. 25, fo. 115v; MS. Dd. 3. 26, sect.4, fo. 4r; Paris, Bibliothèque Nationale, Fonds Latin, MS. 3375, i. fos 277r–88v; Grenoble, AD Isère, MS. B4350, fos 303v, 342v; B4351, fos 299v, 357v; Fornier, *Histoire générale*, vol. 2, pp. 204–5; a severely damp-damaged part of Grenoble MS. B 4350 appears to contain a reference to one *barbe* from Burgundy. For more on the *barbes* of the Dauphiné and their visits, see the meticulous analysis of the Grenoble registers in Paravy, *De la Chrétienté romaine*, pp. 1,059–68.

early as 1432 it was reported that supporters of the Waldenses had been gathering money from their number to pay for promoting lawsuits to prevent the inquisitor Pierre Fabri from investigating them.[157] Around the same time, John of Segovia reported at the Council of Basel that the Dauphinois Waldenses had raised money to support the cause of the Bohemian rebels.[158] By the late fifteenth century this fiscal levy on heretic households had become, apparently, an established tax on landed property. Freissinières contributed half, and L'Argentière and Vallouise the other half. Pragelato, on the Piedmontese side of the passes, also made a collection. Some of those who objected to this levy protested either to the archbishop or to the inquisitors; one poor farmer called Antoni Blanc, who refused to pay, found that one of his sheep was stolen to cover his dues.[159] With the money thus raised, the Waldensian people of the Dauphiné paid for some of their own people to act as procurators. They continued in this work both before the crusade and afterwards, with the ultimate success described below.[160] Within the villages themselves, decisions were taken by the collective, led by its locally elected magistrates, known in the region as syndics or consuls. These acted as representatives before the archbishop from 1483 onwards, and told their people how to respond to the crusaders in 1488.[161] Even more striking is the fact that the leaders of the village communities exhorted and encouraged their heretic pastors, the *barbes*, to appear before the inquisitors to dispute their case in public – something which the *barbes*, understandably, failed to do.[162] This quasi-legal embodiment of Waldensian protest into the

---

157　Fornier, *Histoire générale*, vol. 2, p. 330.
158　Joannes de Segovia, *Historia Gestorum Generalis Synodi Basiliensis*, ed. E. Birk, vol. 1, in *Monumenta Conciliorum Generalium Seculi Decimi Quinti, Concilium Basiliense, Scriptorum* tomus ii (Vindobonae, 1873), p. 138: 'In Delphinatu esse quandam porcionem inclusam inter montes, que adherens erroribus Bohemorum tributum imposuerat, levaverat, et miserat ad eosdem Bohemos, in quo manifesta fautoria heresis patebat.' Whether the statement is true or not, it reflects contemporary fear that the Bohemian heretical disease was subverting social order through sympathizers elsewhere in Europe.
159　For evidence of the support tax, see Cambridge, University Library, MS. Dd. 3. 25, fo. 111r; MS. Dd. 3. 26, sect.2, fos 2v–3r, sect.4, fos 2r-v, 4r, 5r, 9r, 12r; Dublin, Trinity College, MS. 266, fo. 57r; Grenoble, AD Isère, MS. B4350, fo. 70r; B4351, fos 100r, 118r, 122r; Fornier, *Histoire générale* vol. 2, pp. 330, 355; Marx, *L'Inquisition en Dauphiné*, p. 248; J. A. Chevalier, *Mémoire historique sur les hérésies en Dauphiné avant le xvie siècle* (Valence, 1890), pp. 146, 148, 150, 152.
160　Cambridge, University Library, MS. Dd. 3. 26, sect.3, fo. 1r-v; Grenoble, AD Isère, MS. B4350, fos 99v–100r, 105v; Paris, Bibliothèque Nationale, Fonds Latin, MS. 3375, ii. fo. 479r-v.
161　Cambridge, University Library, MS. Dd. 3. 25, fo. 56r-v; Grenoble, AD Isère, MS. B4351, fos 161v, 164r-v, 173r; Marx, *L'Inquisition en Dauphiné*, pp. 231–5.
162　Grenoble, AD Isère, MS. B4350, fo. 307v; B4351, fo. 247v; Godefroy, *Histoire de Charles VIII*, p. 280; Fornier, *Histoire générale*, vol. 2, pp. 413, 426.

fabric of local society, and its control by the secular leaders of its communities, is unique in the history of the movement, and deserves special notice.[163]

The beliefs of the Waldenses of the Dauphiné appear less complex and more conventionally 'Waldensian' than those of their Piedmontese associates. There appear no signs of the Christological heresy, or doubts about the real presence, which can be glimpsed in the material from fourteenth-century Piedmont. Neither – apart from one bewildering custom – is there any hint of the interpenetration of Cathar and Waldensian ideas found in the teachings of Martin Prestre or Giacomo Bech.[164] The core of the heresy of the Waldenses of the Dauphiné consisted in their *theoretical* rejection of the status of the sacral priesthood, and of the intrinsic holiness claimed for its rites and cult-objects. Related to this anti-sacerdotal sentiment was the familiar refusal to endorse official teachings concerning purgatory and the destiny of the soul after death. In the crudest, most repetitive and stereotypical of evidence, this picture is presented in a fairly conventional way, though even in such evidence there are idiosyncrasies. In the fuller and more detailed registers, a more complex picture emerges. The lay Waldensian followers or friends, like those whom Peter Zwicker had interrogated ninety years before, 'negotiated' their belief, as well as practice, to accommodate both heretical and Catholic influences.[165] For instance, Waldensian heresy in principle excluded prayers to or worship of the saints: *barbes* reportedly discouraged the practice. Yet some ignored this advice and prayed to them anyway; some venerated them 'even though they did not hear prayers'.[166] So unavoidable was the cult of the Virgin Mary that no less than thirteen suspects from Freissinières and L'Argentière prayed to both God and the Virgin Mary.[167] In at least a dozen cases *barbes* were reported to have enjoined saying the Ave Maria as part of a heretic's penance

163 Compare P. Paravy, 'Waldensians in the Dauphiné (1400–1530): From Dissidence in Texts to Dissidence in Practice', in Peter Biller and Anne Hudson (eds), *Heresy and Literacy, 1000–1530* (Cambridge, 1994), pp. 165–7; Paravy, *De la Chrétienté romaine*, pp. 1,015–31.

164 See above, section 7.3. The 'bewildering custom', one reported by only a few witnesses, is that some Waldenses apparently placed a halter around the neck of a dying believer, possibly to prevent the soul expiring from the dead person and transmigrating. See Cambridge, University Library, MS. Dd. 3. 25, fos 54v, 57r, 110r, 111v–13r, 114r-v; Marx, *L'Inquisition en Dauphiné*, p. 24; Fornier, *Histoire générale*, vol. 2, p. 209; discussion in Cameron, *Reformation of the Heretics*, pp. 116–17. There is no other evidence of belief in transmigration of souls in all the copious documentation from this period.

165 See above, chapter 6.5, and notes 230–2.

166 Cambridge, University Library, MS. Dd. 3. 26, sect.4, fos 8v, 10v; Grenoble, AD Isère, MS. B4351, fos 129v, 175v, 180r, 318v–19v.

167 Grenoble, AD Isère, MS. B4351, fos 124v, 126r, 127r-v, 167v, 169r, 170r, 178v, 180r, 218v, 304r, 307v, 345v.

(which flatly contradicts the earlier evidence from Germany and else-where). In only one case, that of Angelin Palon of Freissinières, does one read that he prayed the Ave Maria 'as far as "Holy Mary, Mother of God" only', omitting the request that she pray for him.[168] Some later (albeit unreliable) evidence from the 1500s claimed that many alleged Waldenses knew their Pater, Ave and Credo by heart, in Latin as well as the ver-nacular.[169] The cult of the Virgin Mary had sunk such deep roots in medieval culture that it had subverted even the long-standing Walden-sian aversion to saint-worship.

Something similar happened to the traditional Waldensian disbelief in purgatory. In a striking parallel to statements made by the German Waldenses, many of those of the Dauphiné affirmed that there were only two ways, after this life, to heaven and hell, and that purgatory did not exist; one should not bother with money offerings for the dead, as the Church invented these for profit.[170] Yet Peyre Roux of Freissinières claimed to have objected to a *barbe* that purgatory was mentioned in the Book of Maccabees.[171] Others either rejected the *barbes'* opinions on this point, or were confused as to what they were. In any case, there is evi-dence, both from the Dauphiné and subsequently from Provence, that the Waldensian communities took part in the system of offerings and Masses for the dead, though at a much lower level than contemporary Catholics.[172] Several were alleged to say in ordinary conversation, when they referred to a dead person or prayed for him, 'may God have par-doned him', rather than 'may God pardon him'.[173] They would be dif-

168 Cambridge, University Library, MS. Dd. 3. 25, fo. 67v, 69r; Cambridge, University Library, MS. Dd. 3. 26, sect.2, fo. 4r; sect.4, fos 1r, 4r, 5v, 6r-v, 10v, 11v; Grenoble, AD Isère, MS. B4351, fos 116r-v, 306v; Chevalier, *Mémoire historique*, p. 151.
169 Paris, Bibliothèque Nationale, Fonds Latin, MS. 3375, i, fos 446r, 455r-v, 457r, 458v, 463v; ii, fos 2r, 9v, 12v, 14r-v, 16r-v.
170 Cambridge, University Library, MS. Dd. 3. 25, fos 53r-v, 54v, 57r, 61r-v, 63v, 116v; Cambridge, University Library, MS. Dd. 3. 26, sect. 2, fo. 11r; sect. 4, fos 4r-v, 10v, 11r, 12r, 13r-v, 15r-v; sect. 5, fo. 7r; sect. 6, fo. 4r; Grenoble, AD Isère, MS. B4351, fo. 199r (this is one of a huge number of denials of purgatory in this dossier); Paris, Bibliothèque Nationale, Fonds Latin, MS. 3375, i, fos 244v, 247r, 249v–50r, 261v–2r, 270r, 278v, 281v, 284r-v, 286v, 289r.
171 Cambridge, University Library, MS. Dd. 3. 26, sect. 4, fo. 8v; the reference is to 2 Maccabees 12:43–5, a standard proof-text for the existence of purgatory. See above, chapter 5, note 54. For further ambiguity about the existence of purgatory, see Grenoble, AD Isère, MS. B4351, fos 255r, 285r, 327r.
172 Cambridge, University Library, MS. Dd. 3. 25, fos 29r, 33r, 35v; Grenoble, AD Isère, MS. B4351, fo. 268v; Paris, Bibliothèque Nationale, Fonds Latin, MS. 3375, ii, fos 58v, 70r, 78v; note that ibid., ii, fo. 437r-v, a Catholic legal represen-tation from 1507 specifically sought to deny the suggestion that Waldenses bought Masses for the dead. For practice in Provence (which is indisputable) see below, note 243.
173 Cambridge, University Library, MS. Dd. 3. 25, fos 55r–6r; Paris, Bibliothèque Nationale, Fonds Latin, MS. 3375, ii, 436v–7r.

ferent enough from the majority to stand out, yet not different enough to be consistent.

In a number of other aspects, too, Waldensian religious conduct remained distinctive, yet curiously at odds with the theoretical implications of their belief. The heretics supposedly ignored the fasts and feast-days of the Church, around which so much of the rhythm of medieval religious life revolved.[174] Yet under interrogation, individual Waldenses would admit to a bewildering confusion of practice, observing some major feasts but rejecting others. Some claimed that *barbes* had advised them not to fast in the Ember seasons; others reported that they had been told the opposite.[175] While traditional theory claimed that Waldenses rejected the Lenten fast, along with the rest of the liturgical calendar besides Sunday, the Waldenses of the Dauphiné observed Lent like the Catholics, but with one small but significant modification. They began their fast not on Ash Wednesday but on the following Monday, the start of the 'old Lent' as they called it, according to the Ambrosian rite still practised in the province of Milan.[176] Most difficult of all to assess is the Waldensian attitude to the priesthood. Repeatedly in the Dauphiné material one reads confessions which state that the priests of the Church led too lax and immoral a life, whereas the *barbes* led pure, holy lives, and because of their greater sanctity had greater spiritual power.[177] Yet in applying this attitude, Waldenses faced the same paradox as other late medieval heretics like the later Lollards. Though doubting the worth of the Roman priesthood, their pastors did not themselves consecrate or baptize, even though they might claim the theoretical authority to do so.[178] Moreover, they had no ordained priests of their own. They were thus caught in the paradox which Peter Zwicker demonstrated so well

---

174 On the liturgical rhythms, see for example Ronald Hutton, *The Rise and Fall of Merry England: The Ritual Year, 1400–1700* (Oxford, 1994); Caroline Walker Bynum, *Holy Feast and Holy Fast: The Religious Significance of Food to Medieval Women* (Berkeley, Calif., 1987).

175 Cambridge, University Library, MS. Dd. 3. 25, fo. 111v; Dd. 3. 26, sect. 4, fos 1v, 3r-v, 4v-r, 6r, 8v, 12r; sect. 5, fo. 7r; sect. 7, fo. 8r; Grenoble, AD Isère, MS. B4350, fos 268v, 270v, 273r-v, 276r; B4351, fo. 129v and *passim*; Paris, Bibliothèque Nationale, Fonds Latin, MS. 3375, i, fos 278v, 281v, 284r, 286v. Chevalier, *Mémoire historique*, pp. 146–51.

176 Cambridge, University Library, MS. Dd. 3. 25, fos 67v, 100v; Dd. 3. 26, sect. 4, fos 1v, 3v, 4r, 8v, 10v, 11r; sect. 5, fo. 7r; Grenoble, AD Isère, MS. B4350, fos 117v, 134v; Paris, Bibliothèque Nationale, Fonds Latin, MS. 3375, i, fos 278v–9r, 281v, 284v, 287r, 289v; Marx, *L'Inquisition en Dauphiné*, pp. 21, 247.

177 Cambridge, University Library, MS. Dd. 3. 25, fos 59v, 61r, 63v, 73r; Cambridge, University Library, MS. Dd. 3. 26, sect. 2, fos 11v, 14r; sect. 3, fo. 2r; sect. 4, fos 1v, 8v, 11r, 12r; sect. 5, fo. 7v; sect. 6, fos 4v, 10r; Grenoble, AD Isère, MS. B4351, fos 124v, 181r, 215r, 248r; Paris, Bibliothèque Nationale, Fonds Latin, MS. 3375, i, fos 255r, 261v, 256v–7r, 279r, 282r, 289v–90r.

178 This is made explicit in Grenoble, AD Isère, MS. B4350, fo. 355r: 'si vellent possent consecrare corpus cristi sed ipsi nolunt'.

to the German heretics in the 1390s: to 'screen' the clergy for their sacramental worthiness was simply not feasible.[179] In practice, some priests spoke well of the Waldenses' religious conduct in church, others denounced their 'lack of devotion'.[180] For their part, the Waldenses condemned the clergy in theory; yet when placed under effective interdict in Piedmont in 1453 and in the Dauphiné in the late 1490s, they pushed vigorously to have the full sacramental service restored to their churches and communities.[181]

There is considerable evidence that, in all sorts of ways, the Waldensian followers stood out from their neighbours, in terms of their conduct, manners and social behaviour. Their attitude to oath-swearing is a case in point. It is already clear that throughout the later middle ages Waldensian followers rarely refused absolutely to take a civil oath to tell the truth, before an inquisitor or otherwise. Medieval society was so dependent on oath-taking that such conduct was barely practicable for anyone who had a landlord, or belonged to a guild or town or village corporation. Yet in the case of the German Waldenses in 1330s Bohemia, for instance, real reluctance to take such oaths could sometimes be detected by inquisitors.[182] Nothing of this sort of reluctance can be detected in the Dauphiné material. Not only did the heretics take oaths before the inquisitors without the slightest sign of hesitation; the exhaustive researches of Gabriel Audisio into their everyday conduct, as revealed in the secular archives of Provence, show them taking oaths in all sorts of legal contexts quite freely.[183] Even more striking is the evidence, in full, detailed testimonies, that Waldenses willingly took oaths from each other – something which according to thirteenth-century authorities they were supposed to regard as a worse sin than murder.[184] Pons Brunet met Antoni Blanc of Freissinières while escorting some *barbes* at night near the hamlet of Pallon. When speaking with Blanc afterwards, he made Blanc swear on the scriptures not to reveal their presence. A similar oath

179   See above, chapter 6 and notes 262–3.
180   Such conflicting testimonies are found, for example, in Cambridge, University Library, MS. Dd. 3. 25, fos 29r, 57r.
181   Alessio, 'Luserna e l'interdetto di Giacomo Buronzo', pp. 417–18; and see below, section 7.5.
182   See above, chapter 6, notes 103–5.
183   On the practice of taking civil oaths among the Waldenses of Provence, see G. Audisio, *Les Vaudois du Luberon: une minorité en Provence (1460–1560)* (Aix-en-Provence, 1984), pp. 205–8.
184   M. Nickson, 'The "Pseudo-Reinerius" Treatise, the Final Stage of a Thirteenth-century Work on Heresy from the Diocese of Passau', *Archives d'Histoire Doctrinale et Litteraire du Moyen-Age* 34 (1967), p. 303: 'Immo plusquam homicidam reputant qui cogit iurare, ut confirmator quia confirmando exigit iuramentum, et iudex a testibus, et examinator in fide, et sacerdos qui cogit abiurare peccata, unde multi sunt periuri.'

of secrecy was extracted by one heretic living in the Valentinois from another.[185] It becomes increasingly clear, in the light of such testimonies, that the Dauphiné Waldenses made themselves conspicuous, not by refusing *legal* oaths, but by keeping their speech free from the constant use of *profane* oaths to emphasize a point. 'Swearers and blasphemers of God', a *barbe* told Odin Valoy of St-Crépin, were 'the firebrands of hell'.[186] Their collective refusal to blaspheme would be reported by a whole sequence of witnesses, hostile and friendly alike, through the sixteenth century.[187]

One ought not, therefore, to envisage the Waldensian followers as a clandestine community in the sense of one whose identity was unknown to those around. On the contrary, it was abundantly evident to local observers, not only that the Waldenses saw themselves as different to their Catholic neighbours, but that they were determined to show the fact in their speech and conduct. One of the most conspicuous ways in which they demonstrated this sense of community was by preferring, if at all possible, to marry only partners chosen from other Waldensian families.[188] There were obvious practical attractions to this; but contemporary observers saw it as part of their general attitude of distancing themselves from the common herd.[189] When Odin Valoy married a Catholic, none of his family would attend the wedding. The Catholic Peyre Don of Villaretto lost his intended (Waldensian) bride Jehanette Veylier because he would not convert to her faith.[190] Large-scale evidence from the migrant communities of Dauphinois Waldenses in Provence documents this trend even more graphically: marriages tended to take place between one Waldensian village and another much more often than between Catholic and Waldensian villages.[191]

---

185 Cambridge, University Library, MS. Dd. 3. 25, fos 115v–16r; Dd. 3. 26, sect. 2, fo. 5r; sect. 7, fo. 9v; sect. 6, fos 1v, 5v–6r; Dublin, Trinity College, MS. 266, fo. 48r.
186 Cambridge, University Library, MS. Dd. 3. 26, sect. 2, fo. 8v: the *barbe*'s statement is, most unusually, reported in dialect French rather than Latin: 'juradors et blasphemadors de dieu sont tisons de enfern'.
187 Cambridge, University Library, MS. Dd. 3. 25, fo. 33r; Dublin, Trinity College, MS. 259, p. 48; Oxford, Bodleian Library, MS Barlow 8, pp. 483–4, 496–7; Paris, Bibliothèque Nationale, Fonds Latin, MS. 3375, i, fo. 356v; Claude de Seyssel, *Adversus errores et sectam Valdensium disputationes* (Paris, 1520), fo. 8.
188 Compare the quite frequent mixed marriages among the German Waldenses, as above, chapter 6, notes 186–8.
189 Cambridge, University Library, MS. Dd. 3. 25, fos 53r–v, 54v, 57r, 100v–1r; Paris, Bibliothèque Nationale, Fonds Latin, MS. 3375, ii, fos 442v, 443v–4r; P. Allix, *Some remarks*, p. 301.
190 Cambridge, University Library, MS. Dd. 3. 26, sect. 2, fos 4r, 13r; Grenoble, AD Isère, MS. B4350, fo. 106r.
191 Audisio, *Les Vaudois du Luberon*, pp. 110–14.

Although the *identity* of the Waldensian followers' communities was fairly transparent, their *conduct* was not. From late in the fourteenth century, at the earliest, inquisitors had suspected the Waldenses of holding promiscuous sexual orgies at their nocturnal meetings after the reading and prayers were finished. These charges were revived in the Dauphiné in the late fifteenth century and insisted upon with tasteless pertinacity by clergy who tried to defend the crusade after it had taken place. Given the hundreds of interrogations which survive, relatively few contain details of such allegations; and most have something about them which makes one doubt the evidence. One witness had been tortured; another only admitted the tale after many days' interrogation; another seems to have been on the margins of the movement, despised for his Catholic links and eager to spread scandal.[192] Some crusade victims from around Vallouise confessed to attending orgies, but their statements only survive in the transcriptions of seventeenth-century Catholic propagandists: the originals are lost.[193] On the other hand, the story was not merely the product of literary tradition or a diseased ecclesiastical imagination: it was clearly a scandal current in the Waldensian villages at the time. The Bérard family of L'Argentière was extremely touchy about the allegations and denied them fervently; while Catholics claimed that a particular house in Balboutet had been identified as one of the places used to host such gatherings.[194] However, once the scandal had broken and the heretics had been pursued with merciless force by the crusaders, sympathetic Catholic neighbours fell over themselves to insist, and as far as possible to justify their claims, that there was no truth in the allegations. The Waldenses were in fact morally strict to the point of puritanism and may have attracted hostile suspicion by that very characteristic.[195]

The exceptionally detailed evidence for the late fifteenth-century Dauphiné allows one to raise, and suggest answers to, some of the most important questions about rural dissenters in late medieval society. How well did the Waldenses integrate themselves into Catholic society? Was there great hatred against them from the majority? How much local support did the inquisitors have to draw upon? The evidence taken before the 1487–8 crusade suggests that there were tensions between individuals, suspicion and some scandal. In the main, however, the Waldensian

192 Cambridge, University Library, MS. Dd. 3. 26, sect. 2, fos 12v, 15v; Grenoble, AD Isère, MS. B4350, fos 74v–5r, 104v–5v, 154v.
193 Rorengo . . . di Lucerna, *Memorie Historiche*, pp. 12–13; G. Martin, *Inscription en faux . . . contre le livre intitulé 'De la puissance du Pape' par le sieur Marc Vulson* (Grenoble, 1640), pp. 220–6.
194 Cambridge, University Library, MS. Dd. 3. 26, sect. 4, fo. 11r; Paris, Bibliothèque Nationale, Fonds Latin, MS. 3375, i, fos 307v–8r, 404r; Grenoble, AD Isère, MS. B4351, fos 262r, 278v, 279v–80v, 286r-v, 304v, 319r.
195 See, for example, Paris, Bibliothèque Nationale, Fonds Latin, MS. 3375, i, fos 447r-v, 451v–2r.

followers were accommodated, given that their behaviour was neither offensive nor outrageous, and that they conformed in a minimal way to the social and spiritual expectations of society around them. Attitudes would be changed dramatically by the crusade itself; its impact is crucial to understanding the changes which followed.

7.5 Crusade and Rehabilitation in the Dauphiné, 1487–1509

The Waldensian crusade of 1487–8 does not evoke the same powerful image in the popular mind as the Albigensian crusade of nearly three centuries earlier. Even among the surviving Waldensian Church of Piedmont, it is not exactly a part of their folklore, since it took place not in Piedmont itself, but in the territories of the Dauphiné both east and west of the passes. Yet for its time and within the region where it had its impact, this episode was deeply shocking in many ways. It contributed significantly to patterns of migration from the Alps to Provence and southern Italy. It disrupted religious and even political life in a particularly sensitive region for the kings of France. It temporarily engaged the attention of French kings and Roman popes over a twenty-year period, and led to one of the most bizarre humiliations ever experienced by the processes and structures of ecclesiastical justice. Most intriguingly of all, the whole episode provokes some thoughts about the relationship between heretics and Catholics in the localities where they coexisted.

The story of the Waldensian crusade began with letters issued by Pope Innocent VIII on 21 April 1487, and the bull *Id nostri cordis* of 27 April 1487, which authorized the Archdeacon of Cremona, Albertus de Capitaneis (Alberto Cattaneo or Cattanei) to proceed against heresy in the Dauphiné, Savoy and Piedmont.[196] An unusual aspect of the instruments with which Cattaneo was supplied was that they really did authorize a crusade in the traditional sense of the term. Aiding the inquisition by force of arms was made a religious duty binding on local Catholics. Those who participated in the campaign were promised plenary remission of sins, in the form which had become traditional since the first issuing of a crusade bull in 1095.[197] In practice, the 1487 campaign soon degen-

---

196   The crusade documents survive as Cambridge, University Library, MS. Dd. 3. 25, fos 8ff., 75r-v; Grenoble, AD Isère, MS. B4350, fos 3r–10v (crusade bull) and ibid., fos 11r–18r (letters of Pope Innocent VIII to Cattaneo); Paravy, *De la Chrétienté romaine*, pp. 977–83.

197   Grenoble, AD Isère, MS. B4350, fos 6v–7r: Cattaneo's powers included 'fideles illarum partium, ut contra eosdem hereticos salutiffere crucis signo in cordibus et vestibus assumpto viriliter pugnent per ydoneos verbi dei predicatores crucem sive cruciatam predicantes exhortari et induci faciendi ac cruce signatis et contra eosdem hereticos pugnantibus vel ad id contribuentibus ut plenariam omnium

erated into a squalid plundering raid. That should not conceal the fact that its *formal* ideals were the same as previous attempts to solve the problem of heresy by armed force.

It is far from clear how Alberto Cattaneo became involved in this process. From the fact that he only actually prosecuted his commission within the Dauphiné, it is reasonable to assume that he was called in by members of the Dauphinois petty nobility, who would provide the ensuing crusade with its military muscle and political support. Remarkably, the crusade observed secular rather than religious boundaries: it struck first in the Dauphinois valley of the Chisone east of the passes, within the diocese of Turin rather than the province of Embrun, though no other parts of Turin diocese were attacked. A letter of citation which Cattaneo issued from Pinerolo on 26 June 1487 specifically denounced as illegal the appeal made earlier in that year by the community of Freissinières to the Archbishop of Vienne, in whose proceedings Archbishop Baile had refused to participate.[198] This suggests that the request made to the pope leading to Cattaneo's appointment must have grown out of the frustration of those same nobles with the interminable legal process in which the inquisitions had become bogged down. A papal crusading bull provided the means to cut the legal knot in a most decisive and brutal way. Cattaneo himself was certainly not a vocational, dedicated expert inquisitor like Peter Zwicker or Bernard Gui. He appears to have been a tool in the hands of the nobles who enlisted him. He was alleged by his victims to have been no more than 22 years old and incapable of understanding the local dialect, as he was an Italian speaker.[199] He was a canon lawyer, not a theologian, and his own account of the crusade summarized the heretics' beliefs in an inapposite quotation from a literary source.[200]

The real originators of the 1487–8 crusade can be identified as a small clique of petty aristocrats and landowners from the Embrunais and Briançonnais, several of whom held important political and legal positions which they could exploit. The leaders of the project were Oronce Émé, who by the time of the crusade was the *juge-mage* (senior secular judge) of Briançon, and Jordanon Cordi, the *procureur-fiscal* of Briançon.[201]

---

peccatorum suorum indulgentiam et remissionem iuxta tuam desuper ordinacionem semel in vita et etiam in mortis articulo consequantur concedendi.'

198   Marx, *L'Inquisition en Dauphiné*, pp. 158–9.

199   For complaints against Cattaneo, see Paris, Bibliothèque Nationale, Fonds Latin, MS. 3375, i, fos 294r–305v and 337v–60v, esp. 342v–7r; the former document is ed. in Marx, *L'Inquisition en Dauphiné*, pp. 257–63.

200   Cattaneo's legal qualifications are described in Paris, Bibliothèque Nationale, Fonds Latin, MS. 3375, ii, 446v–7r; for his description of Waldensianism, see his history as ed. in Godefroy, *Histoire de Charles VIII*, p. 278, and compare with Aeneas Sylvius Piccolomini's *Historia Bohemica* as ed. in his *Opera Omnia* (Basel, 1551), pp. 103–4.

201   See above, notes 139, 142.

These two had (as the Waldenses' proctors later alleged) seen their prosecutions of the Waldenses blocked in the time of Louis XI, were arrested because of their excesses and had escaped from prison. They had a score to settle.[202] Two landowners who were also *conseillers* of the Grenoble *parlement*, Pons Pons and Jehan Rabot, were prominent among the persecutors: so were Pierre de Rame, a *coseigneur* of Freissinières, Lanthelme Eynard of Monteynard, *seigneur* of L'Argentière, and Hippolyte de Bardonnèsche, *coseigneur* of Bardonnècchia. Hugues de la Palu, *seigneur* of Varax and lieutenant of the governor of the Dauphiné, led the crusaders' army.[203] Yet it would be quite wrong to see the Waldensian crusade as any sort of class war. Fasion or Fazy de Rame, a relative of Pierre de Rame and also *coseigneur* of Freissinières, tried to mediate between his tenants and the crusaders to prevent bloodshed. For his pains he suffered extortionate exactions from the crusaders to pay their expenses, which are copiously documented in his uniquely surviving book of household accounts.[204] He was by no means unique in this relatively tolerant attitude.

Cattaneo seems to have taken reasonable (though ultimately insufficient) pains to observe the canonical niceties in conducting his crusade. Attention was devoted first of all to the eastern valley of the Chisone. On 28 August 1487 a Franciscan preacher was sent into the Val Chisone to exhort suspected heretics to come to repent. About a month later letters of citation were issued naming the alleged heretics of the valley. About a hundred came to Briançon more or less voluntarily as a result: they were interrogated and sentenced over the winter until March. Those who refused were excommunicated and, on 16 November, formally handed over to the secular arm – in effect, sentenced to death as obstinate heretics even though they had not yet been captured or interrogated. Somewhat later, the same procedure of citation, excommunication and sentence was carried out for the people of the western communities of Vallouise, L'Argentière and Freissinières.[205] Early in March 1488, just

202   Paris, Bibliothèque Nationale, Fonds Latin, MS. 3375, i, fos 381r–2r; for evidence of the cruelties and extortion practised by these two, see Cambridge, University Library, MS. Dd. 3. 25, fos 31r, 38r; Paris, Bibliothèque Nationale, Fonds Latin, MS. 3375, ii, fos 65v–6r, 93r, 98r, 100v–1r; 383r–5r, 390r, 401r–3v, 410v–11r, 416v–17v, 418r–19r, 422r.

203   Cambridge, University Library, MS. Dd. 3. 25, fos 2v, 30v, 34r–v; Paris, Bibliothèque Nationale, Fonds Latin, MS. 3375, ii, fos 31v–2r, 34v–5r, 36r, 43v–4r, 73r–5v, 92v–4v, 98r–9v, 100v–1v.

204   Cambridge, University Library, MS. Dd. 3. 26, sect. 4, fo. 3r; Grenoble, AD Isère, MS. B4351, fos 138r, 162v; Fornier, *Histoire générale*, vol. 2, pp. 434–5; Marx, *L'Inquisition en Dauphiné*, pp. 163–4; G. de Manteyer (ed.), *Le Livre-journal tenu par Fazy de Rame en langage embrunais (6 juin 1471–10 juillet 1507)*, 2 vols (Gap, 1932), vol. 1, pp. 24, 356; vol. 2, pp. 95, 102–3, 109–10, 128–9, 240.

205   The citations and excommunications are found in Grenoble, AD Isère, MS. B4350, fos 53v–68v, 80v–8r, 90r–4v, 107r–12r, 121v–7v; B4351, fos 16r–27v, 29r–30v, 32r–6v, 40v–56r, 60r–74r.

as soon as the weather made it practical to do so, Dauphinois soldiers invaded the Val Chisone. The Waldenses tried to defend themselves against the crusaders. They took provisions and small amounts of weapons, including crossbows and small firearms, and hid themselves in caves in the mountains, known as the *balmas* of Fenestrelle, Traversier and l'Agniel. However, the sieges which ensued lasted at most a few days or a week or so. The Waldenses could not defy properly equipped troops, although there was loss of life on both sides when the caves were stormed.[206] Late in March 1488 the crusaders crossed the passes westwards and herded in the Waldenses of the valleys of the Durance with threats and violence. Here again some were besieged in the caves of the Oréac and Ailefroide, but they were captured quite speedily. Some appear to have surrendered on realizing that they could not withstand assault.[207]

Early Waldensian historiography and folklore has much exaggerated the numbers of heretics killed in the crusade of 1487–8. One account claimed that the storming of one cave alone led to the deaths of 400 children.[208] These figures can be laid to rest by an authentic and contemporary source, the statement made by the Waldenses' own legal representatives in 1507, that 160 suspected Waldenses died violent deaths as a result of the crusade. Those representatives would have had no reason whatsoever to minimize the numbers killed. This loss of life, though less horrifying in sheer numbers than many seen in subsequent religious conflicts, needs to be taken in context. A rough estimate, based on the assumption that the surviving citations for heresy were fairly accurate and included nearly all adult Waldensian followers in the region, might suggest that there were 1,500–1,600 adult believers in the Dauphiné (besides those in Piedmont). The crusade would therefore have led to the deaths of some 10 per cent, an appalling enough proportion without any subsequent exaggeration.[209] Far worse than the actual death toll, in terms of the impression created in the minds of observers, was the

206   Paris, Bibliothèque Nationale, Fonds Latin, MS. 3375, i, fos 277v–87v; ii, fos 378v–9r, 387v–8r, 396v, 400v–1r, 404v, 407v, 414v–15r, 416v, 418r-v, 419v.
207   Grenoble, AD Isère, MS. B4351, fos 267r-v, 269r, 278r-v. For general accounts of the course of the crusade, see Cattaneo's own ed. in Godefroy, *Histoire de Charles VIII*, pp. 281–3; G. Allard's life of Jean Rabot, as ed. in H. Gariel, *Delphinalia*, pt 2 (Grenoble, 1852), pp. 34–9; S. dei Conti di Foligno, *Le Storie de'suoi tempi dal 1475 al 1510* (Rome, 1883), vol. 1, pp. 299–307; Fornier, *Histoire générale*, vol. 2, pp. 429–45; Marx, *L'Inquisition en Dauphiné*, pp. 158–67.
208   Perrin, *Histoire des Vaudois*, bk 2, ch. 3, on the Dauphiné, is the first to have made this claim; see Comba, *History of the Waldenses*, pp. 133–4.
209   Paris, Bibliothèque Nationale, Fonds Latin, MS. 3375, i, fos 386v–7r. The overall numbers for the Waldensian population can be inferred from the surviving letters of citation, as above, note 205; the figure for casualties is endorsed by Paravy, 'Waldensians in the Dauphiné', p. 163; see also Paravy, *De la Chrétienté romaine*, pp. 986–7.

manner in which the crusade was carried out. Regardless of age or sex, suspected heretics were hanged, run through with swords, or thrown headlong from precipices in the mountains. One crusader shut people up in a building and laid burning faggots to it, threatening to burn them all unless they confessed to heresy. Two local landlords extorted money by threatening local heretics with hanging unless they paid ransoms.[210]

Although the fugitive Waldenses were technically already sentenced to death as obstinate heretics, in practice the survivors were treated with greater leniency, for reasons which soon became apparent. The overwhelming majority who survived the crusade and subsequent imprisonment were subjected to a fairly perfunctory interrogation on their beliefs.[211] So large were the numbers involved that Alberto Cattaneo delegated his powers to a group of subordinates, drawn from his own entourage and some of the local clergy. The now formally penitent heretics were sentenced to a range of penances in a grand mass absolution ceremony held before the Grand Real, the great door of the cathedral at Embrun, on 27 April 1488. Cattaneo allegedly extracted from those whom he absolved a promise never to appeal to the pope or the king of France against his sentence, though this detail was omitted from the official record of the absolution.[212] Having shown a taste for hard cash in the ransoms extracted during the crusade, the crusaders now showed even greater readiness to extract money from their victims. Those who had been assigned the traditional humiliating penance of wearing a yellow cross on their outer clothing were offered the chance to buy out of this obligation. Those who fled from the crusaders found their villages occupied and heavy fines levied on the communities. Even the thoroughly Catholic town of Chorges, near Gap, was fined for sheltering fugitive heretics.[213] Those whose properties were confiscated were allowed to buy back their lands, contrary to canon law.[214] As numerous observers

---

210 The evidence for the atrocities is in the sources cited above, note 202; for further evidence relating to other crusaders see also Paris, Bibliothèque Nationale, Fonds Latin, MS. 3375, i, fo. 385v, 386v; ii, fos 61r-v, 64r-v, 378v–9r, 388r–9r, 397r, 411r; Marx, *L'Inquisition en Dauphiné*, pp. 261–2.
211 Note the use of stereotyped phrases in Grenoble, AD Isère, MS. B4350 and B4351, as noted above, note 150.
212 Cambridge, University Library, MS. Dd. 3. 26, sect. 4; Grenoble, AD Isère, MS. B4351, fos 82r–360r, *passim*; Paris, Bibliothèque Nationale, Fonds Latin, MS. 3375, ii, fos 66r, 75r, 94v; the form of abjuration is ed. in Chevalier, *Mémoire historique*, p. 154.
213 Cambridge, University Library, MS. Dd. 3. 25, fo. 30v; Paris, Bibliothèque Nationale, Fonds Latin, MS. 3375, ii, fos 31v–2r, 34v–5r, 36r.
214 Paris, Bibliothèque Nationale, Fonds Latin, MS. 3375, ii, fos 377v–8r, 383r–5r, 386v, 389r–90r, 401r–3v, 410v–11r, 416v–17v, 418r–19r, 422r, 423v, 424v–5r. The commissioners for the rehabilitation were particularly careful to record such breaches of canon law.

remarked a few years later, the Waldenses' heresy lay in their wallets.[215] One might say the same for the crusaders' Catholicism.

The aftermath of the crusade left not only physical devastation and suffering, but a profound and unresolved legal muddle. The Waldensian communities started to appeal to the king almost immediately. Shortly before Archbishop Jehan Baile's death in 1494 a dossier on his inquisitions was sent to the *Grand Conseil* of the King of France. Baile's successor as archbishop, Rostain d'Ancezune, treated the Waldensian communities as being still under collective sentence of excommunication, and refused to allow Catholic services in one of their churches, despite the inhabitants' requests to have them. He presumably knew that many had been absolved by Cattaneo, but may have held that this did not cancel out the sentence imposed on the whole community of Freissinières. Possibly also, the presence of unabsolved heretics who had fled during the crusade justified placing the entire village of Freissinières under interdict. The canonical position of the Waldensian villages was therefore unclear, as was the legal status of the crusade and the prosecutions which preceded it. The ecclesiastical dispute implied a fiscal one. If the status of the prosecution of heretics was doubtful, then so was the title to confiscated lands and other property held by those who had seized money and goods during the crusade. In 1498 it was agreed to refer the whole matter to a commission of senior French churchmen appointed by Pope Alexander VI. This commission was led by Laurent Bureau, confessor to Louis XII and bishop of the Provençal diocese of Sisteron.

In the latter half of July 1501 two of the commissioners visited the valleys of the Durance and conducted a long series of interviews with Catholic and 'formerly' heretical residents alike. The Catholics spoke warmly and supportively of the Waldenses' moral and religious qualities, and the Waldenses reported the atrocities and cruelties of the previous crusade. The commissioners managed to insult and infuriate Rostain d'Ancezune, who wrote a bitter memoir of their proceedings.[216] However, after the commissioners had formed their extremely positive view of the Waldenses' case, their attempts to rehabilitate them fell foul of the particularism and professional jealousies of the lawyers. The *Grand Conseil*, the law-court most intimately connected to the French king, found great difficulty in enforcing its judgements against subjects living

215   Paris, Bibliothèque Nationale, Fonds Latin, MS. 3375, ii, fo. 11v (one of many such comments).
216   The commissioners' register for this period is found in Paris, Bibliothèque Nationale, Fonds Latin, MS. 3375, i, fos 431r–64v, and ii, fos 1r–104r. Alternative records of some of the interviews, taken down by the archbishop's secretary, are found in Cambridge, University Library, MS. Dd. 3. 25, fos 25r–38v; Rostain's memorandum is found in ibid., fos 2r–6v.

within the jurisdiction of the *parlement* of the Dauphiné at Grenoble. The *Grand Conseil* named, in a decree of May 1502, a list of individuals who were ordered to return property unlawfully confiscated from the people of the Waldensian communities. However, since the *parlement* would not allow them to be summoned outside its jurisdiction for failure to respect the sentence, it remained unenforceable. The legal process dragged on for several more years. In July 1507 the new leader of the joint papal–royal commission, Geoffroy Boussart, visited the lands of the crusade and took a further set of testimonies, including representations from the local Church authorities which tried to defend the inquisitions in ever more strident tones.[217] In October 1508 an ecclesiastical court at the bar of Nôtre-Dame at Paris summoned the archbishop, Alberto Cattaneo (then at Milan) and several local Church dignitaries to attend. They all failed to appear; on 27 February 1509 the inhabitants of the Waldensian communities were given a verdict in their favour. The sentence acknowledged that there was ample reason to investigate their religious beliefs. However, since the legal processes had not 'observed the forms of the law' (how exactly was not specified) and since the Waldenses had not been found to be 'pertinaciously' heretical, the entire process was voided. After nearly twenty years, the communities of Waldensian followers had undone the inquisitions led against them.[218]

Why were the Waldenses of the Dauphiné rehabilitated? First, it was partly because they made their legal case so effectively. Over decades, these rural communities had learned to use the legal system to protect themselves. The highly developed system of communal self-government practised in the Briançonnais gave them abundant examples to follow.[219] The collective management of their affairs by these communities suggests analogies with some of the south-German *Gemeinde* in the decades before the Reformation.[220] Rural peasants were by no means like helpless sheep before those who traditionally wielded authority and force. Second, however, spiritual and secular authority in the region was hopelessly divided over how to deal with the Waldenses. A section of the local

217 The texts defending the inquisitions are found in Paris, Bibliothèque Nationale, Fonds Latin, MS. 3375, ii, fos 399r–406r, 430r–71v, 479r–88r.

218 The best narrative of the complex chain of events leading up to the rehabilitation is Marx, *L'Inquisition en Dauphiné*, pp. 179–97; the sentence of rehabilitation itself is ed. in P. Guillaume, 'Sentence de réhabilitation des Vaudois des Alpes françaises', in Comité des travaux historiques et scientifiques, *Bulletin historique et philologique* (1891), pp. 248–65; the text itself on pp. 261–5.

219 On Briançonnais self-government, see esp. A. A. Fauché-Prunelle, *Essai sur les anciennes institutions autonomes ou populaires des Alps cottiennes-briançonnaises*, 2 vols (Paris, Grenoble, 1856–7), vol. 2, pp. 311–33; J. R. Major, *Representative Government in Early Modern France* (New Haven, Conn., 1980), p. 76.

220 See, for example, P. Blickle, 'Peasant Revolts in the German Empire in the Late Middle Ages', *Social History* 4 (1979), pp. 223–31.

nobility and some of the clergy sought to terrorize and exploit them, probably for entirely corrupt reasons. Other ecclesiastics, such as Archbishop Baile, may have genuinely cherished the futile hope of winning converts back to full Catholic obedience. Many others in the region seem to have regarded the Waldenses as acceptable neighbours: at least, that alone can explain the conspiracy of silence mounted around their beliefs in 1501–7 by Catholic witnesses.[221] It has been observed that dissenters whose dissent was obvious, but not outrageous or offensive, could be tolerated rather than persecuted in early modern society.[222] The Waldenses of the Dauphiné further support that observation.

Outside the Dauphiné, the French royal government probably saw the importance of the valley of the Durance as the primary route from France into Italy. Stability in the region, and the support of the native population for armies traversing the territory, were strategically essential.[223] The courtier–ecclesiastics who made up the investigating commission appear to have been mostly theologians, who despised the narrow perspectives of the canon lawyers who made up most of the local hierarchy.[224] On the eve of the Reformation, intelligent churchmen were wondering if after all the Waldenses deserved the brutal treatment meted out to them.

7.6 The Migrant Communities: Calabria, Apulia, Provence

As was remarked near the start of this chapter, the Alps tended to produce a surplus population, which eked out its income from the unrewarding soil with work of other kinds, sometimes in other places.[225] The inhabitants were therefore under considerable pressure to migrate to other regions where life was less hard. When to the pressures of demography and climate was added regular religious persecution from the mid-fourteenth century onwards, it is not surprising that people from the Alpine regions tended to look for other homelands which might accept them. Migration became a social characteristic of the Alpine Waldenses. Once settled in foreign lands, of course, their religious, linguistic and

221   See above.
222   For an intriguing confirmation of this observation, see Christopher W. Marsh, *The Family of Love in English Society, 1550–1630* (Cambridge, 1994), pp. 250ff.
223   On the strategic importance of the Montgenèvre pass, see Y. Labande-Mailfert, *Charles VIII et son milieu (1470–1498)* (Paris, 1975), pp. 277–8; P. Giovio, *Historiae sui temporis* (Paris, 1558), i, fos 168v–9v; R. J. Knecht, *Francis I* (Cambridge, 1982), p. 42.
224   Cambridge, University Library, MS. Dd. 3. 25, fo. 4r; Marx, *L'Inquisition en Dauphiné*, p. 182.
225   See above, note 8. On the history of Alpine migrations, see Pier Paolo Viazzo, *Upland Communities: Environment, Population and Social Structure in the Alps Since the Sixteenth Century* (Cambridge, 1989), pp. 121–52.

social identities tended to merge. They became, to an even greater extent than in their Alpine homelands, a 'people' marked out by their language (in several senses) and by their cohesiveness as a group. As things turned out, the latter half of the fourteenth century was a particularly propitious time to go in search of new lands. The plague which had struck Europe since the late 1340s left landlords nearly everywhere in need of tenants to work their estates. In the earliest histories of the Waldenses it was remarked how they made themselves welcome to landowners by taking over and making profitable what would otherwise have been left to waste.[226]

There were two chief regions to which the Alpine peoples migrated, sometimes moving first to one and then another. The area for which the earliest evidence exists is the extreme south of Italy, in Calabria and Apulia. In 1353, almost at the very outset of the persecutions in the Dauphiné, Pope Innocent VI lamented that many heretics had left the mountains of Embrun diocese for Calabria.[227] Few details are known about the Calabrian Waldenses until the time of their extinction in 1560–1. Two communities had established themselves in the region of Montalto, in the villages of San Sisto and Guardia 'Piemontese', about 12 miles apart; they were also settled in the villages of Vaccarizzo and S. Vincenzo. They became known locally as the 'oltramontani', 'those from beyond the mountains'. They participated in Catholic worship and generally kept their heads down; by this means they survived a very long time more or less undisturbed.[228] They were, however, noted for their custom of only marrying within their own social and religious group, as the Waldenses of the Alps had been.[229] From the accounts of those involved in the sixteenth-century persecutions, their nocturnal meetings seem to have brought on the same suspicion of holding promiscuous sexual orgies as afflicted the Waldenses of the Dauphiné: a Catholic called Lodovico da Apiano referred to some women who believed in 'crescite et multiplicamini', 'be fruitful and multiply'. This was the text supposedly used to justify sexual excess, according to many inquisitors.[230]

The Calabrians seem to have agreed to convert themselves into a public Church at around the same time as the Piedmontese, and inspired by their example. Around c.1556 they resolved to ask for Protestant min-

---

226 The Waldenses' taking up of lands under emphyteusis was remarked on in J. Crespin, *Actes de martyrs* (n. p., 1565 edn consulted), pp. 189ff.; in the region the term often used was 'accapt': see Audisio, *Les Vaudois du Luberon*, pp. 49–57.

227 Marx, *L'Inquisition en Dauphiné*, p. 13 and n. 6.

228 Oxford, Bodleian Library, MS. Barlow 8, pp. 306–8; P. Gilles, *Histoire ecclésiastique des églises réformées . . . autrefois appellées églises vaudoises*, ed. P. Lantaret, 2 vols (Pinerolo, 1881) vol. 1, pp. 29–30.

229 Oxford, MS. Barlow 8, p. 332.

230 Ibid., pp. 333–6.; Gilles, *Histoire ecclésiastique*, vol. 1, p. 32.

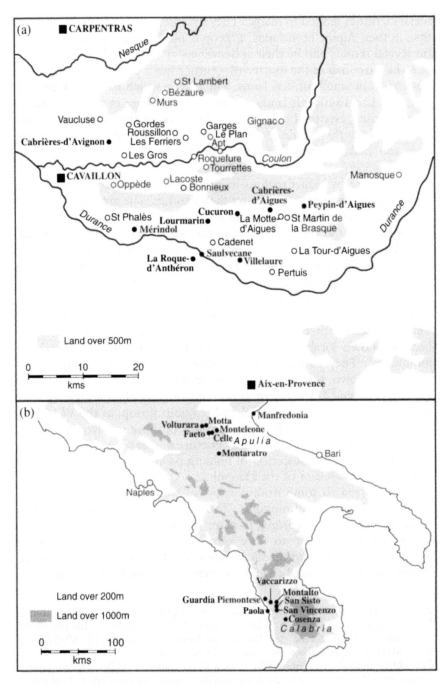

Map VI The Waldensian emigré communities in (a) Provence and (b) southern Italy, 15th–16th centuries.

isters, and shortly received two, Gian Luigi Pascale and Giacomo Bonelli, to supplement the services of Stefano Negrini of Bobbio, a Piedmontese former *barbe*. Pascale was a Piedmontese nobleman from Cuneo, who had studied at Lausanne and Geneva before being called to Calabria by the Italian community at Geneva.[231] The importation of Protestant ministers was a complete catastrophe for the Calabrian Waldenses. They drew the attention of the ecclesiastical and Habsburg authorities just as the end of the Italian wars had left resources free for persecuting heretics. Pascale was captured almost immediately and taken to Cosenza. He was sentenced to death as an obstinate heretic, but was eventually taken to Rome in the hope that he might recant. He refused and even tried to make converts wherever he was held; eventually he was strangled and burned before the Castel San'Angelo at Rome on 9 September 1560.[232] Bonelli would also eventually be executed as a heretic at Palermo. From November 1560 onwards a Dominican inquisitor named Valerio Malvicino set about a systematic persecution of the Calabrian Waldenses.

Malvicino's assault can well be regarded as one of the last thoroughly medieval-style inquisitorial raids on a Waldensian community. From November 1560 he set about the Waldenses of San Sisto and Guardia with the aid of soldiers supplied by the viceroy of the province. The Waldenses put up some resistance and in May 1561 killed a Spanish governor and some fifty of his troops who had tried to ambush them. However, the resistance was half-hearted and too many of the Waldenses were already in Catholic hands for the remainder to match the successes of the Piedmontese in the previous year. Eventually nearly all were captured and sentenced either to death as obstinate heretics, or to the wearing of penitential garments if they had abjured. Some 86 were executed by having their throats cut in June 1561. Children under 15 were separated from their parents and dispersed around the region to be brought up as Catholics.[233]

The communities in Apulia appear to have been more scattered and possibly more numerous. In 1387, according to the testimony of the Pruza brothers, Johan Baridon came from Apulia to preach at Waldensian meetings in Piedmont, having been sent from there by their 'pontiff'.[234] St Vincent Ferrer reported after a visit to the valleys in 1403 that heretic pastors visited Piedmont from Apulia twice a year. A Waldensian layman tried in 1451 reported that the *barbes* who visited

---

231 Oxford, MS. Barlow 8, pp. 464ff., Gilles, *Histoire ecclésiastique*, vol. 1, pp. 32–4.
232 Oxford, MS. Barlow 8, pp. 450–63; the letters of Gian Luigi Pascale were published at the time in *Actes de martyrs* (1565), pp. 969–91; later edn, J. Crespin, *Histoire des martyrs* (n.p., 1619), fos 555r–66r.
233 This narrative is condensed from Oxford, MS. Barlow 8, pp. 306–41.
234 See above, note 52.

Piedmont came either from Freissinières in the Dauphiné or from Manfredonia, a seaport in Apulia.[235] According to the seventeenth-century historian Pierre Gilles, in about 1400 the Apulian Waldenses built for themselves five village strongholds named Monteleone, Montaratro, Faeto, Celle and Motta. They also settled in the town of Volturara *c*.1500.[236] Some evidence suggests that in the late fifteenth century there may have been a fresh wave of migrants from the Dauphiné to southern Italy.[237]

It is possible, moreover, that in Apulia, free from intense scrutiny, the Waldenses embarked on something resembling settled ministry. Pietro di Jacopo, a travelling 'brother of the opinion', i.e. Fraticello, captured and tried at Oulx in 1492, said that he had heard of some churches in Apulia which were 'absolutely white' (presumably without ornaments or decoration) and where the 'priests' were members of the heretical community. Pierre Griot, a trainee *barbe* tried in 1532, reported that 'this sect reigns principally in Calabria and Apulia and there is preached as it were publicly.' Without further evidence it is very hard to comment on these pieces of hearsay: the witnesses did not claim to have seen such things themselves.[238] During the sixteenth century the Waldenses of Apulia disappear from history. It is safe to assume, given their strength in the early years of the century, that they were still active around the time that Gilles des Gilles made his pastoral tour of southern Italy in the middle 1550s. There is not the same detailed martyrological material to account for their disappearance as survives for those of Calabria; there may have been persecutions, but they are not documented.[239] Cut off from the circuit of Genevan ministerial support and deprived of the contact with the *barbes* which they previously had enjoyed, they may simply have dwindled into conformity. By January 1566 an ecclesiastical visitation document reported that Catholic worship had been re-established in Faeto and Celle, where it had previously lapsed.[240]

---

235 Comba, *History of the Waldenses*, pp. 149, 325; J. Jalla, 'Notice historique sur le S. Ministère . . . au sein des églises vaudoises', *Bulletin de la société d'histoire vaudoise* 14 (1897), pp. 8–9; Marx, *L'Inquisition en Dauphiné*, p. 13, n. 9; Gonnet and Molnar, *Vaudois au moyen âge*, pp. 265–6.

236 Gilles, *Histoire ecclésiastique*, vol. 1, p. 30. See the comments of P. Rivoire, 'Les Colonies provençales et vaudoises de la Pouille', *Bulletin de la société d'histoire vaudoise* 19 (1902), pp. 48–54.

237 G. Audisio, *Le Barbe et l'inquisiteur: Procès du barbe vaudois Pierre Griot par l'inquisiteur Jean de Roma (Apt, 1532)* (Aix-en-Provence, 1979), p. 105, n. 1; see also Cambridge, University Library, MS. Dd. 3. 25, fo. 63r, on Barthélemi Blazy's proposed migration.

238 Cambridge, University Library, MS. Dd. 3. 26, sect. 6, fo. 10r; Audisio, *Barbe et l'inquisiteur*, p. 105.

239 Rivoire, 'Colonies provençales et vaudoises', pp. 56–7.

240 Ibid., pp. 58–9, and 59–62 for the document itself.

Finally, in the mid-fifteenth century some Waldenses from the Alps settled much closer to home, especially on waste lands on the southern edge of the massif of the Luberon, east of Avignon in Provence. They settled in the villages of Mérindol, Cabrières-d'Avignon, Lourmarin, Cabrières-d'Aigues and in several dozen other smaller locations. In some villages they represented a preponderance of the population, in others a minority. Given the large numbers who migrated from the Dauphiné to Provence in the later fifteenth century, it is extremely likely that a combination of economic misfortune and the pressure of inquisitions – culminating of course in the crusade of 1487–8 – persuaded them to make the move.[241] The most striking fact about the Waldenses of Provence, ably demonstrated by their most meticulous recent historian, is that the official records say almost nothing about their reputation for heresy until the persecutions of the sixteenth century. One can identify the Waldenses by their social habits. In their business dealings, in their choices of godparents, but above all in their choices of marriage partners, the Waldenses formed a group apart. They maintained relations with their co-religionaries either in Provence or back in the Alps, at the expense of contacts with the Provençal Catholics. Not surprisingly, they baptized their young with their traditional Christian names, avoiding those saints' names favoured in Provence.[242]

In religious terms there is no doubt that, as elsewhere, the Waldenses participated in the prevailing Catholic cult. It is however possible to discern a slight difference in their personal interpretation of it. While the Waldenses undoubtedly made pious bequests and asked for Masses to be said for their souls – notwithstanding the theoretical denial of purgatory which had been a core part of Waldensian teaching – it is evident that their pious gifts were less flamboyant than those of their Catholic neighbours. In particular they showed little taste for the trental, the costly repetition of large numbers of Masses for a departed soul which was so popular in Catholic villages nearby. Conversely, they were more likely to make bequests for the poor.[243] However, it is only in these relatively impersonal documents that one can confirm for the case of Provence what has already been demonstrated for the Alps: a religious practice largely in conformity with Catholic rules, but distinguished by certain visible and somehow deliberate symbolic acts from Catholic patterns of

---

241 Audisio, *Les Vaudois du Luberon*, pp. 45–70; also Audisio, *Barbe et l'inquisiteur*, p. 88, n. 1.
242 Audisio, *Les Vaudois du Luberon*, pp. 101–14, 138–40.
243 Ibid., pp. 202–24, 264–74. Compare Jacques Chiffoleau, *La Comptabilite de l'au-dela: les hommes, la mort et la religion dans la region d'Avignon a la fin du Moyen Age, vers 1320-vers 1480*, Collection de l'École française de Rome, 47 (Rome and Paris, 1980), *passim*, for the development of the cult of the dead in the Avignon region.

behaviour. Combined with that, one finds in all these areas of migration an intense sense of being a people apart. While the Waldensian émigrés were conferring significant benefits on their landlords, it is not surprising that they went unnoticed by the Church and that their minimal deviances from Catholicism were connived at. However, the religious temper of the sixteenth century was very different from that of the fifteenth; and when the Waldenses of these regions resolved to make their dissent more public and more visible, they encountered a hostility against which not even their economic usefulness could protect them.

Part III

The Alpine Waldenses Confront the Reformation

Introduction

The End of Heresy?

Histories of medieval heresy traditionally end with the sixteenth century. It is not that the religious instincts which found expression as popular heresy abruptly changed or evaporated. Rather, the context of medieval Catholicism, against which heresy had been defined, altered out of recognition. Heresy only had meaning if there was an orthodoxy with which to contrast it. After the Reformation, the term could only be used, as it were, in parentheses, by those Catholics who still adhered to the monistic belief that theirs was the only true Christianity, despite the multiple divisions of Christendom; and by some Protestants, who used the term to label those whose dissent wandered even further outside the mainstream.[1]

The disappearance of a unified Christian orthodox establishment offered an alternative to the medieval 'Waldensian' pattern, where furtive rural dissenters were served by secretive itinerant pastors as they carved out a semi-clandestine religious identity at odds with the prevailing culture. Those who were unhappy with the religious position in their homelands could now emigrate, publicly, to another country where conditions were more congenial. Alternatively, they could strive to obtain some sort of legal recognition for their religious practices as a tolerated minority at home. Though the idea of toleration took a very long time to become intellectually and theologically respectable, the political reality of confessional pluralism was almost as old as the reformed Churches themselves. Bipartisan settlements were adopted in Swiss cantons and in the Confederation by 1531, in certain German cities and (in different

---

1 See, for instance, the description of Calvinists and other 'sacramentaries' as heretics in the literature of late sixteenth-century Lutheranism: e.g. Lucas Osiander, *Epitomes Historiae Ecclesiasticae Centuriae* . . . , 8 vols (Tübingen, 1592–1604), *Centuriae Decimae Sextae Pars Prima* (Tübingen, 1602/3), unpaginated prefatory material. On this, see E. Cameron, 'One Reformation or Many: Protestant Identities in the Later Reformation in Germany', in O. P. Grell and R. W. Scribner (eds), *Tolerance and Intolerance in the European Reformation* (Cambridge, 1996), pp. 108–27.

ways) in the Holy Roman Empire by 1555, and in the kingdom of France from 1562 onwards. So in social as much as in semantic terms, 'popular heresy' had no need to exist by the end of the sixteenth century: the conditions which created it had vanished.

These changes in the religious context of Europe would transform Waldensian religious protest out of recognition. Ultimately, both the strategies described above – survival as a dissenting but semi-tolerated minority, and exile to a safer refuge – would play a part in their story. In the course of the century the Waldensian movement would shed its links with Catholic practice. It would become a form of reformed Protestantism; indeed, in the lands of the crown of France it would be subsumed within the French reformed Church. It would acquire learned, ordained ministers (many of them immigrants from elsewhere) and build public, visible places of worship. It would adopt creeds and formulae far more radical in their dissent from medieval Catholicism than ever were the medieval pastors' teachings.

From one point of view, then, the end of the middle ages and the advent of the Reformation does indeed represent the 'end' of Waldensian heresy, as it has been described up to this point.[2] Yet if one considers popular religion to consist as much in people as in Church structures, creeds and procedures, then some at least of the Waldensian peoples did indeed continue, albeit in a very different form. In Germany and Eastern Europe they lost their identity entirely, overtaken by and subsumed in other, newer movements. In the Languedoc, Waldenses had been a memory – and barely that – since the middle of the fourteenth century. In central Italy the silence of the sources has blanketed their history from the fourteenth century at the latest. However, those of the Alps, Dauphiné, Provence and Piedmont continued, as generation after generation of people, some bearing the same surnames as their medieval forebears, maintained their distinctive communal identity, embodied in a non-Catholic religious practice. Part three of this book is about both aspects of the story: discontinuities and transformations in the areas of belief, worship and religious conduct, but subtler continuities at the level of local communities and their stubborn cohesiveness.

---

2   The issue of whether the Reformation does represent the 'end' of Waldensianism is discussed in subtle terms in J. Gonnet and A. Molnar, *Les Vaudois au moyen âge* (Turin, 1974), pp. 316–17; see also G. Audisio, 'La Fin des vaudois (xvie siècle)?', in G. Audisio (ed.), *Les Vaudois des origines à leur fin (xiie-xvie siècles): Colloque international ... Aix-en-Provence, 8–10 avril 1988* (Turin, 1990), pp. 77–99.

8

The Alpine Barbes *and their Culture,* c.*1520–1530*

The evidence from late fifteenth-century Dauphiné and Piedmont was remarkably silent on the *barbes*, the Alpine versions of the traditional itinerant pastors of the Waldenses. This is essentially because the local pastors mostly managed to evade capture in the multiple inquisitions and the crusade: if any were indeed seized, the documents which their capture generated are lost.[1] While very large numbers of the Waldensian lay followers admitted listening and confessing their sins to the *barbes* and described them by name, they said little about their origins, formation, habits or conduct. It is quite possible that they actually knew very little about them.

Quite suddenly in the early sixteenth century, the veil lifts from these people to a considerable extent, though questions remain. Authentic, contemporary and mutually corroborating sources describe in some detail the way in which pastors were chosen and trained, and how they dealt with their followers. More striking, though also problematical, is the survival from the 1520s of a closely knit corpus of manuscript books which appear to have been owned by the Waldensian pastorate. Relatively little of the manuscript material actually originates with the Waldenses themselves: most is derivative from other sources, both Catholic and heterodox. That which does appear to derive from authentically Waldensian sources is often frustratingly anodyne in its content. Because this evidence is so late in date, post-dating the arrival of Martin Luther on the international scene, it is here discussed as part of the prologue to the Reformation, rather than as part of the history of the late medieval Waldenses.

---

1   On the survival of documents, see above, chapter 7, notes 143, 146.

8.1   The Pastorate: The Evidence of Georges Morel
and Pierre Griot

Two individuals from the Waldensian pastorate of the Alps and Provence provided independent and overlapping testimony to the way in which the *barbes* worked in the years around 1530. Georges Morel, a learned *barbe*, wrote a letter to the Basel reformer Joannes Oecolampadius (1482–1531) around the autumn of 1530 in which he described the *barbes'* lifestyle and routine in unique detail.[2] In November–December 1532 an apprentice *barbe* named Pierre Griot, from the region of Cesana Torinese in the Dauphiné east of the passes, was interrogated by the inquisitor Jean de Roma at Apt in Provence. He had been in training and travelling around with other preachers, and revealed much about their customs.[3] It should be added that neither account is entirely free from contaminating influences. Georges Morel was a highly educated person, literate in three languages. He was probably the 'learned *barbe* Georges' from Cabrières-d'Aigues whom Pierre Griot knew.[4] Although traditional accounts claimed that he was a Waldensian from Freissinières in the Dauphiné, there is absolutely no evidence of any inhabitant of that name in the complete, surviving account-book of the *coseigneur* of Freissinières, or in any of the trial records from the end of the previous century, when the entire population of the village was cited for heresy before the inquisitor Cattaneo. All the (numerous) Morels known in the area were both Catholic (including several ordained priests) and relatively prosperous.[5] Morel himself referred to aspects of the *barbes'* customs on which he sought Oecolampadius's advice, saying that 'after he had

2   The letter survives in A. Scultetus, *Annalium Evangelii passim per Europam* . . . *Renovati Decades Duae*, 2 vols (Heidelberg, 1618–20), vol. 2, pp. 295–306; the editor noted in the margin 'from the remains of Oecolampadius's library', implying that this was taken from a manuscript original.

3   G. Audisio, *Le Barbe et l'inquisiteur: Procès du barbe vaudois Pierre Griot par l'inquisiteur Jean de Roma (Apt, 1532)* (Aix-en-Provence, 1979), *passim*.

4   Audisio, *Barbe et l'inquisiteur*, pp. 102, 131.

5   The positive documentation of Catholic Morels is quite copious. See Paris, Bibliothèque Nationale, Fonds Latin, MS. 3375, vol. 2, fo. 223r (Georges Morel, cleric, a representative of Archbishop Baile of Embrun); Gap, Archives Départmentales des Hautes-Alpes, MS. G. 2767, fos 185v–6r (André Maurel, a cleric, given a chaplaincy near Embrun); G. de Manteyer (ed.), *Le Livre-journal tenu par Fazy de Rame en langage embrunais (6 juin 1471–10 juillet 1507*, 2 vols (Gap. 1932), vol. 2, paras 141–2, 223, 364, 385, 1,186, 1,266, 1,273, 1,286, 1,290 (numerous dealings between various Morels and the landlord Fazy de Rame, though none were among his tenants at Freissinières); N. Chorier, *Histoire générale du Dauphiné*, 2 vols (Valence, 1878–9, repr. Grenoble, 1971), vol. 2, p. 512 (an attack on heretics near Bardonècchia abetted by Gabriel and Claude Morel, nobles).

learned of these things since his arrival in the country' he saw that they needed Oecolampadius's input.[6] His remark does not suggest someone born and raised among the Waldenses. Though a committed *barbe*, Morel was also to some extent an outsider. Griot, while very much an insider himself, was heavily influenced by a vagrant married ex-Dominican friar named Anthoine Guérin, who imported news of Luther and sub-Lutheran ideas to the Provençal Vaudois.[7] These exotic aspects of Morel's and Griot's cultures do not impair the value of their eye-witness testimony to the *barbes'* conduct; they do however require their statements about belief and doctrine to be read with some caution.

Neither Morel nor Griot had any clear idea of the Waldenses' origins. Griot thought they dated from the time of the apostles, and was bewildered when told that 'Johannes Valdus' (*sic*) was active only 300 years earlier.[8] Morel noted that 'our people' often claimed they originated with the apostles, while he himself thought they dated to over 400 years ago.[9] The people who supported them, according to Morel, were mostly simple, rustic farmers, scattered widely because of frequent persecutions over a range of 800 miles (approximately the distance from the Waldensian valleys in the southwestern Alps to the tip of Italy). They lived precariously, everywhere subject to the jurisdiction of 'priests of the infidels'.[10] Morel's and Griot's descriptions of the *barbes'* relationship with their 'friends' largely confirms what earlier testimonies from their followers had reported. They visited their flock annually in their homes, read or recited from scripture to them, preached and heard confessions. The pastors travelled around in pairs, an elder being accompanied by one less experienced. Griot reported that the elder commonly addressed the more important and better informed heretic followers, while the junior spoke to the poor.[11] Morel, with unconscious paradox, admitted that the sacraments were given to the people not by the *barbes* but by the 'members of antichrist'; however, the *barbes* tried to interpret the sacraments for the people's benefit. Otherwise Morel reported their giving copious and decidedly puritanical moral advice to the people. Good Waldensian followers were told not to swear, attend dances or

---

6   V. Vinay, *Le Confessioni di fede dei Valdesi riformati, con i documenti del dialogo fra la 'prima' e la 'seconda' riforma*, Collana della Facoltà valdese di teologia, 12 (Turin, 1975), pp. 40–1: 'Haec inter nos ministros, quae tamen post in hanc patriam adventum meum, ut cognovi et edoctus sum, maxime tui spiritus lima indigent'.

7   Audisio, *Barbe et l'inquisiteur*, pp. 72–5, 103–4.

8   Ibid., p. 133.

9   Vinay, *Confessioni di fede... riformati*, pp. 36–7; Dublin, Trinity College, MS. 259, p. 1.

10   Vinay, *Confessioni di fede... riformati*, pp. 42–4; Dublin, Trinity College, MS. 259, pp. 54–5.

11   Audisio, *Barbe et l'inquisiteur*, pp. 124–5.

games such as archery, enjoy lascivious songs or wear sumptuous or gaudy clothes; the married were to be restrained in their sexual activity, avoiding intercourse at unfruitful times. As they had no magistrates, they should try to resolve disputes through arbitration among themselves. Those who ignored the *barbes'* guidance were sometimes 'excommunicated' from the group, but Morel admitted this sanction was often made light of.[12]

The two *barbes'* evidence yields more about how the pastors were selected, instructed and trained for their mission. Prospective *barbes* were taken from herding or husbandry at around the age of 25 or 30 on the encouragement of a sponsor among the pastorate. Pierre Griot was exhorted to train as a preacher by the senior Provençal *barbe* 'Loys': before that he had been a muleteer and a barber.[13] They were then made known to an assembly of the *barbes*; if approved, they entered into a period of testing and education, during which over three to four years they were taught during the winter months and their moral conduct was scrutinized. They learned to read and write, but also learned large portions of the New Testament by rote: Matthew and John's Gospels, the so called 'canonical epistles' and parts of the Pauline corpus.[14] Thereafter, according to Morel (but not Griot) trainees spent some time in a place where celibate sisters of the movement lived. (These 'Waldensian nuns' are attested nowhere else in the evidence for the movement at this late period, though equivalents have been detected much, much earlier, in the early thirteenth century.) At the end of the process the *barbes* laid hands on the trainee, admitted him to the 'priesthood' and sent him out to preach and teach with a senior companion, to whom the junior would always defer.[15]

After this manner of ordination all the *barbes* remained unmarried (though Morel noted that celibacy was not always fully observed); they travelled around teaching, and received food and lodging gratis from those to whom they ministered. Any gifts made by the followers were shared around the *barbes*. They worked at various artisan crafts, presumably in part to explain and justify their itinerancy to suspicious Catholics; but this work occupied them to such an extent that Morel felt that they were ignorant of the scriptures. Certainly Griot found his first elder companion's learning insufficient, which was why he attached himself to the ex-friar Anthoine Guérin.[16] Apart from preaching and teaching, the *barbes'* day

---

12 Vinay, *Confessioni di fede ... riformati*, pp. 42–3; Dublin, Trinity College, MS. 259, pp. 48–50; cf. Audisio, *Barbe et l'inquisiteur*, pp. 71–2, 126ff., 134–5.

13 Audisio, *Barbe et l'inquisiteur*, pp. 70–1.

14 Ibid., p. 105: note that the list of scriptures to be learned varies slightly from Griot to Morel.

15 Vinay, *Confessioni di fede ... riformati*, pp. 36–9; Dublin, Trinity College, MS. 259, pp. 7–8; cf. Audisio, *Barbe et l'inquisiteur*, pp. 106–7, 125–6.

16 Audisio, *Barbe et l'inquisiteur*, p. 107.

was punctuated by periods of repeated praying on bended knee: the Lord's Prayer was always said before anything was eaten or drunk.[17] Once a year the *barbes* met together in a gathering, usually held in the Piedmontese Alps. No mention was made of any *barbes* from outside the Alps and Provence attending: it must be assumed that this included only those of the Franco-Provençal language group (possibly including some from the émigré communities in southern Italy). Griot reported that such meetings were held around the end of August. In these meetings the 'governors' of the synods assigned preaching circuits to the *barbes*, who until they reached great ages were not allowed to remain more than two or three years in one place. Money collected was gathered in and shared out in common at the annual synod. Any *barbe* who had fallen into fornication was ejected from the brotherhood on these occasions.[18]

Morel and Griot both gave indications of the beliefs and teachings of their brotherhood. However, Morel's account tended to mince words, presumably because he had already anticipated Oecolampadius's disapproval or correction of some points. Griot's beliefs were clearly affected by the Protestant Guérin (for instance in his admission of holding reforming views on the eucharist).[19] Morel affirmed the Trinitarian and Christological orthodoxy of the Waldenses. He insisted that Christ was the sole mediator and that the saints, though holy, 'awaited in heaven the resurrection of their bodies'. The sacraments were (in Augustine's phrase) 'visible signs of invisible grace' and Morel admitted that 'they had erred thinking there were more than two sacraments'. Auricular confession was used to strengthen the weak 'without respect to the season': in other words, it was not just for Lent.[20] Human ceremonies linked to the Church's calendar Morel rejected as abominations. He firmly believed that after death there were only heaven and hell, denying the existence of 'purgatory invented by Antichrist'.[21] While calling priests 'limbs of Antichrist', Morel did not expatiate on the state of the Church or the papacy in particular.[22] He added a curious scholastic proviso that followers were exhorted to love first God, then their own soul, then their neighbour's soul, then their own body, then their neighbour's body, then their own possessions.[23]

17   Ibid., p. 109; Vinay, *Confessioni di fede . . . riformati*, pp. 38–9.
18   Ibid., pp. 38–41; Dublin, Trinity College, MS. 259, pp. 11–14; cf. Audisio, *Barbe et l'inquisiteur*, pp. 103–6.
19   Audisio, *Barbe et l'inquisiteur*, p. 81.
20   For conventional pre-Reformation Catholic practice regarding confession, see especially David Myers, *'Poor Sinning Folk': Confession and Conscience in Counter-Reformation Germany* (Ithaca, NY, and London, 1996), pp. 27–60.
21   Vinay, *Confessioni di fede . . . riformati*, pp. 40–1; Dublin, Trinity College, MS. 259, pp. 22ff.; cf. Audisio, *Barbe et l'inquisiteur*, p. 80.
22   But compare Audisio, *Barbe et l'inquisiteur*, pp. 74, 80.
23   Vinay, *Confessioni di fede . . . riformati*, pp. 40–3; Dublin, Trinity College, MS. 259, pp. 46–7].

Morel appended to his first letter to Oecolampadius a list of very spe-
cific technical requests for advice on moral and practical issues, which will
be discussed later.[24] In fact, both Oecolampadius and Martin Bucer of
Strasbourg (1491–1551), whom Morel and his companion Pierre
Masson also visited, took apart every item of Morel's description of
Waldensian belief and conduct and subjected it to critical scrutiny. The
itinerant, celibate ministry, which told people to live within the Catholic
Church but to believe differently from it, would not please the reformers. Morel's letter inaugurated a campaign, albeit an unsuccessful one, to
turn the *barbes* into ministers.

8.2   The 'Waldensian Books'

Neither Morel nor Griot had said a great deal about literature, apart from
the Bible itself. Numerous witnesses referred to *barbes* carrying books
with them on their preaching tours.[25] However, both Morel and Griot
also stressed the *oral* quality of their culture: scriptures were learned by
rote, preaching was done face-to-face. No mention is made in the trial
records or correspondence of written sermons, didactic treatises or any
text at all besides scripture. Yet there survives a significant body of manuscript texts, securely datable to the middle 1520s in several cases, which
is written in the same dialect as the vernacular digest of Morel's correspondence with the reformers and appears to originate from some sort
of Waldensian source. These manuscripts have since the late sixteenth and
early seventeenth centuries been collected as evidence for the Waldensian
religious spirit.[26] It has proved extremely difficult to integrate these into
the history of the movement, even with the aid of all modern scholarly
apparatus; and several accounts have found them unusable for the history
of the Waldenses.[27]

24   See below, chapter 9.1.
25   Cambridge, University Library, MS. Dd. 3. 25, fo. 59v; Grenoble, Archives
Départmentales de l'Isère, MS. B 4350, fos 87v, 119v, 301r.
26   One of the earliest published references to and citations of the Waldensian poetry
is in P. de Marnix, Seigneur de Ste-Aldegonde, *Tableau des differens de la religion*, 2
vols (Leiden, 1603–5), vol. 1, fos 149r–53r. The work first appeared in 1599. Much
more extensive use of the material was made by J.-P. Perrin and his successors, as
discussed in the Epilogue below.
27   G. Audisio, *Les Vaudois du Luberon: une minorité en Provence (1460–1560)* (Aix-
en-Provence, 1984), makes no substantial use of the 'Waldensian books', so difficult
are they to tie in to the rest of the evidence. The reservations against using them as
evidence for the beliefs of the fifteenth-century Dauphiné, expressed in E. Cameron,
The Reformation of the Heretics: The Waldenses of the Alps 1480–1580 (Oxford, 1984),
pp. 66–7, are further justified by the recent assigning of dates in the 1520s for their
compilation. For the fullest recent discussion in print, see Anne Brenon, 'The

Nevertheless, the manuscripts exist and there is just enough evidence, both internal and circumstantial, to link the books (though not all their contents) with the Waldenses of the Alps and Provence. In the form in which they survive (leaving aside the issue of whether several volumes may have been subsequently bound as one) there are six in Cambridge University Library, eight in Trinity College, Dublin, five in the Bibliothèque Publique et Universitaire at Geneva, and one each in the municipal libraries of Carpentras, Dijon and Grenoble, and in the Zentralbibliothek in Zürich. The location of the bulk of these manuscripts can be explained by their being deliberately sought out by Protestant apologists in the seventeenth century.[28] Of the twenty-three volumes, five are incomplete translations of the Bible, usually comprising most of the New Testament and selected moralizing passages from the Old Testament.[29] Four of the Cambridge manuscripts, five of those at Dublin, all five at Geneva (three of which are later copies) and the text in Dijon contain disparate collections of religious texts, comprising in varying proportions basic catechesis, moralizing treatises, sermons and religious poetry of different provenances. There is also a bestiary, entitled 'On the Properties of Animals', apparently intended for didactic purposes, which offers moralistic interpretations of the natures of various animals. It has a long ancestry in similar early Christian and Catholic writings, and appears to be a cousin of a Latin work published in Mondovì, *c.*1510.[30] There is a handful of anomalous pieces. There is a vernacular translation and reorganized digest of the Morel–Oecolampadius–Bucer discussions of 1530, compiled at a slightly later date and based on a body of correspondence originally conducted in Latin, most of which survives in other forms.[31] At Dublin there is also a seventeenth-century copy of

Waldensian Books', in Peter Biller and Anne Hudson (eds), *Heresy and Literacy, 1000–1530* (Cambridge, 1994), pp. 137–59.
28   Those in Cambridge and Dublin were certainly collected to their present locations as part of the process described in chapter 8 above, note 143. Links between the Waldensian congregations and the Genevan Church after 1555 could account for their having been retrieved by Samuel Morland from Geneva in the 1650s. In Cambridge, University Library, MS. Dd xv. 30, at the bottom of the first remaining folio, are the words 'A monsr. Morland par son servit[eu]r. J. Leger, 1656'. On J. Léger see the Epilogue below, notes 35–6.
29   Cambridge, University Library, MS. Dd xv. 34; Dublin, Trinity College, MS. 258; Carpentras, Bibliothèque Inguimbertine, MS. 8; Grenoble, Bibliothèque Municipale, MS. 43, ex 488, ex 8595; Zürich, Zentralbibliothek, MS. C. 169.
30   Cambridge, University Library, MSS. Dd. xv. 29–32; Dijon, Bibliothèque Municipale, MS. 234; Dublin, Trinity College, MSS. 260, 261, 262, 263, 267; Geneva, Bibliothèque Publique et Universitaire, MSS. 206, 207, 208, 209, 209a. On the bestiary, see Gonnet and Molnar, *Vaudois au moyen âge*, pp. 342–3 and references; also A. M. Raugei, *Bestiario valdese* (Florence, 1984).
31   Dublin, Trinity College, MS. 259: note that Brenon, 'The Waldensian Books', p. 145 and n. 16, accepts that Dublin, Trinity College, MS. 269, formerly included

some earlier religious tracts.[32] In Cambridge, classed with the Waldensian manuscripts, is a book which contains a Latin grammar written in the Alps, Latin scriptural extracts, Provençal poetry, an arithmetical text and some moral texts: its multiple hands all look quite different from the others and it appears to have no discernible connection with the Waldenses.[33]

The five scriptural translations and the bulk of the religious collections form a quite homogeneous group in various ways. The dialect in which they are written, called 'Vaudois' by some commentators and 'Occitan' by others, is a clearly defined version of the many diverse patois which existed between Provence and Piedmont. For present purposes it is best called 'Franco-Provençal': a northern version of Provençal, probably comprehensible on both sides of the Alpine passes and among the Alpine migrants to Provence.[34] The handwriting of the bulk of the pieces is remarkably similar: it is a stylized, archaic, rounded book-hand characterized by extremely thick pen-strokes. The presentation of the manuscripts varies: some are quite large, formal volumes with lavish illumination, as in some of the Bibles.[35] On the other hand, some are extremely small, compact volumes: Cambridge, University Library MS. Dd. xv. 31 and 32 are both approximately 9 cm tall by 6–7 cm across. Nevertheless the handwriting style is recognizably the same despite differences in size.[36] Finally, the manuscripts show remarkable homogeneity as to date. Dublin, Trinity College MS. 260 is internally dated to 1524, Dublin, Trinity College MS. 263 to 1523;[37] others can securely be dated to the 1520–30 period either by their contents or by explicit dating somewhere in the manuscript.[38] In themselves, then, these texts testify only to the Waldensian culture of the first

in the corpus, is not a Waldensian text. Content, language and date are all different to those of the remainder.

32   Dublin, Trinity College, MS. 264.
33   Cambridge, University Library, MS. Dd. xv. 33. Lists and descriptions of the whole corpus are found in Gonnet and Molnar, *Vaudois au moyen âge*, pp. 443–50, and Brenon, 'The Waldensian Books', p. 159. E. Montet, *Histoire littéraire des Vaudois du Piémont* (Paris, 1885), is now superseded.
34   Brenon, 'The Waldensian Books', pp. 141–3 and references. For a discussion of the linguistic problems specific to this part of the Alps, see G. Jochnowitz, *Dialect Boundaries and the Question of Franco-Provençal* (The Hague and Paris, 1973). An older discussion of the 'Waldensian dialect' is E. Comba, *History of the Waldenses of Italy*, trans. T. E. Comba (London, 1889), pp. 160–6.
35   Cambridge, University Library, MS. Dd. xv. 34; Carpentras, Bibliothèque Inguimbertine, MS. 8. The Carpentras Bible is reproduced on the wrapper of G. Audisio, *The Waldensian Dissent: Persecution and Survival, c.1170–c.1570*, translated by Claire Davison (Cambridge, 1999). The Cambridge Bible is quite similar.
36   Brenon, 'The Waldensian Books', pp. 140–1.
37   Dublin, Trinity College, MS. 260 is dated to 1524, since that date is given as the basis for the ecclesiastical calendar on the first leaf. Dublin, Trinity College, MS. 263, fo. 124r, the colophon to the manuscript, carries the date 1523.
38   Brenon, 'The Waldensian Books', p. 144.

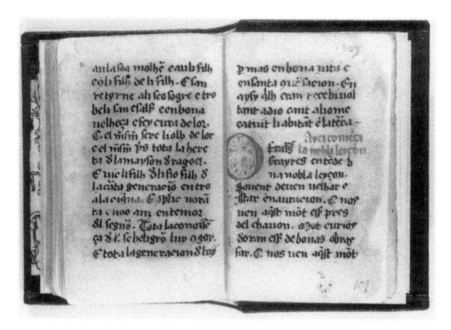

Plate 3 This opening in one of the smaller books of treatises shows the end of an exposition of the Book of Tobit, followed by the beginning of a fragment of the dialect poem *La Nobla Leyçon*. The most notable feature of this manuscript is its diminutive size (each page is less than 9 cm × 7 cm), which is in marked contrast to the much larger editions of the Bible. (Reproduced by permission of the Syndics of Cambridge University Library.)

half of the sixteenth century, the period when other forms of heterodoxy were exerting powerful influence on the dissenting movements of the Alps and Provence. Given that many include copies of earlier treatises, they may testify to a longer-standing tradition; however, the inclusion of renderings of some very recent material, such as a précis of late works of Lukas of Prague (d. 1528), warns against pushing this literature too far back into the Waldensian past.[39]

Besides the biblical translations, the texts found in these manuscripts can be divided into various categories, though it must be stressed that they are all mixed together in the collections, usually without any apparent order. Broadly speaking, there is a range of what may be called catechetical material, of which one of the largest and most often copied texts is a version of the *Somme le Roi* composed by Laurent de Bois, or Laurent d'Orléans, *c.*1279.[40] The contents are Catholic and uncontroversial: the

39 Gonnet and Molnar, *Vaudois au moyen âge*, p. 365 and notes, demonstrates that the work entitled *Qual cosa sia Antichrist* contains material based on a work by Lukas of Prague dating from 1525. See below.
40 Cambridge, University Library, MS. Dd. xv. 30, fos 125r–237v.

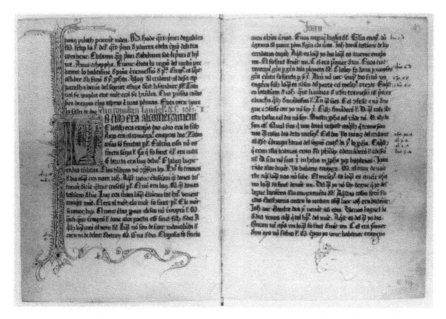

Plate 4 This opening shows some of the partial translation of the Bible into Franco-Provençal dialect, which is now in Cambridge University Library. At top left the translation of Luke's Gospel ends abruptly at chapter 3:6, at which point John's Gospel follows on immediately. This may suggest that the manuscript was copied from an earlier, damaged exemplar. The text of John appears originally to have been complete, though seventeen leaves are missing from the manuscript as it now exists. The translation of 'the Word' as 'lo filh', 'the Son' in the early verses is surprising. Unlike the Bible now in Carpentras, this text is written in a single column, though the detail and style of the illumination is quite similar to the Carpentras Bible. (Reproduced by permission of the Syndics of Cambridge University Library.)

Ten Commandments, the twelve articles of faith, the seven deadly sins, the gifts of the Holy Spirit, the cardinal virtues. There are numerous associated pieces, Catholic in content and probably in derivation, which expatiate on the sins of the flesh to be avoided and the ascetic virtues to be cultivated.[41]

A second range of material comprises sermons, of which more than 200 have been identified.[42] In some cases the text includes the gospel or epistle passage on which it is based; in others it is merely cited. Some sermons make general moral points rather than expounding a scriptural passage in detail. *Mesquins*, for example, is a general warning to avoid the vices and exhortation to cultivate the virtues. 'All you who labour'

41   These include expositions of the Lord's Prayer, treatises on penance and the pains and joys of the afterlife, and similar homiletic material.
42   Brenon, 'The Waldensian Books', p. 146.

('O vos tuit li qual lavoran') makes a call for the hearer to avoid the distractions of worldly life, business, family, and so forth and to cultivate prayer, almsgiving and fasting.[43] These sermons have only recently been subjected to serious scrutiny. They were poorly regarded by nineteenth-century commentators and historians because of their medieval character, embodying as they did far-fetched allegories, moralizing and mnemonics.[44] The much-copied 'Sermon on the infant Jesus', for example, draws from the story of Jesus's separation from his parents at Jerusalem a series of somewhat fanciful moral analogues. These explain the sins which cause one to lose sight of Jesus and then the virtuous practices and contemplation which allow the believer to find him again.[45] Except for one huge sequence for the whole liturgical year in a Dublin manuscript,[46] the sermons are habitually intercalated with the short moralizing religious treatises, which suggests that the compiler or compilers saw little difference in their purpose or use.

Related to the sermons are two short pieces of pastoral advice. The 'Letter of the friends' ('Pistola de li amic') contains nothing which a Catholic could not have written, but testifies to the pastoral realities of rural life. It exhorts its readers to live in charity with each other and to supply their needs by honest labour. It warns against the deceits often practised in commerce and manufacturing. It dwells on the evils of usury, condemning those who accept fields or vines as security for loans and then take the fruits of those fields for themselves. It makes practical recommendations for healing agricultural disputes, warns against contentiousness over marriages and inheritances, and exhorts everyone to be inoffensive and harmless.[47] The letter of *Barbe* Bartolomeo Tertian of Meana di Susa, from around 1500, contains comparable exhortations to peaceful and moral living, avoidance of superfluities and occasions to sin. His readers were told to avoid 'games, greed, ribaldry, dancing, and other disorders; quarrels, deceits . . . usury, ill-will, discord'. The style is reminiscent of the pastoral epistles of the New Testament, which may have served as models.[48]

Rather different are the Waldensian poems, five of which are transcribed together in one of the manuscripts at Cambridge.[49] These are not entirely independent of the Catholic tradition, but their rhyming couplets and call for the persecuted minority to endure tribulations are

---

43 Cambridge, University Library, MS. Dd. xv. 32, fos 51r–66v.
44 See Gonnet and Molnar, *Vaudois au moyen âge*, pp. 366–7.
45 Cambridge, University Library, MS. Dd. xv. 30, fos 252r–256r.
46 Dublin, Trinity College, MS. 267, fos 49r–338r.
47 Cambridge, University Library, MS. Dd. xv. 30, fos 64r–79v.
48 The text is in the original and in Italian translation in B. Pazè Beda and P. Pazè, *Riforma e cattolicesimo in val Pragelato 1555–1685* (Pinerolo, 1975), pp. 33–5.
49 Cambridge, University Library, MS. Dd. xv. 30, fos 79v–118v.

distinctly evocative. The 'New Comfort' ('Novel Confort') warns its hearers against dreaming through life, then discovering that late in life is too late to repent of their sins. One cannot serve God and the world; everything worldly is damnable. The poem lists all the sins to be avoided and calls on the hearer to cultivate all the virtues, including perseverance and patience in tribulation and persecution. It uses the New Testament image of heaven as a wedding feast, contrasting the deceivers, hypocrites, persecutors and antichrists who are to be cast out, with the true persecuted lambs of Christ, who will be rewarded in heaven.[50] The 'New Sermon' ('Novel Sermon') adopts a similarly homiletic tone. Most people leave off doing good and live in error: the poems lists the covetous (including false clerics, though 'good servants of the Lord' are excused), those devoted to the pleasures of the senses, the idle, gluttonous and lecherous, the angry and vengeful, murderers and robbers. All will be punished in hell. Instead, one is to serve God in one of three classes: the best of all, the contemplatives who live in poverty; or the second class who are chaste and live by work; or the third, that of the married who live well.[51] Service to Christ brings tribulations but will ultimately be rewarded.[52]

The longest and most ambitious of the poems is the 'Noble Lesson' ('Nobla Leyçon'), which is no less than a verse summary of the entire Bible story. It evokes the coming end of the world; signs of the last days are multiplying and death may come at any time. Therefore one must protect the soul with the virtues; the many sinners are contrasted with the few who keep the law. The Old Testament from Abraham to the Babylonian captivity is then briefly summarized; then the Annunciation of Jesus's birth to the Virgin, his nativity and his life. Jesus's mission is summed up as 'perfecting the law': Jesus made the law of Moses more demanding and more complete, forbidding even adulterous thoughts and looks as well as the act, forbidding divorce, encouraging virginity, forbidding all swearing and all vengeance, and commanding forgiveness to evil-doers. Christ's persecution and passion, resurrection and ascension are described, then Pentecost and the rise of the early Church. The true Church was persecuted and still is up to the present. At this point one finds almost the only reference in the entire literature to the title 'Waldensian':

Scripture says and we can see / that if there is any good person who wishes to love God and fear Jesus Christ / who does not wish to curse or swear

50   Ibid., fos 79v–86v.
51   This classification of three hierarchies of Christians was a *topos* of medieval homiletic literature, and is found in Durand of Osca as well. See K.-V. Selge, *Die ersten Waldenser mit Edition des Liber antiheresis des Durandus von Osca*, 2 vols (Berlin, 1967), vol. 2, pp. 63–9 and references.
52   Cambridge, University Library, MS. Dd. xv. 30, fos 86v–96v.

or lie / or commit adultery or kill or take what is another's / or revenge himself on his enemy / they say he is a Waldensian [*vaudes*] and worthy to be punished / and find accusations with lies and with deceit.[53]

The poem ends with a call to true penitence, which is described as interior contrition and repentance: only God forgives, not popes, cardinals or prelates, so one must repent and do penitence in the present life. It exhorts the reader to follow Christ in a life of spiritual poverty and chastity.[54]

The remaining poems are somewhat shorter. The 'Father eternal' is an extended prayer in the form of an acrostic poem organized around the three persons of the Trinity, comprising a series of verses of mostly three lines.[55] The 'Ship' ('Barca') echoes the moralizing themes of the first two. Its first part comprises a mordant and depressing lament on the miseries of the human condition: humankind is made of earth, the vilest of the elements, conceived in sin, weakest of all the animals at birth, dominated by corruption and sin. This part of the poem has long been recognized as a paraphrase, in some places a nearly exact translation of *On the Miseries of the Human Condition* written by Pope Innocent III, a fashionable text throughout the later middle ages.[56] In the latter part of the poem human life is compared to a merchant's voyage: the dying person (the merchant) sailing into the port of heaven will be in great fear if his ship is laden with worthless goods, but confident of reward if he is carrying precious things (the virtues). There follows an exhortation to call on God for help, to make a full confession of sins compared against the seven deadly sins and the Ten Commandments, to resolve to live better and perform penance.[57]

What can one conclude from this material about the religiosity of the Waldensian *barbes* on the eve of the Reformation? There is no clear line which divides the material drawn from Catholic sources and that which appears to be indigenous to the Waldenses themselves. The ethical standards of the Waldenses were no different, in principle, from those of the late medieval Church. The call to fortitude in persecution may, because of the context in which it is found, appear specific to a persecuted heresy; yet in truth the idea that true Christians were a scorned minority was

---

53   Ibid., fo. 105r.
54   Ibid., fos 96v–107v.
55   Ibid., fos 107v–111r.
56   See Gonnet and Molnar, *Vaudois au moyen âge*, p. 331 and note; for the original text, see Lotario dei Segni (Pope Innocent III), *De miseria condicionis humane*, ed. Robert E. Lewis (Athens, Ga., 1978); on its reception, see Jean Delumeau, *Sin and Fear: The Emergence of a Western Guilt Culture, 13th–18th Centuries*, trans. Eric Nicholson (New York, 1990), pp. 44–7.
57   Cambridge, University Library, MS. Dd. xv. 30, fos 111r–118v.

always part of the heritage of the Church. In so far as one can draw conclusions from this part of the literature, it is the *principle of selection* used in selecting material from the Catholic inheritance, more than any specifically Waldensian content, which may be of help.

The first point which demands attention is the relentless ethical emphasis of the overwhelming majority of the texts. Christianity is *law*: it is a list of things to be done and not done, of vices to be shunned and virtues to be cultivated.[58] In complete contrast to the way in which the reformers would interpret Christ and the gospel, the Waldensian texts portray Christ as the bringer of a stricter, more severe system of moral law. Christ took the law of the Old Testament and made it tougher. Even apparently unlikely texts are subordinated to this pitiless drive for moral perfection. The exposition of the Lord's Prayer in one of the Cambridge manuscripts, for example, interprets every petition of the Lord's Prayer in terms of the seven deadly sins. 'Your name be hallowed' is a prayer to escape the sin of lechery and cultivate chastity; 'your kingdom come' asks for freedom from avarice and the gift of spiritual poverty; 'your will be done' asks to escape from sloth; 'give us this day or daily bread' seeks to avoid gluttony; 'forgive us our sins . . .' asks to escape anger; 'lead us not into temptation' is a prayer to avoid pride. 'Deliver us from evil' provokes a recapitulation of a whole list of sins.[59]

This emphasis on avoiding the deadly sins might appear merely self-evident and platitudinous. In the context of Waldensian attitudes to ritual, however, it is more than that. In the medieval Church, one could harp on the omnipresence of sin and corruption, in order to encourage the people to look for grace and help through the sacraments of the Church. Indeed, the whole homiletic endeavour of the medieval Church was based around a balance: human moral effort is weak, temptations to sin are everywhere, but if one will only turn to Christ's Church, the sacraments, the sacramentals, the intercession of saints, and all the other spiritual helps, one can mitigate the consequences of sin. This latter, countervailing element is largely absent from the Waldensian literature. It is not that there is any consistent attack on the Church; rather, the ministrations of the Church to reassure and cleanse are simply passed over. The last section of the 'Noble Lesson' contains a warning that those who now believe themselves forgiven will be disillusioned at the last judgement. One cannot turn to the popes and the clergy thinking that they have power to pardon any single mortal sin; only God forgives, so everyone must do true penance for themselves, in this life.[60] One can, however, clear the Waldenses of one charge which might be laid against

58   Cf. ibid., fo. 106v.
59   Ibid., fos 6r–24v.
60   Ibid., fos 105r–106r.

them, that of works-righteousness or an excessive confidence in the power of human moral virtue. The texts are not Pelagian in the sense that believers are thought able to satisfy the law of themselves. Prayer for strength, for the gift of the Holy Spirit, is always encouraged. In fact, there is not really any speculative theological exploration in these texts as to *how* the believer is to satisfy the demands of the law. He or she is simply told to do so.

In so far as these texts were probably copied and conserved among the *barbes* rather than the people, one is justified in locating them within a tradition of ascetic, quasi-monastic piety typical of the Christian middle ages. The *barbes* incorporated the belief that those who lived chastely in the celibate life were inherently superior to the majority of the married living in ordinary society. Everyday life, let alone married life, is full of dangers and temptations, and those who seek and attain purity will please God better. The *barbes* therefore associated themselves with the separation from and contempt for the world cultivated by the priesthood and the regular orders. They presumably believed themselves to be better at it, at least in terms of their poverty, the dangers and inconvenience of their life-style, and the need for fortitude.

In one respect one might turn to the literature to clarify a question which remains unclear. Waldenses in theory 'did not swear': yet, as was shown earlier, Waldensian followers not only swore civil oaths readily before Catholics, but even used them among themselves, though they were otherwise famous for the cleanliness and lack of profanity in their ordinary speech. Can the Waldensian books help out on this question? Unfortunately, the evidence both supports the traditional view and raises new questions. In the 'Treatise on the Seven Deadly Sins' contained in one of the Dublin manuscripts, there is a discussion of the evils of swearing which draws on Catholic sources such as Augustine: someone who swears runs the risk of perjuring himself; one who forces another to swear can kill the soul as well as the body, and therefore is worse than a murderer who kills only the body. Jerome is also quoted to the effect that 'the truth of the Gospel does not receive oath-swearing'. These passages were traditionally interpreted to dissuade profane and repetitious swearing; and indeed the text from which these warnings are extracted is part of Laurent de Bois's *Somme le Roi*![61] Both this passage and the Waldensian sermon *Mesquins* quote two favourite texts against profane swearing, from Ecclesiasticus 23:9: 'Do not accustom your mouth to oaths' and 23:11: 'One who swears is full of iniquity, and the scourge will not leave his house'. It is interesting to note that these same texts were quoted by the Piedmontese Waldensian 'Bruna' in

---

61   Dublin, Trinity College, MS. 260, fo. 135 r-v; compare with the rejection of profane swearing in ibid., fo. 206v.

1335;[62] but in truth such authorities were part of the medieval mainstream. The 'Noble Lesson' identified as one of the 'perfections' of the law that Christ said 'do not swear at all'; but the key question, unanswered in this literature, was what that text actually meant and how it could be applied to everyday life.

8.3   The Puzzle of Hussite Influence

The manuscript literature testifies to one aspect of the Waldensian experience in the early sixteenth century which is otherwise tantalizingly poorly documented. From the response of some *barbes* to the discussions with the reformers in 1530–2, it is clear that contacts existed between the *barbes* and the Bohemian Brethren. The latter would send a critical letter to the former reproaching them for their discussions with the reformers in 1533.[63] Otherwise, the contacts between the Bohemians and the *barbes* are shrouded in obscurity, which even the meticulous researches of Amedeo Molnár failed to elucidate.[64] Previous research into the local trial evidence has failed to discover any evidence of Bohemian ideas at work in the Alps; indeed, the great differences between the priestly and monastic style of the Unity of Brethren and the preaching mission of the *barbes* among their followers would have made such cross-fertilization very difficult.[65]

Yet the manuscripts prove that there was an awareness and a use of the religious writings of the Hussite tradition and the Unity of Brethren

---

62   G. G. Merlo, *Eretici e inquisitori nella società piemontese del trecento* (Turin, 1977), p. 220; as above, chapter 7, note 31.

63   See below, chapter 9, note 90.

64   Apart from Gonnet and Molnar, *Vaudois au moyen âge*, pp. 211–82, the most important articles on this point are those by A. Molnar, 'Luc de Prague et les Vaudois d'Italie', *Bollettino della Società di Studi Valdesi* 90 (1949), pp. 40–64; 'Les Vaudois et l'Unité des Frères Tchèques', *Bollettino della Società di Studi Valdesi* 118 (1965), pp. 3–16; 'L'Internationale des Taborites et des Vaudois', *Bollettino della Società di Studi Valdesi* 122 (1967), pp. 3–13; 'Les Vaudois et les hussites', *Bollettino della Società di Studi Valdesi* 136 (1974), pp. 27–35.

65   G. Audisio, *Les 'Vaudois': naissance, vie et mort d'une dissidence (xiie–xve siècles)* (Turin, 1989), pp. 82ff., testifies to an inability, despite exhaustive research, to uncover any evidence of Hussite influence among the Mediterranean Waldenses in the fifteenth century. P. Paravy, 'Waldensians in the Dauphiné', in Peter Biller and Anne Hudson (eds), *Heresy and Literacy, 1000–1530* (Cambridge, 1994), pp. 174–5, detects evidence of the interpenetration of Hussite ideas in the works of the Catholic theologians Samuele da Cassini and Claude de Seyssel, who wrote anti-Waldensian polemics in the first decades of the sixteenth century. The evidence of these authors is, however, far from clear or conclusive. See also P. Paravy, *De la Chrétienté romaine à la réforme en Dauphiné*, Collection de l'École Française de Rome, 183, 2 vols (Rome, 1993–4), pp. 1,109–21.

in Provence and the Alps. One finds, dispersed throughout eight of the manuscript collections of religious treatises, more or less elaborate versions of dogmatic and controversial pieces which derive both from the early age of Hussitism and from the Taborites and the Unity of Brethren.[66] Many of these form part of a fluid but identifiable theological *summa* entitled in some of the manuscripts 'Treasure and Light of Faith' ('Tresor e lume de fe').[67] Other important treatises of post-Hussite inspiration include a short catechism known as the 'Lesser interrogations' ('Enterrogacions Menors') translating a catechism written by Lukas of Prague in 1501;[68] and an important controversial piece derived from Lukas of Prague's later writings, here entitled 'Antichrist'.[69] It is important to stress that the presence of these texts interleaved with the other material in the Waldensian literature is inherently problematic. Incorporating post-Hussite religious literature entailed internal conflicts and contradictions within the Waldensian manuscripts: doctrines were upheld in one text which were then denounced in another.[70] One must presume that the copyists and translators who prepared these manuscripts were not setting out to store up dogmatic puzzles for themselves. They clearly thought that there was something in the Bohemian material which was useful to them. The best way to analyse this element in the literature is to try to see it from the Waldensian point of view.

First of all, much of the religious writing of Hussite inspiration in the manuscripts provided its users with basic, uncontroversial catechetical material for instruction in the agreed documents of medieval Christianity. The 'Tresor e lume de fe', for example, contained a straightforward translation of the Athanasian Creed and an exposition of the Apostles' and Nicene Creeds.[71] The 'Enterrogacions Menors' offered a catechism which echoed Catholic exemplars in numerous respects: man was a creature of God, rational and mortal, created for the purpose of knowing God, worshipping him, and being saved by his grace.[72] The remainder

---

66   Such material is found in Cambridge, University Library, MSS. Dd. xv. 29, 32; Dijon, Bibliothèque Municipale, MS. 234; Dublin, Trinity College, MSS. 267, 260, 262, 263; Geneva, Bibliothèque Publique et Universitaire, MS. 208.
67   See especially Dublin, Trinity College, MS. 260, fos 176v–226v; and analysis in Gonnet and Molnar, *Vaudois au moyen âge*, pp. 353–61; Brenon, 'The Waldensian Books', pp. 153ff. and references, names it the *Exposé*.
68   Dublin, Trinity College, MS. 260, fos 284v–291v.
69   Dublin, Trinity College, MS. 267, fos 365v–377v; for discussion, see Gonnet and Molnar, *Vaudois au moyen âge*, p. 365.
70   See Brenon, 'The Waldensian Books', pp. 157–8. The contradictions arise between both Catholic and heretical material and between different sorts of heretical teachings.
71   Dublin, Trinity College, MS. 260, fos 179r–182r.
72   Ibid., fos 284v ff.

of the catechism was organized around a three-fold structure of faith, hope and charity, with Trinitarian overtones. Second, a great deal in the post-Hussite material echoed and reinforced the insistent moralizing tone found in the Waldenses' sermons and their adaptations of Catholic literature. The exposition of the Ten Commandments in 'Tresor e lume de fe' echoed the Catholic *Somme le Roi* to a remarkable extent: this is particularly evident in the discussion of swearing under the rubric 'do not take the name of the Lord in vain'.[73] The 'Enterrogacions Menors', like the 'Noble Lesson', attributed to Christ the foundation of a new set of commandments, which forbade anger against a brother, lustful looks at a woman, divorce, swearing, etc.[74] A Taborite tract on marriage found in two of the Dublin manuscripts presented its readers with the classic scholastic position on sexual ethics: sexual intercourse might be engaged in by married couples to 'avoid fornication' and to bear children, but was subject to a host of provisos and things to be avoided by pious spouses.[75] A treatise on the upbringing of children exhorted parents to use appropriate discipline and warned against the toleration of sins and faults within the family; it was accompanied by fervent exhortations to protect the chastity of daughters.[76]

The Taborite material presented its Waldensian users with a literate, articulate presentation of anti-clerical, anti-sacerdotal and anti-ritualist arguments. These could have been used by preachers faced with the paradox of teaching followers who continued to receive the sacraments from Catholic priests, and who needed to maintain a sense of their spiritual superiority to the priesthood. The 'Enterrogacions Menors', for example, draws a distinction between true and false ministers in the Church: the true ministers showed faith, sound doctrine and examples of good living. False ministers could be recognized by ignorance, manifest sins, idolatry and the attributing of power to purely human rituals, false religion and the acts of simoniac priests. Many priests erroneously thought that the power of the sacraments was tied up in the external rituals rather than the spiritual state of the recipient.[77] 'False prophets' led the people astray to worship created things, through prayers, fasts, sacrifices, offerings, pilgrimages and so forth.[78] The work called 'Antichrist', based like the 'Enterrogacions' on Lukas of Prague's writings, in its first part listed a whole series of 'works of Antichrist'. The first

---

73   Dublin, Trinity College, MS. 260, fos 197r–230r, esp. 206v; the same point is noted by Brenon, 'The Waldensian Books', p. 153.
74   Dublin, Trinity College, MS. 260, fo. 287r.
75   Ibid., fos 85r–91r; cf. MS. 263, fos 34v–38r; on this topic, see James A. Brundage, *Law, Sex and Christian Society in Medieval Europe* (Chicago, 1987).
76   Dublin, Trinity College, MS. 260, fos 78v–85r.
77   Ibid., fos 288r ff.
78   Ibid., fo. 290v.

was the diverting of worship from God to created things, whether the saints, or the sacraments, or other blessed and consecrated objects. Antichrist deprived Christ of the sufficiency of grace and transferred it to human rituals. He turned religion into a matter of outward and ceremonial forms.[79] The second part of the work, based on a piece written by Lukas as late as 1525, expatiated on the corruption of true worship in the 'ministerial Church'.[80]

This sort of critique would in theory have enabled *barbes* to fulfil Morel's ambition of instructing the people to understand the sacraments which they received in a different way to that which the priests taught.[81] However, the Bohemian restatement of medieval Christian worship actually fitted most uneasily into the Waldensian context. The exposé of the seven sacraments in 'Tresor e lume de fe' contained a series of prescriptions for reforming and simplifying liturgical practice. Baptism required water, someone to baptize, and verbal exhortation; it did not need exorcism, breathing into the nostrils, the sign of the cross, salt, saliva or anointing.[82] Ordination to priesthood required prayer, fasting, almsgiving and diligent self-examination; other rituals commonly used, such as anointing and the ceremonial presentation of instruments, were unnecessary.[83] Extreme unction as commonly practised did not conform to the New Testament. Jakoubek of Stribro had argued that the oil used was originally intended for the use of all Christians, not just priests; John Wyclif ('the evangelical doctor') argued in the *Trialogus* that many could be saved without it.[84] This discussion of the sacraments, with its quotations from Hussite leaders and John Wyclif, called for a reformation of ritual, not for a reinterpretation of rituals as they stood. Even more awkward for Waldensian readers was the critique in the same text of auricular confession. The Hussite authors argued that external confession of sins to a priest was merely an accompaniment to the essential act of interior contrition; that it was impossible to argue that auricular confession was necessary to salvation; and therefore the method introduced by Innocent III and normally practised by 'simoniac priests' was to be shunned.[85] One need hardly add that a chief part of Waldensian ritual had been built around mimicking precisely this auricular confession which the Bohemian texts sought to modify out of existence. The discussion of the eucharist, a few pages on, appeared to argue for a spiritual presence of Christ in the elements, whereas the exposition of the

79 Dublin, Trinity College, MS. 267, fos 369r–370r.
80 Ibid., fos 373v–377v.
81 See above, note 14; Vinay, *Confessioni di fede . . . riformati*, pp. 42–3.
82 Dublin, Trinity College, MS. 260, fos 182v–184r.
83 Ibid., fos 190v–191v.
84 Ibid., fos 192v–194v.
85 Ibid., fos 184v–187v.

Lord's Prayer in another of the manuscripts argued for something very much like transubstantiation.[86]

Apart from their comments about ritual, the Hussite texts helped to reinforce Waldensian rejections of the official cult in two other important respects. The treatise entitled the 'Dream of Purgatory' in 'Tresor e lume de fe' dismantled one of the most potent embodiments of priestly and sacral power. The fables about purgatory had caused an immense growth in church building and a multiplication of altars. Those destined to be saved were truly 'purged' in various ways during their lives, such as the Word, good works, bearing adversity and converting sinners. Above all, Christ's blood was the true purgation. None of the early Fathers knew of a third, intermediate state besides heaven and hell; and their position was supported by 'Master John of blessed memory', that is, Jan Hus. Prayers for the dead were of doubtful authority, supported only by the deuterocanonical book of Maccabees; their supposed efficacy was mostly supported by fables and deceptions.[87] The Hussite treatise 'On the Invocation of saints' noted how the belief in the need for intercession by saints before the Godhead led to idolatry and superfluous ritual. Christ was the sole, accessible and perfectly sufficient mediator for the sinner with God, and it was foolish to look for any other, as Wyclif had demonstrated in the *Trialogus*, which was summarized at some length.[88]

What does this Hussite material in the midst of the 'Waldensian books' suggest? If the Hussite texts had been clearly distinct from the other, presumably older material, one might plausibly argue for an attempt by some *barbes* to reconstruct Waldensian protest along Bohemian models. However, the organization of the manuscripts makes this hard to believe. Taborite and Catholic materials are jumbled together, with no evident sense that the two contradict each other at several points.[89] One might then conclude that the translators and copyists saw in the Hussite texts a useful *addition* to a mostly Catholic literary corpus, which otherwise matched rather ill with the Waldensian position on Church rituals. Hussite texts would have seemed to offer an intellectually respectable theological diet, which was also usefully anti-sacerdotal and anti-ritual in its tone and arguments. If this hypothesis is correct, then it flatters the Waldenses unduly to speak, as some historians do, of

---

86   Ibid., fos 187v–189v; cf. Cambridge, University Library, MS. Dd. xv. 30, fos 14r ff.
87   Dublin, Trinity College, MS. 260, fos 373v–378r.
88   Ibid., fos 378r–383r.
89   Note that Gonnet and Molnar, *Vaudois au moyen âge*, in their description of the manuscripts, pp. 443–50, list the contents separated by theological provenance, which is misleading. As Brenon, 'The Waldensian Books', p. 147, remarks, 'the entanglement of these texts with one another is total'.

a 'Waldensian–Hussite international'. The Alpine Waldenses received an entirely one-way traffic in advice and literary support from the Bohemian Brethren; indeed, Lukas thought too poorly of the Italian heretics whom he had met to adopt anything from them.[90] Moreover, its impact seems to have occurred far too late to do more than scratch the surface of the *barbes'* religious ideas, before the Reformation supervened. That must surely explain the generally agreed fact that 'Hussite' ideas are undetectable in the trial evidence from Waldensian followers in the late fifteenth century, despite the fact that such evidence constitutes the largest archive in the history of the movement.[91]

90   See Gonnet and Molnar, *Vaudois au moyen âge*, pp. 279–80.
91   Gonnet and Molnar, *Vaudois au moyen âge*, p. 266, observe that a detailed trial from the Piedmontese valleys in 1451 revealed no sign whatever of the interpenetration of Hussite ideas. The same holds for the trials from the 1480s and 1490s.

9

The Encounters of 1530–1532 and their Outcomes

News of the Reformation breaking out across central and western Europe did not take long to reach the Waldenses of the Alps and Provence. According to one later account, '*barbe* Martin' brought news and books about the Reformation back to the Alps as early as 1526.[1] Thereafter there is evidence, between 1530 and 1532, of a complex, multi-faceted exchange of views between various Waldensian leaders and a diverse spectrum of reforming churchmen and theologians. In the past, historians of Waldensianism quite understandably tried to construe a logical sequence out of these encounters. They envisaged a gradual but coherent and collective decision-making process through which the *barbes* found out what the Reformation was about, discussed its implications with its proponents, and eventually decided to adhere to it. The discovery of several important new documents in the past twenty years, and the re-examination of all the others, forces one to question the coherence and unity of this process. What is suggested here is emphatically *not* that the discussions did not happen, or that they were of no consequence. Rather, the evidence suggests that they were inconclusive. Various aspects of nascent Protestant theology were discussed by different people and evoked a range of responses from committed enthusiasm, through prudent and cautious interest, to outright hostility and scandal. The consequence of these discussions seems to have been a degree of doctrinal and practical confusion in the life and work of the *barbes* – a confusion which can be paralleled in the life of many proto-Protestant communities at the same

---

1 Reported in P. Gilles, *Histoire ecclésiastique des églises réformées . . . autrefois appellées églises vaudoises*, ed. P. Lantaret, 2 vols (Pinerolo, 1881), vol. 1, p. 47. Around this the story of a 'Synod of Laux' reported (undated) by a later sixteenth-century commentator has been constructed. See E. Cameron, *The Reformation of the Heretics: The Waldenses of the Alps 1480–1580* (Oxford, 1984), pp. 134–5 and references.

time – which was only resolved when the Waldensian congregations of the Dauphiné and Provence were subsumed in the French 'Huguenot' Church of the region, and those of Piedmont acquired their own, largely non-indigenous and imported cadre of Protestant ministers as a free-standing Savoyard Protestant Church. The contacts made in the early 1530s, therefore, only reached their ultimate outcome in the 1550s and early 1560s.[2]

9.1 The Correspondence of Georges Morel and the Reformers

In the autumn of 1530 *barbes* Georges Morel and Pierre Masson travelled, probably from Mérindol in Provence, to make a tour of reforming centres. They visited Neuchâtel, Morat and Bern, and from Bern were sent to Basel to meet Oecolampadius.[3] To Oecolampadius Morel presented the long letter or memorandum describing the *barbes*' lives, customs and beliefs which was analysed in the last chapter. He appended to the letter a long list of detailed requests for advice on a range of ethical and doctrinal issues. On 13 October 1530 Oecolampadius penned his first, long reply to the 'brethren' who, it may be assumed, had sent Morel on his tour: this responded and adjudicated on not only Morel's specific questions but also their entire description of their way of life.[4] A few days later Oecolampadius wrote a short addendum addressing a few further issues.[5] He gave both letters to the *barbes*, along with a letter of introduction to Martin Bucer, dated 17 October, which asked Bucer to look over his replies and make any amendments which he thought necessary; or if he wished to pass the task on to Wolfgang Capito.[6] Morel himself wrote a brief letter asking for advice.[7] Around the end of October Bucer wrote the first of his replies, which survives in the Thomassarchiv in Strasbourg and was not, unlike Oecolampadius's letters, published in the

---

2   This is the conclusion of Cameron, *Reformation of the Heretics*, pp. 129–66; the substantive conclusion as to chronology was supported, quite independently, by G. Audisio, *Les Vaudois du Luberon: une minorité en Provence (1460–1560)* (Aix-en-Provence, 1984), pp. 178–93, 409ff. Debate over the precise significance of the events of 1532 seems set to continue nevertheless.

3   V. Vinay, *Le Confessioni di fede dei Valdesi riformati, con i documenti del dialogo fra la 'prima' e la 'seconda' riforma*, Collana della Facoltà valdese di teologia, 12 (Turin, 1975), pp. 72–3; Cameron, *Reformation of the Heretics*, pp. 135–6 and references.

4   Vinay, *Confessioni di fede . . . riformati*, pp. 52–62 and references. The original is in J. Oecolampadius and H. Zuinglius, *Epistolarum libri iv* (Basel, 1536, though thought to date from 1548), fos 2r–3v.

5   Vinay, *Confessioni di fede . . . riformati*, pp. 64–8.

6   Ibid., pp. 70–1.

7   Ibid., pp. 72–3.

sixteenth century. It bears no date.[8] Bucer was, notoriously, one of the most verbose and prolix of reformers, both in speech and in writing.[9] Far from shuffling off the responsibility to his colleague Capito, he clearly expended much thought, time and ink on the *barbes'* questions. Some time after the *barbes'* mission was over, a sort of digest of Morel's questions and the two reformers' replies was prepared in a Franco-Provençal manuscript, whose handwriting is mostly quite similar to that of the treatises and sermons discussed above. This digest testifies to a more extensive exchange of views than the surviving Latin letters document. It adds many minor and two significant passages of Bucer's advice which do not survive elsewhere. Accordingly, it is not possible to reconstruct the precise chronology of the Morel–Bucer discussions from the surviving documents.[10]

Nevertheless, one may infer from the surviving texts something about the different ways in which *barbes* and reformed theologians regarded the encounter. Georges Morel seems to have regarded most of his description of the *barbes'* practices and life-style as a matter of information rather than discussion, save for his admission that they had perhaps 'erred' over the number of the sacraments. On the other hand, he approached the reformers with a shopping-list of 'cases of conscience', most of which were to do with ethics, although some were doctrinal in character. The questions were as follows:

1 Whether the orders of bishop, priest and deacon ought to be used in ordaining ministers, as they were not among the Waldenses; and whether such ordained ministers might pass judgement.
2 Whether it was right to put criminals to death.
3 Whether secular laws had validity before God.
4 Whether the *barbes* were right to advise their followers to kill those who betrayed them to the Catholic authorities.
5 Whether someone might furtively seize back his own property held unjustly by another.
6 Whether the mother of orphan children whose father had died intestate might inherit their property, notwithstanding Numbers 27 (verses 8–11).
7 Whether anything added to the principal of a loan was usury; and whether any business which brought profit without labour was a sin.

---

8   Ibid., pp. 74–117.
9   See, for instance, the comments on Bucer's style in T. H. L. Parker, *Calvin's New Testament Commentaries*, 2nd edn (Edinburgh, T & T Clark, 1993), pp. 78ff., 86–90.
10   This conclusion was reached, among others, by V. Vinay, 'Mémoires de Georges Morel', *Bollettino della Società di Studi Valdesi* 132 (1972), pp. 35–48.

8 Whether every oath was forbidden on pain of mortal sin.
9 Whether the division of sins into original, venial and mortal was valid.
10 Whether the division of ignorance into invincible, negligent and crass was valid.
11 Whether it was lawful to pray for the dead, since the stories of the saints gave contradictory evidence.
12 Whether all infants below the age of reason of any race were saved by the merits of Christ; and whether all above the age of reason who did not believe in Christ were damned.
13 Whether young women wishing to enter a religious life might do so.
14 Whether marriage might be contracted between relatives outside the degrees specified in Leviticus 18 (verses 6–20).
15 What one should make of the debate over free will and predestination between Luther and Erasmus.
16 What were the ceremonial and judicial laws (of the Old Testament) and whether they were entirely abrogated after Christ's coming.
17 Whether allegorical senses in scripture might be allowed and used in preaching.
18 What were the canonical books of scripture.
19 What books ought to be bought for the exposition of scripture.
20 What manner should be followed in teaching the people.[11]

In the second reply of Oecolampadius to Morel,[12] four further questions were answered:

1 Whether the saints earned merit before God.
2 Whether one might defend oneself against a robber, as a last resort, by killing him.
3 Whether one might work on festal days.
4 What was the power of the keys (given to Peter).

In the dialect digest a number of other questions were posed, which do not appear to survive in the extant Latin versions of the correspondence. These include:

• Whether ministers of bad and corrupt life can profitably teach the people, even if they teach doctrine correctly.[13]

---

11 Vinay, *Confessioni di fede . . . riformati*, pp. 44–8; the numeration of these questions is not followed through consistently in the original.
12 Ibid., pp. 64–9.
13 Dublin, Trinity College, MS. 259, p. 58.

- Whether there can be ministers who teach only through example of good life rather than teaching doctrine.[14]
- Whether ministers can have private property.
- What was the difference between ministers of the word in the Old and New Testaments.[15]
- Whether all parts of scripture can be used for teaching, even those including details which might scandalize hearers, such as the number of Solomon's wives and concubines.[16]
- Whether children below the age of reason can be married off.[17]
- A range of questions about marriage and sexual ethics: can a woman remarry if she has been long uncertain whether her husband is alive or dead? What are the proper reasons for marriage? Can a woman dispose of any of her husband's property without his knowledge?[18]
- Are there commandments and counsels in scripture?[19]
- Should the *barbes* administer the sacraments?[20]
- How does one reconcile justification by faith with New Testament passages which exhort people to do good works?[21]
- Can an oppressed farmer keep back some of the rent he has promised?[22]
- Does ignorance excuse a sin?[23]
- Did the Passion of Christ only cancel out original sin? Does the Passion profit those who persist in sin, and are such people's good works profitable?[24]
- How to advise someone who has sinned grievously, e.g. by murder, or fathering a child on another man's wife.
- Whether deathbed repentance through fear is of any use.
- How to advise someone who has found lost property and does not know the rightful owner.

These often very circumstantial questions appear to represent the first stage of Morel's approach to the reformers. In the subsequent digest of their debates, a number of additional 'questions' would be created through the juxtaposition of Morel's short statements about Waldensian

14   Ibid.
15   Ibid., p. 61.
16   Ibid., p. 64.
17   Ibid., p. 66.
18   Ibid., pp. 67–71.
19   Ibid., p. 71.
20   Ibid.
21   Ibid., pp. 81–3.
22   Ibid., p. 101.
23   Ibid., p. 106.
24   Ibid.

practice or belief with the reformers' replies to these. For the purposes of analysing Morel's attitude to the discussions, however, one ought to confine oneself to the above.

Several points are particularly striking about Morel's questions. First, Morel was distinctly well-informed, both about the issues of the Reformation and about many of the clichés of medieval theology. He introduced the Erasmus–Luther debate as something which greatly perturbed himself and his companions, then raised pertinent texts on the issue between faith and good works. Moreover, he knew the different categories of sin and ignorance, the distinction between commandments and counsels, the scholastic advice about the moral order of priorities to be followed,[25] and the issue over allegorical interpretations of scripture. None of this need have required huge theological erudition, but it does demonstrate familiarity with traditional late medieval catechesis.

Second, Morel evinced the intense preoccupation with practical ethics which has already been noted in the sermon and catechetical literature discussed above.[26] Like the reader of a confessional manual, he sought specific answers to practical questions relating to things like marriage, property, rent, usury and self-defence. Such issues were surely raised through the daily experience of advising his followers in private confession.[27] Third, Morel mentioned the classic 'issues' of Waldensian protest and 'heresy': judicial execution, oaths, prayers for the dead, the value of the ministry of corrupt priests (or *barbes*?). However, he raised these as questions, ostensibly open for discussion, and intermingled these points with other issues of casuistry in a jumbled way. There is little sense from the documents that Morel had a clear concept of the distinctively 'Waldensian' nature of his religious vocation, let alone of any sense of 'heresy' or 'protest' (beyond his explicit rejection of purgatory). Rather, he was trying to be a more moral and more ascetic type of priest, informed by both the Waldensian and Catholic traditions.

On the other hand, the reformers' responses, if predictable to our eyes, must have presented Morel with a series of shocks. First and most devastating was their initial response to the Waldenses' practising their religion in secret, under the shadow of Catholic conformity. Oecolampadius thought that the Waldenses should be ready to face martyrdom rather than 'deny Christ'. 'Those who know that they are redeemed by the blood of Christ should be stronger.'[28] Bucer – at least initially – regarded

---

25 See above, chapter 8.1.
26 See above, chapter 8.2.
27 Compare the analysis of contemporary manuals for confessors in T. N. Tentler, *Sin and Confession on the Eve of the Reformation* (Princeton, NJ, 1977), *passim*.
28 Dublin, Trinity College, MS. 259, pp. 2–5; Vinay, *Confessioni di fede . . . riformati*, pp. 52–4.

the taking of Catholic sacraments as a great sin and a weakness.[29] With further discussion, Martin Bucer moderated his position in this respect, though still likening the papal Mass to the 'table of demons'. He told the *barbes* that, until the time when they could be delivered from their 'captivity' (their worshipping within the Catholic Church) they ought to teach the people how to interpret the eucharist. They should regard it as an ordinance of Christ, but 'depraved by ministers of Antichrist'. Since the *barbes* did not dare to consecrate the eucharist, it was better to take the papal eucharist in the name of Christ rather than in that of Antichrist (i.e. with a reformed rather than a Catholic understanding of it). As there was only one baptism, one should never rebaptize those baptized by Catholic priests.[30] This typically tortuous, verbose piece of advice seems to show Bucer facing up to the Waldenses' long-established reluctance to administer the sacraments, and finding a means to accommodate with it. One presumes that Morel had made it abundantly clear that public profession of Waldensian religious affiliations was not on the agenda.

Second, the Waldenses' equation of sexual with religious purity found no echo among the new generation of reformers. When told that neither the *barbes* nor the celibate 'sisters' who cared for their needs (the 'Waldensian nuns') were married, Oecolampadius responded:

> We do not think it is of the spirit of Christ that marriage should be forbidden to the ministers. For this supreme, angelic life in the flesh is not given to many. Hence it happens that the consciences of many are hardened and corrupted, and the worst of scandals arise. Brothers, do not prize so much the reputation of such sanctity with such great risk. In marriage also there is a continency which is greatly pleasing to God.[31]

Bucer regarded the trainees' spending time among celibate sisters as a risk best avoided: the company of even chaste women would soften the holiest of men. He cited a range of texts supporting marriage and noted that Paul himself had not recommended his life-style for everyone else. Marriage should be a matter of free choice for everyone.[32] Given the intense practical and theoretical praise heaped on the life of

29   Dublin, Trinity College, MS. 259, pp. 53–4; Vinay, *Confessioni di fede . . . riformati*, p. 84; see discussion in C. Ginzburg, *Il Nicodemismo: Simulazione e dissimulazione religiosa nell'Europa del '500* (Turin, 1970), p. 108.
30   Dublin, Trinity College, MS. 259, pp. 71–5.
31   Ibid., p. 16; Vinay, *Confessioni di fede . . . riformati*, p. 58.
32   Dublin, Trinity College, MS. 259, pp. 17–20; Vinay, *Confessioni di fede . . . riformati*, pp. 76–8.

virginity among the Waldenses and in the literature which they used, to have marriage commended as a more realistic option clearly was a shock.[33]

Not only did the reformers respond to the Erasmus–Luther issue which Morel had raised. They both, but especially Bucer, ensured that the *barbes* were fully instructed in the essential points of Reformation teaching. In a large excursus added to the dialect digest, Bucer expounded the essential points of justification by faith, as he understood it.[34] As God was the creator and original of all, it followed that all knowledge of his nature must come from his Spirit, and therefore be his work. God fills those whom he has justified with good works; therefore scripture speaks of good works being rewarded. All the proof-texts relating to rewards for 'good works' referred to the elect: they were 'rewarded' for the good works which they did; but they could only do these because of the faith and other benefits with which God had endowed them. At times, Bucer allowed his preoccupations with the Strasbourg context to run away with him. Although there is no suggestion that the Alpine–Provençal Waldenses doubted the value of infant baptism, or rebaptized infants,[35] Bucer still felt it necessary to justify infant baptism at prodigious length. The only reason for this huge excursus must be that the Anabaptists at Strasbourg had recently challenged it, and their arguments had come close to swaying one of Bucer's closest associates, Wolfgang Capito; Bucer evidently feared that something similar might happen to the Waldenses unless they were forearmed against it.[36]

The reformers' Protestant aversion to legalism made it difficult for them to reply to many of Morel's most circumstantial ethical questions. Oecolampadius and Bucer alike refused to offer strict legal guidelines in response to the *barbes*' enquiries; instead, they said that one must decide in accordance with the rule of charity and the guidance of the Spirit. This was entirely consistent with the reformed principle that those who are

33　Compare the response to the same suggestion as reported by Pierre Griot, as below, note 44.
34　Dublin, Trinity College, MS. 259, pp. 81–96; Vinay, *Confessioni di fede . . . riformati*, pp. 118–37.
35　Martin Luther, in his *Postils* for Lent 1525, seemed to have formed the impression that the Bohemian Brethren rebaptized German Catholics who joined their number. There is certainly no evidence in the trials or the literature that such things happened in the Alps.
36　Dublin, Trinity College, MS. 259, pp. 25–46; Vinay, *Confessioni di fede . . . riformati*, pp. 86–102; for Anabaptism at Strasbourg, see for example George Huntston Williams, *The Radical Reformation*, 3rd edn, Sixteenth Century Essays and Studies, vol. 15 (Kirksville, Mo., 1992), pp. 363–430.

justified by faith need no specific code of law to guide them, because the Spirit teaches them how to live according to the law of love.[37]

9.2 1532

The year 1532 is a key one in traditional Waldensian history. It has been presented as the time when the Waldenses, collectively, decided to associate themselves with the reformed Protestant Church. The vision of such a voluntary, conscious joining of forces is enormously symbolic. The older and senior Reformation decides to merge its heritage with the ideas and intellectual strength of the new movement, and move on.[38] Stone monuments at the hamlet of Chanforan in the Valle d'Angrogna, and paper monuments in the shape of conference proceedings and journals, commemorate this formal, official, disbandment and re-establishment of the Waldensian Church.[39]

It is in some ways easier to question this vision in relation to the reformed Churches than it is in relation to the Waldenses. There was, in 1532, no firmly established 'reformed Church' for Waldensianism to merge into. In conformity with Luther's vision of 'community churches', there were nascent reformed communities, towns, principalities or cantons, which had each one by one taken the decision to adopt some kind of reformed order. They had no overarching confessional structure to compare with the national reformed Churches of the modern era.[40] Yet by Luther's standards, the Waldensian followers in the Alps were not whole communities, even if in the émigré communities in Provence or Apulia they came very close to being so. Rather, they were *sections* of communities, sometimes majorities (as in Freissinières or Angrogna) but more usually minorities, which followed additional, dissenting and illegal

---

37 See, for example, Luther's observations in M. Luther, *Werke: Kritische Gesamtausgabe*, 58 vols (Weimar, 1883–1948), vol. 7, p. 53, and *Luther's Works*, US edn, ed. J. Pelikan and H. T. Lehmann, 55 vols (Philadelphia and St Louis, 1955–), vol. 31, pp. 349–50.

38 Compare, for example, the remark of E. Comba, *History of the Waldenses of Italy*, trans. T. E. Comba (London, 1889), p. 300: 'The idea of Waldo springs up like a fountain, it runs into the river of the Reformation, and the river flows on.'

39 See, for instance, *Bulletin de la société d'histoire vaudoise* 58 (1932), 'Bollettino Commemorativo del Sinodo di Cianforan (Angrogna) 1532–1932', where the entire issue was dedicated to the 400th anniversary of the synod. A similar commemorative number of the journal (now entitled *Bollettino della Società di Studi Valdesi*) was issued for the 450th anniversary in 1982.

40 See E. Cameron, *The European Reformation* (Oxford, 1991), pp. 210–313. The point must be emphasized that the creation of far-reaching confessional leagues among Protestant communities occurred *after* the establishment of community churches.

religious customs alongside their Catholic worship. For such communities to become like 'reformed Churches' would involve social and political change, as well as confessional or theological decisions. This was precisely the kind of change to public profession which Morel plainly refused to countenance in his discussions with Martin Bucer.

In reality, 1532 saw, not clear-cut decisions, but *contacts*: contacts between various different proto-reforming leaders, especially from the Pays de Vaud in western Switzerland, and meetings of the Alpine *barbes*. These meetings are complex and the sources for them are not free of problems or contradictions.

There is an eye-witness account from the trial of Pierre Griot, the trainee *barbe* from Cesana Torinese,[41] to this effect:

> He [Griot] said and confessed that all the *barbes* and preachers of the said sect assemble once a year between the mountains and the land of Piedmont. That year past[42] they assembled in Piedmont, in Val Luserna, in a place called Il Serre, where there are ten or twelve houses. They always assemble in August around the end of it [the month]. He has heard that they always assemble in that country. The speaker [Griot] has been this year in the said congregation; there was present Anthoine Guérin, hatter of Avignon. . . .
>
> This present year[43] there were great clerks and doctors at their congregation. Amongst others there was one in a black habit, and another in white: they were [of] religious [orders]. And two others, who were gentlemen from the land of Grenoble. They held a disputation amongst them about faith. The two religious said that faith alone justified, and the two others said that faith without works was dead. Against that, the religious said that works served for no purpose in justification, but were only evidence of the faith; and that works were nothing but a superstition which had been invented, and that God in no way asked for external works but only asked for a person's heart.
>
> The two religious also said: 'You are more concerned and restricted by your ceremonies and external works than those of the Roman Church', as though meaning that it is a waste of time and useless burden to bother with such works, and God took no pleasure in them, because [doing] that stopped one taking care of doing worldly works.
>
> Such that after these disputations had been made by the said religious and gentlemen, the *barbes* were left scandalized, because the said *barbes* have a custom and teach the people not to drink or eat or do anything without first praying to God.

41 For Griot himself see above, chapter 8.1.
42 G. Audisio, *Le Barbe et l'inquisiteur: Procès du barbe vaudois Pierre Griot par l'inquisiteur Jean de Roma (Apt, 1532)* (Aix-en-Provence, 1979), p. 103, n. 1, suggests this event may have taken place in 1531.
43 The French original contrasts the two years as 'présente' in this paragraph and 'passé' in the preceding extract.

QVI·DOVE OR SONO QVATTRO
SECOLI L'ANTICA CHIESA VALDE
SE RACCOLTA NEL SINODO DI
CHANFORAN CONSACRAVA LA
PROPRIA SOLIDARIETA CON LE
CHIESE DELLA RIFORMA E OFFRI
VA LORO IN DONO REGALE LA
BIBBIA TRADOTTA DA OLIVETA
NO·LE VNIONI CRISTIANE DEL PIE
MONTE·A RICORDO SOLENNE DEL
FATTO·QVESTO MONVMENTO
ELEVANO E DEDICANO

XII SETT MD   XII SETT. MCMXXXII

5

Plates 5 and 6   The monumental *stele* erected in 1932 in the small cleft in the hill-side at Chanforan, near Il Serre, Valle d'Angrogna, commemorates the discussions between Waldenses and reformers believed to have taken place there in September 1532. The traditional explanation of what happened there is recorded in a plaque in the main European languages. This chapter argues that the traditional account of the 'synod of Chanforan' rests on the conflation of a number of sources which are not entirely easy to reconcile. These large monuments show how much collective memory has been invested in that account. (Photographs by the author.)

They were also scandalized because the said religious told them that there is no need of divine service save with the heart, and not with external gestures, because God in no way asks for these. Thus it appears that the religious wished the world to be all secular and all spiritual. The said religious and gentlemen also disputed about the sacrament

Plate 6

of marriage. Because the said *barbes* promised to God poverty, chastity and obedience, the said religious said it was ill done by them to promise chastity, and that they ought all to marry, because Saint Paul said that one who teaches should be the husband of one wife, and likewise the deacon. By this means, the *barbes* were left all scandalized, saying that they were not accustomed to marry, and others said that they were already old. . . .

The four disputants . . . were called . . . Charles and Adam, gentlemen, and the religious Augustin and Thomas.[44]

The Genevan chronicler Antoine Fromment wrote in his *Actes et gestes merveilleux de la cité de Genève*, probably written before 1550, as follows:

44 Audisio, *Barbe et l'inquisiteur*, pp. 103, 107–9, 119–20.

Guillaume Farel and Antoine Saunier, both from the Dauphiné, ministers under the lordship of Bern, were asked by certain other ministers, Georges Morel of Freissinières, and Pierre Masson of Burgundy, ... to be present at a synod ... which was to be held in Piedmont, and there were to be assembled a certain number of faithful Christians, who used to be called Waldenses, or Poor of Lyons, and now Lutherans, from Calabria, Apulia, Piedmont, Provence, Dauphiné, Lorraine, and several other regions of the world.... After they had gathered, they discussed ... regarding the affairs of their religion ... to the great benefit of Christianity ... even if only by the printing of the Bible at Neuchâtel, translated at their expense from Hebrew into French by Pierre Robert, called Olivetanus.[45]

Fromment located this event just before Guillaume Farel's first and tempestuous visit to Geneva in late September 1532. With less detail, Fromment's account of a visit by Farel and Saunier to Piedmont in September 1532 was echoed in the chronicle of Michel Roset, former secretary to the *Petit Conseil* of Geneva, the sixteenth-century annalist Savion, the early seventeenth-century German historian Abraham Scultetus, and the *Geneva Restituta* of F. Spanheim (1635).[46]

In the correspondence of the French-speaking reformers there is a letter signed by 'Adam' to Guillaume Farel, dated 5 November 1532. It reads as follows:

The brethren at *Mureta* and *Tulinum* received us happily, likewise the people, though their leaders, who have been suborned by false brethren, are hostile to us and resist us in certain respects. But God will bring his own people round into the right way when it pleases him. We are teaching the ministers and the people, though not openly; they hear us willingly, and some travel from distant places, as much as two days' journey away, only for the sake of hearing the words of truth. We do not yet have public schools, but we soon shall have. About this we have had a council and gathering summoned, but it is not yet concluded [*or* it is not yet resolved].[47]

The brethren wish you every happiness and are most grateful that you have sent us to them again. The printer has been given five hundred gold pieces by Martin, to have things printed as soon as possible. See to a

---

45   A. Fromment, *Les Actes et gestes merveilleux de la cité de Genève ...* , ed. G. Revilliod (Geneva, 1854), pp. 2–3.

46   M. Roset, *Les Chroniques de Genève*, ed. H. Fazy (Geneva, 1894), p. 163; P. F. Geisendorf, *Les Annalistes genevoises du début du dix-septième siècle, Savion, Piaget, Perrin: Études et textes* (Geneva, 1942), p. 401; A. Scultetus, *Annalium Evangelii passim per Europam ... Renovati Decades Duae*, 2 vols (Heidelberg, 1618–20), vol. 2, p. 383; F. Spanheim, *Geneva Restituta, Oratio* (Geneva, 1635), p. 42.

47   The Latin original reads 'nondum exclusum est'. The meaning of this is not entirely clear: Herminjard corrects it to 'conclusum'. It does, however, seem most unlikely to refer to a meeting held nearly a month earlier.

Unio,[48] well corrected, in French, for it will be of the greatest use to us. I left behind some books with you, or with Fromment, or with Simon at Aigle; if this is convenient, see to having them sent to me (for the real problem here is a shortage of books) together with Olivétan's baggage. See to the Bible being corrected and printed as I suggested, one column in large letters of French, and another smaller column in small letters in Latin, both on the same page.[49]

It has been traditional to identify 'Adam' as a pseudonym of Antoine Saunier,[50] but the reasons for this identification are not clear, other than the fact that Saunier reportedly visited the Alpine valleys with Farel a month earlier.

What is one to make of these pieces of evidence? The 'Adam' of Griot's trial testimony may have been the same as the 'Adam' who wrote to Farel in November, but one cannot be quite sure. 'Charles' and 'Adam', gentry from the Dauphiné, *could* have been Farel and Saunier, who were both Dauphinois; but if so, why were they apparently debating *against* justification by faith?[51] Who were the religious brethren 'Augustin and Thomas', spokesmen for the reformed message? Is one of them connected with the 'Thomas the Italian' who wrote to Guillaume Farel in November 1532?[52] These three testimonies appear to describe three different encounters, one in August, one in September and one in November. If one allows that 'late August' was a mistake for 'September',[53] one might conflate Griot's testimony with Fromment's, though in that case the problem of who 'Augustin' and 'Thomas' were still remains. In any case, the letter of 'Adam', which speaks of the brethren's gratitude that (Farel) had 'sent us to them again', makes it clear that the November visit was a follow-up to some earlier contacts. Again, Fromment's chronicle claims that the project for printing the Bible originated with a meeting in September; the letter from 'Adam' implies that it ensued from the November encounter, which was still ongoing when the letter was written. Griot's testimony makes no mention of the Bible whatsoever. We are dealing here with two, possibly three meetings, none of which was conclusive.

---

48 H. Bodius, *Unio dissidentium in sacris literis locorum* (Cologne, 1531; further edns at Lyon, 1532, Basel, 1557, and subsequently). The work is often, though not universally, attributed to Martin Bucer and provides summaries of Reformation doctrine with scriptural and patristic texts to support each point. It was therefore a potent preaching and disputing manual.
49 A.-L. Herminjard (ed.), *Correspondance des réformateurs dans les pays de la langue française*, 9 vols (Geneva and Paris, 1866–97), vol. 2, pp. 452–4.
50 See ibid., p. 455, n. 29.
51 See the discussion in Audisio, *Barbe et l'inquisiteur*, pp. 55–60.
52 Herminjard, *Correspondance des réformateurs*, vol. 2, p. 463.
53 As suggested by Audisio, *Barbe et l'inquisiteur*, p. 103, n. 2.

The subject-matter of the encounters is also different (though here one might perfectly well admit that different witnesses would recall different things). Griot speaks of a meeting dominated by justification by faith, the uselessness of external religious practice, and the attack on celibacy. It states that the *barbes* remained 'scandalized' by the encounter. Fromment and 'Adam', on the other hand, do not specify what doctrines were discussed, but give a much more optimistic picture of the reformers teaching and discussing with their new allies. This complex picture is now made yet more confusing when one includes the key contemporary statement to emerge from the 1532 discussions, which will now be translated.

9.3   The Propositions of Angrogna

In the last pages of Trinity College, Dublin MS. 259, there is a short, somewhat scrappy and inconsistently written document appended to the record of Georges Morel's discussions with Oecolampadius and Bucer. The document has been known in a reorganized and bowdlerized form since the work of the Dauphinois historian Jean-Paul Perrin in the early seventeenth century.[54] The original manuscript reading was recovered by the German historian Karl Benrath in the nineteenth century, and has subsequently been carefully edited. What follows is a translation of this important text.

The Angrogna Propositions of 12 September 1532[55]

The propositions which were disputed in Angrogna the year of the Lord 1532. And the 12th day of September. In presence of all the ministers and also of the people. The first day it was disputed whether it is lawful to a Christian to swear in any way.

C. 1   The Christian may lawfully swear in the name of God without acting against the words which are written in St Matthew, Chapter 5.[56] The conclusion is established in this[57] way, that someone who swears does

---

54   The heavily edited and rearranged version is found in J. P. Perrin, *Histoire des Vaudois, divisée en trois parties* (Geneva, 1618 and 1619), pp. 157–61: many of the crossings-out in the original manuscript are probably the result of Perrin's preparing it for the press.

55   This version has been translated from Vinay, *Confessioni di fede . . . riformati*, pp. 139–43, and checked against the manuscript original, Dublin, Trinity College, MS. 259, pp. 118–25. Other modern editions exist, e.g. Audisio, *Les Vaudois du Luberon*, pp. 510–12, based on Vinay.

56   Compare Matthew 5:33–7.

57   'don modo': from later uses in context this appears the best rendering.

not take the name of God in vain, so that he may swear. He does not take the name of God in vain when his oath redounds to the greater glory of God and the benefit of his neighbour and God; one may swear in a court of law, because one who holds authority, whether he is faithful or unfaithful, exercises the authority of God, and by this reason in a certain way the oath is given. We intend to swear by the name of God etc.

C. 2   No work is called good save that which God has commanded. No work is called evil save that which God has forbidden. As far as concerns external works which are not forbidden by God, a man may do them or not according to the conclusion given without sin, etc.[58] The two first propositions are known for themselves by faithful people intuitively.[59] You shall not do all those things which seem well done in your sight, but shall do that which I command you, to the end of the c[hapter].[60] You shall do only and alone that which I command you, neither adding nor removing anything to my word, but do only all that which I command you.[61] You shall not turn away to the right or the left; do only that which I command you,[62] and that shall be your rule in all your external works; you may do all things as far as external works of whatsoever kind they are. In this way, that they may not lead you to go against the commandment of God which is that of love. Nor also against that which is forbidden, that is not to do to our neighbour that which you would not wish to be done to yourself.[63]

C. 5[64]   Auricular confession is not commanded by God. It is concluded according to Holy Scripture that the true confession of a Christian is to confess to God alone, to whom belongs honour and glory. And to him likewise only is confession etc. The second confession is to be reconciled to one's neighbour, as we see in St Matthew chapter 5,[65] and St James last [chapter],[66] we confess etc. The third is in St Matthew 18, about someone who sins in regard of me: that is, that I knowing that I ought to go to him, and not he to me. And if he does not wish to be corrected neither by me, nor by testimonies, nor even by the whole congregation. And thus since

---

58   The previous sentence is crossed out in the manuscript, probably in the seventeenth century.
59   'deontiuone': meaning suppositious.
60   There appears to be a biblical reference here, which has not so far been traced.
61   Compare Deuteronomy 4:2.
62   Compare Deuteronomy 5:33.
63   The negative version of the Golden Rule, which originates with the first-century BCE rabbi Hillel, and is found in a variant reading of Acts 15:20 and 29.
64   The number '3' appears to have been written here first, then '5' over the top. All the heading numbers after this point are added in the margin rather than the body of the text as in the first three, save for C. 9, C. 17 and C. 18 below.
65   Compare Matthew 5:23–4.
66   Compare James 5:16.

he has publicly sinned, publicly he has to confess his sin.[67] Other manner of confession we do not find in the Holy Scripture etc.

C. 6 The cessation of work on Sundays is not forbidden by God to a Christian. The conclusion is reached that even though a person may work on a Sunday without sin, as we find in the Gospels. And also in Galatians in the 4th chapter,[68] and Colossians in the 2nd chapter;[69] nevertheless to show charity to our servants. And also to take time for the Word of God we ought to stop work on that day as one who respects [?][70] the honour and glory of God.

C. 7 Words are not necessary for prayer.

C. 8 Kneeling down, or specific hours, or uncovering of the head or other external things are not necessary or required in prayer.[71] It is concluded that divine worship may not be done unless in spirit and in truth, as we find in St John in the 4th chapter: God is spirit and one who wishes to speak with him, it is necessary that he speaks with the spirit.[72] Words and other external things do nothing save to express and demonstrate great affection for one's neighbour etc. like that which someone has towards his God.

C. 9[73] The imposition of hands is not necessary. The conclusion is reached that for all that the apostles used it. And the ancient fathers: nevertheless because it is an external thing, it will be in the free choice of each person.

C. 10 It is not lawful for a Christian to take revenge on his enemy in any manner whatever.

The present proposition is clear of itself, as we find in St Matthew in the 5th chapter.[74] And St Paul Romans 12,[75] and Saint Peter in the first etc.[76]

C. 11 The Christian can exercise magistracy over Christians who are criminals.[77] The proposition is clear as we find in St Paul Romans 13,[78] Corinthians 6,[79] and St Peter in his first epistle.[80]

---

67 Compare Matthew 18:15–17.
68 Apparently a reference to Galatians 4:10.
69 Compare Colossians 2:16, 20–2.
70 'cellatore': meaning not clear: possibly from Latin 'cultor'.
71 From C. 6 down to this point has been crossed out, again probably in the seventeenth century.
72 Compare John 4:24.
73 This number, unlike those around it, is in the body of the text.
74 Compare Matthew 5:38–41.
75 Compare Romans 12:19–21.
76 Compare 1 Peter 3:9.
77 'deliquenti': word scored out in the manuscript.
78 Compare Romans 13:1–3.
79 Compare 1 Corinthians 6:1–7.
80 Possibly a reference to 1 Peter 2:13–17.

C. 12 The Christian does not have fixed times when he must fast. This is clear through the whole of Scripture, because it is not found that God has commanded it.

C. 13 Marriage is not forbidden to anyone of whatsoever order they may be.

C. 14 Whosoever forbid marriage to those whom they wish teach a devilish doctrine.

C. 15 To establish a state or order of virginity is a devilish doctrine.

C. 16 Someone who does not have the gift of continency is obliged to marry.

The conclusions are sufficiently clear in so far as concerns doctrine: first we have in Genesis that it is not good for man to be alone. The second is clear as we find in St Paul, 1 Timothy chapter 4.[81] The third moreover is manifest because it is without foundation in Scripture.
The fourth is most true, as Paul writes to the Corinthians in the 7th [chapter] of the first [epistle].[82]

C. 17[83] Not all usury is forbidden by God. This is clear because God did not forbid [it] save for that usury which harms one's neighbour, as is contained in the law not to do to another that which you would not wish to be done to yourself.

C. 18 The words which are in St Luke 'give'. . . etc., do not refer to usury.[84]

The proposition is clear because Christ did not mean anything other than to teach only the manner which we ought to keep with our neighbour, and to lend one to the other in the office of charity which we ought to practise one to another: that is, that he ought not only to lend to the poor but also to give if necessity requires it.

C. 19[85] All those who are already and will be saved were pre-elected before the foundation of the world.

C. 20 Those who are saved cannot be not saved.
The first is clear as we find in St Paul to the Ephesians chapter 1.[86]
The second also in Romans in the 8th and 9th chapters.

Whosoever would establish free will denies entirely the predestination and the grace of God. This is more than clear as we find in Romans, also throughout the epistle to the Galatians, also through all that to the Ephesians. . . .

---

81 Compare 1 Timothy 4:3.
82 Compare 1 Corinthians 7:2–7.
83 C. 17 and C. 18 are inserted at the end of the line of the preceding paragraph.
84 Possibly a reference to Luke 6:38.
85 From this point the numbers are in the margin: from here to the end the writing is cursive, quite different to the book-hand of the rest of the text.
86 Compare Ephesians 1:4–6.

C. 22 The ministers of the Word of God ought not to move from place to place unless this may be of great utility to the Church.

C. 23 For the ministers to have some private goods to nourish their families is not contrary to apostolic sharing [of goods].

These two conclusions are clear as we find in the Acts of the Apostles.

Around the matter of the sacraments, it is concluded by the Scripture that we have only two sacramental signs which Christ has left: one is baptism, the other is the eucharist, which we use as a demonstration of our perseverance in the faith which we have promised in baptism when we were children; and also in memory of that great benefit which Jesus Christ has done for us by dying for our redemption, and washing us with his precious blood.

Therefore, brethren, since it has been the good pleasure of God to gather [us] together through his most holy Scripture; and that with his help we have come to take a declaration of the present conclusion,[87] in everything we are united and of one same spirit. And publicly they have been expounded not as commanded by men but as commanded by the Holy Spirit, as they truly are. Therefore we should perjure ourselves in the bowels of that charity,[88] if after we have shared it together, we were discordant in teaching, both in the conclusions stated above, as also in the interpretation of the Scripture: and so, as one same Spirit has composed it, let us ensure that it is interpreted by that same Spirit.

One final point should be added about this document. There is a subtle but very discernible difference between the dialect in which the Angrogna propositions are written, and the dialect of the Alpine–Provençal Vaudois which is used in the rest of Trinity College, Dublin MS. 259, and the remainder of the 'Waldensian books' dating from the 1520s. In effect, the Angrogna propositions are in a Piedmontese form of Italian rather than Provençal.[89] It is therefore unlikely that they were written by the same scribe as compiled the rest of the manuscript, even if the handwriting of the early part of the propositions is broadly similar.

The Angrogna propositions may be a memorandum from the meeting attended by Pierre Griot. With no names in the former document, one can only compare the issues addressed in the two pieces of evidence:

87 The context suggests it should read 'the present conclusions', as this obviously purports to be a conclusion to the entire document. However, the reading 'dechiaratione dela presente conclusione' is quite clear in the manuscript.
88 Possibly a reference to Colossians 3:12.
89 See Comba, *History of the Waldenses*, pp. 163–4, discussing the comments of E. Montet: 'he states that "the acts of the Synod of Angrogna of 1532 are written in a language greatly resembling the Italian". But the language in which these acts are recorded not only *resembles* Italian, it *is* Italian, as it was then spoken.'

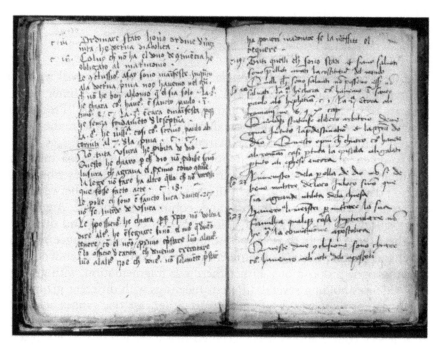

Plate 7 One of many puzzles posed by the text of the Angrogna propositions is the sudden change of handwriting in the middle of clause 19. On the left-hand page the hand resembles the stylized calligraphy used in the manuscripts described in chapter 8 (and in the earlier part of this text), although the language is significantly closer to Italian. If the same scribe wrote both pages, the change in style may show his abandoning the attempt to copy a form of writing which was not natural to him. From this point to the end the theological contents of the text are more explicitly and positively reformed. (The Board of Trinity College Dublin.)

Angrogna propositions	_Griot trial evidence_
	Justification by faith, not works
Oath-taking accepted	
Good works restricted	Good works restricted
Auricular confession unnecessary	
Sunday observance optional	
Formal worship unnecessary	Formal worship unnecessary
Laying-on of hands unnecessary	
Revenge forbidden	
Magistracy lawful	
Regular fasting not obligatory	
Marriage permitted to all	Marriage obligatory for
Some usury permissible	ministers
Predestination affirmed	

Mobility of ministers rejected
Private property allowed to ministers
Two sacraments affirmed and defined

The ultra-reforming, almost sectarian insistence that all formal worship is unnecessary, and that one need only worship with the inner heart, appears to be the same in both texts; yet this is not a 'core' Protestant teaching in this form. This suggests that the two meetings were the same, even if Griot's recollections were extremely selective.

However, one cannot have it both ways. If the Angrogna meeting beginning 12 September was the same as that which Griot described and [mis-?] dated to late August, then there is a clear difference between the apparent expressions of concord and commitment in the Angrogna propositions on one hand, and Griot's reports of scandal and divisions on the other. Nor is there any absolutely compelling evidence to link Farel and Saunier *either* to the meeting which Griot had attended *or* to the Angrogna propositions. Either there was fragmentation, with groups of Waldenses holding several different meetings with different groups of reformers; or there was disagreement. In either case one cannot speak of a clear collective decision to adhere to the Reformation.

It has of course always been accepted that a section of the *barbes* was angered by the negotiations with the reformers and fragmented the brotherhood as a result. Daniel and Jean, two of the *barbes*, found their way to Bohemia and described what had passed. The Bohemian brethren as a result wrote on 25 June 1533 a scathing letter to the Waldenses, now preserved at Neuchâtel, which commented that some 'meddlers or corrupters of Christian doctrine from Switzerland' had associated with the Waldenses and had provoked a schism which in turn led to a persecution. The anonymous authors expressed surprise that the Waldenses had allowed people unknown to them to impose on them to that extent.[90] Seventeenth-century tradition claimed that this letter was discussed and rejected at an assembly in the Val Germanasca on 15 August 1533.[91]

One footnote ought to be added to the story of 1532. The meeting at 'Angrogna' where the propositions were adopted was described by seventeenth-century historians from Jean-Paul Perrin onwards, and by their successors, as a 'synod' held 'in Angrogna'. Only in 1847 did Antoine Monastier, in the *Histoire de l'église vaudoise*, for the first time claim that it took place at a specific point in the Valle d'Angrogna, a tiny hamlet called Chanforan. From Monastier's references, it is clear that he transferred to 1532 a piece of evidence relating to a six-day 'chapter' of the

90 Herminjard, *Correspondance des réformateurs*, vol. 3, pp. 63–9; Vinay, *Confessioni di fede . . . riformati*, pp. 144–51.
91 Gilles, *Histoire ecclésiastique*, vol. 1, pp. 56–7.

barbes held 'in the *bourgade* of the Chanforans in the middle of Angrogna' which had actually taken place three years later, in September 1535.[92] Although Monastier's misuse of that particular piece of testimony was noticed and corrected by the end of the nineteenth century, that did not prevent a tradition growing up according to which the 1532 meeting[93] also took place at Chanforan, where there now stands a huge stone column to commemorate the event. The location of the 1532 meetings is not in itself of any great significance; the small cleft in the hillside at Chanforan may have been a regular meeting-place or it may not. The building up of the 'Synod of Chanforan' into a symbolic and decisive turning-point for the movement is, however, a deeply misleading piece of historical construction, and as such to be avoided.[94]

9.4   The Farels and their Circle from 1533 Onwards

By the end of the middle ages the 'Waldensian books' included some partial copies of the Bible, usually containing a large portion of the New Testament and selected books of the Old Testament. The Old Testament books especially favoured appear to have been those with clear, epigraphic moral messages, such as Proverbs, Ecclesiasticus or Job. In any event, one could not argue that knowledge of the entire Bible determined the religious experience of the medieval Waldenses, even though selected books were learned by heart for teaching purposes. One of the first measures of the early reformers was to encourage the Waldenses to obtain a Bible of their own, arguing that 'sects and heresies . . . came from ignorance of the word of God'.[95] The letter from 'Adam' of 5 November 1532 specified a bilingual Latin–French edition in parallel columns,[96] and implied that 'Martin' (possibly the Piedmontese *barbe* Martin Gonin) had given five hundred gold pieces to fund the project.[97] The Bible project appears to originate with a close-knit group of friends: *barbe* Martin

---

92   A. Monastier, *A History of the Vaudois Church* (London, 1848), p. 146, mis-citing Gilles, *Histoire ecclésiastique*, vol. 1, pp. 65–6. Monastier's work appeared first in French in 1847. For further details, see Cameron, *Reformation of the Heretics*, pp. 264–7.

93   E. Comba, having spotted the misreading, then postulated, in his 'L'Introduction de la réforme dans les vallées de Piémont', *Bulletin de la société d'histoire du protestantisme français* 43 (1894), pp. 7ff., not one 'synod of Chanforan' but a total of three.

94   For the publication enterprise which this approach has entailed, see above, note 39.

95   Herminjard, *Correspondance des réformateurs*, vol. 2, p. 453, n. 19.

96   See above, note 49.

97   For more details on the elusive references to Martin Gonin, see Cameron, *Reformation of the Heretics*, pp. 183–4 and references.

Gonin, the Dauphinois reformer Antoine Saunier, the biblical scholar Pierre Robert Olivétan, and the printer Pierre de Vingle. In 1533 Olivétan published an edition of his *Instruction des enfans* in 1533 at Geneva on the press of Pierre de Vingle, set up in the house of one Jehan Chautemps, for whom Olivétan worked ostensibly as a tutor. The dedicatory epistle to this edition was written by 'M. [possibly Martin Gonin] to his good brother Ant[oine] Son[nier]'.[98] This tight-knit group set about producing a French edition of the Bible, which eventually appeared at Pierre de Vingle's presses in Neuchâtel in 1535.

Much scholarly work has been done on Olivétan's edition of the Bible, the title-page of which made the ambitious claim that the translation was based on the Hebrew and Greek originals. There is, in fact, no real doubt that Olivétan derived most of his version from the earlier French Bible of Jacques Lefèvre d'Étaples, though with a very large number of amendments and alterations.[99] For the historian of the Waldenses, however, the scholarly merits of the Olivétan Bible, or its relationships to its antecedents and successors, are beside the point. As a contribution to 'Protestantizing' the Waldensian communities or their *barbes*, the Olivétan Bible was a somewhat doubtful asset. In the first place, it was in French (and only in French), not Franco-Provençal or any other form of Occitan. This was a language barely, if at all, more comprehensible to the bulk of the Waldensian communities than Latin was. The speaking of French in the Dauphiné or Provence was a social marker: the noble, mercantile or clerical elites used it, not the general populace.[100] Second, the Olivétan Bible was a massive folio volume, elegant, expensively produced, but also unwieldy and impossible to conceal. It was therefore appropriate to a settled church, but quite unsuitable for the Waldensian context where heretical activities took place in semi-secret. Anyone who has handled one of the surviving copies of Olivétan's Bible in a library

98   H. Delaure, 'Olivétan et Pierre de Vingle à Genève, 1532-3', *Bulletin d'humanisme et renaissance* 8 (1946), pp. 115–18.

99   On the 1535 Bible, see J. Jalla, 'La Bible d'Olivétan', *Bulletin de la société d'histoire vaudoise* 58 (1932), pp. 76–92; E. Pétavel-Olliff, *La Bible en France, ou les traductions françaises des Saintes Escritures* (Paris, 1864), pp. 89–117. Some parts of the Olivétan Bible are thought to be almost entirely independent of Lefèvre, especially in the Old Testament, while others are more clearly a revision of the earlier version. Olivétan also departed from Lefèvre's ordering of the OT, separating out the apocryphal from the canonical books, whereas Lefèvre had intermingled them. See also B. Roussel, 'La Bible d'Olivétan: la traduction du livre du prophète Habaquq', in *Études théologiques et religieuses* 4 (1982), pp. 537–57.

100   This is evident from the restriction of French to certain elite and official documents in the region at this period. The Edict of Villers-Cotterets of 1539 sought to proscribe the use of Occitan in formal documents. Note, however, that even a minor nobleman like Fazy de Rame of Freissinières kept his accounts in dialect. See above, chapter 7, note 204.

will find the idea of a missionary preacher concealing it in his knapsack or the folds of his clothing frankly ludicrous.[101] Third, the prefaces make it clear that this was a pet project of the reformers of the Pays de Vaud, to whom the Waldenses were merely a convenient and necessary source of funds. The 'Christian churches, our good brethren' were referred to only obliquely. One preface, on the other hand, devoted several thousand words to the cause of converting the Jewish people to Christianity.[102]

There are, alas, signs that the Waldenses realized quite soon that they had been used as financiers by ambitious, highly motivated but commercially inept evangelists. In 1533 Saunier described how he had been 'reproached' by the Waldenses because a year had passed after the money was handed over for the printing, and nothing had been done.[103] Once it was published in 1535, there is little evidence that many Waldenses actually bought the edition.[104] It remained in print until Pierre de Vingle's death; but before then, in 1549, the Waldenses had some of his property sequestered at Neuchâtel to protect their investment.[105] On 12 September 1561 it was reported to the reformer Pierre Viret that the remaining books of the now deceased printer de Vingle would be sold, and the money used to repay the money (now estimated at 800 écus) which the 'good people' had paid to have the Bible printed.[106]

What was happening meanwhile in the Waldensian valleys after 1532? While events in Provence up to the atrocity of 1545[107] are relatively well documented, there are only scraps of information about what happened

---

101   Copies which survive include Oxford, Bodleian Library, Bib. Fr. 1535 c.1; there is also a copy in Lambeth Palace Library. The Oxford copy belonged to the daughter of a Limburg magistrate.

102   In Olivétan's translator's preface to the 1535 Bible, one finds, sig. * iiv: 'Ce paoure peuple qui te faict le present fut deschasse et banny de ta compagnie plus de trois cens ans y a / et espars aux quatre parties de la Gaule / tenu depuis et repute (a tort et sans cause toutesffoys pour le nom de Christ et selon sa promesse) le plus meschant / execrable / et ignominieux que iamais fut / voire tant que le nom diceluy a este comme en fable et proverbe aux autres nations et usurpe pour extreme injure et reproche'. Olivétan goes on to refer, apparently, to Louis XI's changing of the name of Valpute, in the Dauphiné, to Vallouise. However, the word 'Vaudois' is scrupulously avoided by Olivétan, as by most French writers of the period. The preface entitled 'O. F. C. a nostre allié et confedere le peuple de lalliance de Sinai' follows this and a further prefatory letter.

103   Herminjard, *Correspondance des réformateurs*, vol. 3, p. 81.

104   Though the Provençal heretic Collin Pellenc did apparently acquire one: see M. Villard, 'Vaudois d'Apt au xvie siècle', in Comité des travaux historiques et scientifiques, *Bulletin philologique et historique* (for year 1965, pub. 1966), pp. 649–51.

105   Jalla, 'La Bible d'Olivétan', p. 87.

106   *Joannis Calvini Opera quae supersunt Omnia*, ed. G. Baum, E. Cunitz and E. Reuss, Corpus Reformatorum, vols 29–87, (Berlin, 1853–1900), vol. 18, col. 712.

107   See below, section 9.5.

in the Alpine heartlands at the same period. In the light of later events, it seems clear that no substantial practical consequences followed from the discussions with the reformers in the early 1530s. The *barbes* presumably continued their itinerant moralizing mission much as before. To some extent, things may have been made rather easier by the effects of the Franco-Habsburg Italian wars on the region after 1536. For a brief period in 1535 the Duke of Savoy authorized the lord of Roccapiatta, Pantaleone Bersatore, to seize heretics by secular (rather than inquisitorial) authority. Bersatore conducted a brief persecution which was soon cut short, first by objections from the widow of the Count of Luserna, and then by François I's invasion of the region.[108] The French invasion conveniently secured the release of Antoine Saunier, who had spent a short period in the Duke of Savoy's prison.[109] It then led to the imposition of military rule in the valleys of Piedmont under the German mercenary Captain Wilhelm von Furstenberg. Von Furstenberg appointed the Dauphinois nobleman Gauchier Farel (brother of Guillaume Farel, the stormy reformer of Geneva) as his representative in the Piedmontese valleys of Angrogna, Luserna, Perosa and Germanasca. Gauchier Farel seems to have shared his brother's interest in and concern for the Alpine Waldenses. He visited them, in the company of Antoine Saunier, in July 1535 and again, it would appear, in September of that year.[110] In 1537–8 he reportedly had the Catholic churches in the Valle d'Angrogna destroyed and punished the lords of Luserna for harassing the Waldenses. In 1538, however, Farel was elsewhere, and the French governor in Turin, René de Montjehan, took advantage of his absence to lead a plundering raid into the Luserna and the Germanasca. Von Furstenberg quarrelled bitterly with Montjehan over this, and when Montjehan died in 1539 the valleys were again left in peace.[111]

108   L. C. Bollea, 'Alcuni documenti di storia valdese (1354–1573)', *Bulletin de la société d'histoire vaudoise* 45 (1923), pp. 5–7; Gilles, *Histoire ecclésiastique*, vol. 1, pp. 58–67.
109   Herminjard, *Correspondance des réformateurs*, vol. 3, pp. 321–5, 351, 355 n. 4, 370, 398.
110   Ibid., pp. 83, 321ff., 352 n.
111   Documents for this period are in Gilles, *Histoire ecclésiastique*, vol. 1, pp. 71–5; F.-X. Provana di Collegno, 'Rapports de Guillaume Farel avec les Vaudois du Piémont', *Bulletin de la société d'études ... des Hautes-Alpes* (1891), pp. 257–78; P. E. Martin, 'Une Lettre inédite de Guillaume Farel relative aux Vaudois du Piémont', *Bulletin de la société d'histoire du protestantisme français* 61 (1912), pp. 204–13; Herminjard, *Correspondance des réformateurs*, vol. 5, pp. 149, 170ff., 281; vol. 6, pp. 122–3; vol. 9, pp. 459ff.; A. Pascal, 'Le Ambascerie dei cantoni e dei principi protestanti di Svizzera e Germania al Re di Francia in favore dei Valdesi durante il periodo della dominazione francese in Piemonte (1535–1559)', *Bollettino storico-bibliografico subalpino*, vol. 18, nos 1–3 (1913), pp. 83–9, and vol. 19, nos 1–3 (1914), pp. 26–7; see also R. Peter, 'Le Conte Guillaume de Furstenberg et les Vaudois', *Bollettino della Società di Studi Valdesi* 143 (1978), pp. 30–2.

What this encounter suggests is that warfare and the resulting disintegration of local spiritual and secular authority may have done more to enable the establishment of the 'Piedmontese Church' than delicate discussions with the reformers in 1530–2. The destruction of churches and the cowing of the more hostile of the local aristocracy were vital precursors to the transformation of the Waldensian valleys into a Protestant enclave. The disruption of secular and presumably also of ecclesiastical authority due to the Franco-Habsburg wars will have made effective harassment of the travelling preachers much more difficult. On the other hand, there was no positive establishment of a reformed 'settled Church' in the valleys at this period. Cardinal Innocenzo Cibô carried out a pastoral visitation in 1545 in the Waldensian heartland parishes in Piedmont. This led to a decree forbidding the receiving of 'foreign preachers' but made no mention of resident heretics.[112] In fact, so far from the reformers changing the Waldenses into parish ministers, the reverse may have occurred. Early Protestants, like the Provençal Anthoine Guérin, may have acted, for the time being, more like *barbes*. They travelled around in semi-secret, carried illicit literature and taught their people as occasion and opportunity offered. Even this activity was fraught with considerable danger. Antoine Saunier and a companion were captured at Pinerolo in 1535, though they were released by April of the following year. Martin Gonin was captured in the Champsaur region near Gap, interrogated at Grenoble, and drowned as a heretic on 26 April 1536. Étienne Brun, a layman from the Embrunais who had learned Latin to read his Bible, was burned for heresy at Embrun in 1540.[113] The French *parlement* established at Turin in 1539 began to work against heresy with the inquisitor-general of Turin, Tommasso Giacomelli, from around 1550 onwards. The people of Angrogna were briefly harassed by this court, though after the inhabitants had ambushed the inquisitor and frustrated his mission, the authorities seem to have concentrated on heretics nearer hand, from places in the plain of Piedmont such as Fenile, Vigone, Barge and Bagnolo Piemonte.[114]

112 A. Pascal, 'Communità eretiche e chiese cattoliche nelle valli valdesi secondo le relazioni delle visite pastorali del Peruzzi e della Broglia (secolo xvi)', *Bulletin de la société d'histoire vaudoise* 30 (1912), p. 62.

113 Gonin's martyrdom is reported in J. Crespin, *Actes de martyrs* (n. p., 1565 edn consulted), pp. 138–40, and in subsequent editions and adaptations; Étienne Brun's in ibid., pp. 154–5.

114 Gilles, *Histoire ecclésiastique*, vol. 1, pp. 81–2; L. Romier, 'Les Vaudois et le parlement français de Turin', *Mélanges d'archaeologie et d'histoire* 30 (1920), pp. 193–221; A. Pascal, *I Valdesi e il parlamento francese di Torino* (Pinerolo, 1912).

9.5   The Luberon and its Sufferings, 1530–1550

One of several attractions of the empty lands of the Luberon for the Waldensian migrants from Piedmont and the Dauphiné was the peace and quiet which these regions afforded in the fifteenth century. The lack of disturbance has been an equally unmitigated nuisance to their historians, who find no significant trial registers or other such material to illuminate their beliefs and practices. Their most meticulous historian to date has been forced to limit himself, through a study of their names, residence, marriage contracts and other civil evidence, to establishing who they were, where and how they lived in comparison with the rest of the population.[115] All this changed quite dramatically in the 1530s. The Luberon region became notorious, first as a place where the new heresies of Lutheranism and 'sacramentarianism' (as François I persisted in calling it) were taught; then as the place where whole communities were savagely massacred, in an episode which brought the Waldenses to the sympathetic notice of the literate of Europe for the first time.

Two factors predisposed the Provençal Vaudois to a more public expression of heresy from the 1520s onwards. First, Protestant immigrants settled and taught among the Waldensian communities, like Anthoine Guérin; several can be shown to have known and read Protestant literature.[116] Second, the Luberon appears to have attracted a series of renegades from the Catholic clergy, including several former Franciscan friars, an ex-nun and some secular priests. Hélion Barberoux of Tourves, based at Mérindol, 'kept a school' in which he disseminated new and old heresies to his hearers, including an ex-priest.[117] These Catholic religious may have carried over their public ministry from Catholicism into Protestantism, and have taught in a more sedentary, public fashion than even the Provençal *barbes* had done – though not, of course, in anything resembling a settled, regular 'parish' structure. On the other hand, the Waldensian communities of the Luberon provided a preformed body of anti-clerical, anti-sacerdotal listeners for the new doctrines. The 'Lutherans' in Provence did not need to win communities over by laboriously weaning their people from trust in the rituals of the old Church, as Farel and his associates had to do in the Pays de Vaud.

---

115   See Audisio, *Les Vaudois du Luberon, passim*, and esp. pp. 543–5 for his establishing of 'criteria' to identify those who were probably Vaudois.
116   Audisio, *Barbe et l'inquisiteur*, pp. 96, 104, 107, 126; see also note 104 above.
117   Audisio, *Les Vaudois du Luberon*, p. 308; also J. Aubéry, *Histoire de l'execution de Cabrières et de Mérindol* (Paris, 1645), pp. 22–31. Aubéry's work comprises the case for the prosecution in the trial of the leaders of the 1545 massacre in the Paris *parlement*.

It is easy to assume that heretic communities in the middle ages were routinely, normally persecuted and that no explanation for the process is needed. The Waldenses of Provence belie this assumption: they escaped notice for several generations. One may therefore reasonably assume that it was the additional attention attracted by the informal Protestant preaching of the late 1520s which drew the ecclesiastical authorities' attention down on them. The hunt for heretics was conducted by several distinct authorities. The Dominican friar Jean de Roma began seeking out heretics in Provence in 1528, apparently after being evicted from the papal enclave of the Comtat Venaissin. He embarked on a furious campaign against his targets in the autumn of 1532; he appears to have used torture fairly indiscriminately to secure scandalous confessions, although the surviving dossier of the trial of the *barbe* Pierre Griot, which de Roma presented in his own justification, appears quite careful and meticulous. In any event, in spring 1533 he was stopped and investigated by a combination of royal and episcopal authority, and died of plague at Avignon the following summer.[118]

Royal and episcopal authority combined their forces in the main investigation of 'Lutherans' in the diocese of Aix, which appears to have begun in July 1531. The Archbishop of Aix sent his official, his *procureur-fiscal* and the inquisitor of the province, while Carmelite friars were sent to the region to warn the people against the errors being taught there. In 1532–3 the investigations were traditional in nature: village by village, individuals were summoned and called on to abjure, from the communities of Lourmarin, Villelaure, La Roque, Peypin, Cucuron and Cabrières-d'Aigues.[119] In 1535, however, signs appeared of trouble to come. Officers of the Aix ecclesiastical court tried to seize a suspected *barbe*: they were attacked by forty or fifty armed heretics; the prisoner was rescued; his captors were chased to the abbey of Saulvecane and besieged there. The possibility of further violence was enhanced by the presence of Wilhelm von Furstenberg, who had also acted as a protector to the Waldenses in Piedmont. He used his influence in 1537 to protest at the harassment of married priests at Tourves.[120] During interrogations of heretics in 1539 it was discovered that the Waldenses intended to

118 Jean de Roma's persecution is documented in Audisio, *Barbe et l'inquisiteur,* esp. pp. 7–35; for the furore which he generated see the documents in Herminjard, *Correspondance des réformateurs*, vol. 7, pp. 465–88.
119 For the official narrative of the 1530s persecutions see the edition of Archives Départmentales des Bouches-du-Rhône, MS. G. 161, in J.-H. Albanès, 'Un Nouveau document sur les premières années de protestantisme en Provence', in Comité des travaux historiques et scientifiques, *Bulletin historique et philologique* (1884), pp. 30–41 and esp. pp. 32–7; see also P. Gaffarel, 'Les Massacres de Cabrières et de Mérindol en 1545', *Revue historique* 107 (1911), pp. 241–71, esp. pp. 243–4.
120 See Peter, 'Guillaume de Furstenberg et les Vaudois', pp. 30, 35–6.

defend themselves by force and join von Furstenberg's mercenary corps.[121] Further skirmishes would take place at local level between Waldenses and Catholics in 1541[122] and in 1543; the heretics' leader Eustache Marron latterly became something of a feared guerrilla leader.[123]

The dynamics of persecution thereafter depended on French royal foreign policy. In the summer of 1535 François I had issued the Edict of Coucy, which suspended persecutions of heretics for six months; the clause which excluded the abhorred 'sacramentarians' from its terms was generally ignored (as being, one suspects, too difficult for theologically illiterate lawyers to administer) and it was extended beyond its original terms well into 1536.[124] This amnesty was evidently intended to clear the decks before the 1536 invasion of Piedmont, part of François's long-running and wasteful duel with Charles V in the cockpit of northern Italy. In contrast, royal letters of 24 June 1539 gave jurisdiction over heresy to the local secular courts, to act in collaboration with ecclesiastical authorities.[125] This change of jurisdiction affected the politics of dealing with heresy in two ways. First, attention shifted somewhat, away from pure religious error, and towards the threat which the Waldenses posed to good order and loyalty. Second, the personal attitudes of the *présidents* of the *parlement* of Provence became crucial.

On 18 November 1540 the *parlement* of Aix-en-Provence issued the infamous 'Mérindol edict' which declared that the entire population of Mérindol, Cabrières-d'Avignon and a number of surrounding villages were obstinate heretics, sentenced them all to death, and decreed that the village of Mérindol itself should be razed to the ground and never rebuilt.[126] From the way in which the decree was used at first, it does not appear to have been intended to be put into execution, at least not immediately: it was rather a massive threat, intended to cow the Provençal heretics into submission. In any event, the *président*, Barthélemi Chassanée, suspended the edict while further enquiries were made. François

---

121   Ibid., p. 33; Aubéry, *Histoire de l'execution*, pp. 22–7.

122   See E. Arnaud, *Protestants de Provence, du Comtat Venaissin et de la Principauté d'Orange*, 2 vols (Paris, 1884), vol. 1, pp. 45–51.

123   Aubéry, *Histoire de l'execution*, pp. 21–3, 25–6, 30–2; Arnaud, *Protestants de Provence*, vol. 1, pp. 9ff., 50ff.; Gaffarel, 'Les Massacres', pp. 250–1.

124   Albanès, 'Premières années de protestantisme', pp. 37–9; Arnaud, *Protestants de Provence*, vol. 1, pp. 14–15; Gaffarel, 'Les Massacres', p. 245; R. J. Knecht, *Francis I* (Cambridge, 1982), pp. 390–7; N. M. Sutherland, *The Huguenot Struggle for Recognition* (New Haven, Conn.,1980), pp. 30–3.

125   Albanès, 'Premières années de protestantisme', pp. 39–40; Knecht, *Francis I*, pp. 397ff.; Sutherland, *Huguenot Struggle*, pp. 33ff.

126   The text of the edict is in Audisio, *Les Vaudois du Luberon*, pp. 531–3.

I obtained from his then lieutenant in Piedmont, Guillaume du Bellay, a favourable report on the Waldenses' life and morals; accordingly the sentence was mitigated as long as they recanted their errors within three months.[127] The Waldensian villagers for their part embarked on a campaign of persuasion to have the edict lifted. In spring 1541 they protested to the *parlement*, appending an irenic, moderate and largely orthodox profession of faith to their protests.[128] Meanwhile, Protestants abroad, gathered for the colloquy of Regensburg, wrote to François on 23 May in their support.[129] The letters of grace suspending the edict were renewed in 1542 and 1543.[130]

Barthélemi Chassanée (whose concern for due process of law became legendary)[131] was dead by 1543, and was succeeded after a short interval by a landlord from the region of Cabrières and Mérindol named Jean Meynier, Sieur d'Oppède. Meynier does not appear to have had Waldenses as his own tenants; jealousy of those of his neighbours who did, and fear of the Waldenses' growing political and military threat in the region, may explain the personal interest which he took in bringing the decree into execution. The measures taken by the villagers to fortify and defend their communities only made the calls for military intervention more plausible. Eventually, and with much lobbying, Meynier and the Aix *parlement* secured letters patent from François I on 1 February 1545 which ordered that the decree, with its wholesale killing and destruction of villages, be put into effect.[132] An army was assembled under a captain named Polin de la Garde. From 18 April they led a punitive and destructive raid across the southern edge of the Luberon massif where the Waldenses were settled, devastating one town after another. Large numbers of the inhabitants were killed; many others were taken

127   For the suspension of the edict, see Gaffarel, 'Les Massacres', p. 247; Arnaud, *Protestants de Provence*, vol. 1, pp. 27–34; V.-L. Bourrilly, *Guillaume du Bellay, Seigneur de Langey* (Paris, 1905), pp. 314–17.
128   The protests of the people of Mérindol are in Crespin, *Actes de martyrs*, pp. 202–5; Herminjard, *Correspondance des réformateurs*, vol. 7, pp. 80–2.
129   Arnaud, *Protestants de Provence*, vol. 1, pp. 43–5, based on *Calvini Opera*, vol. 11, letter no. 311.
130   Arnaud, *Protestants de Provence*, vol. 1, pp. 52ff.
131   Chassanée or Chasseneuz was celebrated at the time for a legal opinion, reported in Barthelemy de Chasseneuz, *Catalogus Gloriae mundi* . . . (Lyons, 1529, and subsequent edns), in which he had argued at Autun that a decision to order the extermination of the local rats was unjust, as the rats had not had the opportunity to defend themselves in court, especialy due to the large numbers of cats abroad in the region.
132   Crespin, *Actes de martyrs*, pp. 212–15; Gaffarel, 'Les Massacres', pp. 249–51; Audisio, *Les Vaudois du Luberon*, pp. 355–60, with intriguing details of the contemporary political and socio-economic background.

prisoner, some sent to the French galleys, and others banished into exile. The leader of the massacres, Jean Meynier, was praised by the king and honoured by the pope.[133] Some five years later, however, the outrage caused by the massacres led Henri II to have Meynier, Polin de la Garde and others involved in the massacres tried in the *parlement* of Paris. The perpetrators were eventually acquitted (given that they had manifestly acted under royal orders, any other outcome would have been bizarre), but Meynier had a long struggle to regain possession of his lands, which he only succeeded in doing shortly before his death.[134]

The Waldensian communities of the Luberon survived even this appalling carnage. Large numbers of their people migrated to Geneva during the 1550s, and a few years afterwards some of these returned to their homes. Meanwhile, the Genevan presses publicized the scandal of the massacres in a series of publications from 1556 onwards; these accounts of the massacres were duly incorporated into all the major Protestant martyrologies.[135] In the early 1560s 'settled churches' were set up in the Luberon, in the manner of Protestant churches elsewhere in France at the same time. Mérindol was rebuilt, in a slightly different location, despite the terms of the edict, and recalled its former minister in 1563. A particularly vigorous Huguenot church grew up at Lourmarin from the early 1560s onwards, and even survived the Revocation of the Edict of Nantes into the eighteenth century.[136] From that point onwards the Luberon churches formed part of the Huguenot Church of Provence, with its synodal structures and its Genevan customs and rituals. Unusually for the Protestant Church of the Languedoc, they were based in country villages rather than significant towns; their Alpine origins, names and social cohesion will have marked them off from other Huguenots.[137] On the other hand, in this form they can no longer truly be regarded as

---

133   *Calvini Opera*, vol. 12, cols 79–81; Audisio, *Les Vaudois du Luberon*, pp. 360–99.

134   Gaffarel, 'Les Massacres', pp. 265–70; Arnaud, *Protestants de Provence*, vol. 1, pp. 89ff., 98ff.; Audisio, *Les Vaudois du Luberon*, pp. 402–5.

135   Jean Crespin's account of the massacres was published separately as *Histoire mémorable de la persécution et saccagement du peuple de Mérindol et Cabrières et autres circonvoisins, appelez Vaudois* (n.p., 1556), as well as in the *Actes des Martyrs*; for the very widespread dissemination of the story, see Cameron, *Reformation of the Heretics*, pp. 237–9 and references. See also Audisio, *Les Vaudois du Luberon*, pp. 405–7.

136   Audisio, *Les Vaudois du Luberon*, pp. 421–6, analyses the parish register of the Huguenot church of Lourmarin; on the early history of Protestantism in 1560s Provence, and the role of former Vaudois, see also Cameron, *Reformation of the Heretics*, p. 155 and notes.

137   In general, Protestantism was associated with towns rather than the country-side in Languedoc. See E. Le Roy Ladurie, *Les Paysans de Languedoc*, abridged edn (Paris, 1969), pp. 178–85, with the otherwise curious exception of the Cévennes (ibid., pp. 186–93).

part of the 'Waldensian' story. That identity would in years to come shrink ever more closely around the Waldensian communities of Piedmont and the lands of the Duke of Savoy. The reasons why this was so will be explored next.

Calvin's Geneva takes over in Piedmont, 1555–1565

There is now quite general agreement between historians that the real, decisive transformation of the Waldensian communities of the Alps into a rural minority Protestant Church took place after 1555. By this period, the Reformation was just sufficiently stable in Geneva itself to allow the Compagnie des Pasteurs (Company of Pastors) to respond to requests to support and supply Churches elsewhere. The decade after 1555 was, across western Europe, the turning-point in establishing the Genevan paradigm for reforming local, regional and even national Churches: in France, Flanders, the Rhine Palatinate and Scotland. Against this background, one should not be surprised that the establishment of 'Waldensian churches' took place later than used to be thought. Rather, one should note how early, how precocious, were the Alpine churches in taking shape, when compared to developments elsewhere in Calvin's sphere of influence. In fact, the Waldenses, especially in Piedmont-Savoy, received an exceptional, even disproportionate amount of attention and support from the Church of Geneva. How these tenacious and self-reliant communities responded to being thus placed in the spotlight of international Protestantism was another matter.

10.1   The Mission of Vernou and Lauversat, 1555

On 22 April 1555 Jean Vernou of Poitiers, an associate of Calvin, wrote a letter to the Genevan ministers which described a missionary visit to the Piedmontese Alps. Vernou and a companion (whose surname is variously reported as Lauversat, Lauvergeat or Laborie) had visited the Val Chisone in the eastern promontory of the Dauphiné, then moved on to Angrogna:

We have arrived in this country safe and sound. First, we arrived in a hamlet called Barbotté [Balboutet] where, for the space of five or six days we spent a good part of the day and the night in proclaiming [God's] Word, both in public sermons (amongst the faithful who are in good numbers there) and by secret means. From there we came to a village called Fenestella [Fenestrelle]. On the way we had a body of good people who escorted us, and because in the said place of Fenestella three or four of the leading people had made some difficulty about receiving us, thinking that we were public preachers from Geneva, several of these good people were very angry. Amongst others, a good old man of strong spirit came before us, but his heart was struck with fear at the thought of trying to prevent us, and he could do no more than withdraw and weep. So it was that in despite of Satan, we were so well received there that we could not satisfy their enthusiasm, even though each day we delivered two great sermons, each one for two full hours, quite apart from private exhortations. The houses could not hold all the people [who attended]; we had to meet in barns. Also, on Easter day, we celebrated the Lord's Supper among a greater number of people than we had hoped; after dinner, at their beseeching, we allowed ourselves to go to the extent of agreeing to their opinion that we should preach out in the open fields against all the abuses of popery. I said 'their opinion' deliberately: because there and in the country around they generally share this insane fancy that it would be better to go into the countryside and preach the Gospel in public than in secret. We pointed out to them the captivity in which they stand, and the great danger into which they are putting not only us but also themselves and their households; also, the example of the nightly gatherings of the primitive Church; also, that for our part we were keener to spare them [risk] than they were themselves, and we did not wish to be bold at their expense, and only [wished] that they should leave all the abominations of Antichrist, and each one should progress towards confessing Jesus Christ according to the limits of his faith and his calling. Moreover, [we said] that in future we should take care not to allow ourselves to be carried as far as their rashness, and that the only reason why we did it was so that they should not think that fear made us hold such an opinion. By remonstrances like these we think that some of them have corrected that insane opinion.

So, to return to our journey: from Fenestella we arrived in the Valle d'Angrogna, where we were led by night by a good number of brethren well armed with staves; this was at the instruction of the governors of Fenestella (even of those who at the beginning had been quite inhospitable towards us) and also of those of Angrogna, who sent three brethren well armed in front of us. We have been here ever since; each day we preach a sermon (apart from private meetings) in the house of one of their ministers, except on Sundays, when so many people come from all directions, even from great distances, that one is obliged to give the sermon in a great courtyard surrounded by galleries, and the Supper in so far as one can give it, because the multitude there is so great. For this reason, we have advised them that they should make efforts to have more harvesters to help those people whom they already have, since there is such a great harvest in these valleys. For our part we have promised them that if they would give us a note of the number of places which wish to have ministers and how many of them they wish for, we would inform you on our return, assuring them of your affection and diligence to assist them in this place and in everything possible for you. Already Fenestella asks for nothing other than a minister; also, the good people said to him who led us to that old man, that if one of us wished to take over the charge [of the parish], their bodies and goods would be at his command.[1]

Vernou's account suggests, on the face of it, that he began the attempt to draw the Piedmontese Waldenses into the Genevan orbit more or less from scratch; and that he related directly to 'ministers' and people alike, rather than negotiating with the *barbes* in advance of mass meetings. On the other hand, there are some signs that the behaviour of the Waldenses had already changed somewhat from medieval norms. No mention is made of encounters between Vernou and the Catholic priests; possibly the Catholic cult had already been severely curtailed during Furstenberg's time. In later years, Melchior di Dio of Torre Pellice, minister at Villar, was reported to have been an ex-priest; so there may even have been some prior conversions or defections among the local priesthood.[2] The 'minister' in whose house Vernou preached at Angrogna was a sedentary individual with his own home, rather than a travelling mendicant. It is remarkable that Vernou should have had a struggle to *dissuade* the Waldenses at Fenestrelle from holding worship in public. Two conclusions may be drawn from this account. First, by 1555 the Alpine Waldenses seem to have become even more confident in expressing their dissent than they had been at the time of Buronzo's interdict, *c.*1450. Second, some at least seem to have been aware of and ready to deal with Protestant ministers. Some such preparedness, even if only felt by a minority of the Piedmontese Waldenses, may explain the haste with which their transformation into a reformed Church now proceeded. Nevertheless, one gains no sense from Vernou's account that his reception was in any way affected by any 'policy decisions' taken by the *barbes* 23 years before.

1 'Une Mission en Piémont', a document edited anonymously in *Bulletin de la société d'histoire du protestantisme français* 17 (1868), pp. 16–19.
2   S. Foà (ed.), 'Valli del Piemonte soggette all'Altezza di Savoia, infette d'heresia et suoi luoghi', *Bulletin de la société d'histoire vaudoise* 24 (1907), pp. 8–9: this Catholic document from the 1570s describes one of the ministers of Villar Pellice as 'Marchioto Didio prete della Torre'. Given that other ministers are listed by their *Catholic* status as either 'prete', 'frate' or 'laico', one can be fairly sure that Di Dio had indeed received Catholic orders. Several other ministers were by this period former Augustinians or Carmelites.

10.2   Churches Built and Ministers Sent

In 1555, according to the account in Crespin's martyrology, the schoolmaster at Angrogna, who had been leading preaching meetings in the valley, found that the numbers attending his sermons were too great for an ordinary house to accommodate. In August 1555, therefore, two 'temples' were built, one near the church of San Lorenzo (which is now the main village centre of the valley) and another 'a mile higher up', probably at the hamlet of Il Serre near Chanforan.[3] Later in the same year other churches were built in the valleys of the Pellice and the Luserna; in March 1556 a church was built in the Val Germanasca.[4]

Are we dealing here with an explosion of self-help among the Waldenses, or was this wave of building carried out in anticipation of the arrival of foreign ministers to lead the congregations? The latter explanation may be the more persuasive. At exactly the same time, the Company of Pastors of Geneva, the administrative body for the Genevan clergy, began to despatch significant numbers of ministers to the region. The first attempt to settle ministers was a disaster. Jean Vernou, following his report to the Company, was sent at once in summer 1555. However, he was almost immediately captured along with four companions and taken to Chambéry; that autumn he and the others were burned as heretics.[5] The first Huguenot minister who actually settled at Angrogna was Étienne Noel from Troyes in Champagne.[6] In 1555 he met the Waldensian pastor Gilles des Gilles (who divided his time between Piedmont and southern Italy) at Lausanne. Noel had just been expelled from Montbéliard and agreed to take over the Angrogna congregation. He thereafter spent his career shared between Angrogna and the much more important charge of

---

3   Simple church buildings still exist on both these sites.
4   The original martyrological account of this whole period is found in J. Crespin, *Histoire des martyrs* (n.p., 1619), fos 583r–600r; also published independently as *Histoire des persecutions et guerres faites depuis l'an 1555 jusques en l'an 1561 contre le peuple appelé Vaudois* (n.p., 1562); modern edition as E. Balmas and C. A. Theiller (eds), *Storia delle persecuzioni e guerre contro il popolo chiamato valdese che abita nelle valli del Piemonte, di Angrogna, Luserna, San Martino, Perosa e altre, a far temp dall'annp 1555 fino al 1561* (Turin, 1975), comprising an Italian translation and a photographic reproduction of the original French text. On the church-building see Crespin, *Histoire des Martyrs*, fo. 584r; *Storia delle persecuzioni*, pp. 73–4, 232–3.
5   The story of the martyrdom of Vernou and his companions is recorded in Crespin, *Histoire des martyrs*, fos 345r–60v; also Crespin, *Actes des martyrs*, 1565 edn, pp. 624–56; see the letters in *Joannis Calvini Opera quae supersunt Omnia*, ed. G. Baum, E. Cunitz, and E. Reuss, Corpus Reformatorum, vols 29–87, Braunschweig (Berlin, 1853–1900), vol. 15, cols 689–91, 694–7, 707–9, 740–5, 805–7, 808–9.
6   On Troyes at this period see Penny Roberts, *A City in Conflict: Troyes During the French Wars of Religion* (Manchester, 1996).

Plate 8 The first churches built in the Valle d'Angrogna in 1555 were simple rec-
tangular structures in the same basic shape as the traditional housing of the region.
The Waldensian *tempio* at Angrogna San Lorenzo is believed to contain the shell of
this first building. The decorative plasterwork and inscription on the facade are of
course more recent. (Photograph by the author.)

Grenoble. He supported the Grenoble Protestants during the first War of
Religion while he served there between 1562 and 1565; he returned to
Angrogna between 1565 and 1574, reverting to Grenoble subsequently,
and ending his ministry at Gap.[7]

   Noel reported on the state of the Piedmontese churches to Calvin and
Farel in spring 1556.[8] In the summer of 1556 five further ministers were
nominated for Piedmont (though not all were sent immediately); two
more were sent in 1557, and another (Scipione Lentolo of Naples, of

7   P. Gilles, *Histoire ecclésiastique des églises réformées . . . autrefois appellées églises
vaudoises*, ed. P. Lantaret, 2 vols (Pinerolo, 1881), vol. 1, pp. 86–8; T. de Bèze (?),
Histoire ecclésiastique des églises réformées au royaume de France, 3 vols ('Antwerp',
i.e. Geneva, 1580), vol. 3, pp. 284–5.
8   *Calvini Opera*, vol. 15, cols 102–4, 108–10, 146–7; T. de Bèze, *Correspondance
de Théodore de Bèze*, ed. H. Aubert and others (Geneva, 1960–), vol. 2, pp. 41–2
and notes.

Plate 9 A *tempio* was almost certainly built at Il Serre at the same time as the one in Angrogna San Lorenzo. The present structure is a nineteenth-century rebuilding, but gives some idea of how the *tempio* nestled among the vernacular buildings of the hamlet. (Photograph by the author.)

whom much more later) in November 1559.[9] A further three were sent to the Val Chisone in 1557–8.[10] Shortly afterwards, the nascent Protestant churches of the Marquisate of Saluzzo, in the valleys of the Po, the Varaita and the Màira, also asked for ministers. Étienne Noel recommended their cause in a letter to Geneva in 1561; two Genevan alumni were sent to be ministers at Dronero shortly afterwards.[11] A congregation of valley parishes held at Combe de Villar in autumn 1557 included 24 ministers, of whom it was reported that the majority had been sent by Calvin and the Genevan clergy; so, allowing for those lost through capture, the numbers of missionaries known by name may well understate the true total figure.[12]

9 *Calvini Opera*, vol. 15, col. 189; vol. 16, cols 153–4, 532; vol. 17, cols 667–8; R. M. Kingdon, J.-F. Bergier, O. Fatio and O. Labarthe (eds), *Registres de la compagnie des pasteurs de Genève au temps de Calvin*, vols 1–3 (Geneva, 1962–5), vol. 2, pp. 68–70, 74, 79.
10 Ibid., pp. 70, 74, 81, 83; vol. 3, pp. 264–6.
11 *Calvini Opera*, vol. 20, col. 476; Bèze, *Correspondance*, vol. 4, p. 274, n. 8; Gilles, *Histoire ecclésiastique*, vol. 1, pp. 409–11.
12 Crespin, *Actes des martyrs*, 1565 edn, pp. 895–6; J. Jalla, 'Synodes vaudois de la réformation à l'exil, 1536–1686', *Bulletin de la société d'histoire du protestantisme français* 50 (1901), pp. 471ff.

Bearing in mind that the total number of ministers known to have been sent out by the Company of Pastors to the whole of France between 1555 and 1562 is 88, the commitment of at least 19 ministers to the extremely uncomfortable, dangerous and often lethal posting of the Piedmontese Alps testifies to the seriousness with which Geneva took the former Waldensian communities.[13] Most of the new ministers were French; two, however, the former Capuchin Giafredo Varaglia and the Neapolitan theologian Scipione Lentolo, were Italians. There may have been an attempt here to bridge the linguistic gap between the educated and the Franco-Provençal speakers, as it were from both sides. The intellectual quality of the ministers sent was also very high. Scipione Lentolo was a Doctor of Theology; he was also a humanist scholar who described his first encounter with the Waldenses at Angrogna in florid, mannered Latin.[14] Humbert Artus, minister of Bobbio Pellice, was literate in Latin, Greek and Hebrew. Giafredo Varaglia, a former Capuchin and friend of Bernardino Ochino, came from the most elevated circles of Italian spirituality.[15] In contrast, only a few former Waldensian pastors appear to have acted as ministers under the new dispensation. Gilles des Gilles, the itinerant *barbe* who had enticed Étienne Noel to Piedmont, ultimately served the churches of Villar Pellice, Pinasca and Tagliaretto in succession.[16] François Laurens, minister in the Val Germanasca, was also an ex-*barbe*.[17] Laurenzo Pignatello and the brothers Philippe and Hugues Pastre, ministers in the Val Chisone by 1564, bore Waldensian family surnames; given the early date, they *may* have been ex-*barbes*.[18]

With a cadre of ministers in place, the Waldensian valleys of Piedmont soon became, in effect, a presbytery of their own. A synod held on 13 July 1558 adopted articles of ecclesiastical discipline in the Genevan manner. They provided for the regular holding of synods and colloquies. They envisaged the consistories of the congregations being permitted to

13   See E. G. Léonard, *A History of Protestantism*, ed. H. H. Rowley, trans. J. M. H. Reid and R. M. Bethell, 2 vols (London, 1965–7), vol. 2, pp. 104–9; M. Greengrass, *The French Reformation* (Oxford, 1987), pp. 38ff. and references; R. M. Kingdon, *Geneva and the Coming of the Wars of Religion in France 1555–1563* (Geneva, 1956).

14   *Calvini Opera*, vol. 17, cols 668–9.

15   Crespin, *Actes des martyrs*, 1565 edn, p. 891; Gilles, *Histoire ecclésiastique*, vol. 1, pp. 88–9; *Registres de la compagnie des pasteurs*, vol. 2, p. 74.

16   Jalla, 'Synodes vaudois', p. 475, n. 12; Gilles, *Histoire ecclésiastique*, vol. 1, pp. 88, 113; Foà, 'Valli del Piemonte', p. 8.

17   Jalla, 'Synodes vaudois', p. 475, n. 16.

18   Ibid., pp. 475, 481; Pazè Beda and P. Pazè, *Riforma e cattolicesimo in val Pragelato 1555–1685* (Pinerolo, 1975), pp. 30–1, 45–6, 49. On earlier members of those families, see Paris, Bibliothèque Nationale, Fonds Latin, MS. 3375, i, fos 253v, 258r, 263r; ii, fos 396r–8r, 404v.

administer excommunication when needed, and the establishment of the orders of deacons, elders and 'superintendents' to assist the ministers. They undertook to follow the *Ordonnances* of Geneva on issues regarding the reforming of the old canon law on marriage. A further synod at Angrogna in September 1563, after the 1560–1 war, ratified the decisions taken in 1558. On 18 April 1564 a meeting at Villar Pellice resolved to follow the Genevan *Ordonnances* as far as possible.[19]

Investment of such quantity and quality of clergy as the Genevans made, in serving a rural population of a few thousand people, was probably not sustainable for very long. In the longer term, the answer would be to educate the offspring of Waldensian peoples themselves at Geneva, and then to send them back to their home congregations. After a suitable interval, this seems to have been done to some extent. From 1559 onwards one finds Piedmontese and Saluzzese students, and one Dauphinois, enrolled at the Genevan academy.[20] While not every one of them will have become a minister and returned to his home district, it seems probable that the majority did so, and this can be positively stated in several cases. Notwithstanding, a devastating attack of plague in 1630 would force a further investment of new, francophone ministers into the Piedmontese valleys; the 'Waldensian' churches would continue indefinitely to need assistance and support from the wider reformed community.[21]

10.3   Threats and Intercession: International Interest

The attempts made by the civil authorities to stamp out this efflorescence of rural Protestantism elicited further powerful evidence of international Protestant interest in the cause of the Waldenses. Up to 1559 French provincial *parlements* administered lay justice in the southwestern Alpine region: that of Grenoble dealt with the Dauphiné including the Val Chisone, while the *parlement* set up in Turin was responsible for Piedmont. Between December 1555 and March 1556 the Turin *parlement* ordered the imprisonment of those who had received ministers from Geneva during the previous Lent. It sent two of its judges to the valleys to investigate, who directed on 23 March 1556 that the inhabitants must

19   Jalla, 'Synodes vaudois', pp. 476–8.
20   P. F. Geisendorf, *Le Livre des habitants de Genève*, 2 vols (Geneva, 1957–63), vol. 1, pp. 79, 163, 166, 189; Sven and Suzanne Stelling-Michaud (eds), *Le Livre du recteur de l'académie de Genève*, 6 vols (Geneva, 1959–80), vol. 1, pp. 81–5, 88; vol. 2, p. 183; V. Vinay, *Facoltà valdese di teologia (1855–1955)* (Torre Pellice, 1955), p. 17.
21   On the plague, see A. Armand-Hugon, *Storia dei valdesi ii: Dall'adesione alla Riforma all'Emancipazione (1532–1848)* (Turin, 1974), pp. 63–7.

live and worship according to Catholic rites. The inhabitants replied with a conciliatory but nonetheless resolute confession of faith. In November Henri II issued an edict ordering that the prosecution of heresy be proceeded with; the following year, on 22 March 1557, further orders required the congregations to surrender their ministers, and 43 named inhabitants to present themselves at Turin.[22] From March 1556 onwards the Grenoble *parlement* was making similarly threatening noises.[23]

News of these events reached the Swiss almost immediately.[24] In the spring of 1557 Guillaume Farel and Théodore de Bèze travelled around first the Swiss reformed city-states, then the south-German cities and principalities of Strasbourg, Württemberg and the Palatinate. The objective was to persuade the international Protestant powers that the Waldenses were good fellow-Protestants and that they ought to bring as much moral pressure to bear on the King of France to desist from his threats against them.[25] The Waldensian cause strained Protestant solidarity nearly to breaking point. In the 1540s François I had tried to break up the opposition of foreign Protestants to his policies by claiming that the Waldenses held radical, exotic heresies which other Protestants would not wish to support.[26] Documents produced during the 1557 embassies show just how concerned the Swiss were to avoid such ambiguities. Heinrich Bullinger even encouraged his delegates to claim that the Waldenses of Piedmont were quite different to those of Provence.[27]

22   Balmas and Theiller, *Storia delle persecuzioni*, pp. 75–86, 234–40; J. Jalla, *Storia della riforma in Piemonte fino alla morte di Emanuele Filiberto 1517–1580* (Florence, 1914), pp. 80–90; A. Pascal, 'Le Ambascerie dei cantoni e dei principi protestanti di Svizzera e Germania al Re di Francia in favore dei Valdesi durante il periodo della dominazione francese in Piemonte (1535–1559)', *Bollettino storico-bibliografico subalpino*, vol. 18, nos 1–3 (1913), pp. 91–2.

23   Pazè Beda, *Riforma e cattolicesimo*, pp. 45–52; J. J. Hemardinquer, 'Pour le 403me anniversaire de la prédication publique à Fenestrelles: Les Vaudois du Dauphiné et la résistance à l'insurrection d'après des documents inédits', *Bollettino della Società di Studi Valdesi* 103 (1958), pp. 54–5, 57–63.

24   See A. Dufour, 'Un Document sur les vallées vaudoises en 1556', *Bollettino della Società di Studi Valdesi* 128 (1970), pp. 57–63.

25   Pascal, 'Le Ambascerie', *Bollettino storico-bibliografico subalpino*, vol. 18, nos 1–3 (1913), pp. 91–119, nos 5–6 (1913), pp. 314–36; vol. 19, nos 1–3 (1914), pp. 27–38; A. Hollaender, 'Eine schweizer Gesandtschaftsreise an den französischen Hof im Jahre 1557', *Historische Zeitschrift* NS 33 (1892), pp. 385–410; the detailed correspondence regarding this embassy is also edited in *Calvini Opera*, vol. 16, cols 459–61, 462–3, 469–81, 481–6, 499–503, 538–41, 545–8, 571, 586–7, 590–6, 609–17, and Bèze, *Correspondance*, vol. 2, pp. 73–5, 82–3, 86–94, 118–20, 238–42, 251.

26   François I's letter is printed in C. Schmidt, 'Aktenstücke besonders zur Geschichte der Waldenser', *Zeitschrift für die historische Theologie* 22 (1852), pp. 258–9; note also the reaction to it in *Calvini Opera*, vol. 12, cols 133–6.

27   *Calvini Opera*, vol. 16, cols 459–61; Bèze, *Correspondance*, vol. 2, pp. 62ff., 238–42; Pascal, 'Le Ambascerie', *Bollettino storico-bibliografico subalpino*, vol. 19, nos 1–3 (1914), pp. 27–30.

The situation was made more delicate by the way in which the southern German states had been 'Lutheranized' following the Augsburg 'Interim' of 1548 and especially the Peace of Augsburg in 1555.[28] Lutheran theologians reared in the tradition of Johannes Brenz and the *Swabian syngramma* were especially pernickety about taking the side of those who might turn out to be 'sacramentaries', that is, to espouse eucharistic beliefs which minimized the real bodily presence of Christ in the communion. It was only by cautious mediation that Calvin himself (at least before the debate with Westphal, *c.*1559) contrived not to be irreparably tarred with this brush.[29] At Göppingen in Württemberg in May 1557, Farel and de Bèze tried to prove the orthodoxy of the Waldenses to sceptical Lutherans by presenting them with a eucharistic confession allegedly shared by the churches of 'Switzerland and Savoy'.[30] The problem, now, was that to please the Württemberg Lutherans Farel had tried to represent all of Switzerland – including Zürich, where the memory of Zwingli was still fresh – as adhering to an almost 'Lutheran' eucharistic doctrine. As soon as Heinrich Bullinger heard of the confession, he wrote a furious letter to Geneva denouncing it and blaming it for problems which he was experiencing within Switzerland.[31] From the Waldenses' point of view, this inter-Protestant wrangling was a waste of time and effort. It does demonstrate, though, how important the Waldensian cause had become to the wider Protestant community. Farel and de Bèze could risk opening the rawest of raw sores in the Protestant flank, simply in the hope of obtaining the most powerful and broadly based intercession on the Waldenses' behalf.

Although Henri II met both the Swiss and German embassies in 1557, he gave no concrete assurances. Perhaps aware that his rule over Piedmont was winding down, though, the king seems to have allowed the Waldenses to be left alone, since the Turin *parlement* did little more than make threatening noises thereafter.[32] The Protestants themselves learned

---

28 See E. Cameron, *The European Reformation* (Oxford, 1991), pp. 346–9 for the background.

29 On Calvin's subtle mediation between the Germans and the Zürich Swiss in the 1540s and 1550s, see especially Bruce Gordon, 'Calvin and the Swiss Reformed Churches', in A. Pettegree, A. Duke and G. Lewis (eds), *Calvinism in Europe 1540–1620* (Cambridge, 1994), pp. 64–81.

30 *Calvini Opera*, vol. 16, cols 470–1; Pascal, 'Le Ambascerie', *Bollettino storico-bibliografico subalpino*, vol. 19, nos 1–3 (1914), pp. 33–4.

31 *Calvini Opera*, vol. 16, cols 538–9, 472–81, 539–41, and as above, note 25. See further discussion in E. Cameron, 'One Reformation or Many: Protestant Identities in the Later Reformation in Germany', in O. P. Grell and R. W. Scribner (eds), *Tolerance and Intolerance in the European Reformation* (Cambridge, 1996), pp. 111–13.

32 Gilles, *Histoire ecclésiastique*, vol. 1, pp. 99–100. For the letter of thanks, see A. Vinay, 'Lettre de Busca', *Bulletin de la société d'histoire vaudoise* 7 (1890), pp. 43–60, esp. pp. 44–7.

lessons by their experience. Further embassies would be despatched through the 1560s to raise support against the persecuting acts of the restored Duke of Savoy, Emanuele Filiberto. These were not disrupted by diplomatic or theological rows and appear to have achieved some of their objectives.[33] Moreover, the attitude that one group of Protestants ought to care about the fate of another, even if they were not of precisely the same confession, took deep roots in the later sixteenth century. For good or bad, it had much to do with the rise of 'internationalist' Protestantism in the years around 1600.[34]

10.4 The War of the Edict of Nice

Two incidents in the middle of the sixteenth century projected the Waldenses on to the European stage through the printing press. The first was the massacre of the communities of the Luberon in 1545.[35] The second was the small war waged between the Waldenses of Piedmont and Duke Emanuele Filiberto in 1560–1. However, whereas the Luberon incident was unmitigated tragedy, the story of the Piedmontese Waldenses was one of qualified triumph. It was the story of how, for the first time in their history, the Waldensian communities defended themselves against a threat to their religious identity, in such a way that they won the right to a *public* and *exclusive* profession of their dissenting creed. This story raised all sorts of interesting and challenging issues to the wider Protestant community. Not only was it the story of the true faith under persecution; it was also the story of armed rebellion against a ruler for the sake of the gospel.

Duke Emanuele Filiberto, after some years as the titular but dispossessed Duke of Savoy, was restored to his duchy in 1559 under the terms of the Peace of Cateau-Cambrésis, which had brought to an end the long agony of the Habsburg–Valois Italian wars. It would have been quite comprehensible if Emanuele Filiberto had entered into his inheritance with a deep resentment of organized Protestantism. Not only was Geneva long since lost to Savoyard control; it was also by then a notorious nest of heretical expansionism. Protestant soldiers in French pay had weakened the Church in Piedmont since 1536. In contrast, the participants to the 1559 peace were (it was widely believed) resolved to purge all their lands of heresy now that they were no longer distracted by fight-

---

33 *Calvini Opera*, vol. 17, cols 600–2; Bèze, *Correspondance*, vol. 3, pp. 125–6, 130–1; vol. 6, p. 186; vol. 7, pp. 66, 126, n. 7, 141–6.
34 Cameron, 'One Reformation or Many', pp. 113–14, 126–7.
35 See above, chapter 9.5.

ing each other.[36] For whatever complex of reasons, on 15 February 1560 the duke promulgated the Edict of Nice. It forbade, on pain of a fine and being sent to the galleys, listening to 'Lutheran' preaching in the Val Pellice or elsewhere.

The Waldensian churches' leaders responded as they had done in 1556–7, with a diplomatic initiative. In May they submitted a Prefatory letter, Apology and Confession of Faith to the duke.[37] The Apology and Confession were translated by Scipione Lentolo from the French *Confessio Gallicana* of 1559, but with certain amendments which Calvin himself had proposed to them.[38] There was no question of pretending to be other than reformed; however, such confessions sought to convince rulers of the essential respectability and Christian character of their subscribers. Lentolo's preface to the duke argued that, if the pagan emperors Trajan and Hadrian had mitigated their persecution of Christians when they learned of their good moral conduct, how much more should a Christian prince bear with those whose customs were different, but with whom he shared so much. It appealed to a sense of common nationhood between the duke and his subjects, and insisted on the Waldenses' political loyalty despite differences of creed. The preface even tried to play on the fact that Emanuele Filiberto was descended from the princely house of Saxony, 'by means of which in our times the Lord wished to introduce the Gospel into the world'. It justified the right of princes to make decisions regarding religion and reassured the duke that reading the confession would disprove all the calumnies laid against the Protestants.[39]

In July 1560 a disputation was held in Angrogna between the ministers, led by Scipione Lentolo, and the Jesuit Antonio Possevino, commendator of San Antonio at Fossano, still only 27 and yet to build up his later reputation. These disputations were fairly common in the early stages of the Reformation, though there were no precedents for them in Waldensian history. Rarely were they genuine contests in which the outcome – politically speaking at least – was not predetermined.[40] They gave whichever side administered them the hope of demonstrating the

36   Pascal, 'Le Ambascerie', *Bollettino storico-bibliografico subalpino*, vol. 18, nos 5–6 (1913), p. 334. For a typical Savoyard justification of the campaign, see for example J. Tonsi, *Vita Emmanuelis Philiberti* (Turin, 1596), pp. 144–5.
37   V. Vinay, *Le Confessioni di fede dei Valdesi riformati, con i documenti del dialogo fra la 'prima' e la 'seconda' riforma*, Collana della Facoltà valdese di teologia, 12 (Turin, 1975), pp. 155–78.
38   For the history of the French documents on which the Piedmontese versions were based, see Greengrass, *French Reformation*, pp. 47–54; Léonard, *A History of Protestantism*, vol. 2, pp. 111–20; N. M. Sutherland, *The Huguenot Struggle for Recognition* (New Haven, Conn., 1980), pp. 63–73.
39   Vinay, *Confessioni di fede . . . riformati*, pp. 155–9.
40   On early Reformation disputations, see Cameron, *The European Reformation*, pp. 237–9 and references.

rightness of their cause, and thereby of justifying the policy which it had already been resolved to implement. Often, especially by the later sixteenth century, the disputants found themselves arguing past each other, on the basis of mutually irreconcilable presuppositions. Nevertheless, the disputation of 1560 anticipates, in an uncanny way, the Colloquy of Poissy in the following year in France.[41] Lentolo was sufficiently pleased with his own performance to write it up in his own *History* of the Waldensian churches.[42] Possevino appears to have chosen the themes for debate. He argued, first of all, that the Mass as practised in the Roman Church was of vast antiquity, and indeed that the word 'Mass' could be traced back to a Hebrew word meaning 'consecration'. By implication, this authenticated the consecration of the eucharist, transubstantiation and the sacrificial private Mass. Second, Possevino reproached Lentolo for breaking his vow of celibacy and claimed that the rule of religious celibacy was of vast antiquity in the Church. The debate descended into invective. Possevino refused to believe the claims made by the Waldenses about their own moral standards; he then criticized the allowing of usury in Geneva, the fact that Luther had changed his mind over many issues, and the reformers' calling the pope Antichrist. There was a brief discussion about the respective authority to be accorded to scripture and the Church, after which the debate ended. Afterwards both sides sent pamphlets around the valleys detailing their views; Lentolo even had his rebuttal of Possevino published at Geneva.[43]

It must be doubtful whether these preliminaries did anything more than give the duke time to muster his forces. According to the various narrative accounts compiled at the time, some local landlords in the Val Germanasca by the name of Truchets or Trucchietti rather jumped the gun, attacking the inhabitants of the valley on their own initiative. The duke then commissioned a professional soldier, the Conte della Trinità, to bring the people of the valleys to heel once and for all. This had been done, of course, in the Val Chisone and in the valleys of the Dauphiné in 1487–8; but it seems never to have been attempted in the valleys of Piedmont since the Waldensian movement had been ensconsed there.[44] Della Trinità attacked the Waldenses ferociously; but they defended

41   Léonard, *A History of Protestantism*, vol. 2, pp. 121–8; Sutherland, *Huguenot Struggle*, pp. 73–136.
42   S. Lentolo, *Historia delle Grandi e Crudeli Persecutioni fatti ai tempi nostri . . . contro il Popolo che chiamano Valdese*, ed. T. Gay (Torre Pellice, 1906), pp. 171–6; also Oxford, Bodleian Library, MS Barlow 8, pp. 188ff. The Oxford manuscript, checked and corrected by the author's nephew, is much more complete than the Gay edition or the original manuscript, now in Bern, Stadtsbibliothek, MS. 716.
43   Oxford, Bodleian Library, MS Barlow 8, pp. 188–94. Lentolo included copies of Possevino's treatise (ibid., pp. 194–6) and his own (ibid., pp. 196–221).
44   See above, chapter 7, notes 74–6.

themselves not only with equal fierceness, but also to striking effect. Early in 1561, during a battle for control of Pradeltorno in the Val Germanasca, the Waldenses made use for the first time of their *compagnia volante* or 'light company', a body of a hundred harquebusiers accompanied by a minister, who turned the tide of the fight.[45] By the early summer Emanuele Filiberto must have decided that he had had enough. After negotiations he issued the Edict of Cavour on 5 June 1561. The Edict of Cavour became as it were the prototype of all the pacification documents produced in the French Wars of Religion thereafter. It gave the people of specific named communities a geographically restricted right to exercise their religion in peace, subject to certain conditions; and it gave them an amnesty for their previous rebellion against their sovereign.[46]

The War of the Edict of Nice caused something of a sensation in Europe. Like the epic resistance of Magdeburg to Charles V,[47] it took resistance to the persecuting ruler out of the realm of theoretical speculation and into that of actual experience. It seems likely that the warfare had a crucial effect on relations between ministers and people, and on the solidarity of the formerly 'Waldensian' communities. At the early stages, when conflict seemed likely, the reformers were explicitly anxious to prevent armed resistance. In 1556–7 Calvin and de Bèze had already been worried by the rumours that the Waldenses intended to fight back if they were attacked by the *parlement* of Turin. The Waldenses apparently regarded flight to the mountains as a waste of time, since they would soon be forced down by hunger: resistance was the only option.[48] Nevertheless, at the outset of the 1560–1 war the ministers apparently once again instructed the people to escape to the mountains with their belongings. Within a few days, however, other ministers apparently protested that self-defence, even armed self-defence, to protect true religion and one's own life was permissible. In an interesting echo of Luther's final argument about the emperor as the 'pope's henchman', it

---

45 Balmas and Theiller, *Storia delle persecuzioni*, pp. 168, 288.
46 The text of the Edict of Cavour is edited in Balmas and Theiller, *Storia delle persecuzioni*, pp. 194–200, and also cited by Lentolo, MS Barlow 8, pp. 294–302. Other accounts of the war include a brief manuscript by Lentolo in Cambridge, University Library, MS. Dd. 3. 33, fos 1r–2v; and the contemporary *Histoire mémorable de la guerre faite par le duc de Savoye contre ses subjectz des vallées* (n. p., 1561); modern edition by E. Balmas and V. Diena (Turin, 1972).
47 On the siege of Magdeburg and the theoretical implications of its resistance, see O. K. Olson, 'Theology of Revolution: Magdeburg, 1550–1551', *Sixteenth Century Journal* 3 (1972), pp. 56–79; Q. Skinner, *The Foundations of Modern Political Thought*, 2 vols (Cambridge, 1978), vol. 2, pp. 207–9.
48 *Calvini Opera*, vol. 16, cols 102–4, 719–20; Bèze, *Correspondance*, vol. 2, pp. 41–2, 141–2.

was argued that since the pope was stirring up the war, not the duke himself, armed resistance was permissible.[49] By the later stages of the war a minister was regularly accompanying the light company to lead the Waldensian soldiery in prayers before battle; such prayers apparently terrified their enemies when heard from a distance.[50]

It seems extremely likely that the co-operation between ministers and people in the war of 1560–1 played a vital role in bonding the pastors to their flocks. One minister actually said as much, in a letter of October 1561: until the persecutions of the previous year it had been difficult for the ministers to get through to their people and instruct them; now, however, they were responding more favourably.[51] When confronted by an attacking army, the new Protestant clergy had stood by their congregations in a way which, it must be said, none of the old Waldensian *barbes* had done. It would have been easy enough for the immigrant clergy to take flight before the war had broken out, but they had stayed with their people. That in no way eliminated the pastoral problems of relationships between ministers and lay people, but it must at least have set their relations on some sort of stable footing.

10.5 The French Wars of Religion in the Dauphiné

Because the conflict in the Duchy of Savoy was relatively compact and brief, it is sometimes favoured in Waldensian historiography over the much more confusing story of the establishment of a Huguenot stronghold in the territories of the Dauphiné. Here sporadic armed conflicts began even earlier than elsewhere in France and the spin-offs from that conflict played a significant part in establishing the Huguenot Protestant Church in regions of former Waldensian influence and activity. Nevertheless, these conflicts marked a real change in the relationship between religious dissent and rural society. In the late middle ages, heretics and Catholics had coexisted, worshipped together though in some respects differently, and had only been polarized under the extreme conditions of the 1487–8 crusade. In the 1560s and afterwards, the two religious communities were set at odds in a much more graphic and violent way. Districts were forcibly removed from Catholic control and placed under that of bands of armed Protestants.

---

49 Balmas and Theiller, *Storia delle persecuzioni*, pp. 121–3, 258–9. On the Lutheran equivalents to this argument, see W. D. J. Cargill Thompson, *The Political Thought of Martin Luther*, ed. P. Broadhead (Brighton, 1984), pp. 108–11.
50 Balmas and Diena, *Histoire mémorable*, pp. 100–2.
51 *Calvini Opera*, vol. 19, cols 28–9.

As early as 1560 the *parlement* at Grenoble was aware that Huguenot leaders were taking advantage of the isolated nature of the Val Pragelato, which formed part of the salient of the Dauphiné east of the Alpine passes, to build up a stronghold. By March of that year the Protestant minister in the district, Martin Tachard, led a band to invade and despoil the Catholic churches at Fenestrelle, Pragelato and Usseaux. The ornaments were smashed and the buildings converted for the use of Protestant congregations. In April Tachard led some 150 men across into the Val Germanasca in Savoy, to help the people of the hamlet of Riclaretto.[52] By around the middle of the year the Pragelato was being used by the Huguenot captains Paulon de Mauvans and Charles du Puy de Montbrun. An armed expedition planned by the *parlement* of Grenoble in the winter of 1560–1 failed to materialize. In January 1561 the people of Pragelato formed a defensive pact with those of Piedmont. Even in military matters, the old heretical associations counted for more than national political frontiers. Later in 1561 the Protestants of the Upper Val Chisone spread their creed by force into the lower valley as well.[53]

Reciprocal aid between former Waldenses in different districts was offered on subsequent occasions also. In April 1569 Protestants from Angrogna in Piedmont went to the assistance of the Huguenot soldiers who had captured the fort of Exilles, in the upper Valle di Susa near the passes. Although the Protestants still lost control of Exilles, this mission inaugurated regular arrangements for assistance from the Piedmontese, negotiated by the ministers of the Val Chisone, who included the former *barbe* Philippe Pastre.[54] In July 1573 ministers and people under François Guérin of Dronero routed the Catholic Carlo Birago at San Germano Chisone. In late March 1574 Guérin invaded the Catholic valley of the Queyras with 200 men from Angrogna and converted it to Protestantism by armed force. Catholic historians reported a series of atrocity stories about Guérin's group. Whatever the truth of these, it seems clear that this Genevan trainee from the marquisate of Saluzzo had discovered a talent for spreading the reformed gospel with sudden force and terror. When the Queyras was under attack from the Catholics in the early 1580s, they sought and received further help from those of Angrogna. This assistance allowed them to hold out until the upper valley of the

52   Balmas and Theiller, *Storia delle persecuzioni*, pp. 103–5, 248–9; Hemardinquer, 'Les Vaudois du Dauphiné', pp. 62–3.
53   On this episode, see especially Pazè Beda, *Riforma e cattolicesimo*, pp. 52–62.
54   Ibid., pp. 71–2; A. Pascal, 'La lotta contro la riforma in Piemonte al tempo di Emmanuele Filiberto, studiata nelle relazioni diplomatiche tra la corte Sabauda e la Santa Sede (1559–1580)', *Bulletin de la société d'histoire vaudoise* 53 (1929), pp. 77–80.

Durance was captured by the Huguenot grandee the Duc de Lesdiguières, who seized Embrun in 1585.[55]

Such violent solidarity in defence of the reformed faith radically transformed the social structure of the Waldensian communities. In the late fifteenth century the *barbes* had provided some of the spiritual services of the Waldensian followers; but it was their own community leaders who saw to the collecting of funds for legal and physical defence.[56] After the formation of settled churches the pastor assumed a much more controlling role, as both the religious and the political leader of the community.

10.6   Pastors and Flocks in a 'Heretical' Community

Yet it would be a mistake to assume that in every case the relationship between pastors and people was a tranquil or an easy one. It is widely accepted among historians of the Reformation that something quite unprecedented happened to the social relationships of minister and people when the first generation of university- or academy-educated reformed ministers were installed in their parishes. Intellectuals who would previously have been confined to the comfortable seclusion of monasteries, cathedral chapters or university colleges now took their creed to real people in their real-life predicaments. For ministers and people alike, the result was often a rude shock. The new clergy were dismayed to discover just how ignorant their people really had become; the people were alarmed by the sky-high expectations in terms of mental effort and attentiveness which their new incumbents made of them.[57] For a while – at least until a generation or so had passed, and relations between ministers and their people adjusted and settled down – one finds clergy writing what has been called a 'literature of complaint', in which the ministers lamented the thankless and distasteful aspects of their ministries.[58]

The Waldensian churches offer a particular and very special kind of case-study in this phenomenon. On the one hand, these parishes were not unwilling victims of a religious policy determined from above by a

---

55   On the Queyras and its forced reformation, see E. Cameron, *The Reformation of the Heretics: The Waldenses of the Alps 1480–1580* (Oxford, 1984), pp. 225–7 and references; sources include Marc'Aurelio Rorengo de' Conti di Lucerna, *Memorie Historiche dell'introduttione dell'heresie nelle valli di Lucerna, Marchesato di Saluzzo, e altre di Piemonte . . .* (Turin, 1649), pp. 81–9; P. Gioffredo, *Storia delle Alpi Marittime*, ed. C. Gazzera, Monumenta Historiae Patriae, Scriptorum vol. 2 (Turin, 1839), cols 1,510ff., 1,516ff.

56   See above, chapter 5, note 18; chapter 7, notes 157–63.

57   On this large subject, see Cameron, *The European Reformation*, pp. 389–410 and references.

58   Ibid., pp. 411–16 and references.

remote and unaccountable sovereign, a duke of Württemberg or a queen of England. On the contrary, the peoples of Piedmont had been born into a non-Catholic religious tradition with which they identified fiercely and which they defended to the point of bloodshed. There was no question of 'alienation' between the Waldensian laity and their special confessional position after the Peace of Cavour. Yet, on the other hand, the Waldensian people had not been 'converted' to the specific message of Calvin and Geneva as had, say, the Huguenots of the Languedoc, or the bourgeois of Antwerp or Edinburgh. They had accepted an offer of help from a new class of religious leaders who promised to lead them into a better form of religion. Their identity was still, to some extent, bound up with their heretical past as well as their reformed present. In such circumstances they might have been even more difficult to handle than those who came to Protestantism by more conventional routes.

For the most part, one depends on reading between the lines of the surviving sources to discern how ministers related to their congregations. The ministers sent by Geneva to the Waldensian valleys were an extremely diverse set of characters, who responded to the challenges of their new charges in very different ways. As was discussed earlier, a significant proportion of the new ministers soon adopted the militant, even violent habits which proved necessary to defend and extend the scope of the new churches.[59] Others responded differently. Étienne Noel seems to have conformed as closely as possible to the ideal of the peaceful, conscientious parish minister, learned and highly esteemed wherever he served. He found Angrogna an extremely difficult and painful charge. Travelling around the mountains took a great toll on him. By 1563 he had lost all the books which he had originally taken there (presumably in the 1560–1 war); at that point he plainly wished to bring his family away from Angrogna to join him in Grenoble.[60]

Another minister tried to keep hold of his congregation by means other than sheer moral prestige. According to a letter sent to Geneva in July 1563, Cosme Brevin, the minister at Fenestrelle in the Val Chisone, had resorted to stand-up comedy. His sermons appear to have been a riot of jokes, exaggerated gestures and word-play. Most dangerously for the church, he devised satirical names and puns with which to make fun of the military leaders in the district, Catholic and Protestant alike, as well as the kings of France and Spain. The Huguenot soldiery who attended his sermons in light-coloured felt hats he called 'white pigs'. Nearer home, he quarrelled with the local syndic, refused to baptize his son and mocked him in his sermons. Moreover, when removed from Fenestrelle he gravitated down the valley to Pinasca, where he preached in compe-

---

59   See, for example, the case of Martin Tachard above, note 52.
60   Bèze, *Correspondance*, vol. 4, pp. 272–3; cf. *Calvini Opera*, vol. 16, cols 532–3.

tition to the settled pastor and drew his congregation away.[61] Eventually he returned to Geneva and was then sent to cause as little harm as possible as minister of Sark in the Channel Islands.[62]

In complete contrast to Cosme Brevin, the Piedmontese Waldensian valleys offer one spectacularly detailed instance of the 'literature of complaint'. Scipione Lentolo, minister in Piedmont from late 1559 until c.1566, wrote a history of the Waldensian Church shortly after his departure from his parish. This history remained in manuscript until 1906, when a printed edition was prepared, which extensively edited and trimmed the text.[63] Some time after its compilation an authenticated copy of the manuscript was made, which now seems to constitute the only complete and authentic copy of Lentolo's text.[64] The significance of the original text of Lentolo's history for this part of the story lies in the entirely unedited and unpublished eighth book of the work. In this book, Lentolo explained why the Waldenses had suffered so many persecutions and hardships down the ages, as the previous books of the history had just recounted. The explanation was that they committed five principal sins. They despised the word of God; they lacked fear of God; they were not zealous for the honour of God; they did not respect their pastors; and they were avaricious and dedicated to worldly goods.[65]

This devastating and minutely detailed diatribe occupies the last hundred pages or so of the Oxford copy of Lentolo's manuscript. Clearly Lentolo found his seven years or so in Piedmont vexing in the extreme. The people were reluctant to come to hear his sermons more than once a week; Sunday was their maximum. When they alleged poverty and work as the reason for their absence, Lentolo asked sarcastically if they would attend if the minister were to give a *scudo* to everyone who attended.[66] He also pointed out that for large parts of the year the land was unworkable because of snow (apparently not considering that snow might interrupt church attendance as well!).[67] The people reacted angrily to sermons which denounced their vices, especially avarice; in the manuscript he told stories of landowners who cheated their tenants, or families who put off children's marriages because of haggling over property.[68] More serious than their truculence was the Waldensian laity's invincible ignorance. They resented being told to buy Bibles and even resisted sending their

---

61   *Calvini Opera*, vol. 20, cols 79–84.
62   See A. H. Ewen and A. R. De Carteret, *The Fief of Sark* (Guernsey, 1969), pp. 42, 46, 57–8.
63   Lentolo, *Historia delle Grandi e Crudeli Persecutioni*, ed. T. Gay.
64   Oxford, Bodleian Library, MS Barlow 8; see above, note 42.
65   Lentolo, MS Barlow 8, pp. 473–5, 482–3, 491–511.
66   Ibid., pp. 493–4.
67   Ibid., p. 494.
68   Ibid., pp. 497–8, 523–5.

children to school to read.[69] They were mostly illiterate and even such documents as the Creed which they knew by heart, they needed to have explained to them by the pastor.[70] In consequence, Lentolo appears to have taught by an intimidating, repetitive method of rote learning, based on the framing of a simple catechism on one or two of the clauses of the Apostles' Creed for each Sunday. He then tried to have as many as possible of the congregation rehearse this short catechism to him during a series of gatherings during the following week.[71]

Lentolo was eventually forced to leave the valleys after he had attempted to interfere in the election of syndics and *conseillers* for his community, and had stormed in a rage at the people when the election did not go in favour of his approved candidates.[72] Lentolo's account (which has hardly been vigorously exploited in recent Waldensian historiography!) raises intriguing questions about the relationships between ministers and people. Essentially, how typical was this sort of confrontation between learned urban minister and self-reliant, obstinate mountain people? Lentolo was certainly not the first or the last Protestant minister to find that weekday services were poorly attended, or that catechism classes were hopelessly unpopular, especially among the adult laity.[73] However, not all pastoral relationships broke down quite so spectacularly as Lentolo's. More striking is the fact that Lentolo himself, on the evidence of his later career, does not seem to have been without political skill. After leaving Piedmont he was settled at Sondrio in the Valtelline by September 1567. There he involved himself in the debates surrounding the heterodox Italian theologians who settled in the Valtelline after leaving Italy: intelligent, fractious individuals influenced by Camillo Renato and the Sozzini. In 1570 he prevailed upon the Grisons governors of the Valtelline to impose a standard of Calvinist orthodoxy on their Protestant subjects, and brought a discipline hitherto absent to the Italian-speaking reformed churches of the region. Lentolo may have been pathologically earnest, but he was not absolutely impossible.[74] The clear implication is therefore that Lentolo and the indomitable peasants of the Waldensian valleys were spectacularly ill-suited. Each grated on the other, and there were probably faults on both sides. In Lentolo's eyes, the Waldenses wore their Protestantism like a badge of allegiance: they would

69 Ibid., p. 495.
70 Ibid., pp. 506–12.
71 Ibid., pp. 513–14, 518–20.
72 Ibid., pp. 580–1.
73 See especially G. Strauss, *Luther's House of Learning: Indoctrination of the Young in the German Reformation* (Baltimore, Md., 1978), pp. 268–99.
74 On Lentolo's later, more successful career in reformed church politics see Mark Taplin, 'The Italian Reformers and the Zurich Church, c.1540–1620', St Andrews Ph.D. thesis, 1999, pp. 204–44.

fight for it, but they were not keen to learn it, and they would certainly avoid dying for it if at all possible.[75]

One issue signally fails to make any sort of appearance in the eighth book of Lentolo's history. Absolutely nothing is said about any continuing role for the *barbes*, the former medieval pastors of the Waldenses. From reading his text – and indeed the vast body of the correspondence generated by the reformers dealing with the Waldenses after 1555 – one is given the impression that there were ministers and there was the undifferentiated mass of the lay people. The experience of being drawn into the international association of Protestant Churches had homogenized the Waldensian laity into a mass of rural people, to be educated and disciplined. Did this mean the end of medieval Waldensianism? In a sense, it certainly did; just as the advent of the Reformation overwhelmed and obliterated all popular heresies in western Europe. There were no more Waldenses in the old sense, just as there were no more Lollards or Free Spirits. On the other hand, the self-awareness of the Waldenses as a people, their peculiar identity and the long ancestry ascribed to them, made them a unique kind of heretic. They became, not just a people to be instructed and cared for, but a debating tool to be used in the confessional polemics of the later sixteenth century. As the 'Waldenses' were becoming ever more thoroughly merged into the Calvinist world, they were brought more and more into the limelight as factors in the history of the 'True Church', through which the Reformation traced its ancestry back to the time of the apostles and the Church Fathers.

75   Lentolo, MS Barlow 8, p. 492.

Epilogue

The Waldenses as Persecuted Martyrs and the 'True Church'

As was seen earlier, the Waldenses were, in actual practice, extremely unclear about their own origins and history. The combination of myth and legend with their collective memory, and the loss of whatever documents might have existed, conspired to prevent the growth of any specific or detailed historical consciousness.[1] It is all the more ironic, therefore, that the Waldenses became, in the 150 years or so after their incorporation into the reformed Churches, a very potent and important debating tool in Church history. The reasons for the Waldenses' involvement in the confessional debates are rooted in inter-sectarian polemic and apocalyptic. Initially, many Catholic writers who opposed the first Protestant theologians argued that the Protestants were doing no more than reviving old heresies. Luther's opponent at the Leipzig debate of 1519, Johannes Maier von Eck, claimed that Luther was echoing the condemned errors of Jan Hus.[2] In his *Enchiridion* Eck pressed the argument still further: the Protestants were resuscitating the teachings of Wyclif, even of the Albigenses.[3] In imagery borrowed from the Old Testament prophets, the Protestants were accused of digging out the old, cracked cisterns of error in place of the clear spring of truth.[4] As a debating ploy to humiliate a few contentious academics, this argument might have been expected to be adequate. As the Reformation spread and its adherents multiplied, however, the idea of embarrassing the thousands of Protestant followers by associating them with disreputable, misguided

1 For example, see above, chapters 6.4, 7.1.
2 For the Leipzig debate, see for example B. J. Kidd (ed.), *Documents Illustrative of the Continental Reformation* (Oxford, 1911), pp. 47, 49–50.
3 Johannes [Maier von] Eck, *Enchiridion locorum communium* (Ingolstadt, 1541), fo. 5v; cf. also fos 11v, 162v. The original edition appeared in 1535.
4 'Lutherani relinquentes verum et vivum fontem ecclesiae, fodiunt cisternas dissipatas haereticorum, Wikleff, Husz, Albigentium etc.' This is a reference to Jeremiah 2:13.

forebears became less plausible. Instead, another quite contradictory argument took its place. Everyone agreed that the prophecy of Christ, that he would be with his Church forever, could not but be true.[5] Yet such a prophecy implied that there must be a continuous, visible succession of the Church from the time of the apostles to the present. Only the Roman Catholic Church (so it was argued from the western Europe-centred viewpoint of the sixteenth century!) fulfilled that prophecy. The Church of the Reformation was no older than the time of Martin Luther. How, therefore, could the reformers claim to represent the 'True Church'?[6]

The reformers' answer, from the 1550s onwards, was that the True Church and the visible hierarchy of Rome, with its popes and its prelates, were not the same thing. By general consent, there were unedifying and embarrassing episodes in the history of the medieval papacy. When to disciplinary failings one added the theological 'errors' of papal primacy, canon law, scholastic theology, purgatory, saint-worship and so forth, it became possible to claim that the True Church had altogether ceased to exist within the Catholic dispensation.[7] Therefore, if the True Church had not existed within Catholicism, where was it? At this point the Protestant theologians discovered the Waldenses, as just one of a whole mass of anti-papal, anti-sacerdotal heretics whose condemnation and exclusion from the Church coincided very neatly with the apogee of papal power and medieval scholasticism. If the Church was not truly with the pope and his minions, it must have been with the persecuted minorities, with the little tradition, hidden but not altogether invisible.[8] For some authors, the interpretation of the Book of Revelation supported this view.

---

5   Matthew 28:20.
6   See John Foxe, *Acts and Monuments*, ed. J. Pratt, 4th edn (London, n. d.), vol. 1, p. 8, who summarizes his opponents' arguments in the form of a syllogism: 'Forasmuch as an ordinary and known church visible must here be known continually on earth, during from the time of the apostles, to which church all other churches must have recourse: and seeing there is no other church visible, orderly known to have existed from the apostles' time, but only the church of Rome: they conclude, therefore, that the church of Rome is that church whereunto all other churches must have recourse.'
7   See, for instance, Calvin's denunciation of Rome in *Institutes*, IV, ii, 2: 'in withdrawing from deadly participation in so many misdeeds [i.e. Roman belief and worship] there is accordingly no danger that we may be snatched away from the church of Christ'.
8   See Foxe, *Acts and Monuments*, vol. 1, p. xxi: '[in the later middle ages] the true church of Christ, although it durst not openly appear in the face of the world, oppressed by tyranny; yet neither was it so invisible or unknown, but, by the providence of the Lord, some remnant always remained from time to time, which not only showed secret good affection to sincere doctrine, but also stood in open defence of truth against the disordered church of Rome.'

After the dragon, the devil, was bound in the pit for a thousand years, it was predicted that he 'must be let out for a little while'.[9] The period during which the Church existed in the persecuted minorities could be said to coincide with this 'loosing of Satan', an indefinite but limited period of mischief which had been brought to an end by the Reformation.[10]

Protestant theologians were therefore given potent reasons to investigate the Waldenses and hold them up as evidence of the continuity of the True Church during years of popish darkness. However, the debate did not stop there. Roman Catholic theologians and polemicists, especially in the late sixteenth and early seventeenth centuries, refused to accept the Protestant argument lying down. They studied the documentary evidence for medieval heresies, including Waldensianism, with enthusiasm and care, then gleefully pointed out that the heretics of the middle ages were not, after all, the antecedents of the reformers. Some, like the Cathars, had taught *outré* and bizarre errors which Protestants and Catholics alike disowned; others, like the Waldenses, had been far closer to Catholicism in many aspects of their belief and practice than they were to the Protestants.[11] The thrust of Catholic argument was to show the diversity, the plurality, the inconsistency of medieval heretics, where before they had been tempted to point out their general consistency and common features.

This debate formed the intellectual context in which the Waldensian heresy was written about in the early modern period. Histories were written about the Waldenses on their own. Their sufferings, the stories of their martyrdoms both individual and collective, were written into the corpus of hagiographic literature which spread across Protestant Europe and helped to build up a sense of pan-Protestant solidarity. Finally, articles on the medieval Waldenses were written into theological histories and treatises, which sought to demonstrate the continuity of the True Church within the dissenting tradition. All of these historical traditions

---

9 Revelation 20:1–3, 7–8.

10 Foxe, *Acts and Monuments*, vol. 1, pp. 4–5; vol. 2, pp. 724–6; James Ussher, *Gravissimae quaestionis, de Christianarum ecclesiarum in occidentis praesertim partibus, ab apostolicis temporibus ad nostram usque aetatem, continue successione et statu, Historica explicatio* (London, 1613), sigs A2v–A3r, and pp. 142–9.

11 See, for example, the English Jesuits' answers to Foxe, in N. Sanderus, *De visibili monarchia ecclesiae* (Würzburg, 1592), pp. 469–81; (Robert Parsons), *A Treatise of Three Conversions of England*, 3 vols (n.p., 1603), vol. 1, pp. 513–46. For discussion see E. Cameron, 'Medieval Heretics as Protestant Martyrs', in D. Wood (ed.), *Martyrs and Martyrologies: Papers read at the 1992 summer meeting and the 1993 winter meeting of the Ecclesiastical History Society*, Studies in Church History, vol. 30 (Oxford, 1993), pp. 203–4 and references.

began at roughly the same time, in the latter half of the 1550s, as Protestant historical writing was taking off.[12]

The earliest accounts of the Waldenses were, in terms of chronology, those which documented the latest chapters in their history. They were the writings prompted by the massacres in Provence in 1545 and by the War in Piedmont of 1560–1. Narratives of these events were issued under separate covers, as small books or pamphlets.[13] Some of the same texts were then incorporated into the larger martyrological collections: the most widely circulated narratives of Provence and Piedmont were, for instance, transcribed one after another into John Foxe's *Acts and Monuments*, the official martyrology of the Church of England.[14] In fact, so generally was it accepted that the Waldenses of Provence and Piedmont should be numbered among the martyrs, that even relatively even-handed or secular histories of the sixteenth century retold their story in much the same manner as the martyrologists: accounts of their experiences were included by such historians as Johannes Sleidan, Henri-Lancelot de la Popelinière, Théodore-Agrippa d'Aubigné and Jacques-Auguste de Thou.[15]

Alongside the martyrological accounts, a separate tradition developed which described the Waldenses in general, without regard to specific places or people, as an example of early resistance to Roman Catholicism. In this tradition, the Waldenses were essentially a list of beliefs, or rather unbeliefs: similar to the reformers in the negative sense that they rejected purgatory, the Mass, clerical celibacy (*sic*) and the primacy of the pope; and in the positive sense that they believed in the primacy of the Bible and the sole mediation of Christ. These 'articles' of Waldensianism gained circulation through their inclusion in the *Catalogue of Witnesses to the*

---

12 On early Reformation historiography the standard authority remains A. G. Dickens and J. M. Tonkin, *The Reformation in Historical Thought* (Oxford, 1986); see also Bruce Gordon (ed.), *Protestant History and Identity in Sixteenth-century Europe*, 2 vols (Aldershot, 1996).

13 See, for example, (Jean Crespin), *Histoire mémorable de la persécution et saccagement du peuple de Mérindol et Cabrières et autres circonvoisins, appelez Vaudois* (n.p., 1556); *Histoire mémorable de la guerre faite par le duc de Savoye contre ses subjectz des vallées* (n. p., 1561); *Histoire des persecutions et guerres faites depuis l'an 1555 jusques en l'an 1561 contre le peuple appelé Vaudois* ... (n.p., 1562); and entries in the martyrologies, as for example, J. Crespin, *Histoire des martyrs* (n.p., 1619), fos 141r–55v, 195v–7v, 583v–600r.

14 Foxe, *Acts and Monuments*, vol. 4, pp. 474ff., 507ff.; for martyrological histories where these accounts are included, see E. Cameron, *The Reformation of the Heretics: The Waldenses of the Alps 1480–1580* (Oxford, 1984), pp. 237ff.

15 J. Sleidanus, *De statu religionis et reipublicae ... commentarii* (Strasbourg, 1556), fos 217r–19r; H.-L. V. de la Popelinière, *L'Histoire de la France* (La Rochelle, 1581), fos 24r–9v, 245r–54v; E. Agrippa d'Aubigné, *Histoire universelle* (Maillé, 1616–20), vol. 1, pp. 66–81; J. A. Thuanus, *Historiarum sui temporis* (Paris, 1604–8), vol. 1, pp. 455–73; vol. 3, pp. 19–50.

Truth published in 1556 by the ultra-Lutheran theologian and Church historian Matthias Flacius Illyricus (1520–75).[16] The attempt to reduce the Waldenses to an idealized schema of theological statements forced the Protestant theologians to delve into the medieval literature, in a way that the narratives of the sixteenth-century persecutions did not. Flacius Illyricus included large extracts from the last version of the thirteenth-century treatise on the German Waldenses by the Passauer Anonymous.[17] Flacius then had to explain away elements of this text which described the Waldenses as holding beliefs not shared by the Protestants, such as voluntary religious poverty, or the rejection of excommunication, oaths or marriage. This was largely done by inserting marginal comments designed to discredit the Catholic source. However, at times he argued that the Catholic sources could be disproved by comparison between each other. Here the semantic confusion between Waldenses and Hussites proved extremely convenient. Pius II, in his *History of Bohemia*, had included a brief paragraph describing 'Waldensian' beliefs, which actually listed some of the 'errors' of the Hussites.[18] These 'Bohemian' errors were comfortably closer to the Reformation than those of the thirteenth-century Waldenses, and a range of historians used them.[19]

The Protestant claim of a continuous but hidden succession of the True Church through the heresies of the middle ages aroused the ire of Catholic controversialists, especially those from the Jesuit order. Nicholas Sanders, for example, in his *On the Visible Monarchy of the Church*, argued that the Waldenses had been shown to reject all oaths and capital punishment and to justify sexual libertinage.[20] Robert Parsons or Persons, in his *Of the Three Conversions of England*, mocked Foxe's 'ridiculous succession of the Church': he argued that it was as though one were to write the history of London out of the lives of all the criminals hanged at

16   M. Flacius Illyricus, *Catalogus Testium Veritatis qui ante nostram aetatem reclamarunt papae* (Basel, 1556), pp. 704–12. Although Flacius was a rabid and sectarian Lutheran, his work was also current in the Calvinist world in 'S. G. S.' (= S. Goulart, ed.), *Catalogus Testium Veritatis, qui ante nostram aetatem Pontifici Romano atque Papismi erroribus reclamarunt* (Lyon, 1597; later edition, Geneva, 1608).

17   Flacius Illyricus, *Catalogus Testium Veritatis* (1556), pp. 723–57; for the Passauer Anonymous, see above, chapter 6, notes 14, 18.

18   Aeneas Sylvius Piccolomini, *Historia Bohemica*, as edited in his *Opera Omnia* (Basel, 1551), pp. 103–4.

19   Bohemian evidence for the 'Waldenses' is used, for example, in Flacius Illyricus, *Catalogus Testium Veritatis* (1556), pp. 760–1; M. Freherus, *Rerum Bohemicarum antiqui scriptores* (Hanover, 1602), pp. 238–68; Ussher, *Gravissimae quaestionis, de . . . successione et statu*, pp. 154–8, 234–5, 296–9; even in J. Chassanion, *Histoire des Albigeois* (Geneva, 1595), pp. 37–48. See Cameron, 'Medieval Heretics as Protestant Martyrs', pp. 199–202.

20   Sanderus, *De visibili monarchia ecclesiae*, pp. 469–81.

Tyburn in the past few centuries.[21] However, none of the English Jesuits approached the enthusiasm for recovering documents of medieval heresy displayed by the Ingolstadt scholar Jakob Gretser (1561–1625). In a raft of volumes Gretser published in their entirety a large proportion of the surviving late medieval literary texts written against the Waldenses; indeed, his editions remain in many instances the most accessible versions of those texts.[22] The burden of evidence far outweighed the point to be made, which was a very simple one: the sources did not support the idea that the Waldenses were forerunners of the reformers.

The Jesuit enterprise in no way dismayed the Protestant scholars, who still wished to claim the Waldenses as their own. James Ussher (1581–1656) in his first major work, the *Historical Exposition of the Unbroken Succession and State of the Christian Church*, published in 1613, made the Waldenses pivotal to his argument that the True Church had existed among the heretics through the later middle ages. However, unlike the apologists of the 1550s, he addressed a large range of the texts which had been adduced by the Catholic controversialists. Ussher used some ingenuity here. Whereas the Catholics had simply argued that the vast range of witnesses proved that Waldensian beliefs were not proto-Protestant, Ussher pointed out the great diversity of opinion found in those witnesses. Since *ex hypothesi* there was a 'Waldensian tradition' which reached back into the very remote past, and that tradition was more or less homogeneous,[23] then the diversity of the medieval testimonies raised a problem. Simply, some of them must be wrong; and after all, did not the Catholic authors of such documents have every reason to falsify and traduce the beliefs of their opponents and the victims of their persecutions?[24] Having demonstrated the inconsistencies in the sources, Ussher steered his description of the Waldenses back to the safe

21   Parsons, *A Treatise of Three Conversions*, vol. 1, pp. 513–46.
22   Gretser's most important services to editing the sources for Waldensian history were J. Gretser, *Lucae Tudensis episcopi, scriptores aliquot succedanei contra sectam Waldensium: nunc primum in lucem editi cum prolegomenis et notis; in quibus de Waldensium factionibus, peruersisq[ue] dogmatis copiose disseritur* (Ingolstadt, 1613), but here consulted in M. de la Bigne (ed.), *Magna Bibliotheca Veterum Patrum*, 15 vols (Cologne, 1618–22), vol. 13, pp. 297–342; and *Trias scriptorum adversus Waldensium sectam* (Ingolstadt, 1614); for a more fragmentary study of German literary remains to prove Germany's Catholic past, see J. Gretser, *Murices catholicae et Germanicae antiquitatis, sectariorum predicantium pedibus positi et sparsi* (Ingolstadt, 1608). Of Gretser's *Opera Omnia*, 17 vols (Ratisbon, 1734–41): volume 12 is partly devoted to writings about the Waldenses.
23   Ussher, *Gravissimae quaestionis, de . . . successione et statu*, pp. 209–55.
24   Ibid, p. 153. Ussher accuses the Catholics of systematic falsification because of the allegations of libertinage made against the Waldenses: 'Hisce maxime sunt gemina quae, licet non eadem elegantia, pari tamen malitia, de Waldensibus declamare consueverunt Pontificiorum Fraterculorum mendicabula'. On pp. 159–73 he dissects minutely nine 'errors' which he finds in Parsons's description of the Waldenses.

territory of some of the late Bohemian evidence and the conciliatory, irenic, Protestant-influenced confessions derived from Provence in the 1540s.[25]

By this means Ussher was able, not only to make the Waldenses appear moderate and respectable in their beliefs, but also to make them paradigmatic for other medieval heretics. He did so by introducing the idea of critical, selective use of the surviving medieval evidence, based on the assumption that records left by inquisitors were subject to exaggeration, falsification, or the distorting effects of prejudice and torture. This line of argument made the possession of the records – obtaining the physical evidence of the trials of heretics – an important goal for reformed historians, who wished to gain extra ammunition for the polemical debate. In the case of the trial records generated by the Dauphiné inquisitions of the fifteenth century, religious conflict and scholarly controversy are curiously interwoven. In November 1585 the Huguenot warlord Lesdiguières was besieging Embrun, and the defenders of the archbishop's palace retired across a wooden gallery to the 'Tour Brune' (originally the archbishop's prison, where suspected heretics had been held). The defenders cut down the gallery to try to escape pursuit, and the records of the archbishop's inquisitions, which had been stored in the gallery, spilled into the street. They were collected by two Huguenot nobles, Soffrey de Calignon and Marc Vulson.[26] Lesdiguières appears to have taken charge of the documents, and the synods of the Dauphiné cast around to find a historian to write them up. Eventually in 1605 the minister of Nyons, Jean-Paul Perrin, was assigned the task: he completed his two-volume work on the Waldenses and Albigenses by 1617, and the book was published two years later. It was subsequently translated into English and German.[27] Perrin, and later Marc Vulson, argued on the basis of some scraps surviving in the trial dossiers that the scribes' initial 'notes' taken at interrogation were much less detailed than the final version of

25   Ibid., pp. 154, 173, 301–3.
26   J.-P. Perrin, *Histoire des Vaudois, divisée en trois parties* (Geneva, 1618 and 1619), preface and p. 128.
27   Daniel Chamier, a distinguished theologian, was the first to turn down the task of writing up the material: see M. Fornier, *Histoire générale des Alpes maritimes ou cottiennes et . . . de leur métropolitan Embrun*, ed. J. Guillaume, 3 vols (Paris, 1890–2), vol. 2, p. 195; J. Jalla, 'Synodes vaudois', *Bulletin de la société d'histoire vaudoise* 21 (1904), pp. 62–3; G. Miolo, *Historia breve e vera de gl'affari de i valdesi delle valli*, ed. E. Balmas (Turin, 1971), pp. 7–9. The work was translated as *The Bloudy rage of that Great Antichrist of Rome, and his superstitious adherents, against the true Church of Christ* (also entitled in some editions *Luther's fore-runners, or a Cloud of Witnesses, deposing for the Protestant faith*), trans. S. Lennard (London, 1624); and partially as J. J. Grassern, *Waldenser Chronick . . .* (Basel, 1623). For the historiography of Perrin's work, see also J. H. Todd, *The Books of the Vaudois: The Waldensian Manuscripts Preserved in the Library of Trinity College, Dublin* (London, 1865), pp. 116–25.

the inquisitorial registers, and that such 'sumpta' showed inquisitorial falsification at work.[28]

The story of the Dauphiné dossiers did not stop there. James Ussher,
installed as Primate of Ireland, appears to have corresponded with Jean-
Paul Perrin at some date after the completion of his work, and to have
obtained a significant proportion of his dossier. This, at least, is the most
plausible explanation for the presence in the library of Trinity College,
Dublin, of seventeenth-century copies of two of the Dauphiné trial registers,[29] besides the original of the dialect Morel-Bucer dossier of 1530
and a large proportion of the surviving dialect tracts. Many of the marginal notes, excisions and deletions in the Dublin manuscripts are in the
same spindly, thin hand which is very likely to be that of Perrin himself;
and in most instances the clear purpose of the notes is to remove from
the record pieces of evidence which were unhelpful to the argument that
the Waldenses were really Protestants.[30] Then, in 1655, Ussher met a
young diplomat in the service of the Cromwellian Protectorate, Samuel
Morland, who was on his way to Piedmont to protest to the court of
Savoy about the notorious massacre perpetrated against the Piedmontese
Waldenses in the *Pasque Piemontesi* or 'bloody spring' of that year.[31]
Ussher evidently urged Morland to see if he could acquire further manuscripts. Morland appears to have made contact with the descendants of
the Duc de Lesdiguières (who unlike the duke himself had not converted
to Catholicism) based at Geneva. It is most likely from this source that
Morland acquired the manuscript collection which is now in Cambridge
University Library, and which comprises most of the original material
from Archbishop Jean Baile's inquisitions, as well as further dialect religious tracts and sermons.[32]

28   Perrin's discovery of these 'sumpta' (which were probably in fact summaries
made after the trial) is described in M. Vulson, *De la Puissance du pape* (Geneva,
1635), pp. 204–12.
29   Dublin, Trinity College, MSS. 265 and 266.
30   Todd, *Books of the Vaudois*, pp. 8–21, analyses Dublin, Trinity College, MS. 259,
and comments (p. 20) of what are almost certainly Perrin's crossings-out of parts of
the text: 'in the erasures made in the MS. by some early possessor of it, the object
apparently was to omit everything, properly speaking, Waldensian; and if these erasures were made with a view to publication of the document, I have no hesitation in
saying that they were made with the dishonest intention of concealing the original
difference in doctrine and discipline between the Vaudois and the reformed, and of
representing the ancient state of the former as identical with that to which the reformers of Germany, at the beginning of the sixteenth century, were anxious to reduce
the Church.'
31   For the massacre of 1655, see A. Armand-Hugon, *Storia dei valdesi ii:
Dall'adesione alla Riforma all'Emancipazione (1532–1848)* (Turin, 1974), pp.
73–102.
32   On Morland, see *Dictionary of National Biography*, art. Morland, Sir Samuel.

On his return, the Protectorate secretary John Thurloe urged Morland to write his material up, in what became the *History of the Evangelical Churches of Piedmont.*[33] This large work incorporated in a somewhat indiscriminate way long extracts from the manuscripts which Morland had obtained. With lack of precision (or scruple) Morland arbitrarily dated many of the dialect tracts (now known to be of the early sixteenth century in the surviving copies) to 1120, a date antecedent even to Valdesius himself.[34] The story of the documents went full circle when the Piedmontese Waldensian pastor Jean Léger issued his *Histoire Générale des églises évangeliques des vallées de Piémont* in 1669.[35] Léger, in effect, translated Morland from English into French wholesale. By this means a work incorporating not only the alpine manuscripts of both heretical and Catholic provenance, but also the complex arguments drawn from inter-confessional polemic, became the reference work of Waldensian history which appeared to derive authentically from the Piedmontese churches themselves.[36]

By the middle of the seventeenth century the Piedmontese Walden-sian Church was well established as a prime area for concern both in the-ological debate and in practical religious diplomacy. Numerous academic theses continued to discuss the argument that the Waldenses demon-strated the continuity of the Church.[37] On the other hand, the history of the Waldensian Church in the seventeenth century was punctuated by several serious crises, which might have obliterated it but for the con-stant support and interest of the wider reformed Church. In 1630 the clergy of the valleys and many of the inhabitants were nearly wiped out by the savage plague which devastated Europe at that time. As a result, the Church had to be re-staffed with ministers almost from scratch.[38] Then, in 1655, there came the dreadful massacre instigated by a local military leader. News of this spread throughout the Protestant world; pamphlets denounced the cruelty of the persecutors, collections were made to help the survivors, and the Duke of Savoy had his ears well and

---

33   S. Morland, *History of the Evangelical Churches of the valleys of Piemont* (London, 1658).

34   For example, a confession of faith, which Perrin had concocted out of two of the early sixteenth-century manuscripts now in Dublin, was assigned a date of 1120 in Morland's work, which long became accepted as fact.

35   Jean Léger, *Histoire Générale des églises évangeliques des vallées de Piémont,* 2 vols (Leiden, 1669).

36   Léger's work has long been recognized as substantially a translation of Morland (e.g. in an article in the *Bulletin de la société d'histoire vaudoise* many years ago). However, it was for many years still customary to cite Léger as though he were an independent authority.

37   Many of these are described in Cameron, *Reformation of the Heretics,* pp. 250ff.

38   On the plague, see A. Armand-Hugon, *Storia dei valdesi ii,* pp. 63–7.

truly bent by embassies like that of Samuel Morland.[39] In 1686 Vittorio
Amedeo II, under pressure from Louis XIV who had revoked the Edict
of Nantes and expelled his Huguenot subjects in the previous year,
ordered the cessation of the Protestant worship which had been formally
permitted since 1561. Many of the Piedmontese Waldenses were converted by force to Catholicism; several thousand died in prison in Piedmont. A small group of 'invincibili' stayed in the mountains and defied
the ducal forces long enough to obtain permission to emigrate to
Switzerland: they duly went to Genevan territory in early 1687, and from
thence were dispersed around Switzerland. While some despaired of ever
returning to Piedmont, a group remained in Geneva hoping to return.
When William III was invited to strike at the English throne in 1688 and
succeeded in deposing James II, the balance of international politics
surrounding Louis XIV changed dramatically. An anti-Louis XIV coali-
tion was formed, with William at its head. In this atmosphere a section
of the Waldensian people, among whom the pastor Henri Arnaud took
a leading part, decided to fight their way back into their homelands in
August 1689. After a series of skirmishes they reached Bobbio Pellice at
the end of that month. They then spent a tense winter in readiness to
defend their valleys, only to find that Vittorio Amedeo II had changed
sides and joined the forces ranged against Louis XIV in the spring of
1690. In consequence the Vaudois were given back their rights of residence and worship.[40] The 'glorious return' added another chapter to the
epic of the Waldenses. Like the events of 1560–1, its ambiguous lustre
made them seem at one and the same time persecuted victims and
victorious warriors for the gospel.

Despite the Duke of Savoy's temporary favour in 1690, persecution
lasted, in theory and often in practice, until the Edict of Emancipation
of 1848, which gave the Protestant subjects of Savoy civil rights. Both
before and since the Emancipation, these churches have received, and at
times needed, a level of support and interest from the wider reformed
community altogether disproportionate to their size. From the mid-
nineteenth century they became the focus of the wider (though still very
small) reformed Church in Italy as a whole, with links to Italian émigré

39   See, for instance, the tract *Relation véritable de ce qui s'est passé dans les persecutions et massacres faits cette année aux églises réformées de Piémont* (n. p., 1655) and
numerous others with similar titles, in all major European languages; J. J. Sudermann, *Waldenser Chronick* (n. p., 1655).
40   On the exile and the return, see A. Armand-Hugon, *Storia dei valdesi ii*, pp.
119–95; recent research on 1689 and its international impact is set out in A. de
Lange, *Dall'Europa alle valli valdesi: Atti del xxix convegno storico internazionale 'il
glorioso rimpatrio'* . . . , Collana della Società di Studi Valdesi, 11 (Turin, 1990); on
the author of the expulsion, see Geoffrey Symcox, *Victor Amadeus II: Absolutism in
the Savoyard State 1675–1730* (London, 1983).

Plate 10 Henri Arnaud, a leader and a historian of the 'glorious return' of 1689, is commemorated by this imposing sculpture near the *Casa valdese* in Torre Pellice. It may be unique among statues commemorating Protestant clerics, in showing its subject with sword unsheathed ready for battle. (Photograph by the author.)

churches overseas. Torre Pellice became and remains at one and the same time the centre of the churches of the Piedmontese valleys, and an educational and conference centre for a much wider reformed missionary effort. The Società di Studi Valdesi is a genuinely international body which holds an annual conference. In recent years, while the scholarly interest in these churches and their history has remained lively and if anything increased in volume and stature, the numbers of worshipping members of the churches have suffered with those of religious minorities nearly everywhere in the modern world. The two-fold nature of the 'Waldenses' – as both an academic subject for historical debate, and a body of real people with spiritual needs and a unique social background – is, however, rooted in the very circumstances in which their Church came into being.

Conclusions and Reflections

The story as told up to this point is necessarily incomplete, for a whole host of reasons. Some of what could have been the best historical evidence has never existed as such. Many important communities of Waldenses – above all the émigré colonies in Provence and the southernmost extremities of Italy – escaped the attention of ecclesiastical justice for long periods, and their spiritual lives therefore went unrecorded. Given that inquisition shaped or even distorted the life-style of the heretics, it would have been fascinating to have known how they lived and believed when shaded from its glare. Vast swaths of evidence certainly did once exist, but do so no longer. Records of the trials conducted in Burgundy by Guy de Reims in the late thirteenth century, and many German trial registers from the fourteenth century, no longer survive: Gallus of Neuhaus's huge register is known from only six fragmentary leaves. The surviving registers of the Waldensian crusade of 1487–8 in the Dauphiné, large as they are, represent only the first and sixth volumes of what was once a six-volume dossier. Some records of interrogations of authentic *barbes* which were known to have taken place have also disappeared. Finally, many surviving pieces of documentation, from various corners of Europe, could not be incorporated in a coherent way into the present account without turning it into a confusing mosaic of fragments, and expanding the book excessively. Here emphasis has been placed on those groups of Waldenses who were sufficiently well documented to offer something like a rounded image of their religious and social life.

A residue of questions cannot be answered with any certainty at the present level of knowledge. The most important question, or rather bundle of questions, concerns the identity, continuity and coherence of the 'Waldensian' movement. Were the Waldenses one dissent or several? Did they have a conscious 'identity', transcending the distances of space and time between their various manifestations? Even to ask such questions, to call into doubt the continuity and unity of Waldensianism, risks drawing down on one the ire of many historians of the movement. Yet the question must be asked, not out of a spirit of controversy, but because the sources require it. After all, did not a German source of *c.*1400 liken the Waldenses to a three-headed monster, whose Italian, German and Piedmontese leaders all acted independently of each other?

Clear evidence exists of continuous Waldensian belief and practice within Austria between the middle of the thirteenth century and the end of the fourteenth; within Brandenburg between the late thirteenth and mid-fifteenth centuries; and within the southwestern Alps from shortly before 1300 through to the Reformation era. These communities were well rooted in the soil of their respective countries, and resisted or evaded for many decades the efforts of churchmen to convert them. The real historical problem lies in knowing where they came from and how they arose in the first place. Lombardy, the probable source for the German Waldensian diaspora, and Burgundy, which produced the late thirteenth-century Occitan colonies and *possibly* transmitted heresy to the Alps, are both far too poorly documented to allow firm conclusions about how those regions spread heresy to elsewhere in Europe. It is equally uncertain how the Lombards and the Burgundians were related to Valdesius and his companions, as the disputes over the origins of the early thirteenth-century Lombard Waldenses demonstrate.

If the Waldenses had been an order of monks or friars, they might have kept a record of their successions, of an ordination to headship handed down through the generations, or a catena of documents and charters to embody their continuity. No such record exists, nor is it likely ever to have existed. Clearly, the Waldenses themselves, 'brethren' and 'followers' alike, did not know where they came from, and tended to imagine for themselves a history reaching far back into the early Christian past. Contact with ecclesiastical culture and its relatively precise chronologies was fatal to the Waldenses' perception of their history. The acid historical critiques of the convert German brethren of 1368 mercilessly exposed the implausibilities of the Italians' largely mythical version of Waldensian origins.

The identity of Waldensianism, then, may be sought more in the shared purpose, attitudes and beliefs of the movement, rather than in any formal continuity or quasi-apostolic succession. How far has the story examined here supported the idea of such a shared identity?

(1)   The distinction, remarked on by several Italian churchmen and at the root of dispute at the Conference of Bergamo, between (a) the 'non-Donatist' followers of Valdesius and (b) the 'Donatist' Italians led by Johannes de Ronco, appears to be much more important than has often been allowed. In thirteenth-century France, Waldensian dissent seems to have followed a non-Donatist line: it argued that the Catholic Church was valid, but mistaken in denying to the Waldensian preachers the right

to preach. This attitude is found in the writings of Durand of Osca. It seems to have determined the views of Raymond de Sainte-Foy at his trial before Jacques Fournier. Raymond's persistent refusal to avow Donatist beliefs clearly surprised and confused his inquisitor; accordingly, it almost certainly derived from the heretic himself. This French style of dissent, which was really just stubborn disobedience to the Church's rules on preaching and hearing confessions, appeared in the Languedoc at the time of the earliest inquisitions in the 1240s, and reappeared under the influence of the 'Burgundian' immigrants in the 1280s–1320s. However, it appears to have perished not long afterwards.

On the other hand, the Lombard Donatist tradition justified receiving spiritual ministrations from itinerant laymen, on the grounds that the priests were simply too sinful to do their job. Paradoxically, brethren in this tradition almost never felt comfortable administering any of the sacraments other than confession: even in the primitive years laymen who consecrated eucharists aroused bitter debate. This tradition thus condemned itself to half-measures and internal inconsistencies. It denounced the clergy, but its representatives sought their services. Donatist Waldensianism was very strong in Lombardy in the early and mid-thirteenth century. It probably continued beyond that date, though evidence from central Italy is extremely sparse thereafter. The German strand of medieval Waldensian dissent almost certainly derived from the Lombard rather than the French; and there is just enough evidence of links between Germany and Milan to make that filiation extremely likely.

(2) How far did persecution determine the shape of the movement? The most radical discontinuity in terms of practice – and even of belief – in the whole history of Waldensianism is that which divides the early anti-heretical poor preachers of the 'first phase' in the late twelfth century from the clandestine, anti-sacerdotal ministry of the mid-thirteenth century onwards. In the beginnings, the Waldenses as voluntary preachers, lay and clergy, undertook to resist Catharism through public testimony and disputation. Their criticism of the Church was more implicit than theoretical: they held their mission to be necessary because the clergy were not up to the task. Rejection by the hierarchy and subsequent pursuit by inquisitors soon transformed the public ministry of preaching into the private, secret one of hearing confessions and preaching to concealed groups of supporters behind closed doors. Among the Lombards at least, persecution can only have accentuated the anti-clericalism which led to vehement disbelief in and rejection of the Church's 'holiness'. Such rejection of the Church was not essential to the movement in its first years: it was something which only grew on it over time.

(3) At various times Waldensian dissenters appear to have been influenced, or even seduced, by ideas from other heresies. The early Occitan Waldenses adopted patterns of behaviour very similar to those of the

Cathars when under attack from the Church, above all the two-tier structure of itinerant ascetic pastors and sedentary lay supporters. They also prayed in a similar way. In fourteenth-century Piedmont some alleged 'Waldenses' may even have been attracted by the Cathar dualist mythology, which within Catharism may perhaps have been kept concealed as a secret knowledge for initiates only. Likewise, the Alpine Waldenses received into their literature some input from late Hussitism on the very eve of the Reformation. Although that input appears to have made no difference to the beliefs and affirmations of its followers, it left its imprint on their books.

(4)   The term 'Waldensian' was prone to misuse in the later middle ages. In various places and at various times it was used as a synonym for a demonic witch. It is usually not difficult to separate out such spurious Waldenses (as most notoriously the 'Vaudois' of Arras of c.1460) from the authentic Waldensian tradition. On the whole, Waldenses were not consistently accused of witchcraft and their supposed licentious 'congregations' or 'synagogues', which many have seen as precursors of the witches' sabbat in the inquisitorial mind, were usually just thought to be dens of vice, rather than dens of witchcraft, in the later middle ages. However, such misuse of the word 'Waldensian' must warn one to beware of the term just a little. Not everyone called by this name necessarily shared all the same characteristics.

(5)   Some aspects of Waldensian religion are frequently represented as bringing cohesiveness and purpose to the movement. It is often said that the Waldenses were biblicist: that they were animated by a profound respect for scripture and determined to shape their religion by scriptural norms. The brethren certainly wished to know and possess the Bible. In thirteenth-century France and Germany, and also in sixteenth-century Provence, one finds Waldenses learning large chunks of the Bible, especially of the New Testament, by rote. The Passauer Anonymous, while mocking the errors of the German vernacular Bibles ('the swine received him not'), testified to how widespread such translations were. From the very end of the story, in the early sixteenth century one finds surviving Franco-Provençal translations of nearly all the New Testament and selected moralistic books of the Old.

The Waldenses, then, had scripture. On the other hand, so had the Catholic Church. It read scripture as the gospels and epistles in the Mass, commented on it in the *Glosa Ordinaria* and lectured on it in the theology faculties of the universities and *studia*. Scripture, interpreted according to its literal sense, was accepted as the sole formal basis for Catholic theology. To argue that the Waldenses found their focus and identity in loyalty to scripture either is a truism or a platitude, or it implies that somehow contemporary Catholicism was 'unscriptural'. Such a critique needs to be explored and justified, and cannot be taken as read.

The question is, what did the Waldenses do with scripture? What attitudes did they bring to scripture which were distinctive from those of the official Church?

Two observations may be made about the Bible in medieval Catholicism. First, the western Church affirmed that scripture was authoritative, but only when it was interpreted within the tradition of the Church. Not the bare text alone, but the text as understood and interpreted by the succession of councils, Fathers and doctors of the Church, was the rule of Christian teaching. Since the text only operated within the Latin tradition, the Latin Vulgate stood as the authoritative version. Second, the Church allowed to accrue around scripture a mass of additional teachings and traditions, often held to have been transmitted orally from the first apostles; in practice this gave the medieval Church space to develop a range of rituals and cults through a process of extrapolation and evolution.

How did the Waldenses use scripture? The most compelling pieces of evidence for the use of biblical texts in controversy come from (a) the *Rescriptum* of the Bergamo conference of 1218, which heaped up authorities to justify a Donatist rejection of the value of the ministries of sinful priests; and (b) the correspondence of the Italian Waldenses and the Austrian brethren who had just defected to Catholicism *c*.1368. In each case abundant scriptural authorities were invoked, but (ironically) this was to make debating points not against the Church as a whole, but rather between one group of brethren and another. The approach which they used, essentially the citing of short extracts, combined with the use of patristic authorities, appears very close to that followed by Catholic theologians in disputation. These Waldenses used scripture in a very similar way to that of their Catholic counterparts. They were distinctive only in that they exploited the techniques of the Catholic tradition as a weapon against that tradition. They therefore rejected the idea that only *within* the universal Church was any given interpretation of scripture binding.

On the other hand, in most of the rest of Waldensian literature, especially the Franco-Provençal sermons, scripture was expounded for one primary purpose: to make an ethical point. This constant stress on scripture as a set of *rules* allowed the hybrid literature of the very end of the middle ages to combine Catholic, Hussite and indigenous elements without the incongruities being too obvious. If the Bible was a source of *law* to follow, then moral homilies from many different sources were grist to the mill. This legalism implicitly – and sometimes explicitly, as for instance in the Hussite treatises – rejected many of the sacramental means of grace which helped a Christian to make up for his or her inability always to keep the law. The distinctiveness of this sort of Waldensian biblicism lay in that it rejected the Church's role as a sacramental institution, through which the forgiveness of God was made effective.

Waldensian 'biblicism' amounts, therefore, to rejection of the universal, ideal and institutional Church. The late medieval Waldenses could not believe that the Church was either the custodian of true interpretation of scripture, or the 'well of grace' from which one could draw resources against the harshness of the moral law. This was a very hard, demanding creed. If one wishes to characterize the life-style of those who followed this creed, 'puritanical' is as good a term as any. If they had been utterly consistent, the only reason why Waldenses should have attended church services was for concealment. Yet they evidently did not conceal themselves by doing so; and it is hard to resist the suspicion that many lay followers, at least, must have hoped to acquire some tangible 'grace' through the Church's services to mitigate the moral demands made by their Waldensian beliefs.

(6) The way of life of the travelling brethren was often likened to the apostolic ideal, from the earliest chroniclers onwards. Numerous lay followers from the fifteenth-century Dauphiné likened the *barbes* to the apostles, as they travelled around spreading the word in poverty and self-denial. In the correspondence of 1368 the Italian brethren regarded themselves as successors to the apostolic ministry, because they preached in simplicity and without 'worldly learning' (though their denials of worldly knowledge rang rather hollow in such an erudite text). Yet the *vita apostolica*, like *Scriptura sola*, was not something with an agreed meaning and terms of reference, but rather a deeply contested and controversial concept. The correspondence of 1368 records an intense debate over who had the better claim to represent the apostles. For those who had converted to Catholicism, one knew that one was 'apostolic' when one joined with the apostolic succession, a tradition thought to derive authentically from the Church's foundation. For those who persisted in Waldensian belief and practice, in contrast, the 'apostolic life' consisted of witness *against* those in that same tradition who had renounced the ancient style of life. However, the Waldenses' claim that apostolicity rested in living and acting like the apostles, rather than inheriting their mantles, invited hostile scrutiny. The converts of 1368 and the inquisitors of 1390s Germany made great play with the fact that the brethren did not preach in public and did not spread the word; rather, they restricted their ministry to those of whom they already felt secure, and relied on other 'friends' cautiously to insinuate them into the confidence of new believers. One cannot, therefore, simply assert that the Waldensian life-style represented the 'apostolic ideal'; rather, it represented an *interpretation* of that ideal, which was at odds with the interpretation prevailing in the official Church.

It is important to preserve some detachment and relativism with regard to the issues which divided Waldenses from Catholics. It is not for the historian to decide whose understanding of scripture, the priestly ministry or the apostolic ideal was the more authentic or correctly Christian. The thought-policing of inquisitors rightly appals the post-Enlightenment mind. Equally, the resilience of those who ran such risks for their beliefs may excite understandable admiration. Yet neither of those responses necessarily justifies passing any sort of confessional verdict on the issues raised by the Waldensian rejection of the Catholic Church.

When one considers the everyday life of the followers rather than the theories of their teachers, medieval popular heresy seems to be the exception which proves the rules about the later medieval Church. As a life-style lived by its lay followers, it reacted against the prevailing religious culture, and yet selected from it. It rejected some of the most fashionable cultic trends, but could not cut itself off from the system as a whole. In this light, the very *differences* between medieval Waldensian dissent and early Protestantism are illuminating. For people to turn finally and decisively away from medievalism, they needed some other focus for their belief and their worship. In practice, they needed well-educated preachers armed with a distinctive, pre-existing and self-sufficient theology, which empowered them to build places of worship, celebrate eucharists, baptize children and hold disciplinary synods. When that intellectual and ministerial confidence was superimposed on the social cohesiveness and tenacity of the dissenting tradition of the southwestern Alps, a rural Protestant Church was born. In the valleys of Piedmont its 'Waldensian' character was sufficiently recent and distinctive for the name and the identity to survive. Elsewhere in France or beyond, Waldensianism simply merged and dissolved in the reformed tradition. Its time was past.

Bibliography

1 Manuscript Sources

This is not in any way a comprehensive list of the manuscripts concerning the Waldenses across Europe: it is simply a formal description of those manuscript materials consulted directly towards the writing of this book. Many other manuscript sources have been consulted in the relevant printed editions listed below.

Cambridge, University Library

Dd. 3. 25, 26	Materials from the Embrun archive relating to inquisitions against Waldenses, late fifteenth- to early sixteenth centuries.
Dd. xv. 29	Biblical fragments, pastoral and didactic writings and a short historical piece on the origins of the Vaudois, in dialect.
Dd. xv. 30	Pieces of biblical exposition, moral treatises, poems and sermons in dialect.
Dd. xv. 31	Three sermons, one moral treatise, biblical fragments and part of a poem, in dialect.
Dd. xv. 32	Medical recipes, moral treatises and some sermons, in dialect.
Dd. xv. 33	A Latin grammar, Latin biblical extracts, patristic quotations in Latin and French, Provençal poetry, Latin moral pieces and French poetry, and a commonplace book. None of this manuscript is in the usual 'Vaudois' dialect.
Dd. xv. 34	Partial bible: Matthew, Luke (extracts), John 1:1 – 6:32, 13:29 – 15:20, 20:29 – end, 1 Corinthians, Galatians, Ephesians, Philippians, 1 and 2 Timothy, Titus, Hebrews 11, Proverbs 5, Wisdom 5, Acts 1 – 26:4.

Dublin, Trinity College

The digest of the discussions between Morel, Oecolampadius and Bucer from 1530, in dialect, including some material not found in the known Latin texts; the propositions of Angrogna from September 1532, in Piedmontese Italian.

260 Moral treatises and sermons, from both Catholic and Hussite provenances, intermingled with each other; also some sermons, in dialect.

263 Didactic treatises, mostly of Catholic origin, some Taborite; and a large range of sermons, in dialect.

265, 266 Sixteenth/seventeenth-century copies and translations in French and Latin of material relating to inquisitions against Waldenses, mostly derived from Cambridge, University Library, MSS. Dd. 3. 25 and 26, with a little unique material.

267 Four moral treatises and a very long set of sermons on biblical texts, in dialect.

Grenoble, Archives Départmentales de l'Isère

B 4350 and B 4351 Incomplete and damaged but very substantial dossiers from the 1487–8 crusade, comprising the legal instruments and letters relating to the campaign, and a proportion of the protocols of interrogations of suspects.

Paris, Bibliothèque Nationale, Fonds Latin

3375, vols 1–2 Complete dossier of the lawsuit for rehabilitation of the Vaudois of the Dauphiné, 1501–7, including transcripts of earlier trial and legal materials.

2 Printed Literature

As many books and articles in this subject also contain editions of primary sources, separation of primary and secondary printed literature would not be helpful, or even possible. The following are simply those items of a very large corpus which have proved most useful for the present work. This list makes no claims to comprehensiveness.

Alain of Lille, *De fide catholica: contra haereticos sui temporis, praesertim Albigenses*, in J.-P. Migne, *Patrologiae Cursus Completus*, Series Latina, vol. 210, cols 305ff.

Albanès, J.-H., 'Un Nouveau document sur les premières années de protestantisme en Provence', Comité des travaux historiques et scientifiques, *Bulletin historique et philologique* (1884), pp. 25–41.

Alberigo, G. (ed.), *Conciliorum Oecumenicorum Decreta: The Decrees of the Ecumenical Councils*, 2 vols, trans. N. P. Tanner (London and Washington, DC, 1990).

Alessio, F., 'Luserna e l'interdetto di Giacomo Buronzo', *Bollettino storico-bibliografico subalpino*, vol. 8, no. 6 (1903), pp. 409–24.

Allix, P., *Some remarks upon the Ecclesiastical History of the Ancient Churches of Piedmont* (London, 1690).

Amati, G., 'Processus Contra Valdenses in Lombardia Superiori, Anno 1387', in *Archivio Storico Italiano*, series 3, vol. 1, pt 2 (1865), pp. 3–52, and vol. 2, pt 1, pp. 3–61.

Annales Marbacenses, ed. R. Wilmans, in *MGH Scriptores* 17 (1861).

Armand Hugon, A., Molnar, A. and Vinay, V., *Storia dei Valdesi*, 3 vols (Turin, 1974–80).

Arnaud, E., *Protestants de Provence, du Comtat Venaissin et de la Principauté d'Orange*, 2 vols (Paris, 1884).

Arnaud, E., 'Histoire des persecutions endurées par les Vaudois du Dauphiné aux xiiie, xive et xve siècles', *Bulletin de la société d'histoire vaudoise* 12 (1895), pp. 17–140.

Aubéry, J., *Histoire de l'execution de Cabrières et de Mérindol* (Paris, 1645).

Aubigné, T.-Agrippa d', *Histoire universelle* (Maillé, 1616–20).

Aubry, des Trois-Fontaines, *Chronica Albrici Monachi Trium Fontium*, ed. P. Scheffer-Boichorst, in *MGH Scriptores* 23 (1874).

Audisio, G., *Le Barbe et l'inquisiteur: Procès du barbe vaudois Pierre Griot par l'inquisiteur Jean de Roma (Apt, 1532)* (Aix-en-Provence, 1979).

Audisio, G., *Les Vaudois du Luberon: une minorité en Provence, 1460–1560* (Aix-en-Provence, 1984).

Audisio, G., *Les 'Vaudois': naissance, vie et mort d'une dissidence (xiie-xve siècles)* (Turin, 1989).

Audisio, G. (ed.), *Les Vaudois des origines à leur fin (xiie-xvie siècles): Colloque international . . . Aix-en-Provence, 8–10 avril 1988* (Turin, 1990).

Audisio, G., *The Waldensian Dissent: Persecution and Survival, c.1170–c.1570*, trans. Claire Davison (Cambridge, 1999).

Balmas, E. and Diena, V. (eds), *Histoire mémorable de la guerre faite par le duc de Savoye contre ses subjectz des vallées* (Turin, 1972).

Balmas, E. and Theiller, C. A. (eds), *Storia delle persecuzioni e guerre contro il popolo chiamato valdese che abita nelle valli del Piemonte, di Angrogna, Luserna, San Martino, Perosa e altre, a far temp dall'annp 1555 fino al 1561* (Turin, 1975).

Barnum, P. H. (ed.), *Dives and Pauper*, vol. 1, pts 1–2, Early English Text Society, Old Series, 275, 280 (Oxford, 1976–80).

Bernard, of Fontcaude, *Adversus Waldensium Sectam Liber*, ed. in J.-P. Migne, *Patrologiae Cursus Completus*, Series Latina, vol. 204, cols 793–840.

Betts, R. R., *Essays in Czech History* (London, 1969).

(Bèze, T. de ?), *Histoire ecclésiastique des églises réformées au royaume de France*, 3 vols ('Antwerp', i.e. Geneva, 1580).

Bèze, T. de, *Correspondance de Théodore de Bèze*, ed. H. Aubert and others (Geneva, 1960–).

Biller, P., 'Aspects of the Waldenses in the fourteenth century including an edition of their correspondence' (Oxford University D. Phil. thesis, 1977).

Biller, P., '*Curate infirmos*: The Medieval Waldensian Practice of Medicine', *Studies in Church History* 19 (1982), pp. 55–77.

Biller, P., '*Multum jejunantes et se castigantes*: Medieval Waldensian Asceticism', *Studies in Church History* 22 (Oxford, 1985), pp. 215–28.

Biller, P., 'The Cathars of Languedoc and Written Materials', P. Biller and A. Hudson (eds), *Heresy and Literacy, 1000–1530* (Cambridge, 1994), pp. 61–82.

Biller, P., 'The Preaching of the Waldensian Sisters', in *La Prédication sur un mode dissident: laics, femmes, hérétiques . . .*, in *Heresis* 30 (1999), pp. 137–68.

Biller, P., 'The Waldenses 1300–1500', *Revue de l'histoire des religions*, vol. 217, fasc. 1 (2000), pp. 75–99.

Biller, Peter, and Hudson, Anne (eds), *Heresy and Literacy, 1000–1530* (Cambridge, 1994).

Blickle, P., 'Peasant Revolts in the German Empire in the Late Middle Ages', *Social History* 4 (1979), pp. 223–31.

Bodius, H., *Unio dissidentium in sacris literis locorum* ('Cologne', 1531).

Boffito, G., 'Eretici in Piemonte al tempo del Gran Scisma', *Studi e Documenti di Storia e Diritto* 18 (1897), pp. 381–431.

Bollea, L. C., 'Alcuni documenti di storia valdese (1354–1573)', *Bulletin de la société d'histoire vaudoise* 44 (1922), pp. 71–87; 45 (1923), pp. 5–14.

Bolton, Brenda (ed.), *Innocent III: Selected Documents on the Pontificate 1198–1216* (Manchester, 1999).

Bourrilly, V.-L., *Guillaume du Bellay, Seigneur de Langey* (Paris, 1905).

Brenon, A., 'The Waldensian Books', in P. Biller and A. Hudson (eds), *Heresy and Literacy, 1000–1530* (Cambridge, 1994), pp. 137–59.

Briggs, R., *Witches and Neighbours: The Social and Cultural Context of European Witchcraft* (London, 1996).

Brooke, C. N. L., *The Medieval Idea of Marriage* (Oxford, 1989).

Brundage, J. A., *Law, Sex and Christian Society in Medieval Europe* (Chicago, 1987).

Burchard, of Ursperg, *Chronicon*, in *MGH Scriptores rerum Germanicarum in usu scholarum*, vol. 16, 2nd edn, ed. O. Holder-Egger and H. von Simson (Hanover and Leipzig, 1916).

Bynum, C. W., *Holy Feast and Holy Fast: The Religious Significance of Food to Medieval Women* (Berkeley, Calif.,1987).

Calvin, J., *Joannis Calvini Opera quae supersunt Omnia*, ed. G. Baum, E. Cunitz and E. Reuss, Corpus Reformatorum, vols 29–87, Braunschweig (Berlin, 1853–1900).

Cameron, E., *The Reformation of the Heretics: The Waldenses of the Alps 1480–1580* (Oxford, 1984).

Cameron, E., *The European Reformation* (Oxford, 1991).

Cameron, E., 'Medieval Heretics as Protestant Martyrs', in D. Wood (ed.), *Martyrs and Martyrologies: Papers read at the 1992 summer meeting and the 1993 winter meeting of the Ecclesiastical History Society*, Studies in Church History, vol. 30 (Oxford, 1993), pp. 185–207.

Cameron, E., 'One Reformation or Many: Protestant Identities in the Later Reformation in Germany', in O. P. Grell and R. W. Scribner (eds), *Tolerance and Intolerance in the European Reformation* (Cambridge, 1996), pp. 108–27.

Cargill Thompson, W. D. J., *The Political Thought of Martin Luther*, ed. P. Broadhead (Brighton, 1984).

Carutti, D., *La Crociata valdese del 1488 e la maschera di ferro, con alcune appendice alla storia di Pinerolo* (Pinerolo, 1894).

Chassanion, J., *Histoire des Albigeois* (Geneva, 1595).

Chasseneuz, Barthelemy de, *Catalogus Gloriae mundi*... (Lyons, 1529).

Chaunu, P. (ed.), *The Reformation* (Gloucester, 1989).

Chevalier, J. A., *Mémoire historique sur les hérésies en Dauphiné avant le xvie siècle* (Valence, 1890).

Chiffoleau, J., *La Comptabilite de l'au-dela: les hommes, la mort et la religion dans la region d'Avignon a la fin du Moyen Age, vers 1320–vers 1480*, Collection de l'École française de Rome, 47 (Rome and Paris, 1980).

Chorier, N., *Histoire générale du Dauphiné*, 2 vols (Valence, 1878–9; repr. Grenoble, 1971) .

Chronicon universale anonymi Laudunensis, ed. G. Waitz, in *Monumenta Germaniae Historica, Scriptores*, vol. 26 (1882), pp. 442–57.

Clark, S., *Thinking with Demons: The Idea of Witchcraft in Early Modern Europe* (Oxford, 1997).

Cohn, N., *Europe's Inner Demons* (London, 1977).

Comba, E., *History of the Waldenses of Italy*, trans. T. E. Comba (London, 1889).

Comba, E., 'L'Introduction de la réforme dans les vallées de Piémont', *Bulletin de la société d'histoire du protestantisme français* 43 (1894), pp. 7–35.

Conti di Foligno, S. dei, *Le Storie de'suoi tempi dal 1475 al 1510*, ed. and trans. D. Zanelli and F. Calabro, 2 vols (Rome, 1883).

Cowdrey, H. E. J., 'The Papacy, the Patarenes and the Church of Milan', in *Transactions of the Royal Historical Society*, 5th series, vol. 18 (1968), pp. 25–48.

Crespin, J., *Histoire mémorable de la persécution et saccagement du peuple de Mérindol et Cabrières et autres circonvoisins, appelez Vaudois* (n.p., 1556).

Crespin, J., *Actes de martyrs* (n. p., 1565).

Crespin, J., *Histoire des martyrs* (n.p., 1619).

Cronica S. Petri Erfordensis Moderna, ed. O. Holder-Egger, in *MGH Scriptores* 30, pt 1 (1896) .

Cross, F. L. and Livingstone, E. A. (eds), *The Oxford Dictionary of the Christian Church*, 3rd edn (Oxford, 1997).

Delarue, H., 'Olivétan et Pierre de Vingle à Genève, 1532-3', *Bulletin d'humanisme et renaissance* 8 (1946), pp. 105–18.

Delumeau, J., *Sin and Fear: The Emergence of a Western Guilt Culture, 13th–18th Centuries*, trans. Eric Nicholson (New York, 1990).

Dickens, A. G. and Tonkin, J. M., *The Reformation in Historical Thought* (Oxford, 1986).

Döllinger, J. J. Ignaz von (ed.), *Beiträge zur Sektengeschichte des Mittelaters*, 2 vols (Munich, 1890).

Dondaine, A., 'Aux origines du valdéisme. Une profession de foi de Valdès', in *Archivum Fratrum Praedicatorum* 16 (1946), pp. 191–235.

Douie, D. L., *The Nature and Effect of the Heresy of the Fraticelli* (Manchester, 1932).

Duffy, E., *The Stripping of the Altars: Traditional Religion in England, 1400–1580* (New Haven, Conn., and London, 1992).

Dufour, A., 'Un Document sur les vallées vaudoises en 1556', *Bollettino della Società di Studi Valdesi* 128 (1970), pp. 57–63.

Duvernoy, J. (ed.), *Le Registre d'inquisition de Jacques Fournier, évêque de Pamiers (1318–1325)*, 3 vols (Toulouse, 1965).

Duvernoy, J., 'Le Mouvement vaudois: origines', in *Mouvements dissidents et novateurs, Heresis*, nos 13–14 (1990), pp. 173–98.

Eck, Johannes [Maier von], *Enchiridion locorum communium* (Ingolstadt, 1541).

Ewen, A. H. and De Carteret, A. R., *The Fief of Sark* (Guernsey, 1969).

Farmer, D. H., *The Oxford Dictionary of Saints*, 3rd edn (Oxford, 1992).

Fauché-Prunelle, A. A., *Essai sur les anciennes institutions autonomes ou populaires des Alps cottiennes-briançonnaises*, 2 vols (Paris, Grenoble, 1856–7).

Flacius Illyricus, M., *Catalogus Testium Veritatis qui ante nostram aetatem reclamarunt papae* (Basel, 1556); also as 'S. G. S.' [= S. Goulart, ed.], *Catalogus Testium Veritatis, qui ante nostram aetatem Pontifici Romano atque Papismi erroribus reclamarunt* (Lyon, 1597; later edition, Geneva, 1608).

Foà, S. (ed.), 'Valli del Piemonte soggette all'Altezza di Savoia, infette d'heresia et suoi luoghi', *Bulletin de la société d'histoire vaudoise* 24 (1907), pp. 8–9.

Fornier, M., *Histoire générale des Alpes maritimes ou cottiennes et . . . de leur métropolitan Embrun*, ed. J. Guillaume, 3 vols (Paris, 1890–2).

Foxe, John, *Acts and Monuments*, ed. J. Pratt, 4th edn, 8 vols (London, n. d.).

Freherus, M., *Rerum Bohemicarum antiqui scriptores* (Hanoviae, 1602).

Fromment, A., *Les Actes et gestes merveilleux de la cité de Genève . . .*, ed. G. Revilliod (Geneva, 1854).

Fudge, T. A., *The Magnificent Ride: The First Reformation in Hussite Bohemia*, St Andrews Studies in Reformation History (Aldershot, 1998).

Gabotto, F., *Roghi e vendette: Contributo alla storia della dissidenza religiosa in Piemonte prima della riforma* (Pinerolo, 1898).

Gaffarel, P., 'Les Massacres de Cabrières et de Mérindol en 1545', *Revue historique* 107 (1911), pp. 241–71.

Gariel, H., *Delphinalia*, pt 2 (Grenoble, 1852).

Geisendorf, P. F., *Les Annalistes genevoises du début du dix-septième siècle, Savion, Piaget, Perrin: Études et textes* (Geneva, 1942).

Geisendorf, P. F. (ed.), *Le Livre des habitants de Genève*, 2 vols (Geneva, 1957–63).

Gesta Treverorum Continuatio IV, ed. G. Waitz, in *MGH Scriptores* 24 (1879).

Gilles, P., *Histoire ecclésiastique des églises réformées . . . autrefois appellées églises vaudoises*, ed. P. Lantaret, 2 vols (Pinerolo, 1881).

Gilmont, J.-F., 'Sources et critique des sources', in G. Audisio (ed.), *Les Vaudois des origines à leur fin (xiie–xvie siècles): Colloque international . . . Aix-en-Provence, 8–10 avril 1988* (Turin, 1990), pp. 105–13.

Ginzburg, C., *Il Nicodemismo: Simulazione e dissimulazione religiosa nell'Europa del '500* (Turin, 1970).

Gioffredo, P., *Storia delle Alpi Marittime*, ed. C. Gazzera, Monumenta Historiae Patriae, Scriptorum vol. 2 (Turin, 1839).

Giovio, P., *Historiae sui temporis* (Paris, 1558).

Godefroy, D., *Histoire de Charles VIII* (Paris, 1684).

Gonnet, G. (ed.), *Enchiridion fontium valdensium (Recueil critique des sources concernant les Vaudois au moyen âge) du IIIe Concile de Latran au Synode de Chanforan (1179–1532)*, vol. 1 (Torre Pellice, 1958).

Gonnet, G., *Le Confessioni di fede valdesi prima della riforma* (Turin, 1967).

Gonnet, J. and Molnar, A., *Les Vaudois au moyen âge* (Turin, 1974).

Gordon, B., 'Calvin and the Swiss Reformed Churches', in A. Pettegree, A. Duke and G. Lewis (eds), *Calvinism in Europe 1540–1620* (Cambridge, 1994), pp. 64–81.

Gordon, B. (ed.), *Protestant History and Identity in Sixteenth-century Europe*, 2 vols (Aldershot, 1996).

Greengrass, M., *The French Reformation* (Oxford, 1987).

Gretser, J., *Murices catholicae et Germanicae antiquitatis, sectariorum predicantium pedibus positi et sparsi* (Ingolstadt, 1608).

Gretser, J., *Lucae Tudensis episcopi, scriptores aliquot succedanei contra sectam Waldensium: nunc primum in lucem editi cum prolegomenis et notis; in quibus de Waldensium factionibus, peruersisq[ue] dogmatis copiose disseritur* (Ingolstadt, 1613); here consulted in M. de la Bigne (ed.), *Magna Bibliotheca Veterum Patrum*, 15 vols (Cologne, 1618–22), vol. 13, pp. 297–342.

Gretser, J., *Trias scriptorum adversus Waldensium sectam* (Ingolstadt, 1614).

Grundmann, H., '*Litteratus-illitteratus*: Der Wandel einer Bildungsnorm vom Altertum zum Mittelalter', in *Archiv für Kulturgeschichte*, vol. 40 (1958), pp. 1–65.

Grundmann, H., *Religiöse Bewegungen im Mittelalter: Untersuchungen über die geschichtlichen Zusammenhange zwischen der Ketzerei, den Bettelorden und der religiöse Frauenbewegung im 12. und 13. Jahrhundert und über die geschichtlichen Grundlagen der deutschen Mystik*, 2nd edn (Hildesheim, 1961).

Gui, Bernard, *Practica inquisitionis heretice pravitatis*, ed. C. Douais (Paris, 1886).

Gui, Bernard, *Manuel de l'inquisiteur*, ed. and trans. G. Mollat and G. Drioux, 2 vols (Paris, 1964).

Guillaume de Puylaurens, *Historia Albigensium*, ed. J. Beyssier, in Université de Paris, Bibliothèque de la Faculté des Lettres (Mélanges d'histoire du moyen âge) 18 (Paris, 1904).

Guillaume, P., 'Sentence de réhabilitation des Vaudois des Alpes françaises', in Comité des travaux historiques et scientifiques, *Bulletin historique et philologique* (1891), pp. 248–65.

Hamilton, B., *The Medieval Inquisition* (London, 1981).

Hamilton, B., *Religion in the Medieval West* (London, 1986).

Harmening, D., *Superstitio: Ueberlieferungs- und theoriegeschichtliche Untersuchungen zur kirchlich-theologischen Aberglaubensliteratur des Mittelalters* (Berlin, 1979).

Haupt, H., 'Waldenserthum und Inquisition im südöstlichen Deutschland bis zur Mitte des 14. Jahrhunderts', *Deutsche Zeitschrift für Geschichtswissenschaft* 1 (1889), pp. 285–330.

Haupt, H., 'Waldenserthum und Inquisition im südöstlichen Deutschland seit der Mitte des 14. Jahrhunderts', *Deutsche Zeitschrift für Geschichtswissenschaft* 3 (1890), pp. 337–411.

Hemardinquer, J. J., 'Pour le 403me anniversaire de la prédication publique à Fenestrelles: Les Vaudois du Dauphiné et la résistance à l'insurrection d'après des documents inédits', *Bollettino della Società di Studi Valdesi* 103 (1958), pp. 53–63.

Herminjard, A.-L. (ed.), *Correspondance des réformateurs dans les pays de la langue française*, 9 vols (Geneva and Paris, 1866–97).

Histoire des persecutions et guerres faites depuis l'an 1555 jusques en l'an 1561 contre le peuple appelé Vaudois (n.p., 1562).

Histoire mémorable de la guerre faite par le duc de Savoye contre ses subjectz des vallées (n. p., 1561).

Hollaender, A., 'Eine schweizer Gesandtschaftsreise an den französischen Hof im Jahre 1557', *Historische Zeitschrift* NS 33 (1892), pp. 385–410.

Hudson, A., *The Premature Reformation: Wycliffite Texts and Lollard History* (Oxford, 1988).

Hutton, R., *The Rise and Fall of Merry England: The Ritual Year, 1400–1700* (Oxford, 1994).

Innocent III, Pope, *Opera*, in J.-P. Migne, *Patrologiae Cursus Completus*, Series Latina, vols 214–17.

Innocent III, Pope (Lotario dei Segni), *De miseria condicionis humane*, ed. Robert E. Lewis (Athens, Ga., 1978).

Institoris, H. and Sprenger, J., *Malleus Maleficarum* (Frankfurt 1582).

Jalla, J., 'Notice historique sur le S. Ministère . . . au sein des églises vaudoises', *Bulletin de la société d'histoire vaudoise* 14 (1897), pp. 3–22; 16 (1898), pp. 3–22.

Jalla, J., 'Synodes vaudois de la réformation à l'exil, 1536–1686', *Bulletin de la société d'histoire du protestantisme français* 50 (1901), pp. 471–89; continued in *Bulletin de la société d'histoire vaudoise* 20 (1903), pp. 93–133; 21 (1904), pp. 62–86.

Jalla, J., *Storia della riforma in Piemonte fino alla morte di Emanuele Filiberto 1517–1580* (Florence, 1914).

Jalla, J., 'La Bible d'Olivétan', *Bulletin de la société d'histoire vaudoise* 58 (1932), pp. 76–92.

Joannes, de Segovia, *Historia Gestorum Generalis Synodi Basiliensis*, ed. E. Birk, vol. 1, in *Monumenta Conciliorum Generalium Seculi Decimi Quinti, Concilium Basiliense, Scriptorum*, tomus ii (Vindobonae, 1873).

Jochnowitz, G., *Dialect Boundaries and the Question of Franco-Provençal* (The Hague and Paris, 1973).

Kamen, H. A. F., *The Spanish Inquisition* (London, 1965); revd edn, *The Spanish Inquisition: An Historical Revision* (London, 1998).

Kamen, H. A. F., *The Phoenix and the Flame: Catalonia and the Counter Reformation* (New Haven, Conn., 1993).

Kaminsky, H., *A History of the Hussite Revolution* (Berkeley and Los Angeles, 1967).

Kidd, B. J. (ed.), *Documents Illustrative of the Continental Reformation* (Oxford, 1911).

Kieckhefer, R., *European Witch Trials: Their Foundation in Popular and Learned Culture, 1300–1500* (London, 1976).

Kieckhefer, R., *Repression of Heresy in Medieval Germany* (Liverpool, 1979).

Kingdon, R. M., *Geneva and the Coming of the Wars of Religion in France 1555–1563* (Geneva, 1956).

Kingdon, R. M., Bergier, J.-F., Fatio, O. and Labarthe, O. (eds), *Registres de la compagnie des pasteurs de Genève au temps de Calvin*, vols 1–3 (Geneva, 1962–5).

Knecht, R. J., *Francis I* (Cambridge, 1982).

Kurze, D., 'Zur Ketzergeschichte der mark Brandenburg und Pommerns vornehmlich im 14. Jahrhundert, Luziferaner, Putzkeller und Waldenser', *Jahrbuch für die Geschichte Mittel- und Ostdeutschlands* 16/17 (1968), pp. 50–94.

Kurze, D. (ed.), *Quellen zur Ketzergeschichte Brandenburgs und Pommerns*, Veröffentlichungen der historischen Kommission zu Berlin, Bd. 45, Quellenwerke Bd. 6 (Berlin, 1975).

Labande-Mailfert, Y., *Charles VIII et son milieu (1470–1498)* (Paris, 1975).

Lambert, M., *Medieval Heresy: Popular Movements from the Gregorian Reform to the Reformation*, 2nd edn (Oxford, 1992).

Lambert, M., *The Cathars* (Oxford, 1998).

Lange, A. de, *Dall'Europa alle valli valdesi: Atti del xxix convegno storico internazionale 'il glorioso rimpatrio'* . . . , Collana della Società di Studi Valdesi, 11 (Turin, 1990).

Lansing, C., *Power and Purity: Cathar Heresy in Medieval Italy* (Oxford, 1998).

La Popelinière, H.-L. V. de, *L'Histoire de la France* (La Rochelle, 1581).

Lea, H. C., *History of the Inquisition of the Middle Ages*, 3 vols (London, 1888).

Lea, H. C., *A History of Auricular Confession and Indulgences in the Latin Church*, 3 vols (Philadelphia, 1896).

Léger, Jean, *Histoire Générale des églises évangeliques des vallées de Piémont*, 2 vols (Leiden, 1669).

Le Goff, J., *The Birth of Purgatory*, trans. A. Goldhammer (London, 1984).

Lentolo, S., *Historia delle Grandi e Crudeli Persecutioni fatti ai tempi nostri* . . . *contro il Popolo che chiamano Valdese*, ed. T. Gay (Torre Pellice, 1906).

Léonard, E. G., *A History of Protestantism*, ed. H. H. Rowley, trans. J. M. H. Reid and R. M. Bethell, 2 vols (London, 1965–7).

Le Roy Ladurie, E., *Les Paysans de Languedoc*, abridged edn (Paris, 1969).

Le Roy Ladurie, E., *Montaillou: village occitan de 1294 à 1324* (Paris, 1975; revd edn 1982); translated in abridged form as *Montaillou: Cathars and Catholics in a French village, 1294–1324*, trans. B. Bray (London, 1978).

Levison, W., 'Konstantinische Schenkung und Silvester-Legende', in *Miscellanea Francesco Ehrle*, 2 (*Studi e Testi*, 38, 1924), pp. 159–247.

Limborch, Philippus van, *Historia Inquisitionis. Cui Subjungitur Liber sententiarum inquisitionis Tholosanae ab anno Christi MCCCVII ad annum MCCCXXIII* (Amsterdam, 1692).

Luther, M., *Werke: Kritische Gesamtausgabe*, 58 vols (Weimar, 1883–1948).

Luther, M., *Luther's Works*, ed. J. Pelikan and H. T. Lehmann, 55 vols (Philadelphia and St Louis, 1955–).

Lyndwood, W., *Lyndwood's Provinciale*, ed. J. V. Bullard and H. C. Bell (London, 1929).

McSheffrey, S., *Gender and Heresy: Women and Men in Lollard Communities 1420–1530* (Philadelphia, 1995).

Major, J. R., *Representative Government in Early Modern France* (New Haven, Conn., 1980).

Manteyer, G. de (ed.), *Le Livre-journal tenu par Fazy de Rame en langage embrunais (6 juin 1471–10 juillet 1507*, 2 vols (Gap. 1932).

Map, W., *De nugis curialium*, ed. M. R. James (Oxford, 1914).

Marnix, P. de, Seigneur de Ste-Aldegonde, *Tableau des differens de la religion*, 2 vols (Leiden, 1603–5).

Marsh, C. W., *The Family of Love in English Society, 1550–1630* (Cambridge, 1994).

Martene, E. and Durand, U. (eds), *Thesaurus Novus Anecdotorum V* (Paris, 1717).

Martin, G., *Inscription en faux . . . contre le livre intitulé 'De la puissance du Pape' par le sieur Marc Vulson* (Grenoble, 1640).

Martin, P. E., 'Une Lettre inédite de Guillaume Farel relative aux Vaudois du Piémont', *Bulletin de la société d'histoire du protestantisme français* 61 (1912), pp. 204–13.

Marx, J., *L'Inquisition en Dauphiné: Étude sur le développement et la répression de l'hérésie et de la sorcellerie du xvie siècle au début du regne de François Ier*, Bibliothèque de l'École des Hautes Études, Sciences Historiques et Philologiques, 206e fasc. (Paris, 1914).

Merlo, G. G., *Eretici e inquisitori nella società piemontese del trecento, [con l'edizione dei processi tenuti a Giaveno dall' inquisitore Alberto di Castellario (1335) e nelle valli di Lanzo dall'inquisitore Tommasso di Casasco (1373)]* (Turin, 1977).

Merlo, G. G., *Valdesi e valdismi medievali: itinerari e proposte di ricerca* (Turin, 1984).

Merlo, G. G., 'Le Mouvement vaudois des origines à la fin du xiiie siècle', in G. Audisio (ed.), *Les Vaudois des origines à leur fin (xiie–xvie siècles): Colloque international . . . Aix-en-Provence, 8–10 avril 1988* (Turin, 1990), pp. 21–33.

Merlo, G. G., *Valdesi e valdismi medievali II: Identità valdesi nella storia e nella storiografia: studi e discussioni* (Turin, 1991).

Miolo, G., *Historia breve e vera de gl'affari de i valdesi delle valli*, ed. E. Balmas (Turin, 1971).

Molnar, A., 'Luc de Prague et les Vaudois d'Italie', *Bollettino della Società di Studi Valdesi* 90 (1949), pp. 40–64.

Molnar, A., 'Les Vaudois et l'Unité des Frères Tchèques', *Bollettino della Società di Studi Valdesi* 118 (1965), pp. 3–16.

Molnar, A., 'L'Internationale des Taborites et des Vaudois', *Bollettino della Società di Studi Valdesi* 122 (1967), pp. 3–13.

Molnar, A., 'Les Vaudois et les hussites', *Bollettino della Società di Studi Valdesi* 136 (1974), pp. 27–35.

Monaster, A., *A History of the Vaudois Church* (London, 1848).

Moneta, of Cremona, *Adversus Catharos et Valdenses libri v*, ed. T. A. Ricchinius (Rome, 1743).

Montet, E., *Histoire littéraire des Vaudois du Piémont* (Paris, 1885).

Monumenta Germaniae Historica, Epistolae Saeculi XIII Selectae, vol. 1 (Berlin, 1883).

Moore, R. I. (ed.), *The Birth of Popular Heresy*, Documents of Medieval History 1 (London, 1975).

Moore, R. I., *The Origins of European Dissent* (London, 1977).

Moore, R. I., *The Formation of a Persecuting Society: Power and Deviance in Western Europe, 950–1250* (Oxford, 1987).

Morland, S., *History of the Evangelical Churches of the valleys of Piemont* (London, 1658).

Morris, C., *The Papal Monarchy: The Western Church from 1050 to 1250* (Oxford, 1989).

Murray, A., *Reason and Society in the Middle Ages* (Oxford, 1978).

Myers, D., *'Poor Sinning Folk': Confession and Conscience in Counter-Reformation Germany* (Ithaca, NY, and London, 1996).

Naz, R. (ed.), *Dictionnaire de droit canonique*, 7 vols (Paris, 1935–65).

Nickson, M., 'The "Pseudo-Reinerius" Treatise, the Final Stage of a Thirteenth-century Work on Heresy from the Diocese of Passau', *Archives d'Histoire Doctrinale et Littéraire du Moyen-Age* 34 (1967), pp. 255–314.

Nider, J., *De Visionibus ac revelationibus . . .* (Helmstedt, 1692).

Noonan, J. T., *The Scholastic Analysis of Usury* (Cambridge, Mass., 1957).

Ochsenbein, G. F., *Aus dem schweizerischen Volksleben des 15. Jahrhunderts. Der Inquisitionsprozess wider die Waldenser zu Freiburg i. A. im Jahre 1430 nach den Akten dargestellt* (Bern, 1881).

Oecolampadius, J. and Zuinglius, H., *Epistolarum libri iv* (Basel, '1536', though thought to date from 1548).

Olson, O. K., 'Theology of Revolution: Magdeburg, 1550–1551', *Sixteenth Century Journal* 3 (1972), pp. 56–79.

Osiander, Lucas, *Epitomes Historiae Ecclesiasticae Centuriae . . .*, 8 vols (Tübingen, 1592–1604).

Osuna, Franciscus de, *Flagellum Diaboli, oder Dess Teufels Gaisl, darin gar lustig und artlich gehandelt wird: Von der Macht uund Gewalt dess boesen Feindts: von den effecten und Wirckungen der Zauberer / Unholdter und Hexenmaister . . .* (Munich, 1602).

Paolini, L., 'Italian Catharism and Written Culture', in Peter Biller and Anne Hudson (eds), *Heresy and Literacy, 1000–1530* (Cambridge, 1994), pp. 83–103.

Paravy, P., *De la Chrétienté romaine à la réforme en Dauphiné*, Collection de l'École Française de Rome, 183, 2 vols (Rome, 1993–4).

Paravy, P., 'Waldensians in the Dauphiné (1400–1530): From Dissidence in Texts to Dissidence in Practice', in Peter Biller and Anne Hudson (eds), *Heresy and Literacy, 1000–1530* (Cambridge, 1994), pp. 160–75.

Parker, T. H. L., *Calvin's New Testament Commentaries*, 2nd edn (Edinburgh, 1993).

Parsons, R., *A Treatise of Three Conversions of England*, 3 vols (n. p., 1603).

Pascal, A., 'Comunità eretiche e chiese cattoliche nelle valli valdesi secondo le relazioni delle visite pastorali del Peruzzi e della Broglia (secolo xvi)', *Bulletin de la société d'histoire vaudoise* 30 (1912), pp. 61–73.

Pascal, A., *I Valdesi e il parlamento francese di Torino* (Pinerolo, 1912).

Pascal, A., 'Le Ambascerie dei cantoni e dei principi protestanti di Svizzera e Germania al Re di Francia in favore dei Valdesi durante il periodo della dominazione francese in Piemonte (1535–1559)', *Bollettino storico-bibliografico subalpino*, vol. 18, nos 1–3 (1913), pp. 80–119, and nos 5–6, pp. 316–36; and vol. 19, nos 1–3 (1914), pp. 26–38.

Pascal, A., 'La lotta contro la riforma in Piemonte al tempo di Emmanuele Filiberto, studiata nelle relazioni diplomatiche tra la corte Sabauda e la Santa Sede (1559–1580)', *Bulletin de la société d'histoire vaudoise* 53 (1929), pp. 5–88, and no. 55 (1930), pp. 5–108.

Patschovsky, A., *Der Passauer Anonymus: Ein Sammelwerk über Ketzer, Juden, Antichrist aus der Mitte des 13. Jahrhunderts*, Schriften der MGH, Deutsches Institut für Erforschung des Mittelalters, Bd. 22 (Stuttgart, 1968).

Patschovsky, A., *Die Anfänge einer Ständigen Inquisition in Böhmen; Ein Prager Inquisitoren-Handbuch aus der ersten Hälfte des 14. Jahrhunderts*, Beiträge zur Geschichte und Quellenkunde des Mittelalters, Bd. 3 (Berlin, 1975).

Patschovsky, A. (ed.), *Quellen zur böhmischen Inquisition im 14. Jahrhundert*, MGH Quellen zur Geistesgeschichte des Mittelalters, vol. 2 (Weimar, 1979).

Patschovsky, A., 'The Literacy of Waldensianism from Valdes to *c*.1400', in Peter Biller and Anne Hudson (eds), *Heresy and Literacy, 1000–1530* (Cambridge, 1994), pp. 112–36.

Patschovsky, A. and Selge, K.-V. (eds), *Quellen zur Geschichte der Waldenser*, Texte zur Kirchen- und Theologiegeschichte, 18 (Gütersloh, 1973).

Pazè Beda, B. and Pazè, P., *Riforma e cattolicesimo in val Pragelato 1555–1685* (Pinerolo, 1975).

Perrin, J. P., *Histoire des Vaudois, divisée en trois parties* (Geneva, 1618 and 1619); English trans. as *The Bloudy rage of that Great Antichrist of Rome, and his superstitious adherents, against the true Church of Christ* (also entitled in some edns, *Luther's fore-runners, or a Cloud of Witnesses, deposing for the Protestant faith*), trans. S. Lennard (London, 1624); partial German trans. as J. J. Grassern, *Waldenser Chronick . . .* (Basel, 1623).

Pétavel-Olliff, E., *La Bible en France, ou les traductions françaises des Saintes Escritures* (Paris, 1864).

Peter, R., 'Le Comte Guillaume de Furstenberg et les Vaudois', *Bollettino della Società di Studi Valdesi* 143 (1978), pp. 27–36.

Piccolomini, A. S. [Pius II], *Opera Omnia* (Basel, 1551).

Pierre de Vaux-Cernay, *Petrum Vallium Sarnaii Hystoria albigensis*, 3 vols, ed. P. Guébin and E. Lyon (Paris, 1926–39).

Plantsch, M., *Opusculum de sagis maleficis* (Phorce, 1507).

Power, E., *Medieval Women*, ed. M. M. Postan (Cambridge, 1975).

Preger, W., *Beiträge zur Geschichte der Waldesier in Mittelalter*, Abhandlungen der historischen Classe der königlich Bayerischen Akademie der Wissenschaften, 13, pt 2 (Munich, 1875).

Preger, W., *Der Tractat des David von Augsburg über die Waldesier*, Abhandlungen der königlichen bayerischen Akademie der Wissenschaften, historische Klasse, vol. 14, pt 2 (Munich, 1879).

Provana di Collegno, F.-X., 'Rapports de Guillaume Farel avec les Vaudois du Piémont', *Bulletin de la société d'études . . . des Hautes-Alpes* (1891), pp. 257–78.

Raugei, A. M., *Bestiario valdese* (Florence, 1984).

Relation véritable de ce qui s'est passé dans les persecutions et massacres faits cette année aux églises réformées de Piémont (n. p., 1655).

Richter, A. L. and Friedberg, E. A. (eds), *Corpus Juris Canonici* (repr. Graz, 1955).

Rivoire, P., 'Les Colonies provençales et vaudoises de la Pouille', *Bulletin de la société d'histoire vaudoise* 19 (1902), pp. 48–62.

Roberts, P., *A City in Conflict: Troyes during the French Wars of Religion* (Manchester, 1996).

Robinson, I. S., 'Gregory VII and the Soldiers of Christ', in *History* 58 (1973), pp. 169–92.

Romier, L., 'Les Vaudois et le parlement français de Turin', *Mélanges d'archaeologie et d'histoire* 30 (1920), pp. 193–221.

Rorengo, Marc'Aurelio, de' Conti di Lucerna, *Memorie Historiche dell'introduttione dell'heresie nelle valli di Lucerna, Marchesato di Saluzzo, e altre di Piemonte* . . . (Turin, 1649).

Roset, M., *Les Chroniques de Genève*, ed. H. Fazy (Geneva, 1894).

Roussel, B., 'La Bible d'Olivétan: la traduction du livre du prophète Habaquq', *Études théologiques et religieuses* 4 (1982), pp. 537–57.

Rubellin, M., 'Au temps oú Valdès n'était pas hérétique: hypothèses sur le rôle de Valdès à Lyon (1170–1183)', in M. Zerner (ed.), *Inventer l'hérésie? Discours polémiques et pouvoirs avant l'inquisition*, Collection du Centre d'Études médiévales de Nice, vol. 2 (Nice, 1998).

Rubin, M., *Corpus Christi: The Eucharist in Late Medieval Culture* (Cambridge, 1991).

Sanderus, N., *De visibili monarchia ecclesiae* (Würzburg, 1592).

Schmidt, C., 'Aktenstücke besonders zur Geschichte der Waldenser', *Zeitschrift für die historische Theologie* 22 (1852), pp. 238–62.

Schneider, M., *Europäisches Waldensertum im 13. und 14. Jahrhundert*, Arbeiten zur Kirchengeschichte, 51 (Berlin, 1981).

Scribner, R. W., 'Ritual and Popular Belief in Catholic Germany at the Time of the Reformation', *Journal of Ecclesiastical History* 35 (1984), pp. 47–77.

Scultetus, A., *Annalium Evangelii passim per Europam* . . . *Renovati Decades Duae*, 2 vols (Heidelberg, 1618–20).

Segl, P., *Ketzer in Österreich: Untersuchungen über Häresie und Inquisition im Herzogtum Österreich im 13. und beginnenden 14. Jahrhundert*, Quellen und Forschungen aus dem Gebiet der Geschichte, Neue Folge, Heft 5 (Paderborn, 1984).

Selge, K.-V., 'Caractéristiques du premier mouvement vaudois et crises au cours de son expansion', *Cahiers de Fanjeaux*, vol. 2, 'Vaudois languedociens et pauvres catholiques' (1967), pp. 110–42.

Selge, K.-V., *Die ersten Waldenser mit Edition des Liber antiheresis des Durandus von Osca*, 2 vols (Berlin, 1967).

Seyssel, Claude de, *Adversus errores et sectam Valdensium disputationes* (Paris, 1520).

Skinner, Q., *The Foundations of Modern Political Thought*, 2 vols (Cambridge, 1978).

Sleidanus, J., *De statu religionis et reipublicae ... commentarii* (Strasbourg, 1556).

Šmahel, F., *La Révolution hussite, une anomalie historique* (Paris, 1985).

Šmahel, F., 'Crypto- et semi-vaudois dans la Bohême hussite', *Revue de l'histoire des religions*, vol. 217, fasc. 1 (2000), pp. 101–20.

Spanheim, F., *Geneva Restituta, Oratio* (Geneva, 1635).

Stelling-Michaud, Sven and Stelling-Michaud, Suzanne (eds), *Le Livre du recteur de l'académie de Genève*, 6 vols (Geneva, 1959–80).

Strauss, G., *Luther's House of Learning: Indoctrination of the Young in the German Reformation* (Baltimore, Md., 1978).

Sudermann, J. J., *Waldenser Chronick* (n. p., 1655).

Sutherland, N. M., *The Huguenot Struggle for Recognition* (New Haven, Conn., 1980).

Symcox, G., *Victor Amadeus II: Absolutism in the Savoyard State 1675–1730* (London, 1983).

Tanner, N. P. (ed.), *Heresy Trials in the Diocese of Norwich, 1428–1431*, Royal Historical Society, Camden 4th Series, vol. 20 (London, 1977).

Taplin, M., 'The Italian Reformers and the Zurich Church, c.1540–1620' (St Andrews Ph.D. thesis, 1999).

Tentler, T. N., *Sin and Confession on the Eve of the Reformation* (Princeton, NJ, 1977).

Thomson, J. A. F., *The Later Lollards 1414–1520* (Oxford, 1965).

Thouzellier, C., 'Le "Liber antiheresis" de Durand de Huesca et la "Contra haereticos" d'Ermengaud de Béziers', *Revue d'Histoire Ecclésiastique*, vol. 55 (1960), pp. 130–41.

Thouzellier, C., *Catharisme et valdéisme en Languedoc à la fin du xiie et au début du xiiie siècle* (Paris, 1966).

Thouzellier, C., *Hérésie et hérétiques* (Rome, 1969).

Thuanus, J. A., *Historiarum sui temporis*, 5 vols (Paris, 1604–8).

Todd, J. H., *The Books of the Vaudois: The Waldensian Manuscripts preserved in the Library of Trinity College, Dublin* (London, 1865).

Tonsi, J., *Vita Emmanuelis Philiberti* (Turin, 1596).

Tourn, G., *L'Étonnante aventure d'un peuple-église* (Tournon and Turin, 1980).

Tremp, Kathrin Utz, *Waldenser, Widergänger, Hexen und Rebellen: Biographen zu den Waldenserprozessen von Freiburg im Uechtland (1399 und 1430)* (Fribourg, 1999) (special number of the *Freiburger Geschichtsblätter*).

Tremp, Kathrin Utz, 'Les Vaudois de Fribourg (1399–1430): état de la recherche', *Revue de l'histoire des religions*, vol. 217, fasc. 1 (2000), pp. 121–38.

'Une Mission en Piémont', a document ed. anonymously in *Bulletin de la société d'histoire du protestantisme français* 17 (1868), pp. 16–19.

Ussher, J., *Gravissimae Quaestionis, de Christianarum Ecclesiarum ... continua successione et statu, Historica Explicatio* (London, 1613).

Viazzo, Pier Paolo, *Upland Communities: Environment, Population and Social Structure in the Alps since the Sixteenth Century* (Cambridge, 1989).

Vidal, J. M., 'Notice sur les oeuvres du Pape Benoît XII', *Revue d'histoire ecclésiastique* 6 (1905), pp. 557–65, 785–810.

Villard, M., 'Vaudois d'Apt au xvie siècle', in Comité des travaux historiques et scientifiques, *Bulletin philologique et historique* (for year 1965, pub. 1966), pp. 641–53.

Vinay, A., 'Lettre de Busca', *Bulletin de la société d'histoire vaudoise* 7 (1890), pp. 43–60.

Vinay, V., *Facoltà valdese di teologia (1855–1955)* (Torre Pellice, 1955).

Vinay, V., 'Mémoires de Georges Morel', *Bollettino della Società di Studi Valdesi* 132 (1972), pp. 35–48.

Vinay, V., *Le Confessioni di fede dei Valdesi riformati, con i documenti del dialogo fra la 'prima' e la 'seconda' riforma*, Collana della Facoltà valdese di teologia, 12 (Turin, 1975).

Viora, M., 'Le persecuzioni contro i valdesi nel secolo xvo: la crociata di Filippo II', *Bulletin de la société d'histoire vaudoise* 47 (1925), pp. 5–19.

Vulson, M., *De la Puissance du pape* (Geneva, 1635).

Wakefield, W. L. and Evans, A. P. (eds), *Heresies of the High Middle Ages: Selected Sources Translated and Annotated* (New York and London, 1969).

Weitzecker, G., 'Processo di un valdese nell'anno 1451', *Rivista Cristiana* 9 (1881), pp. 363–7.

Williams, G. H., *The Radical Reformation*, 3rd edn, Sixteenth Century Essays and Studies, vol. 15 (Kirksville, Mo., 1992).

Zerner, M. (ed.), *Inventer l'hérésie? Discours polémiques et pouvoirs avant l'inquisition*, Collection du Centre d'Études médiévales de Nice, vol. 2 (Nice, 1998).

Zika, C., 'Hosts, Processions and Pilgrimages: Controlling the Sacred in Fifteenth-century Germany', *Past and Present* 118 (1988), pp. 25–64.

Index